Behavioral Economics and Finance Managerial

high quality & original research with empirical evidence and realistic analysis

this book, with the focus on creating a scientific and practical view of the opportunities and challenges facing of the Iranian economy, is compiled and published the result of examining the empirical evidence and realistic analysis in most important field related to the Behavioral Economic and Financial Management on a large part of Iranian industries . so The main audience of this book are foreign organizations and categories of different levels of international firms and other entities that need the information about Iranian financial economics or interested to start trade with Iran and investing in it.

This series contain ten high quality & original research dedicated to MOSTAFA EMAMI(master of science in financial economic from Michigan Technological University).

in addition all the Essays have been selected under scientific supervision of Professor Amrollah Amini(Associate Professor of Economics Faculty Allameh Tabataba'i University) and in some cases are accompanied by his valuable opinions, which are the result of more than thirty years of teaching at Allameh University, so we believe this book can be used as a reference by respected professors in the master's degree program. Related disciplines should be used as the main source of teaching

Author of this Book:

Mostafa Emami:(M.S.C Finance, Michigan Technological University)

Researchers:

- K.Nazari
- A.Shakarbeigi
- H.Fardmanesh,
- H.Maleki
- H.Khanifar
- F.Eavani
- S.Teymorpor
- M.Darabi
- H.Soltani
- A.Khanifar
- Al Ansari
- H.bordbar
- Z.Alizadeh
- S.vafaei
- E.Rayegan
- M.Parveizi
- M.Veisi
- K.Veisi
- M.Doroodgar
- S.Teymorpor
- M.Saiedi
- M.Nikjoo
- A.ghasemi
- H.Hassanzadeh
- M.Malmira
- M.Esfahanib
- M.Malmira
- H.Tajnesaeic

Book details:

ASIN: B00K9BP65Y ISBN-10: 9798578061189

Publisher : Amazon and Kindle are trademarks of Amazon.com Inc. or its affiliates

Language: English

Content

1. A COOPERATIVE GAME THEORY SOLUTION IN AN UPSTREAM-DOWNSTREAM RELATIONSHIP
2. ACTIVITY BASED COSTING MODEL FOR COST CALCULATION IN GAS COMPANIES: EMPIRICAL EVIDENCE OF IRAN
3. BANK PRODUCTIVITY ANALYSIS: AN EMPIRICAL EVIDENCE FROM IRANIAN BANKING INDUSTRY
4. EMPIRICAL INVESTIGATION OF FACTORS MODERATING IT-PERFORMANCE RELATIONSHIP IN DEVELOPED AND DEVELOPING COUNTRIES
5. EMPLOYEES' SOCIAL STATUS IN IRANIAN PUBLIC & GOVERNMENTAL ORGANIZATIONS: THE EFFECTS OF INDIVIDUAL, ORGANIZATIONAL & SOCIAL FACTORS
6. EVALUATING THE COMPARATIVE EFFECTIVENESS OF STAFF IN-SERVICE TRAININGS ON IMPROVING THE SERVICE QUALITY(BEFORE AND AFTER THE IN-SERVICE TRAININGS)
7. FACTORS MODERATE IT DIFFUSION-PERFORMANCE RELATIONSHIP IN DEVELOPING AND DEVELOPED COUNTRIES: AN EMPIRICAL EVIDENCE
8. FUZZY PARTITIONING AND ITS APPLICATION TO RESERVOIR OPERATION PROBLEM (A MULTISTAGE APPROACH USING MARKOV CHAIN)
9. IT ABSORPTION & DIFFUSION READINESS INDEX (ITADRI): CONCEPTUAL MODEL, FACTORS AND MEASURES
10. IT ABSORPTION & DIFFUSION READINESS INDEX (ITADRI): CONCEPTUAL MODEL, FACTORS AND MEASURES
11. IT DIFFUSION IN DEVELOPING AND DEVELOPED COUNTRIES: A CONCEPTUAL ANALYTICAL MODEL
12. STOCK MARKETS EFFICIENCY, ATTACTIVENESS AND THE NATURE OF INFORMATION INVESTORS USE TO TRADE: AN EVIDENCE FROM THE TEHRAN STOCK EXCHANGE(TSE)
13. PROMOTING ORGANIZATIONAL AGILITY: AN APPLIED FRAMEWORK
14. SERVICE QUALITY MEASUREMENT: AN EMPIRICAL INVESTIGATION AND A CRITICAL EVALUATION

A COOPERATIVE GAME THEORY SOLUTION IN AN UPSTREAM-DOWNSTREAM RELATIONSHIP

AMROLAH AMINI (Ph.D)

Associate Professor, Allameh Tabatabaei University (ATU), Tehran, Iran.

aminij@atu.ac.ir

ALIREZA EMAMI

Master of Science , Tehran University, Tehran, Iran

memami@alumni.ut.ac.ir

MOSTAFA EMAMI*

Master of Science, Michigan Technological University (MTU)

memami@mtu.edu

***Corresponding Address**

Applied Research and Technology Office, Michigan Technological University

1400 Townsend Dr, Houghton, MI 49931

Tel & Fax : +1-(816) 237-0018

E-mail: memami@mtu.edu

A COOPERATIVE GAME THEORY SOLUTION IN AN UPSTREAM-DOWNSTREAM RELATIONSHIP

Abstract
What happens when a firm does not want to be vertically integrated? Within a buyer-supplier relationship, and in a context of specific investments, we analyze firm interactions when they decide to cooperate instead of becoming vertically integrated. We develop a model that presents an alternative to vertical integration with firms that cooperate with each other under incomplete contracts. The contribution of our approach is twofold: first, a mathematical component, where we show how to apply the maximum to compute the characteristic functions of the model; and second, an economic element, where we reconsider the upstream-downstream relationship under a cooperative framework and no integration. We find that the total generated value is Pareto optimum if firms cooperate and distribute the benefits following the Shapley value solution. Finally, the Shapley value measures the power that each firm has in the bargaining process.
KEYWORDS: cooperative game, Shapley value, core, incomplete contracts, specific investments, upstream-downstream relations, characteristic functions.

ACKNOWLEDGMENTS
E. Marchi is indebted to Professor Genaro J. Gutierrez who invited him and encouraged him to work in applications of game theory into economic fields. He also appreciates some material provided by Professor Gutierrez. The authors gratefully acknowledge financial support from the Spanish Ministry of Education and Science (SEJ2007-67895-CO4-02).

INTRODUCTION
The theory of the firm deals with the boundaries of a firm and it also focuses on the coordination and motivation problems faced by the different participants. The first definitions of a firm were economic models that considered the firm as a black box where physical inputs and labor came out in an output, at minimum cost and maximum profit (Hart, 1995). This definition had important limitations that gave place to new theories of the firm. Coase (1937) is recognized as the first researcher to provide an explanation about the existence of firms. He suggested that there were market imperfections that generated transaction costs and, in this context, the presence of firms may help to alleviate these market failures. In particular, this author argued that, under some circumstances, transactions could be done through an organization at a lower cost rather than through markets. Later, in 1972, Alchian and Demsetz defined the firm "as a nexus of contracts" and they also provided a description of the "classical capitalist firm".

In 1975 Williamson took the concept of transaction costs given by Coase, and he elaborated it further. In fact, Williamson redefined the concept of transaction costs and applied it to different forms of organizations, not just the market, making a substantial progress in the study of the firm. His most important contribution was to elucidate the roles of imperfect contracts and specific investments (asset specificity, human specificity). Another important contribution was the fact of comparing the transactional efficiency of alternative governance structures, including vertical integration, non-standard contracts and relational contracts (Gibbons, 2000)

Williamson's works opened the door to new investigations based on the ownership of the physical assets. Within this group, one can find the seminal work of Grossman and Hart (1986), who defined the firm as "a collection of physical assets that are jointly owned" (Zingales, 1998).

Although the ownership of physical assets has been used to explain the boundaries of the firm and vertical integration serves as a mechanism to save transaction costs, another important problem remains: the specificity of human assets. The problem of specific human assets in a context of vertical integration was already treated by Klein et al in 1978, at the time of describing the problems between General Motors (GM) and Fisher Body (FB). Human assets cannot be acquired because they are inherent to human beings. Klein revisited the vertical integration between General Motors and Fisher Body and argued that the costs associated with vertical integration are generally incentive costs that are unrelated to the degree of specific investments. Therefore, vertical integration becomes the most plausible solution when the degree of specific investments becomes high (Klein, 1988). Vertical integration avoids transaction costs when the costs are associated with physical assets, but it does not explain what happens when vertical integration is linked to specific human assets.

Rajan and Zingales (2000) indicate that General Motors was, and still is, a vertically integrated firm, which controls the physical assets through ownership. However, they argue the nature of the firms is changing. Large conglomerates have been broken up and their units have been spun-off as stand-alone companies. One example is Nucor, a steel manufacturer that abandoned the tradition of backward integration and out-sourced the entire supply chain of raw material (Holmström and Roberts, 1998).

As a result, vertical integration does not seem to be a good solution any more under certain circumstances. So we wonder if there is another way, different from vertical integration, to solve the problems. In particular, we analyze what happens when some firms decide to cooperate instead of being vertically integrated in a scenario with the presence of specific investments. More specifically, what happens if a supplier does not accept to be vertically integrated and it prefers, instead, to deal with several customers? To answer these questions, we develop a model that attempts to bring a new alternative solution to the problem, a model where the firms negotiate and cooperate to each other in line with the observed practices of many companies.

The contribution of this model is twofold: first, a mathematical contribution where we show how to apply the maximin that is included in the Minimax Theorem (see Marchi, 1967) to compute the characteristic functions of the model; and second, an economic contribution to solve a supplier-manufacturer relationship. Doing this, we present an alternative way to look at the upstream-downstream relationships under a cooperative framework and incomplete contracts.

We find that, under cooperation, the total value generated is Pareto optimum when they cooperate and distribute the benefits following the Shapley value solution. In fact, the Shapley value measures the power that the different participants have in the bargaining process. The bargaining power under cooperative game theory is determined by which player is needed the most (Brandenburger, 2007). In our model, the bargaining power is given by the specificity of the investment. The result of our model is that the supplier's bargaining power is what makes the cooperation between firms possible, making such upstream-downstream relationship enforceable. And, as a consequence, the first best that maximizes the total welfare can be achieved.

This paper proceeds as follows: in section 1, we present the literature review, while in section 2, the economic environment of the model is described. We develop a model under an incomplete and cooperative framework, being the core and the Shapley value the solutions to such model. Finally, in section 3, we present the conclusions of the model, followed by a description of some limitations and future research avenues.

1- LITERATURE REVIEW

The firm, as a black box where physical inputs and labor came out in an output, at minimum cost or maximum profit, has been the basic model of a firm for two hundred years. However, this theory presented important limitations because it takes into account neither the incentives inside the firm, nor its internal structure. In addition, it did not establish the boundaries of the firm. These limitations gave place to the appearance of new theories of the firm. Coase (1937) was the first researcher to give an explanation about the existence of the firms. He suggested that the markets were imperfect and firms existed to solve these market failures. Coase also dealt with the internal organization and suggested that firms would exist only in an environment in which they could perform better than markets (Gibbons, 2000). Furthermore, he argued that, under some circumstances, transactions can be made through the organization at a lower cost rather than through markets. This is so because the organizations ameliorate some market failures and they have the advantage of using employment contracts as a way to save transaction costs.

Later, in 1972, Alchian and Demsetz defined a firm "as a nexus of contracts". They said a firm is characterized by something more than legal status, namely the technology of team production, which means production with an inseparable production function. Thus, they introduced the free-riding problem in team productions. Their solution was to propose the presence of a monitor, who had the right to fire and hire the members of the team and, by doing that, they described the "classical capitalist firm"

In 1975 Williamson took the concept of transaction costs given by Coase and redefined it. In fact, Williamson introduced the transaction cost approach to the study of organizations, suggesting a new way of thinking about the firm and focusing on the analysis of transactions and contracts. In particular, he said that the transaction costs approach relies on two assumptions concerning the individuals: 1) human agents are subject to bounded rationality, and 2) at least some agents may behave in opportunistic way (Williamson, 1981). Furthermore, the characteristics of the transactions, such as their frequency, the presence of specific assets and the presence of information asymmetries may be important sources of transaction costs. Economic exchanges could be efficiently organized by contracts but, due to bounded rationality, the nature of the transactions and the opportunistic behavior of the individuals, contracts are often incomplete.

Williamson made a substantial progress in understanding the nature of the firm, and one key contribution was to elucidate the roles of imperfect contracts and specific investments (asset specificity and human specificity). Asset specificity is critical because, once the investment is made for a determined transaction between a buyer and a supplier, the value of this asset becomes lower if it used in a different transaction. Then, the supplier is "locked into" the transaction (Williamson, 1981). This also applies to a buyer when the buyer cannot make transactions with others suppliers.

Another important contribution was to compare the transactional efficiency of alternative governance structures, including vertical integration, non-standard contracts and relational contracts (Gibbons, 2000). An example of vertical integration was treated by Klein et al in 1978, explaining the relationship between General Motors (GM) and Fisher Body (FB). General Motors signed a contract with Fisher Body in which GM argued to purchase all its closed bodies from FB for 10 years in 1919, and they agreed on a price for delivering based on a cost plus a margin, that also included provisions that GM would not be charged more than other rival automobile manufacturers. As it is well-known, GM faced a much higher demand than the forecasted one, increasing its dependence on FB. As a response to this situation, GM was unsatisfied with the price settled and proposed FB to locate its body plants near the GM assembly plants, an offer that FB refused. As a consequence, GM started to acquire FB stock in 1924 and, finally, it completed a merger agreement in 1926. A GM car needed specific investments, and site specificity implied transaction costs. This vertical integration between GM and FB solved the problems associated with the presence of uncertainty in demand and costs.

Chandler (1977) and Porter and Livesay (1971) analyzed forward integration into distribution activities for the case of manufacturing firms. In retailing, vertical integration was made for those commodities that needed a considerable number of sale information points. In this context, specific human assets were needed to provide service and achieve larger sales, and the integration into wholesaling occurred for those commodities that were perishable and branded. The explanation for the existence of forward integration is that the manufacturer's reputation was at risk: contracts to turn on inventories or to destroy stocks were neither self-enforcing nor incentive compatible. As Williamson (1981) explained "the commodities that had none of these characteristics (perishable and branded) were sold through market distribution channels where no special hazards were posed".

Williamson's analysis encouraged further research based on the ownership of physical assets. The seminal work of Grossman and Hart (1986), who defined the firm as "a collection of physical assets that are jointly owned", is based on Williamson's approach, and along with Moore (1990) these authors developed a theory of incomplete contracts and property rights. There, it is this notion of property rights what determines the right to take decisions concerning all the issues that are not explicitly covered in the contract (Zingales, 1998).

After this, when explaining the boundaries of the firm, most researchers have assumed that the ownership of physical assets confers the right to take decisions. This means that the ownership of physical assets has been used as an incentive mechanism or a control mechanism to induce the agent to make the optimal effort or to carry out the optimal investment.

Our point is that even when ownership of physical assets is used to explain the boundaries of the firm and vertical integration can save transaction costs, another problem still remains: the specificity of human assets. As Klein (1988) pointed out, human assets cannot be acquired because they are inherent to a human being. In fact, this author revisited the General Motors and Fisher Body case and argued that the costs associated with vertical integration are generally incentive costs unrelated with the degree of the specific investments. Therefore, the vertical integration is the most possible solution while the degree of specific investment is high (Klein, 1988). So, vertical integration avoids the transaction costs when the costs are associated with physical assets but, what happens when vertical integration occurs in a context with specific human assets? In this case, vertical integration will not solve the transaction costs problem because the specific human capital is inherent to those human beings and it cannot be owned by a third party. Thus, the opportunistic behavior present in the original organizational arrangement is not eliminated and the benefits of a vertical integration process remain unclear.

In fact, if the conflict between General Motors and Fisher Body was only based on a hold-up problem of the investments in physical assets and specific human assets did not matter, the best solution would have been the acquisition by GM of the Fisher Body's physical assets. But vertical integration, meaning that the Fisher brothers become employees instead of independent contractors, does not eliminate the potential hold-up. Ownership of the specific human asset was still belonging to the Fisher brothers. So, as Klein pointed out, the solution was that General Motors did not buy the closed bodies from Fisher Body, but General Motors had to produce the closed bodies with the assistance of Fisher Body. General Motors was the owner of the plants and could determine where the plants were located, but the Fisher brothers became managers with the capacity to control or hold up GM with regard to specific investments in human assets.

This vertical integration implied that General Motors transformed not only the Fisher brothers into employees but also all the employees of Fisher Body into GM employees. General Motor stopped buying to start producing, acquiring in this way the organizational capital of Fisher Body Corporation. GM became the owner of all employment contracts and also the owner of the knowledge concerning the production of closed bodies. It is in this way that General Motors owned the specific human asset (Klein, 1988).

Furthermore, this solution was a successful one because the number of employees was huge. If few employees are involved, they can leave the firm and the organizational capital will be gone with them. But the threat that all the employees will leave the firm is not credible when the number of employees is so huge. After the vertical integration process, the Fisher brothers could not threat General Motors saying that all their former employees would leave the firm (taking their knowledge with them). In this sense, vertical integration in organizations with large human teams implies the ownership of the human asset as it happens with physical assets. It is in this sense that Klein mentions that specific human capital can be acquired and that the vertical integration could be a solution under some circumstances.

Rajan and Zingales (2000) indicate that General Motors was, and still is, a vertically integrated firm, that controls the physical assets through ownership. However, as these authors point out, the nature of many firms is changing: "Large conglomerates have been broken up and their units have been spun-off as stand-alone companies. Vertically integrated manufacturers have relinquished direct control of their suppliers and have moved toward looser forms of collaboration" (Rajan and Zingales, 2000). One example of this is Nucor, a steel manufacturer that abandoned the tradition of backward integration and out-sourced the entire supply chain of raw material (Holmström and Roberts, 1998). Even General Motors is changing and it has facilitated the spinoff of its major part supplier, Delphi. Toyota, and the relationship with its suppliers, provides another example of new forms of organization to deal with specific assets. In fact, Aoki (1990) talks of quasi-integration to refer to these links between Toyota and its suppliers which remain independent legal entities but exchange information and closely cooperate in the production process and the development of new products.

In summary, vertical integration seems not to be a good solution under some circumstances, as many researchers have already pointed out. This fact makes us wonder if there is another way to solve these problems that vertical integration does not address. In particular, we ask ourselves: *what happens if the firms decide to cooperate instead of being vertically integrated under the existence of specific investments? Additionally, what happens if the supply firm refuses to be vertically integrated?* To answer these questions, we develop a model attempting to bring a new alternative solution to vertical integration. We propose a model where the firms cooperate with each other and we find that the total value generated, under cooperation, is Pareto optimum if they distribute the benefits following the Shapley value solution.

We proceed now to mention briefly some important features of the Cooperative Game theory, before describing the model.

1.1- COOPERATIVE GAME THEORY

The game theory of an arbitrary set of players or agents is created by John von Neumann and Oskar Morgenstern in 1944[1]. The game theory is the study of games, also called strategic situations (Serrano, 2007). The game theory is divided in two main approaches: the cooperative and the non-cooperative game theory. The actors in non-cooperative game theory are individual players who may reach agreements only if they are self-enforcing, while in cooperative game theory, the actors are coalitions, group of players. As Serrano (2007) points out, the fact that a coalition has formed and that it has a feasible set of payoffs available to its members is now taken as given.

These two approaches of game theory imply two different forms to look at the same problem. As Aumann (1959) puts it, "the game is one ideal and the cooperative and non-cooperative approaches are two shadows". Game theory models imply situations in which players make decisions to maximize their own utility, while the rest of the players do the same. The decisions of the latter affect each other utilities. Cooperative game theory looks for the possible set of outcomes, study what the players can achieve, which coalitions will be formed, how the coalitions will distribute the outcomes and whether the outcomes are robust and stable (Sosic and Nagarajan, 2006).

The terms of non-cooperative game theory may, mistakenly, suggest that there is no place for cooperation, and the term of cooperative game theory might suggest that there is no room for conflict or competition. But as Brandenburger (2007) has already pointed out, neither is the case. Part of the non-cooperative game theory studies the possibility of cooperation in ongoing relationships, while many papers that use cooperative game theory also include the possibility of competition among players.

We follow a cooperative game approach that consists of two elements: 1) a set of players and 2) a characteristic function specifying the value created by different subsets of the players involved in the game. The cooperative game theory attempts to answer how the total value is divided up among the players and this answer will depend on their bargaining power. Furthermore, in cooperative game theory, a player's bargaining power depends on how much other players need him to form coalitions, or his marginal contribution. Brandenburger defines it as follows: "the marginal contribution of a particular player is the amount by which the created overall value would shrink if this particular player leaves the game". It is in this way that cooperative game theory captures the idea of competition among different players in bargaining situations.

---

[1] Morgenstern, O., Neumann, von, J., 1944. Theory of Games and Economic Behavior. Princeton University Press.

There are different ways of solving cooperative games and we want to emphasize two of them: the core and the Shapley value. The core was first proposed by Francis Ysidro Edgeworth in 1881, and it was later reinvented and defined in game theoretic terms by Gillies (1953). The core is a solution concept that allocates to each cooperative game the set of payoffs that no coalition can improve upon or block (Serrano, 2007). Concerning the Shapley value, it was first proposed by Lloyd Shapley in his 1953 PhD dissertation. This solution prescribes a single payoff for each player, which is the average of all marginal contributions of that player to each coalition he or she is a member of (Serrano, 2007).

2- THE ECONOMIC ENVIRONMENT

This model is developed under a cooperative game framework and the presence of incomplete contracts. Players take their decisions of buying and producing, depending on their expected benefits. To compute those expected benefits, we have chosen the Shapley value solution because it takes into account what each player could reasonably get before the game starts.

More specifically, we consider a model with three agents, two downstream parties and one upstream party. The upstream party is a supply firm which sells its product to the downstream parties. The supplier has to make specific investments to obtain the product q, which has no alternative use out of these relationships. We assume the existence of a parameter, λ, that measures the degree of investment specificity, where $\lambda \in [0,1]$. The higher the value of λ, the more specific the investment. If $\lambda = 1$, the investment is fully specific, while a value $\lambda = 0$ indicates that the investment becomes totally general. Furthermore, this product q requires a quality process that is not observable to third parties and, therefore, it is not possible to write down an enforceable contract. The supplier gets this q at a cost λc_s.

The downstream parties buy the product from the supplier and they sell it in different markets. Each firm is a monopoly in its market. These downstream firms have incentives to merge or to be vertically integrated with the supplier because this would ensure them the required quality. So we can say the downstream firms compete for the supplier giving him bargaining power, in the sense that both downstream firms need the supplier. In this model, the bargaining power responds to the existence of specific investments. As a result, the incentive problem is twofold: on one hand, the downstream firms want the supplier to produce under a given quality process. On the other hand, the supplier, after having made the specific investments, faces the possibility that the downstream firms may argue that the product has not reached the required quality and, consequently, they will pay less for the product or, in the worst case, they will refuse to buy it.

We consider a one-shot supply transaction. The downstream firm 1 buys q_1 to the supplier and the second firm buys q_2, such that $q_1 + q_2 = q$ and $q_1, q_2 > 0$. The supplier has to make specific investments to produce these quantities at a cost $\lambda c_{s1}, \lambda c_{s2}$ and sells them at prices w_1, w_2, being $w_1, w_2 \geq 0$ and $w_1 \in \left[0, \overline{w_1}\right]$ and $w_2 \in \left[0, \overline{w_2}\right]$

The downstream parties buy the quantities at prices w_1, w_2 and sell them at p_1, p_2, respectively. The prices p_1, p_2 are positive and $p_1 \in \left[0, \overline{p_1}\right]$, $p_2 \in \left[0, \overline{p_2}\right]$ and they are decided by each firm. The downstream firm 1 faces a demand[1] function given by $q_1 = f_1(p_1) = \beta_1 - \gamma_1 p_1$ and the downstream firm 2 faces the demand function $q_2 = f_2(p_2) = \beta_2 - \gamma_2 p_2$. For simplicity, we assume linear demand functions. Additionally, to guarantee that the inverse demand functions exist and they are well defined, we further assume that:
1. the demand functions have negative slopes
2. f_1, f_2 are differentiable functions whose first derivatives are strictly negative and finite for any $p_1 \in \left[0, \overline{p_1}\right]$ and $p_2 \in \left[0, \overline{p_2}\right]$ such that $f_1, f_2 > 0$.

We also assume that $0 \leq w_1 \leq p_1 \leq \dfrac{\beta_1}{\gamma_1}$ and $0 \leq w_2 \leq p_2 \leq \dfrac{\beta_2}{\gamma_2}$

The players of the model have transferable utilities and they are rational, so they take decisions that maximize their expected utilities. The respective utility functions are: $U_s = U(\Pi_s) + \varepsilon_s$ for the supplier, $U_1 = U(\Pi_1) + \varepsilon_1$ for the downstream firm 1 and $U_2 = U(\Pi_2) + \varepsilon_2$ for the downstream firm 2. Furthermore, $\varepsilon_s, \varepsilon_1, \varepsilon_2$ are random variables that follow a normal distribution with $E(\varepsilon_s) = E(\varepsilon_1) = E(\varepsilon_2) = 0$ and variances $\sigma_s^2, \sigma_1^2, \sigma_2^2$, respectively. For simplicity, we also assume the different players are risk neutral.

Finally, the players' expected benefits are given by the following equations.
$\Pi_1 = R_1(q_1, p_1) - w_1 q_1$, for the downstream firm 1, where the revenue is equal to $R_1(q_1, p_1) = p_1 * q_1$
$\Pi_2 = R_2(q_2, p_2) - w_1 q_2$, for the downstream firm 2, where $R_2(q_2, p_2) = p_2 * q_2$, and
$\Pi_3 = q_1 w_1 + q_2 w_2 - \lambda c_{s1} q_1 - \lambda c_{s2} q_2$, for the supplier.

2.1 - THE TIMING

As we mentioned earlier, the players decide to buy and produce in terms of their expected benefits. The timing of the model becomes as follows:

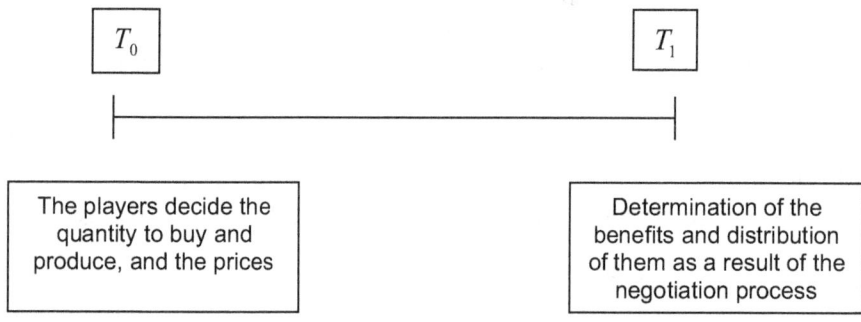

---

[1] For simplicity, it is assumed the demand function is known by the downstream parties. We know this is a strong assumption but if we assume expected demand functions, our results will remain unchanged.

Figure 1: Timing of the Model

At time 0, the downstream firms decide the quantity of product they will buy and the prices they are going to sell it. The supplier decides to produce this level of product, along with the quality and the price it will charge to the downstream parties. At time 1, the three firms will determine the payoffs and the distribution of the benefits according to the negotiation process. Due to the existence of incomplete information and the framework of incomplete contracts, the players decide output level and their prices as a function of their expected future benefits and their distribution

2. 2- BENCHMARK

Under perfect information and complete contracts, we compute the first best. To compute the first best it is assumed there is one player who has perfect information and is the owner of the assets. The firms act as one player who maximizes the total expected benefits (Π_T). The equation of the total expected benefit is:

$\Pi_T = p_1 q_1 - \lambda c_{s1} q_1 + p_2 q_2 - \lambda c_{s2} q_2$, being the demand functions

$q_1 = f_1(p_1) = \beta_1 - \gamma_1 p_1$ and $q_2 = f_2(p_2) = \beta_2 - \gamma_2 p_2$.

$$f_x = f_y = 0$$

To assure the presence of a maximum, it must be satisfied that $f^2{}_{xx} f^2{}_{yy} - 2 f^2{}_{xy} > 0$

$$f^2{}_{xx} < 0$$

So, the maximum is achieved.

$$\frac{\partial \Pi_T}{\partial p_1} = \beta_1 - 2\gamma_1 p_1 + \lambda c_{s1} \gamma_1 = 0$$

$$\frac{\partial \Pi_T}{\partial p_2} = \beta_2 - 2\gamma_2 p_2 + \lambda c_{s2} \gamma_2 = 0$$

From these derivatives, we get the prices and quantities that maximize the total net profit.

$$p_2 = \frac{\beta_2 + \lambda c_{s2} \gamma_2}{2\gamma_2} \quad \text{and} \quad q_2 = \frac{\beta_2 - \lambda c_{s2} \gamma_2}{2}$$

$$p_1 = \frac{\beta_1 + \lambda c_{s1} \gamma_1}{2\gamma_1} \quad \text{and} \quad q_1 = \frac{\beta_1 - \lambda c_{s1} \gamma_1}{2}$$

The total benefit in the benchmark case becomes:

$$\Pi_T = \frac{(\beta_1 - \lambda c_{s1} \gamma_1)^2}{4\gamma_1} + \frac{(\beta_2 - \lambda c_{s2} \gamma_2)^2}{4\gamma_2}$$

Next, we will compare this benchmark solution with the results obtained under incomplete contracts and a cooperative game framework.

2. 3- THE NON-COOPERATIVE OR NASH SOLUTION

Before showing the model under a cooperative game theory framework, we compute the solution under a non-cooperative game framework. To do this, we use the Nash equilibrium definition. In our model, we need:

$$\Pi_1(\bar{p}_1,\bar{p}_2,\bar{w}_1,\bar{w}_2) \geq \Pi_1(p_1,\bar{p}_2,\bar{w}_1,\bar{w}_2) \text{ for all } p_1 \qquad (A)$$

$$\Pi_2(\bar{p}_1,\bar{p}_2,\bar{w}_1,\bar{w}_2) \geq \Pi_2(\bar{p}_1,p_2,\bar{w}_1,\bar{w}_2) \text{ for all } p_2 \qquad (B)$$

$$\Pi_3(\bar{p}_1,\bar{p}_2,\bar{w}_1,\bar{w}_2) \geq \Pi_3(\bar{p}_1,\bar{p}_2,w_1,w_2) \text{ for all } w_1 \text{ and } w_2 \qquad (C)$$

The equations of the model are the following:
$$\Pi_1(p_1,p_2,w_1,w_2) = (p_1 - w_1)(\beta_1 - \gamma_1 p_1) \qquad (1)$$

for the downstream firm 1, where $p_1 \in \left[0, \frac{\beta_1}{\gamma_1}\right]$ and $w_1 \in \left[0, \frac{\beta_1}{\gamma_1}\right]$

$$\Pi_2(p_1,p_2,w_1,w_2) = (p_2 - w_2)(\beta_2 - \gamma_2 p_2) \qquad (2)$$

for the downstream firm 2, where $p_2 \in \left[0, \frac{\beta_2}{\gamma_2}\right]$ and $w_2 \in \left[0, \frac{\beta_2}{\gamma_2}\right]$

$$\Pi_3(p_1,p_2,w_1,w_2) = (w_1 - \lambda c_{s1})(\beta_1 - \gamma_1 p_1) + (w_2 - \lambda c_{s2})(\beta_2 - \gamma_2 p_2) \qquad (3)$$

for the supplier and $\lambda c_{s1} \leq w_1$ and $\lambda c_{s2} \leq w_2$.

To compute the Nash solution we take equation (1) and apply (A) looking for the value p_1 that maximizes equation (1), ceteris paribus.

The Nash solution to the downstream firm 1 is $p_1 = \dfrac{\beta_1 + \gamma_1 w_1}{2\gamma_1}$

We do the same for the downstream firm 2, and the value p_2 that maximizes the function Π_2 is $p_2 = \dfrac{\beta_2 + \gamma_2 w_2}{2\gamma_2}$

Similarly, for the supplier, we must calculate the values w_1 and w_2 that maximize equation (3) given the rest of variables (p_1, p_2). The results are:

$$w_1 = \frac{\beta_1 + \lambda c_{s1}\gamma_1}{2\gamma_1} \qquad w_2 = \frac{\beta_2 + \lambda c_{s2}\gamma_2}{2\gamma_2}$$

Thus, once the prices w_1 and w_2 have been obtained, we replace them in p_1 and p_2, and we get:

$$p_1 = \frac{3\beta_1 + \lambda c_{s1}\gamma_1}{4\gamma_1} \qquad p_2 = \frac{3\beta_2 + \lambda c_{s2}\gamma_2}{4\gamma_2}$$

Replacing this solution in the equations (1), (2) and (3), the players' net benefits become:

$$\Pi_1 = \frac{(\beta_1 - \lambda c_{s1}\gamma_1)^2}{16\gamma_1}$$

$$\Pi_2 = \frac{(\beta_2 - \lambda c_{s2}\gamma_2)^2}{16\gamma_2}$$

$$\Pi_s = \frac{(\beta_1 - \lambda c_{s1}\gamma_1)^2}{8\gamma_1} + \frac{(\beta_2 - \lambda c_{s2}\gamma_2)^2}{8\gamma_2}$$

As it can be seen, the Nash Solution shows us the effects of the double-marginalization. This is not an efficient result and, obviously, we do not reach the first best.

2.4 - INCOMPLETE CONTRACTS AND COOPERATIVE GAME MODEL

Following the timing of the model, at time 0, the three players decide the quantity to sell and produce but these decisions will take into account the future benefits they expect to achieve at time 1. So, the players have to estimate their future benefits. To do this, we are going to use a cooperative game approach based on the subject of the Theorem of the Minimax created by von Neumann (1928). Under cooperative games, the players negotiate and compute their payoffs under different coalitions. The fact of using the maximin to compute the payoffs implies that, in the negotiation process, the actors estimate the least amount they can get if the other players play against them; in other words, they compute the payoffs in the worst scenarios. In order to compute the payoffs or the characteristic functions of the game, we must define first what a characteristic function is. The definition of a **characteristic function**[1] of an n-person game assigns to each coalition, which is a subset S of the players, the best payoff that each one can achieve without the help of other players. In other words, that is the value $v(S)$ that coalition S can guarantee for itself by coordinating the strategies of its members, no matter what the other players do. It is standard to define the characteristic value of the empty coalition, Φ, as 0 so $v(\Phi) = 0$. The characteristic function implies that if X_s is the set of strategies available to the player in S, and Y_{N-S} is the set of strategies available to the players in $N - S$, then

$$v(S) = \max_{x \in X_s} \min_{y \in Y_{N-S}} \sum_{i \in S} e_i(x, y),$$

where $e_i(x, y)$ is the payoff to player i when x and y are the strategies played by the players of the parties S and $N - S$. This is for the mixed extension of finite games. It follows from this definition that if S and T are disjoint coalitions for finite n-person games, we get:
$v(S \cup T) \geq v(S) + v(T)$, if $S \cap T = \{\Phi\}$.
That is, superadditivity.

Once the characteristic function is defined, we present the equations of the model:

$$\Pi_1(p_1, p_2, w_1, w_2) = (p_1 - w_1)(\beta_1 - \gamma_1 p_1) \qquad (1)$$

for downstream firm 1, where $p_1 \in \left[0, \frac{\beta_1}{\gamma_1}\right]$ and $w_1 \in \left[0, \frac{\beta_1}{\gamma_1}\right]$

$$\Pi_2(p_1, p_2, w_1, w_2) = (p_2 - w_2)(\beta_2 - \gamma_2 p_2) \qquad (2)$$

for downstream firm 2, where $p_2 \in \left[0, \frac{\beta_2}{\gamma_2}\right]$ and $w_2 \in \left[0, \frac{\beta_2}{\gamma_2}\right]$ and

$$\Pi_3(p_1, p_2, w_1, w_2) = (w_1 - \lambda c_{s1})(\beta_1 - \gamma_1 p_1) + (w_2 - \lambda c_{s2})(\beta_2 - \gamma_2 p_2) \qquad (3)$$

---

[1] Thomas, L.C., 1984. Games, Theory and Applications. Ellis Horwood Limited

for the supplier and $\lambda c_{s1} \leq w_1$ and $\lambda c_{s2} \leq w_2$. The degree of investment specificity, λ, is high and it could be close to one in this model.

The possible coalitions of the model are:
$v(\phi), v(1), v(2), v(3), v(1,2), v(1,3), v(2,3), v(1,2,3)$.

The computation for the characteristic function for the downstream firm 1 becomes as follows: First, we take equation (1) and apply the maximin

$$v(1) = \max_{p_1} \min_{p_2, w_1, w_2} \Pi_1(p_1, p_2, w_1, w_2) = \max_{p_1} \min_{p_2, w_1, w_2} [p_1(\beta_1 - \gamma_1 p_1) - w_1(\beta_1 - \gamma_1 p_1)] \quad (4)$$

We must find the minimum values of p_2, w_1, w_2 that minimize this function for a given p_1, and then we will maximize that function with respect to p_1. In our context, the minimum value of w_1 that minimizes this function given p_1 is $w_1 = \dfrac{\beta_1}{\gamma_1}$, so we replace this value in the function and look for the p_1 that maximizes the function.

$$v(1) = \max_{p_1} \left[p_1(\beta_1 - \gamma_1 p_1) - \dfrac{\beta_1}{\gamma_1}(\beta_1 - \gamma_1 p_1) \right] = \max_{p_1} \Pi_1(p_1, p_2, w_1, w_2)$$

$$\dfrac{\partial \Pi_1}{\partial p_1} = \beta_1 - 2\gamma_1 p_1 + \beta_1 = 0$$

To ensure the existence of a maximum, we check the second derivative
$\dfrac{\partial^2 \Pi_1}{\partial p_1^2} = -2\gamma_1$. It is negative and, therefore, we have got a maximum.

Thus, $p_1 = \dfrac{\beta_1}{\gamma_1}$ and $q_1 = 0$, and replacing these values in the function (4) we get that the characteristic function for the downstream firm 1 becomes:

$$v(\{1\}) = v(1) = 0. \quad (5)$$

This is the payoff that the player 1 will have in his worst scenario. It means that if the supplier charges him the highest price $w_1 = \dfrac{\beta_1}{\gamma_1}$, which is the highest cost that the downstream firm 1 can face, the downstream firm 1's best response is to set the highest price of $p_1 = \dfrac{\beta_1}{\gamma_1}$ where the demand quantity is equal to 0. In that case, he gets zero profits.

The steps to compute the characteristic function to the downstream firm 2 are similar to the ones already computed for downstream firm 1. We proceed to simply write down the results and present the equation (6).

$$v(2) = \max_{p_2} \min_{p_1, w, w_2} \Pi_2(p_1, p_2, w_1, w_2) = \max_{p_2} \min_{p_1, w_1, w_2} [p_2(\beta_2 - \gamma_2 p_2) - w_2(\beta_2 - \gamma_2 p_2)]$$

$p_2 = \dfrac{\beta_2}{\gamma_2}$ and $q_2 = 0$

The characteristic function or the payoff that downstream firm 2 will receive in case that the other players join themselves against him becomes

$$v_2(\{2\}) = v(2) = 0 \qquad (7)$$

Equations (5) and (7) or the characteristic functions for the downstream firm 1 and the downstream firm 2, indicate the lowest value that they are able to get under the worst scenario.

Similarly, for the supplier, the characteristic function becomes:

$$v(3) = \max_{w_1,w_2} \min_{p_1,p_2} \Pi_3(p_1, p_2, w_1, w_2) =$$

$$\max_{w_1,w_2} \min_{p_1,p_2} [w_1(\beta_1 - \gamma_1 p_1) + w_2(\beta_2 - \gamma_2 p_2) - \lambda c_{s1}(\beta_1 - \gamma_1 p_1) - \lambda c_{s2}(\beta_2 - \gamma_2 p_2)]$$

We have to look for the minimum values of p_1, p_2 that minimize the function. These values are:

$$v(3) = \max_{w_1,w_2}\left[(w_1 - \lambda c_{s1})\left(\beta_1 - \gamma_1 \frac{\beta_1}{\gamma_1}\right) + (w_2 - \lambda c_{s2})\left(\beta_2 - \gamma_2 \frac{\beta_2}{\gamma_2}\right)\right]$$

$$v(3) = \max_{w_1,w_2}[0]$$

The characteristic function for the supplier is:

$$v(\{3\}) = v(3) = 0 \qquad (8)$$

The equation (8) is telling us the value that, in the worst case, the supplier gets. We can think that this is the case that the downstream firms join together and argue that the quality is not the one required and they do not want the product. The supplier's payoff is zero because the supplier cannot force the downstream parties to buy the product.

The characteristic function for the coalition $v(1,2)$ is obtained considering the sum of $\Pi_1 + \Pi_2$ because the coalition $\{1,2\}$ gets the payoff of both players together.

$$v(1,2) = \max_{p_1,p_2} \min_{w_1,w_2} [\Pi_1(p_1,p_2,w_1,w_2) + \Pi_2(p_1,p_2,w_1,w_2)] =$$

$$\max_{p_1,p_2} \min_{w_1,w_2} [p_1(\beta_1 - \gamma_1 p_1) - w_1(\beta_1 - \gamma_1 p_1) + p_2(\beta_2 - \gamma_2 p_2) - w_2(\beta_2 - \gamma_2 p_2)]$$

Looking for the minimum values of w_1, w_2 that minimize the function and replacing them, we obtain (9):

$$v(1,2) = \max_{p_1,p_2}\left[p_1(\beta_1 - \gamma_1 p_1) - \frac{\beta_1}{\gamma_1}(\beta_1 - \gamma_1 p_1) + p_2(\beta_2 - \gamma_2 p_2) - \frac{\beta}{\gamma_2}(\beta_2 - \gamma_2 p_2)\right] = \max_{p_1,p_2}[\Pi_1 + \Pi_2]$$

We have to look for the values of p_1, p_2 that make the function maximum. Thus, we derivate with respect to p_1 and p_2. The first derivatives must be equal to 0 and the second ones must be negative to ensure the presence of a maximum.

$$\frac{\partial[\Pi_1+\Pi_2]}{\partial p_1}=2\beta_1-2\gamma_1 p_1=0 \qquad \frac{\partial^2[\Pi_1+\Pi_2]}{\partial p_1^2}=-2\gamma_1$$

$$\frac{\partial[\Pi_1+\Pi_2]}{\partial p_2}=2\beta_2-2\gamma_2 p_2=0 \qquad \frac{\partial^2[\Pi_1+\Pi_2]}{\partial p_2^2}=-2\gamma_2$$

These values are:

$$p_1=\frac{\beta_1}{\gamma_1} \qquad q_1=0$$

$$p_2=\frac{\beta_2}{\gamma_2} \qquad q_2=0$$

Replacing in equation (9) we get the characteristic function

$$v(\{1,2\})=v(1,2)=0 \qquad (10)$$

This is the payoff that will get the coalition between the downstream parties in the worst condition that the supplier is against them. The supplier will charge them the highest price and their response will be to put the highest prices and they will sell 0. The benefits they get are equal to zero in the worst condition. This equation points out the fact that if the downstream firms cooperate with each other, without any consideration of the third player (the supplier), they will be able to get 0. They cannot force the supplier to invest and sell them the product.

The characteristic function for the coalition $v(1,3)$ is:

$$v(1,3)=\max_{p_1,w_1,w_2}\min_{p_2}[\Pi_1(p_1,p_2,w_1,w_2)+\Pi_3(p_1,p_2,w_1,w_2)]=$$

$$\max_{p_1,w_1,w_2}\min_{p_2}[p_1(\beta_1-\gamma_1 p_1)+w_2(\beta_2-\gamma_2 p_2)-\lambda c_{s1}(\beta_1-\gamma_1 p_1)-\lambda c_{s2}(\beta_2-\gamma_2 p_2)]$$

Looking for the minimum value of p_2 that minimizes the function, we get:

$$v(1,3)=\max_{p_1,w_1,w_2}\left[p_1(\beta_1-\gamma_1 p_1)+w_2\left(\beta_2-\gamma_2\frac{\beta_2}{\gamma_2}\right)-\lambda c_{s1}(\beta_1-\gamma_1 p_1)-\lambda c_{s2}\left(\beta_2-\gamma_2\frac{\beta_2}{\gamma_2}\right)\right]$$

$$v(1,3)=\max_{p_1,w_1,w_2}[p_1(\beta_1-\gamma_1 p_1)-\lambda c_{s1}(\beta_1-\gamma_1 p_1)]=\max_{p_1,w_1,w_2}[\Pi_1+\Pi_3] \qquad (11)$$

Now, we have to find the value of p_1 that maximizes (11)

$$\frac{\partial[\Pi_1+\Pi_3]}{\partial p_1}=\beta_1-2\gamma_1 p_1+\lambda c_{s1}\gamma_1=0 \qquad \frac{\partial^2[\Pi_1+\Pi_3]}{\partial p_1^2}=-2\gamma_1$$

$$p_1=\frac{\beta_1+\lambda c_{s1}\gamma_1}{2\gamma_1} \qquad q_1=\frac{\beta_1-\lambda c_{s1}\gamma_1}{2}$$

Replacing these values in the equation (11), we get the characteristic function

$$v(\{1,3\})=v(1,3)=\frac{(\beta_1-\lambda c_{s1}\gamma_1)^2}{4\gamma_1} \qquad (12)$$

This is the payoff that the coalition between the downstream firm 1 and the supplier can get if the downstream firm 2 is assumed to oppose them. The supplier will produce $q_1=\frac{\beta_1-\lambda c_{s1}\gamma_1}{2}$ and the downstream will sell it at the price $p_1=\frac{\beta_1+\lambda c_{s1}\gamma_1}{2\gamma_1}$. The characteristic function implies that, under any circumstances, the downstream firm 1 and the supplier, together, are sure to obtain the least amount given by this equation. This result is the same as if the supplier and the downstream firm 1 were vertically integrated. It is necessary to note that this coalition makes sense if the investments are specific because, if the investments were general, the players neither need to form coalitions nor to be vertically integrated.

Doing the same for the coalition between the downstream firm 2 and the supplier, we get:

$$v(2,3) = \max_{p_1,w_1,w_2} \min_{p_1} [\Pi_2(p_1,p_2,w_1,w_2) + \Pi_3(p_1,p_2,w_1,w_2)] =$$
$$\max_{p_2,w_1,w_2} \min_{p_1} [p_2(\beta_2 - \gamma_2 p_2) + w_1(\beta_1 - \gamma_1 p_1) - \lambda c_{s1}(\beta_1 - \gamma_1 p_1) - \lambda c_{s2}(\beta_2 - \gamma_2 p_2)]$$

Looking for the minimum value of p_1 that minimizes the function, we get:

$$v(2,3) = \max_{p_2,w_1,w_2} \left[p_2(\beta_2 - \gamma_2 p_2) + w_1\left(\beta_1 - \gamma_1 \frac{\beta_1}{\gamma_1}\right) - \lambda c_{s1}\left(\beta_1 - \gamma_1 \frac{\beta_1}{\gamma_1}\right) - \lambda c_{s2}(\beta_2 - \gamma_2 p_2) \right]$$

$$v(2,3) = \max_{p_2,w_1,w_2} [p_2(\beta_2 - \gamma_2 p_2) - \lambda c_{s2}(\beta_2 - \gamma_2 p_2)] = \max_{p_2,w_1,w_2} [\Pi_2 + \Pi_3] \qquad (13)$$

Now, we have to find the value of p_2 that maximizes (13)

$$\frac{\partial[\Pi_2 + \Pi_3]}{\partial p_2} = \beta_2 - 2\gamma_2 p_2 + \lambda c_{s2} \gamma_2 = 0 \qquad \frac{\partial^2[\Pi_2 + \Pi_3]}{\partial p_2^2} = -2\gamma_2$$

$$p_2 = \frac{\beta_2 + \lambda c_{s2} \gamma_2}{2\gamma_2} \qquad q_2 = \frac{\beta_2 - \lambda c_{s2} \gamma_2}{2}$$

Replacing these values in the equation (13), we get the characteristic function

$$v(\{2,3\}) = v(2,3) = \frac{(\beta_2 - \lambda c_{s2} \gamma_2)^2}{4\gamma_2} \qquad (14)$$

This is the payoff that the coalition between the downstream firm 2 and the supplier can get if the downstream firm 1 acts against them. The supplier will produce $q_2 = \frac{\beta_2 - \lambda c_{s2} \gamma_2}{2}$ and the downstream will sell it at the price $p_2 = \frac{\beta_2 + \lambda c_{s2} \gamma_2}{2\gamma_2}$. The characteristic function implies that, under any circumstances, the downstream firm 2 and the supplier, together, are sure to obtain the least amount given by this equation. As in the previous case, this result is the same as if the supplier and the downstream firm 2 were vertically integrated.

The characteristic function for the coalition $(1,2,3)$ is given by:

$$v(1,2,3) = \max_{p_1,p_2,w_1,w_2} [\Pi_1(p_1,p_2,w_1,w_2) + \Pi_2(p_1,p_2,w_1,w_2) + \Pi_3(p_1,p_2,w_1,w_2)] =$$
$$\max_{p_1,p_2,w_1,w_2} [p_1(\beta_1 - \gamma_1 p_1) + p_2(\beta_2 - \gamma_2 p_2) - \lambda c_{s1}(\beta_1 - \gamma_1 p_1) - \lambda c_{s2}(\beta_2 - \gamma_2 p_2)]$$

And now we must find the values p_1, p_2 that maximize the function.

$$\frac{\partial[\Pi_1 + \Pi_2 + \Pi_3]}{\partial p_1} = \beta_1 - 2\gamma_1 p_1 + \lambda c_{s1} \gamma_1 = 0 \qquad \frac{\partial^2[\Pi_1 + \Pi_2 + \Pi_3]}{\partial p_1^2} = -2\gamma_1$$

$$p_1 = \frac{\beta_1 + \lambda c_{s1}\gamma_1}{2\gamma_1} \qquad\qquad q_1 = \frac{\beta_1 - \lambda c_{s1}\gamma_1}{2}$$

$$\frac{\partial}{\partial p_2} = \beta_2 - 2\gamma_2 p_2 + \lambda c_{s2}\gamma_2 = 0 \qquad\qquad \frac{\partial^2}{\partial p_2^2} = -2\gamma_2$$

$$p_2 = \frac{\beta_2 + \lambda c_{s2}\gamma_2}{2\gamma_2} \qquad\qquad q_2 = \frac{\beta_2 - \lambda c_{s2}\gamma_2}{2}$$

Replacing these values in the equation we get that:

$$v(\{1,2,3\}) = v(1,2,3) = \frac{(\beta_1 - \lambda c_{s1}\gamma_1)^2}{4\gamma_1} + \frac{(\beta_2 - \lambda c_{s2}\gamma_2)^2}{4\gamma_2} \tag{15}$$

This expression is the characteristic function of the grand coalition. This is the maximum payoff that the grand coalition, or total coalition, can achieve if they decide to cooperate with each other. If we compare this payoff with the benchmark, we can observe that we reach the first best if the players decide to cooperate all together. If we also compare this result with the non-cooperative solution, we can argue that the solution under cooperative framework is better than the one under non-cooperative framework where the benefits for the players are lower due to of the presence of double marginalization.

Once we have computed the characteristic function for all the coalitions, we also know that, due to the definition of the characteristic function given by Thomas (1984), if S and T are disjoint coalitions, we get:
$v(S \cup T) \geq v(S) + v(T)$, if $S \cap T = \{\phi\}$. Where ϕ stands for the empty set.
So, in our model, the following expressions are satisfied
$v(1,2,3) \geq v(1) + v(2) + v(3)$
$v(1,2) \geq v(1) + v(2)$
$v(1,3) \geq v(1) + v(3)$
$v(2,3) \geq v(2) + v(3)$
$v(1,2,3) \geq v(1,2) + v(3)$
$v(1,2,3) \geq v(1,3) + v(2)$
$v(1,2,3) \geq v(2,3) + v(1)$
$v(1,2,3) + v(3) \geq v(1,3) + v(2,3)$
$v(1,2,3) + v(1) \geq v(1,2) + v(1,3)$
$v(1,2,3) + v(2) \geq v(2,3) + v(1,2)$

This means that superadditivity holds for the characteristic function. We also know that the presence of superadditivity indicates that the introduction of one player into the coalition adds value to it. Therefore, this means that the marginal contribution of each player added to a coalition, is not null.

To solve this model, we use the core as the solution and then the Shapley Value that is the baricenter of the core. For a convex characteristic function, we determine how the benefits of the model can be split between the players under the negotiation process. In other words, we are going to solve the model taking into account the possible set of rewards that the players can reach. We will consider the entire problem to find the solution, given that the game is essential.

That the game is essential implies that the characteristic function is superadditive and therefore, for two disjoint coalitions the value of the characteristic function of the union is strictly greater that the sum of the value of the individual characteristic functions. This is equivalent to say that $v(1)+v(2)+v(3)<v(1,2,3)$ (Myerson, 1991).

2.5- THE CORE AS A SOLUTION OF THE GAME

Having the characteristic function of the game of the two downstream firms and the supplier, it is important to find a suitable concept of solution. For this reason, first we choose the core as a possible solution. Previous to define the core, it is necessary to define an imputation[1]. An imputation in an n-person game with characteristic function v is a vector $x=(x_1,x_2,....,x_n)$ satisfying the following:

(i) $\sum_{i=1}^{n} x_i = v(N)$;

(ii) $x_i \geq v(i)$, for $i=1,2,.....,n$

Where x_i is obviously the ith player's reward. The condition (i) is a Pareto optimality condition or the rationality of the grand coalition. $v(N)$ is the most the players can get out of the game when they all work together. So, for any possible set of individual rewards x_i; we must have $\sum_{i=1}^{n} x_i \leq v(N)$. If this was a strict inequality, then, by working together, they could always share out the rewards so that everyone got more. The condition (ii) says that everyone must get as much as they could get if they played by themselves.

Once we had defined the imputation concept, we introduce the concept of the core (Gilles, 1953). The core of a game v, denoted by $C(v)$, is the set of imputations which are not dominated for any other coalition. This means that you can not find another imputation y and a coalition S such that

$$\sum_{i \in S} y_i \leq v(S) \text{ and } y_i > x_i \text{ for all } i \in S$$

Thus, if x is in the core, any coalition which forms, either says x is the best imputation for it. Notice there can be more than one imputation in the core. We provide a result which can be found in Thomas (1984).

Theorem: x is in the core if and only if

(i) $\sum_{i=1}^{n} x_i = v(N)$, and

(ii) $\sum_{i \in S} x_i \geq v(S)$ for all $S \subset N$

Once the concepts of an imputation and the core are given, we can apply the core solution in our model. To apply the core, it is feasible to consider in a better way its 0-1 reduction. It must satisfy:

---

[1] Thomas, L.C., 1984. Games, Theory and Applications. Ellis Horwood Limited

$$\overline{w}(S) = kv(S) + \sum_{i \in S} w_i \qquad (16)$$

Such that:
$\overline{w}(i) = 0$;
$\overline{w}(1,2,3) = 1$

Taking the characteristic functions of the model

$v(\{1\}) = v(1) = 0 \qquad v_2(\{2\}) = v(2) = 0 \qquad v(\{3\}) = 0$

$v(\{1,2\}) = v(1,2) = 0$

$v(\{1,3\}) = v(1,3) = \dfrac{(\beta_1 - \lambda c_{s1}\gamma_1)^2}{4\gamma_1}$

$v(\{2,3\}) = v(2,3) = \dfrac{(\beta_2 - \lambda c_{s2}\gamma_2)^2}{4\gamma_2}$

$v(\{1,2,3\}) = v(1,2,3) = \dfrac{(\beta_1 - \lambda c_{s1}\gamma_1)^2}{4\gamma_1} + \dfrac{(\beta_2 - \lambda c_{s2}\gamma_2)^2}{4\gamma_2}$

Next we look for the value $\overline{w}(S)$. To simplify the mathematical calculation, we denote

$\alpha = \dfrac{(\beta_1 - \lambda c_{s1}\gamma_1)^2}{4\gamma_1}$ and $\tau = \dfrac{(\beta_2 - \lambda c_{s2}\gamma_2)^2}{4\gamma_2}$.

Applying equation (16), we get:

$\overline{w}(1) = kv(1) + w_1 = k0 + w_1 = 0$

$\overline{w}(2) = k0 + w_2 = 0$

$\overline{w}(3) = kv(3) + w_3 = k0 + w_3 = 0$

$\overline{w}(1,2,3) = kv(1,2,3) + w_1 + w_2 + w_3 = 1$

$k = \dfrac{1}{v(1,2,3)}$

$\overline{w}(1,2) = kv(1,2) + w_1 + w_2 = 0$

$\overline{w}(1,3) = kv(1,3) + w_1 + w_3 = \dfrac{v(1,3)}{v(1,2,3)} = \dfrac{\alpha}{\alpha + \tau}$

$\overline{w}(2,3) = kv(2,3) + w_2 + w_3 = \dfrac{v(2,3)}{v(1,2,3)} = \dfrac{\tau}{\alpha + \tau}$

These equations are the characteristic functions reduced to 0-1. And once we have reduced the characteristic function, we can then apply the reduced core. It must satisfy the following:

$x_i \geq 0$

$x_1 + x_2 \geq \overline{w}(1,2) = 0$

$x_1 + x_3 \geq \overline{w}(1,3) = \eta$

$x_2 + x_3 \geq \overline{w}(2,3) = \sigma$

$x_1 + x_2 + x_3 = 1 = \varsigma$

Where η, σ and ς denote the characteristic functions in the 0-1 reduced core.

So, we can get the feasible set of payoffs of the model as the figure 2 shows.

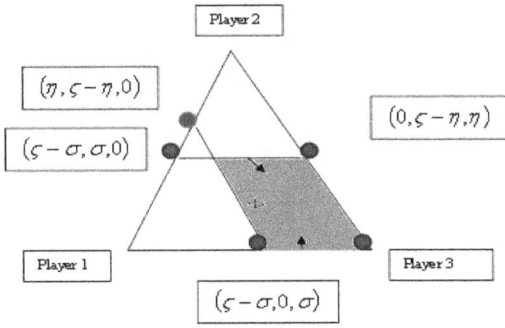

Figure 2: The reduced core solution

The painted area is the reduced core solution. Therefore all the points of the reduced core are possible solutions for the game played by the three agents under consideration. Moreover, under the condition that $\eta+\sigma \leq \eta*\sigma$ in the reduced game, the game is convex in the sense $v(S)+v(T) \leq v(S \cup T)+v(S \cap T)$ for all S and T^1 subsets of $\{1,2,3\}$. The last property is also valid for non-reduced games.

In the case that the characteristic function is convex, then both the reduced and non-reduced core are non-empty, and have a regular structure. In particular, there is the Shapley value which is the center of gravity of the extreme points of the core. If the core is only a point, the Shapley value is unique and coincides with the core (Shapley, 1965).

2.6-THE SHAPLEY VALUE

A solution concept for the game under consideration is the Shapley value (Peleg and Sudhölter, 2003) and (Branzei and Tijs, 2005). Shapley (1953) looked at what each player could reasonably get before the game has begun. He put three axioms, which he called $\phi_i(v)$, player i's expectation in a game with a characteristic function v, should satisfy the following:

S1: $\phi_i(v)$ is independent of the labeling of the players. If π is a permutation of 1, 2,...., n and πv is the characteristic function of the game, with the players numbers permuted by π, then $\phi_{\pi(i)}(\pi v) = \phi_i(v)$.

S2: The sum of the expectations should equal the maximum available from the game, so

$$\sum_{i=1}^{n} \phi_i(v) = v(N)$$

S3: If u,v are the characteristic functions of two games, $u+v$ is the characteristic function of the game playing both games together. ϕ must satisfy $\phi_i(u+v) = \phi_i(u)+\phi_i(v)$.

Given these assumptions, Shapley proved the following theorem:

Theorem. There is only one function which satisfies S1, S2 and S3, namely:

---

[1]Shapley, Lloyd, 1971. Cores of convex games. International Journal of Game Theory 1, 11-26

$$\phi_i(v) = \sum_{S: i \in S} \frac{(\#S-1)!(n-\#S)!}{n!}(v(S) - v(S-\{i\}))$$

Where the summation is over all coalitions S which contain player i and $\#S$ is the number of players in the coalition S. $\phi_i(v)$ is called the Shapley value. The quantity ϕ_i may be interpreted as the "equity value" associated with the position of the i-th player in the game (Shapley, 1965).

In our model, the Shapley value is:
For downstream firm 1,
$$\phi_1(v) = \frac{1}{2}\frac{(\beta_1 - \lambda c_{s1}\gamma_1)^2}{4\gamma_1}$$
For downstream firm 2,
$$\phi_2(v) = \frac{1}{2}\frac{(\beta_2 - \lambda c_{s2}\gamma_2)^2}{4\gamma_2}$$
For the supply firm
$$\phi_3(v) = \frac{1}{2}\left(\frac{(\beta_1 - \lambda c_{s1}\gamma_1)^2}{4\gamma_1} + \frac{(\beta_2 - \lambda c_{s2}\gamma_2)^2}{4\gamma_2}\right)$$

And the total value created is equal to $\frac{(\beta_1 - \lambda c_{s1}\gamma_1)^2}{4\gamma_1} + \frac{(\beta_2 - \lambda c_{s2}\gamma_2)^2}{4\gamma_2}$. As it can be checked, this total value is equal to the first best and to the value obtained when the three firms cooperate with each other. That is, the grand coalition's characteristic function.

The Shapley value indicates how the total benefits can be split in a fair way. We can see that the supplier gets more benefits compared with the benefits that each downstream firm gets. This indicates what we posed in the previous section that the cooperative game theory attempts to answer how the total value is divided up among various players. We remark that this answer will depend on the bargaining power of the players, and this is determined by which players are most needed. In this model, the supplier is the most needed because the firms have incentives to merger or to be vertically integrated with the supply firm, for the reason that a merger or the vertical integration ensures them that the production will have the required quality. In other words, the bargaining power of the supplier relies on the specificity of the investments because it is this specificity what makes the cooperation credible. If the investments were general, non-specific, the cooperation framework would not be enforceable because each player could sell or produce outside the relationship. Such bargaining power is measured by the Shapley value and it is what makes possible the cooperation among the three players, achieving a Pareto optimum solution. Thus, this higher supplier's bargaining power is what makes the upstream-downstream relationship an enforceable one. As a result of this, if the the three firms commit to cooperate and they distribute the benefits as the Shapley value indicates, at time 0, they will decide the quantity level and the prices that maximize total welfare.

3- CONCLUSIONS

In this paper we have developed a model within the upstream-downstream relationship that attempts to find an alternative solution to vertical integration. Our contribution is twofold: first, a mathematical part where we show how to apply the maximin to compute the characteristic functions of the model; and second, an economic contribution, where we explain how cooperation can lead to organizational forms that generate more value. In fact, we set another way to treat the upstream-downstream relationship under incomplete contracts and a cooperative framework, providing an alternative to vertical integration.

As a solution, vertical integration presents some problems and it seems to be a poor solution under certain circumstances. In particular, the existence of these failures made us wonder if there could be another way to solve those problems that vertical integration did not solve. More specifically, what happens if the supply firm does not want to be vertically integrated? What happens if the firms decide to cooperate instead of being vertically integrated under the presence of specific investments? To answer these questions we have developed a model where the firms cooperate with each other. We find that, under cooperation, the total value generated is Pareto optimum if they cooperate and distribute the benefits through the Shapley value solution. The Shapley value measures the power that firms enjoy in the bargaining process, where bargaining power under cooperative game theory is defined in terms of how much each player is needed. The result of our model is that the supplier's bargaining power is determined by the specificity of the investments and this makes the cooperation among the firms possible, and the upstream-downstream relationship enforceable. As a consequence, the first best, that maximizes the total welfare, can be achieved.

In this paper, we have presented a one-shot supply transaction. We want to consider further developments of this model, with n-periods and more participants, in our future research. In such scenarios, one must include relational contracts and the reputation of the firms, increasing the complexity of the analysis. We are also interested in the use of biform games, which combine both the non-cooperative game theory and the cooperative game approach in the same analysis. We believe that more efforts should be implemented in this direction to achieve a better understanding of organizational forms.

5-BIBLIOGRAPHY

Alchian, A., Demsetz, H., 1972. Production, Information Costs and Economic Organization. American Economic Review. 62, 777-795.

Aoki, M., (1988). Information, Incentives and Bargaining in the Japanese Economy. Cambridge University Press, Cambridge, UK (1988).

Aoki, M., (1990). Toward an Economic Model of the Japanese Firm. Journal of Economic Literature 28, 1–27.

Aumann, R.J., 1959. Acceptable Points in General Cooperative n-Person Games. Contribution to the Theory of Games IV. Princeton University Press, pp. 287-324.

Bondareva, O.N., 1962. Certain applications of the methods of linear programing to the theory of cooperative games. Problemy Kibernetiki 10, 119-139 (in Russian).

Brandenburger, Adam, (2007). Cooperative Game Theory: Characteristic Functions, Allocations, Marginal Contribution. Stern School of Business. New York University.

Branzei, R., Dimitrov, D., Tijs, S., 2005. Models in Cooperative Game Theory. Crisp, Fuzzy and Multi-Choice Games. Springer-Verlag Berlin Heidelberg.

Cachon, G., Lariviere, M., 2005. Supply Chain Coordination with Reveneu-Sharing Contracts: Strengths and Limitations. Management Science 51, 30-44.

Cantisani M., Marchi E., 2004. The Weighted Core with Distinguished Coalition. International Games Theory Review 6 (2), 239-246.

Chandler, A., 1962. Strategy and Structure. New York: Doubleday.

Coase, R., 1937. The Nature of the Firm. Economica 4, 357-376.

Edgeworth, F.Y., 1881. Mathematical Physics and Further Papers. Political Economy. Oxford University Press.

Gibbons, R., 2000. Why Organizations are Such a Mess (and What an Economist Might Do About It). Rough Draft. MIT.

Gillies, D. B., 1953. Solutions to general non-zero-sum games. Contributions to the Theory of Games IV. Princeton University Press, pp. 47-85.

Grossman, S., Hart. O., 1986. The Costs and Benefits of Ownership: A Theory of Lateral and Vertical Integration. Journal of Political Economy 94, 691-719.

Grossman, O., Moore, J., 1990. Property Rights and the Theory of the Firm. Journal of Political Economy 98, 1119-1158.

Hart, O., Moore, J., 1990. Property Rights and the Theory of the Firm. Journal of Political Economy 98, 1119-1158.

Hart, O., 1995. Firms, Contracts and Financial Structures. Oxford University Press.

Holmström, B., Roberts, J., 1998. The Boundaries of the Firm Revisited. Journal of Economic Perspectives 12, 73-94.

Klein, B., Crawford, R., Alchian, A., 1978. Vertical Integration, Appropriable Rents and the Competitive Contracting Process. Journal of Law and Economics 21, 297-326.

Klein. B., 1988. Vertical Integration as Organizational Ownership: The Fischer Body-General Motors Relationship Revisited. Journal of Law, Economics and Organization 4, 199-213.

Marchi, E., 1967. On the Minimax Theorem of the Theory of Games. Ann. Mat. Pura ed Appl. Ser. IV, Vol 77, 207-282 (MR 38,1914)

Marchi, E., Matons, M., 2007. Reduced TU-Games. International Journal of Applied Mathematics, Game Theory and Algebra 17, Issue 5/6.

Myerson, R., 1991. Game Theory. Analysis of Conflict. Harvard University Press.

Nagarajan, M., Soŝić, G., 2006. Game-Theoretic Analysis of Cooperation Among Supply Agents: Review and Extensions. European Journal of Operational Research

Neumann, von, J., 1928. Sur Theorie der Gesellschaftsspielle. Math. Annals 100, 295-320

Neumann, von, J., Morgenstern, O., 1944. Theory of Games and Economic Behavior. Princeton University Press, NJ.

Peleg, B., Sudhölter, P., 2003. Introduction to The Theory of Cooperative Games. Kluwer Academic Publishers.

Porter, G., Livesey, H., 1971. Merchants and Manufacturers. Baltimore: John Hopkins University Press.

Rajan, R., Zingales, L., 2000. The Govenance of the New Enterprise. En X. Vives, edr., Corporate Governance: Theoretical and Empirical Perspectives. Cambridge University Press, Cambridge.

Serrano, R., 2007. Cooperative Games: Core and Shapley Value. Encyclopedia of Complexity and Systems Science. Springer. Berlin.

Shapley, Lloyd., 1953. A value for n-person games. Contribution to the Theory of Games II. Princeton University Press, pp. 307-317.

Shapley, L., 1967. On balanced sets and cores. Naval Research Logistics Quarterly 14, 453-460.

Shapley, Lloyd, 1971. Cores of convex games. International Journal of Game Theory 1, 11-26.

Thomas, L.C., 1984. Games, Theory and Applications. Ellis Horwood Limited.

Williamson, O., 1975. Markets and Hierarchies: Analysis and Antitrust Implication: A Study in the Economics of Internal Organization, New York, Free Press.

Williamson, O., 1981. The Economics of Organization.The Transaction Cost Approach. American Journal of Sociology 87, 548-577.

Zingales, L., 1998. Corporate Governance. The New Palgrave Dictionary of Economics and the Law, P. Newman ed, Macmillan, New York, NY.

Emami, M., Amini, Amrollah and Emami, Alireza, . (2011). The Survey of Correlation between Social Capital and Knowledge of Management
(The Case Study in National Oil Refining and Distribution Company in Iran (Shiraz)) Australian Journal of Basic and Applied Sciences

Emami, M., Amini, Amrollah and Emami, Alireza, . (2013).STOCK PORTFOLIO OPTIMIZATION WITH USING A NEW HYBRID EVOLUTIONARY
ALGORITHM BASED ON ICA AND GA : RECURSIVE-ICA-GA(CAS STUDY OF TEHRAN STOCK EXCHANGE),International Conference on Economic, Finance and Management Outlooks

Emami, M., Amini, Amrollah and Emami, Alireza,. (2011). the Impact of Earnings Management and Expectations Management on The
Usefulness of Earnings and Analyst Forecasts in Firm Valuation, International Conference on Economic, Finance and Management Outlooks

Emami, M., Amini, Amrollah and Emami, Alireza, . (2011).Empirical Model for Costing Gas using ABC, Emerging Markets Economics: Industrial Policy & Regulation journal - CMBO

Emami, M., Amini, Amrollah and Emami, Alireza, . (2011). Investment Performance Evaluation Methods: A Mixed Strategy Framework,7th Global Business and Social Science Research Conference

Emami, M., Amini, Amrollah and Emami, Alireza,. (2011). THE IMPACT OF EARNINGS MANAGEMENT AND EXPECTATIONS MANAGEMENT
ON THE USEFULNESS OF EARNINGS AND ANALYST FORECASTS IN FIRM VALUATION, Microeconomics: Decision-Making under Risk

Activity Based Costing Model for Cost Calculation in Gas Companies: Empirical Evidence of Iran

AMROLAH AMINI (Ph.D)

Associate Professor, Allameh Tabatabaei University (ATU), Tehran, Iran.

aminij@atu.ac.ir

ALIREZA EMAMI

Master of Science, Tehran University, Tehran, Iran

memami@alumni.ut.ac.ir

MOSTAFA EMAMI*

Master of Science, Michigan Technological University (MTU)

memami@mtu.edu

*Corresponding Address

Applied Research and Technology Office, Michigan Technological University

1400 Townsend Dr, Houghton, MI 49931

Tel & Fax : +1-(816) 237-0018

E-mail: memami@mtu.edu

Activity Based Costing Model for Cost Calculation in Gas Companies: Empirical Evidence of Iran

Abstract

With the reduction of public funding and the government's emphasis on accountability, output control and cost–effective in the delivery of services, organizations need information to measure their activities, link their inputs with outputs, correct their pricing, and measuring their performance in order to facilitate accomplishing their goals. This research is to explain the steps and the benefits of implementing Activity Based Costing (ABC) in Iranian Gas Company. Using ABC, cost of one cub meter of consuming gas in all regions of capital was determined and compared with the results of the Traditional Costing Systems (TCS). Implementing ABC strongly changed company managers' prospective toward company cost of services, provided more effective system for company internal decision-making, improved the effectiveness of the costing system and cost management and helped the managers to correct company pricing of services and accomplishment of the strategic goals by giving more correct cost information.

Key words:

Activity Based Costing

Traditional Costing Method

Iranian Gas Company

Cost Driver

Cost Center

Indirect Costs

1. Introduction

Nowadays, organizations are involved in more complex situations. Things like tight competitions in market, economic fluctuations, day to day crisis in international ties, the fast progress of technology in most of the fields, sensitivity of human resources in organizations and many other problems have made running the organizations more difficult. Sometimes, management has changed from "a decision for a life" to "a decision for a day". Companies for their survival should set prices in a way that they can compete to others in present markets and at the same time prices guarantee their contribution margin. For this purpose, they should develop effective mechanisms for measuring their performances and for the correct report of costing.

Due to changes in technology, a considerable share of product costs is allotted in overhead costs and consequently an appropriate allotment of overhead costs to products and services regards as a very important matter for all kinds of organizations. Since Traditional Costing System (TCS) utilizes optional bases (such as direct work hour) to share out the overhead costs and ignores the causal relations between used direct work hours and overhead costs, it is weak on allocating and setting costs and can't be accountable for present management needs. As a result, management accountants in order to provide the managers accurate information for optimal decisions in competitive situations have introduced costing based on activity system for calculating cost of products and services. (Hejazi, 2005)

The Islamic Republic of Iran, due to its geo-strategic situation being between the two biggest natural gas rich regions (Soviet Union and the countries around the Persian Golf). Iran is possessing more than 27 trillion cubic meters of natural gas that is considered as the second greatest owner of natural gas resources after Russia. Based on most of the reliable estimations, natural gas because of its inherent properties and especially its adaptation with the environment is one of the energy carriers that will have the highest progress rate among other energy carriers by year 2030. It means that natural gas share of the world's energy consuming basket is continuously increasing. (Khatibi, Tabatabiye, 2006) It is why pricing the natural gas is one of the most important and basic issues in economy of a society. Also, maintenance and appropriate consumption of hydrocarbon resources which are also part of the rights of prospective people increase the importance of gas costing and pricing on the macro level. It is because, the revenue resulting from appropriate pricing of natural gas in every consuming sector will have an influence on not only gas industry interests but also on national and economical interests of the country at the present and in the future. Accordingly, logical and appropriate pricing of natural gas industry, like other industries, should be according to the economical principles and standards. It is well known that in pricing natural gas, several factors such as environmental, social and political considerations as well as its cost should be taken into account. Awareness of the economical cost for setting the economical price of the natural gas is one of the necessary principles in gas pricing model.

In this research, in order to have a model for the correct and exact calculation of the cost of every one cubic meter of the natural gas in different regions, Activity Based Costing (ABC) as a case study was carried out in Tehran Province Gas Company.

The paper is arranged as follows. Next section summarizes the literature on ABC in services and gas industries. In the third section, the research method is described. Section 4 provides the discussions and the result of the analysis. Finally, the paper ends with conclusions and final remarks.

2. Literature Review

Most of studies reveal that ABC system is a useful method for the evaluation of sectors managers' performances, estimation of resource (budget) consumption along the line of giving services, appropriate allocation of resources among public sectors and increase of the quality of the services of public sectors in the central government.

Baxendale and Dornbush (2000) in a study named "ABC for hospice" calculated cost and solutions for decreasing costs in the central hospice of Kentaki. The management of this hospice believes that when the expenses increase, implementing management accounting methods is the only solution for decreasing costs. After studying and counseling with specialists, the management introduced ABC as the most helpful system. In this study, they identified main activities in hospice, grouped the activities, and determined the activities necessary for delivering services to the customers. Results of the study showed that ABC with presenting accurate information about costing has helped the management to decide about decrease of costs, improvement of process, increase of quality, and correct pricing of services.

Tatikonda and Tatikonda (2001), Ellis-Newman et al. (1996), and Mitchall (1996) in a similar research introduced ABC as a good method of performance evaluation, allocating resources, improving process and increasing efficiency of activities in universities. Kelline et al. (2001) and Roberson and Bernasooni (1998) studied the importance of ABC in correct budgeting of university. This study with the application of ABC in the university of Kansas state showed that it in different parts of university can have the following applications:

- Conformity of resources with the units' purposes.
- Increasing efficiency of activities and works in different parts.
- Presenting logical reasons to college and university chancellors about correct method of resources consumption and using more resources if necessary.
- Using logical method of organizing information in units.

University chancellors with implementation of ABC understood that this system in comparison with the TCS is more helpful for budgeting, allocating resources to different parts and also evaluating performances and decision making in attention to costs information.

Lung (2002) in a study named "ABC in Telecom Industry" studied telecom corporations in Australia, Ireland and Panama. They used ABC for costing telephone conversations and setting prices. The results showed that ABC with presenting correct information about the final costs and good pricing led to customers' satisfaction and firms' profitability increase.

Jarvinen (2005), Arnabodia & Lapsly(2005), Arnaboldi & Lapsly (2004), Negrini et al. (2004), Waters et al. (2003), and Rajabi (2001) implemented ABC in different hospitals in the world and introduced this system as a strategy for the correct allocation of direct overheads to products and presentation of helpful information for managers' decision making in competitive situations.

Sap et al. (2005) in a research named "Activity based costing in financial institutions" calculated cost of services in the United States bank. In this study, the reasons for the need of financial institution to exact and complete information about their cost of services are as follow:

- *Deregulation of financial institutions*. Deregulation has intensified competitive pressures on pricing, product mix, delivery, and profitability.
- *Increase in the cost of interest-bearing sources of funds*. This has increased the need for cost information in order to price loans profitably in light of shrinking margins.

- *Expansion of non-fund services.* The introduction of new, non-traditional products and services has complicated the cost\structure and has increased the need for accurate cost information in order to design and price these products and services.
- *Unbundling of products and services.* In days past, banks often relied on a single service charge to cover a bundle of services and hoped that on average the total cost of providing services cost less than the revenue generated by the service charge. The trend over recent years has been to unbundled services and prices each one separately. This has significantly increased the demand for cost information.
- *Automation of many transactions.* While technology has lowered the direct cost per transaction, it has increased the indirect costs. The tracing of these indirect costs to products is a major challenge for a cost system.

Kocakülâh and Crowe (2005), Narasimha and Thampy (2002), Mostaque and Gunasekaran (2001), Innes and Mitchall (1997) with the application of ABC in banking industry, introduced this technique as the one that meet managers information needs and help them to have a correct understanding of costs of services.

Ju Kim (2003) in a study named "Activity based costing in telecommunication industry" calculated cost of internal telephone conversations. The implementation of the ABC in this study was as follow:

- Measuring work hours, statistical data and production.
- Identifying activities in every unit.
- Determining cost drivers.
- Separating cost lacking tariff from cost having specific tariff.
- Codifying based on product unit, recording and measuring statistical data for separating direct costs from indirect costs.
- Allocating indirect costs based on drivers

The results indicated that ABC gives a useful basis for sharing out common costs in telecommunication industry and helps the managers to set the correct price of internal telephone conversations and determine exact loss and profit of the company. Moreover, for the successful implementation in industry, it is necessary to use information technology for measuring statistical data and correct classifying of assets.

Taherkordi (2003) in a study named "The implementation of the activity based costing in Oil Company of Iran continental shelf" calculated cost of one oil barred production of the company. The results indicated that ABC with revealing some of the problems and quantifying company operations make useful information available to optimize operations. Therefore, managers can improve efficacy of their operations by activities and lower the costs.

Muras et al. (2000) believed that ABC was necessary for improvement of process application of managers' goals, standardization and correct pricing of product in oil industry.

Barton and Macarthur (2003) in a research named "ABC and predatory pricing: the case of the petroleum retail industry" which was done due to a legal claim against a petroleum station company about selling petrol with the price cheaper than the price set by America state laws, indicated that final costs of each gallon of petrol based on ABC in comparison with the pervious methods were more accurate and more clear and this technique solved the problems when the final costs of the products are less or more than the real amount.

Arabmazar Yazdi and Naseri (2004) use ABC in banking deposit services. Ellis-Newman (2003) in a study named "ABC in user services of an academic library" in library of Australian university showed that libraries' managers for strategic planning and deciding about the optimal allocation of rare resources needs information about costs behaviors that the best method for understanding this issue and improving costing system is ABC. Detya (2001), Ellis and Robinson (1998) in similar researches evaluated ABC as a helpful technique for the activities of libraries' managers.

Lievens et al. (2003) in a study named "ABC for cost calculation in radiotherapy" calculated radiotherapy costs. These costs include equipment costs which are one of overhead costs in each therapy that their correct tracing to products show correct and precise final cost. Therefore, for the correct allocating of such costs and setting final cost of one day or long term cures, ABC was used. The management of this center after the application of this system introduced ABC as a strong method in setting final prices of services and correct pricing.

Collier (2006) in a study named "Costing of police services " calculated the cost of every crime committed using ABC. In that study with considering the new approach of the management of the public sector toward the rate of resource consumption against services and the importance of police as the supplier of social security, ABC for costing police services has been implemented in England and Wales. The results had considerable benefits for both police and related government because of identifying the activities lacking valued added resulted in process improvement and decrease of organizations. Also the research showed that for giving services, it is essential to profit from more resources.

Kumar (2006) in a research named "Activity based costing in hospital" calculated cost of services in the blood transfusion ward of the American national hospital. With the implementation of the system there, American national hospital managers and directors become aware of the benefits of the ABC in improvement of activities and increase in efficiency. Moreover, according to the researcher, support of the high management, company resources and strategies, good and attractive introduction of the system to the organization and having competitive and instructive environment were among the effective factors that made the implementation of this technique successful.

According to the literature, ABC brings the following advantages:

- ABC with presenting accurate information about costing helps the management to decide about decrease of costs, improvement of process, increase of quality, and correct pricing of services.
- It as a good method of performance evaluation, allocating resources, improving process increases efficiency of companies' activities.
- It is helpful for budgeting, allocating resources to different parts of company and also evaluating performances and decision making in attention to costs information.
- It presents correct information about the final costs and good pricing and leads to customers' satisfaction and increases firms' profitability.
- It is a helpful tool for correct allocation of direct overheads to products and presentation of helpful information for managers' decision making in competitive situations.

- It reveals some of the problems and quantifying company operations make useful information available to optimize operations. Therefore, managers can improve efficacy of their operations by activities and lower the costs.
- It is a strong method in setting final prices of services and correct pricing.
- It identifies the activities lacking value added in process improvement.

3. Research Methodology

Transforming natural gas to the final customers includes some stages as discovery, development and production, transfer and distribution. In this research, in order to calculate cost of services in gas transfer sector, ABC was used. It was examined in Tehran Gas Company as a case of study in the oil and gas industry of Iran. In sampling from Provincial Gas Companies under the supervision of Iran National Gas Company, Tehran Province Gas Company which is the biggest provincial gas companies was selected. Because of the availability of the real information about the year 2005, we have calculated cost of one cube meter of natural gas in all regions of the Tehran province for the year of 2005.

In our study, ABC includes the following eight stages:

Stage 1: Determining cost items and cost drivers: These items are determined by using the company accounting system. The cost items are costs groups of the company included in the profit and loss list. Cost drivers show causes of resources consumption by activities. These cost drivers can be determined using opinions of the managers of the financial affairs.

Stage 2: Identifying main activities and determining cost drivers: In order to identify the main activities, we used of operational process chart, interview with the experts and the researchers. After identifying activities, with attention to the considerations about benefits which were higher than expenses, similar activities put together and related cost drivers were determined. Table 1 shows the main activities, cost drivers and cost items for the company.

[Insert Table 1

Stage 3: Determining the relation between cost items with activities in the Expense-Activity–Dependence Matrix (EADM): This matrix shows how resources consumed by each activity.

Stage 4: Calculating and replacing allocation rates in the EADM: Based on the cost drivers, which are determined in stage 1, share of each activity of company from resources was calculated and put in the matrix cell. According to the calculated numbers, allocation rates of cost items to activities were calculated and placed in matrix cells. Sum of rates in each column of EADM should be equal to one. This matrix is based on the real information in the years 2003, 2004, and 2005 because in Tehran Gas Company, just the financial information of these 3 years was available. The average of allocation rates over three years considered as final rates of resources consumed by activities.

Stage 5: Calculating activities' expenses: Activities' expenses are calculated by the following formula:

$$TCA(i) = \sum_{j=1}^{m} \{ E(j) * EDAM(i,j) \} \qquad (1)$$

Where *TCA (i), m, E (j)*, and *EDA(i,j)* denote the total expenses of activity, number of cost items, the rate of consuming resources by activity and *i*the row and *j*the column in EADM, respectively. After calculating cost of each activity, the new matrix of EADM with monetary values was formed. Table 2 shows completed Expense-Activity–Dependence Matrix (EADM).

[Insert Table 2]

Stage 6: Determining the relation between activities and Activity–Product-Dependence Matrix (APDM): In this stage, the activities consumed by the regions are determined and APDM is formed.

Stage 7: Calculating and replacing allocation rate in APDM: Based on cost drivers determined in stage 2 and applying calculation methods, allocation rates of activity expenses to product are calculated and placed in the APDM cells. Sum of the rates in each of columns of the matrix should be equal to one. To compute indirect overhead costs of regions, the following formula was appalled:

$$OCP(i) = \sum_{j=1}^{n} \{ TCA(j) * APD(i,j) \} \qquad (2)$$

Where *OCP(i), n, TCA (j)*, and *APD(i,j)* are indirect overhead costs of activity, number of activities, total costs of activity, and *i*the row and *j*the column in APDM. After calculating amount of activity overheads for each region, the new APDM with monetary values was formed. Table 3 and 4 show the allocation rates and the monetary values of activity expenses to products.

[Insert Tables 3]

[Insert Tables 4]

Stage 8: Calculating cost of products/services: With allocating indirect overhead costs to the gas transferred regions in the APDM, cost of one cub meter of natural gas in those regions, direct overhead costs, and value of consumed raw materials of each region were calculated by the following formula:

Cost of one cub meter = $\dfrac{\text{Region raw materials} + \text{region direct overheads} + \text{region indirect overheads}}{\text{Cub meters of consuming gas of the region}}$

Table 5 shows cost of one cubic meter of regional gas in ABC system and Table 6 compares cost of one cub meter of gas in ABC and two traditional costing systems. As shows in table 6, there are significant differences among the cost of one cubic meter of gas under three method of calculation. One of the reasons why the amounts of cost of one cubic meter of gas in these two methods are different is that in TCS, some costs are considered in calculating cost of products, but in ABC, all the costs traceable to product are considered in calculating cost. Another reason is the method of tracing indirect costs to products. In the TCS, product consumes organizational resources but in ABC, activities consume organizational resources are traced to products based on drivers related to each activity.

[Insert Table 5]

[Insert Table 6]

4. Results of Data Analysis

Table 7 shows Iranian Gas Company cost model. As it is seen, eighty percent of the Tehran Gas Company resources is used by sustaining activity and main subscribers and the remaining 20 percent is consumed by other activities. In the cost model of Tehran Gas Company, 75% of 80% consuming resources was used by sustaining activities. This means that the managers of Tehran Gas Company should pay attention to this cost center to control and decrease the costs.

[Insert Table 7]

Table 8 analyzes the allocation of the indirect overheads to different regions. In Table 8, the amounts of indirect overheads of regions in ABC have been ordered descending. As it is clear, 80% of the total indirect overheads are dedicated to Karaj, Pakdasht, Shahriyar, Fardis, Nazarabad, Gharchak, Hashtgerd, Chahardange and Shaegods. As shows, Karaj city has the highest share of indirect overheads.

[Insert Table 8]

Table 9 analyzes allocating the cost of main subscribers and sustaining. As it is clear in Table 9, sixty percent of the total costs of sustaining activity, which has the highest cost in Tehran Gas Company cost model, are placed in Karaj, Pakdasht, Varamin, Eslamshahr and Shahriyar. Seventy percent of total cost of main subscribers' activity, which is in the second row of table 7, is placed in Pakdasht, Chahardange, Karaj and Gharchak. Because sustaining activity consist of 75% of the total cost of sustaining and main subscribers, the management of Tehran Gas Company should pay attention to this critical region; in this manner it can control almost 50 percent of the company costs.

[Insert Table 9]

Table10 shows direct overhead costs of regions. In Table 10, the amounts of direct overhead costs of regions are ordered descending. As it is indicated in the Table, 60% of the total direct overheads are placed in Karaj, Eslamshahr, Varamin, Shahriyar and Pakdasht, As seen in table 10, fifty percent of the direct overhead is consumed in Karaj city. Since these cities have most of the share of Tehran Gas Company budget, the management of the company should pay more attention to the resources allocated to these regions and their performances in relation to budget consumption. The management of Tehran Gas Company with using activity based budgeting can make useful decisions about correct budgeting and decreasing costs and use it as a means for evaluating performances of different regions.

[Insert Table 10]

Finally, Table11 shows cost of one cubic meter gas in regions. As shown in Table 11, cost of one cubic meter of the regional gas was ordered descending. In other words, different regions have different costs and in some cases have many differences, while all the subscribers in different regions pay the same price for the consuming gas.

[Insert Table 11]

5. Conclusions and Final Remarks

Traditional single overhead rate method is not concerned with the actual relation between the expenses and their cause of existence because it just makes use of one based in sharing out factory overhead. This method due to the average out to the high and low amount of the overhead costs will result in product cost deviation. Generally, the multi rate method, through the creation of the cost centers based on the similar expenses or cost centers; allocate the collected expenses in these centers to the products/services based on the one of the determined basis. In this system, there is no relation between the necessary activities for producing product or giving services and use of financial resources by these activities. Therefore, cost of products/services does not show the company activities and the value of the resources used by the company.

In the ABC, this fault is removed by the direct arranging of the organizational costs and operational activities. Pragmatically, the ABC determines the causal relations between the creation of expenses and the necessary activities for producing product or giving services, which have the economical value for the company. Instead of one factor, several basis factors determine the activities, the cost center for each activity, find the rates related to expenses and attract these rates to the products based on the resources which are used for producing product or giving services. Therefore, we can say that in the ABC with the more appropriate allocation of the collected expenses in cost centers to given services, these services are costed more exactly. By improving the quality of the information, ABC system can inform the management about the activities which consume company resources. This helps the manager to decide about the process which improve the quality of the activities done (process improvement) and the process which increase the result of those activities (productivity). Generally, the ABC system helps the manager in correct pricing of services and accomplishment of the strategic goals of the organization by giving more correct information about the cost of services.

This paper is aimed to calculate cost of one cubic meter gas in different region of Tehran Gas Company using ABC. In this research, we explained the steps and the benefits of implementing ABC in Iranian Gas Company. Using ABC, cost of one cub meter of consuming gas in all regions of province of Tehran was determined and compared with the results of the TCS. The results showed meaningful differences between ranges of cost deviations in the TCM in the highest and lowest levels. Benefits of implementing ABC strongly changed Iranian Gas Company managers' prospective toward company cost of services, provided a very effective system for company internal decision-making, improved the effectiveness of the costing system and cost management, and helped the managers to correct pricing of services and accomplishment of the strategic goals of the organization by giving more correct information about the cost of services. As a result, we can claim that the information collected from the

ABC, comparing with the present TCS of Tehran Gas Company, was more useful and valuable for the management decision making.

References

1. Arabmazar, M., and Naseri, M. (2004) Using Activity Based Costing (ABC) in Banking Deposit Services, Iranian Accounting and Auditing Review, 10(34), pp. 3-26.
2. Arnaboldi, M., and Lapsley, I. (2004) Modern Costing Innovations and Legitimating: A Healthcare Case Study, *Abacus*, 40(1), pp. 1-20.
3. Arnabodia, M. and Lapsley, I. (2005) Activity Based Costing in Healthcare: A UK Case Study, *Research in Healthcare Financial Management*, 10, pp. 22-34.
4. Barton, T..L., and MacArthur, J. B. (2003) Activity-Based Costing and Predatory Pricing: The Case of the Petroleum Retail Industry, Management Accounting Quarterly, Vol. 4, No 3, pp.1-7.
5. Baxendale, S. J. and Dornbush, V. (2000) Activity-Based Costing for a Hospice, *Strategic Finance* (March 2000), pp. 60-70.
6. Deyta (2001). Activity-based costing: a study to develop a costing methodology for library and information technology activities for the Australian higher education sector. Department of Education, Training and Youth Affairs. Retrieved November 20, 2001, from http://www.detya.gov.au/highered/otherpub/libraries/libraries.pdf
7. Collier, P. M. (2006) Costing Police Services: The Politicization of Accounting, *Critical Perspective on Accounting*, 17(1), pp. 57-86.
8. Ellis-Newman, J. and Robinson, P. (1998) The Cost of Library Services: Activity Based Costing in an Australian Academic Library, *Journal of Academic Librarianship*, 24(5), pp. 373-379.
9. Ellis-Newman, J., Izan, H.Y., and Robinson, P. (1996) Costing Support Services in Universities: An Application of Activity Based Costing, *Journal of Institution Research in Australasia*, 5, pp. 75-86.
10. Ellis-Newman, J. (2003) Activity Based Costing in User Services of an Academic Library, *Australia Library Trends*, 51(3), pp.333-348.
11. Hejazi, R., and Bashiri, N. (2005) Role of Internal Auditing in Correct Costing, *Journal of Hesabdar*, (168).
12. Innes, J. and Mitchall, F. (1997) The Application of Activity based Costing in the UK's Largest Financial Institutions, *The Service Industries Journal*, 17(1), pp. 190-203.
13. Jarvinen, J. (2005) Rational for Adopting Activity Based Costing in Hospitals, University of Oulu.
14. Ju kim, H. (2003) Activity Based Costing System in Telecommunications Industry, http://www.sis.pith.edu
15. Kelline S. C. Downet, R. G. and Smitt L.G. (2001) Activity-Based Costing and Higher Education _ Can it Work?, http://www.iupindia.org/books/ABC%20of%20Activity-Based%20Costing _Cont.asp.

16. Khatibi Tababaye, S. M. A. and Behrouzi Far, M. (2006) A Review on the World Gas Market and Iran Situation, *Review of Energy Economy*, (2).
17. Kocakülâh, M. C. and Crowe B. (2005) Utilizing Activity Based Costing (ABC) to Measure Loan Portfolio Profitability in a Community Bank, *Journal of Cost Management Boston*, 19(4), pp. 40-47.
18. Kumar, A. (2006) Towards the Use Ontology's Activity Based Costing in Healthcare Organizations. http://www.booksonline.iospress.nl/Content/View.aspx?piid=85
19. Lievens, Y. Bogaert, V. D. and Kesteloot, K. (2003) Activity Based Costing Model for Cost Calculation in Radiotherapy, *International Journal of Radiation Oncology Biology Physics*, 57(2), pp. 522-530.
20. Lung, A. (2002) Activity Based Costing in the Telecom Industry, Director & General Manager ABC Technologies (Hong Kong). Available: www.Bettermanagment.com.
21. Major, M. and Hopper, T. (2005) Implementation ABC in a Portuguese Telecommunications Company, *Management Accounting Research*, 16(2), pp. 205-229.
22. Md Mostaque, H. and Gunasekaran A. (2001) Activity Based Cost Management in Financial Services Industry, *Managing Service Quality Bedford*, 11(3), pp. 213-226.
23. Mitchell, F. (1996) Activity Based Costing in UK Universities, *Public Money and Management*, 16(1), pp.51-57.
24. Montgomery, J. R. and Snyder J. K. (1998) Costing a Library: A Generic Approach, *Research in Higher Education*, 30(1), pp. 48-87.
25. Muras, A.D., Calhoun, D. D., and Stripling, W. S. (2000) The ABC's of Activity Based Management (ABM) in the Petroleum Industry, *Petroleum Accounting and Financial Management Journal*, 19(2), pp. 79-100.
26. Narasimha, M. S. and Thampy, A. (2002) Activity Based Costing in Banking Service: A Case Study of a Large Indian Private Sector Bank, *Prajnan*, 31(2), pp. 95-110.
27. Negrini, D., Kettle, A., Sheppard, L., Mills, G.H. and Edbrooke, D. L. (2004) The Cost of a Hospital Ward in Europe: Is There a Methodology Available to Accurately Measure the Costs?, Journal of Health, *Organization and Management*, 18(3), pp. 195-206
28. Rajabi, A. (2001) The Implementation of the Costing Based on Activity System in Shahid Faghihi Hospital of Shiraz, National Research Project of Health Ministry of Iran.
29. Roberson, S. Bernasooni, R. (1998) Costing Methodology for Use within Australian Higher Education Institutions, Ernest &Young, pp. 1-50.
30. Sap, R. W. Crawford, D. M. and Rebisckle, S. A. (2005) Activity Based Information for Financial Institution, *Journal of Performance Management*, 10(1), pp. 61-74.
31. Taherkordi, M. (2003) The Implementation ABC in Oil Company of Iran Continental Shelf, College of Social Science and Humanities of Mazandaran University.

32. Tatikonda, L. and Tatikonda, R. (2001) Activity Based Costing for Higher Education Institutions, *Management Accounting Quarterly*, 16-17(15), Retrieved November 15, 2001, from http://www.mamag.com/winter01/w01tati.htm.
33. Waters, H., Abdollah, Santillian, H. and Richardson, P. (2003) Application of Activity Based Costing in Peruvian NGO Healthcare System, An Operations Research Results Report, University Research Co., LLC•7200 Wisconsin Avenue, Suite 600•Bethesda, MD20814• www.qaproject.org.
34. West, T. D. and West, D. A. (1997) Applying ABC to Healthcare, *Management Accounting*, 78(8), pp. 22-33.

Table 1. Company main activities and cost drivers, cost items and cost drivers,

Row	Cost items	Cost drivers	Main activities	Cost drivers
1	Salary & wage	Cost center personal	Engineering	Net work size
2	Goods	Monetary value of orders	Transportation	Number of automobiles
3	Receivable services	Monetary value of services	Telecommunication	Number of telephone lines
4	Other costs	----------	Measuring & distribution of gas	Number of stations
5	Depreciation	Monetary value of resources	Main subscribers	Number of main subscribers
6	Water & power bill	Monetary value of payments	Computer	Number of computers
7	Automobile rent	Monetary value of transport fare	Sustaining	Number of personnel
8	Training	Training hour		
9	Administrative & organization	Monetary value of office services		

Table 2. Expense-Activity–Dependence Matrix (EADM)

Activities \ Cost items	Engineering	Transportation	Telecommunication	Main subscribers	Measuring & distribution of gas	computer	sustaining	Sum
Water & power bill	24.03%	0.74%	5.27%	3.67%	1.09%	1.49%	63.72%	100%
	102,796,908	3,156,869	22,543,392	15,682,806	4,669,814	6,353,523	272,596,954	427,800,266
Automobile rent	3.15%	91.78%	0.04%	0.54%	0.19%	0.21%	4.08%	100%
	25,534,931	742,938,232	325,615	4,385,466	1,556,946	1,706,451	33,035,763	809,483,350
Administrative and organization	51.70%	2.31%	0.06%	9.97%	2.34%	3.95%	29.13%	100%
	1,860,996,372	83,303,263	21,751,257	358,799,825	84,135,722	142,254,704	1,048,533,883	3,599,775,145
Other costs	6.67%	6.21%	0.02%	6.02%	0.19%	0.11%	79.79%	100%
	38,797,835	31,428,926	107,224	30,432,566	952,872	534,416	403,418,157	505,871,997
Salary & wage	10.46%	0.70%	0.52%	1.64%	0.43%	1.02%	85.24%	100%
	6,553,573,565	440,124,964	326,148,707	1,025,534,346	269,095,466	636,456,931	53,423,131,635	62,674,063,524
Depreciation	2.21%	31.70%	0.55%	53.98%	0.06%	2.59%	8.99%	100%
	792,520,180	11,831,689,875	207,083,767	20,150,196,286	23,106,234	967,982,783	3,355,845,143	37,328,425,512
Receivable services	20.11%	1.66%	0.39%	3.08%	0.75%	1.95%	72.06%	100%
	2,152,116,574	177,603,634	41,477,783	329,711,141	80,478,473	208,457,974	7,710,029,761	10,699,875,698
Training	35.29%	1.62%	12.33%	10.97%	5.93%	2.64%	31.23%	100%
	149,796,038	6,855,694	52,315,946	46,546,567	25,161,248	11,208,906	132,579,091	424,463,490
Goods	17.28%	9.73%	1.30%	2.32%	0.53%	8.26%	60.59%	100%
	335,988,951	189,289,077	25,271,335	45,140,835	10,244,595	160,553,139	1,178,405,418	1,944,893,350
Total	12,011,891,617	13,506,261,257	697,008,847	22,006,399,407	499,394,708	2,135,399,310	67,556,973,516	118,413,328,662

Table 3. Activities- product- dependence matrix (APDM)

Row	Activities / Regions	Sustaining	Computer	Measuring & distribution of gas	Main subscribers	Telecommunication	Transportation	Engineering
1	Eslamshahr	8.79%	9.94%	5.29%	2.02%	7.57%	6.35%	5.90%
2	Pakdasht	2.20%	3.51%	11.06%	38.87%	8.37%	6.35%	5.51%
3	Pishva	4.40%	1.75%	0.96%	1.62%	2.39%	3.17%	1.48%
4	Damavand	2.20%	4.09%	1.44%	0.40%	5.58%	3.17%	3.30%
5	Robat karim	3.30%	2.34%	3.37%	0.81%	1.59%	3.17%	2.69%
6	Gharchak	2.20%	2.34%	1.44%	11.34%	2.39%	3.17%	2.81%
7	Vavan	0.55%	1.75%	0.96%	0.20%	1.20%	1.59%	0.86%
8	Varamin	11.54%	14.62%	6.73%	2.83%	8.76%	9.52%	5.85%
9	Eshtehard	1.65%	0.58%	1.44%	3.85%	3.19%	3.17%	0.52%
10	Shahregods	3.30%	4.68%	1.92%	3.04%	4.78%	4.76%	3.29%
11	Shahriyar	7.69%	7.02%	5.29%	0.61%	3.59%	7.94%	6.91%
12	Fardis	4.95%	2.92%	10.10%	1.82%	1.99%	6.35%	6.86%
13	Karaj	28.57%	22.81%	25.48%	11.94%	25.50%	17.46%	30.42%
14	Nazarabad	3.85%	2.92%	3.37%	4.05%	1.59%	4.76%	5.19%
15	Vardavard	2.20%	2.34%	0.48%	0.81%	2.79%	1.59%	2.08%
16	Hashtgerd	4.40%	3.51%	2.88%	0.61%	3.59%	6.35%	2.90%
17	Bagherabad	0.55%	0.58%	1.44%	0.20%	0.80%	1.59%	0.78%
18	Gheyamdasht	1.10%	2.92%	0.48%	0.20%	7.57%	1.59%	0.59%
19	Chahrdange	0.55%	2.34%	3.37%	13.97%	0.40%	1.59%	5.28%
20	Rodehen	1.65%	1.17%	2.40%	0.40%	3.19%	1.59%	1.82%
21	Golestan	1.65%	2.34%	4.33%	0.20%	0.40%	1.59%	0.20%
22	Nasimshahr	1.65%	1.75%	1.92%	0.00%	1.59%	1.59%	2.19%
23	Malard	1.10%	1.75%	3.85%	0.20%	1.20%	1.59%	2.55%
	Total	1	1	1	1	1	1	1

Table 4. APDM with monetary items

Row	Regions	Sum of Indirect Overhead	Sustaining	Computer	Measuring	Main Subscribers	Telecommunication	Transportation	Engineering
1	Eslamshahr	8,242,049,347	5,939,074,595	212,291,159	26,410,297	445,473,672	52,761,626	857,540,397	708,497,600
2	Pakdasht	11,745,367,432	1,484,768,649	74,926,292	55,221,530	8,553,094,506	58,315,481	857,540,397	661,500,577
3	Pishva	3,991,557,873	2,969,537,297	37,463,146	4,801,872	356,378,938	16,661,566	428,770,199	177,944,855
4	Damavand	2,532,943,923	1,484,768,649	87,414,007	7,202,808	89,094,734	38,876,988	428,770,199	396,816,538
5	Robat karim	3,234,874,982	2,227,152,973	49,950,861	16,806,553	178,189,469	11,107,711	428,770,199	322,897,217
6	Gharchak	4,819,327,433	1,484,768,649	49,950,861	7,202,808	2,494,652,564	16,661,566	428,770,199	337,320,786
7	Vavan	783,808,021	371,192,162	37,463,146	4,801,872	44,547,367	8,330,783	214,385,099	103,087,591
8	Varamin	10,814,242,910	7,795,035,406	312,192,882	33,613,105	623,663,141	61,092,409	1,286,310,596	702,335,372
9	Eshtehard	2,493,669,073	1,113,576,487	12,487,715	7,202,808	846,399,977	22,215,421	428,770,199	63,016,466
10	Shahregods	4,076,828,473	2,227,152,973	99,901,722	9,603,744	668,210,508	33,323,132	643,155,298	395,481,095
11	Shahriyar	7,433,833,655	5,196,690,270	149,852,583	26,410,297	133,642,102	24,992,349	1,071,925,497	830,320,557
12	Fardis	5,550,306,883	3,340,729,460	62,438,576	50,419,658	400,926,305	13,884,638	857,540,397	824,367,849
13	Karaj	28,735,072,635	19,301,992,433	487,020,895	127,249,613	2,628,294,666	177,723,371	2,358,236,093	3,654,555,564
14	Nazarabad	4,846,620,943	2,598,345,135	62,438,576	16,806,553	890,947,344	11,107,711	643,155,298	623,820,325
15	Vardavard	2,198,714,507	1,484,768,649	49,950,861	2,400,936	178,189,469	19,438,494	214,385,099	249,581,000
16	Hashtgerd	4,423,988,286	2,969,537,297	74,926,292	14,405,617	133,642,102	24,992,349	857,540,397	348,944,232
17	Bagherabad	749,435,505	371,192,162	12,487,715	7,202,808	44,547,367	5,553,855	214,385,099	94,066,497
18	Gheyamdasht	1,189,369,406	742,384,324	62,438,576	2,400,936	44,547,367	52,761,626	214,385,099	70,451,477
19	Chahrdange	4,363,706,902	371,192,162	49,950,861	16,806,553	3,073,768,338	2,776,928	214,385,099	634,826,961
20	Rodehen	1,694,872,895	1,113,576,487	24,975,431	12,004,680	89,094,734	22,215,421	214,385,099	218,621,042
21	Golestan	1,470,661,874	1,113,576,487	49,950,861	21,608,425	44,547,367	2,776,928	214,385,099	23,816,707
22	Nasimshahr	1,649,326,174	1,113,576,487	37,463,146	9,603,744	0	11,107,711	214,385,099	263,189,987
23	Malard	1,372,749,530	742,384,324	37,463,146	19,207,489	44,547,367	8,330,783	214,385,099	306,431,321
	Total	118,413,328,662	67,556,973,516	2,135,399,310	499,394,708	22,006,399,407	697,008,847	13,506,261,257	12,011,891,617

Table 5. Cost of one cubic meter of regional gas in ABC

Row	Regions	Cost of One Cubic Gas (4)/(5)	Cubic Gas (5)	Total cost (4)=(1)+(2)+(3)	Consuming Gas (3)	Indirect Overheads (2)	Direct Overheads (1)
1	Eslamshahr	126.03	242,600,000	30,575,629,949	11,359,939,170	8,242,049,347	10,973,641,432
2	Pakdasht	59.05	340,070,000	20,079,449,391	1,269,392,461	11,745,367,432	7,064,689,498
3	Pishva	140.36	64,900,000	9,109,260,698	2,990,935,777	3,991,557,873	2,126,767,048
4	Damavand	54.52	1,300,250,000	70,885,656,290	62,514,770,316	2,532,943,923	5,837,942,052
5	Robat karim	195.71	43,100,000	8,435,221,428	1,982,723,623	3,234,874,982	3,217,622,823
6	Gharchak	109.11	148,800,000	16,235,934,548	7,105,227,713	4,819,327,433	4,311,379,402
7	Vavan	107.55	32,300,000	3,473,980,186	1,685,034,240	783,808,021	1,005,137,925
8	Varamin	391.65	78,750,000	30,842,585,489	9,969,785,922	10,814,242,910	10,058,556,657
9	Eshtehard	190.87	24,100,000	4,599,962,864	1,140,206,503	2,493,669,073	966,087,288
10	Shahregods	97.91	166,060,000	16,258,636,287	7,975,828,737	4,076,828,473	4,205,979,077
11	Shahriyar	136.14	170,430,000	23,202,201,304	7,863,493,121	7,433,833,655	7,904,874,527
12	Fardis	40.5	324,200,000	13,130,000,990	3,510,488,001	5,550,306,883	4,069,206,106
13	Karaj	113.26	1,760,260,000	199,360,839,332	135,364,417,305	28,735,072,635	35,261,349,391
14	Nazarabad	104.95	160,700,000	16,864,840,648	7,807,325,313	4,846,620,943	4,210,894,392
15	Vardavard	333.20	10,600,000	3,531,945,656	454,959,245	2,198,714,507	878,271,904
16	Hashtgerd	179.07	64,940,000	11,628,952,551	3,044,295,194	4,423,988,286	4,160,669,071
17	Bagherabad	26.48	101,110,000	2,677,778,506	1,291,859,584	749,435,505	636,483,417
18	Gheyamdasht	73.32	32,100,000	2,353,653,462	449,342,464	1,189,369,406	714,941,592
19	Chahrdange	92.05	106,800,000	9,830,519,194	5,111,270,529	4,363,706,902	355,541,763
20	Rodehen	166.06	22,430,000	3,724,781,999	645,929,792	1,694,872,895	1,383,979,312
21	Golestan	14.20	311,200,000	4,418,423,228	2,134,376,704	1,470,661,874	813,384,650
22	Nasimshahr	27.76	165,400,000	4,591,924,905	1,460,363,008	1,649,326,174	1,482,235,723
23	Malard	18.06	343,900,000	6,211,814,844	3,707,075,329	1,372,749,530	1,131,989,986
	Total	85.12	6,015,000,000	512,023,993,750	280,839,040,052	118,413,328,662	112,771,625,036

Table 6. Comparing cost of one cub meter of gas in ABC and TCSs

Row	Regions	Cost of One Cub Meter of Gas in TCS (Single Method)	Cost of One Cub Meter of Gas TCS (Multiple Method)	Cost of One Cub Meter of Gas in ABC System
1	Eslamshahr	74.2	110.98	126.03
2	Pakdasht	74.2	29.95	59.05
3	Pishva	74.2	101.13	140.36
4	Damavand	74.2	53.46	54.52
5	Robat karim	74.2	157.31	195.71
6	Gharchak	74.2	89.87	109.11
7	Vavan	74.2	102.00	107.55
8	Varamin	74.2	310.60	391.65
9	Eshtehard	74.2	109.31	190.87
10	Shahregods	74.2	91.33	97.91
11	Shahriyar	74.2	104.53	136.14
12	Fardis	74.2	32.86	40.5
13	Karaj	74.2	105.04	113.26
14	Nazarabad	74.2	86.66	104.95
15	Vardavard	74.2	176.74	333.20
16	Hashtgerd	74.2	136.04	179.07
17	Bagherabad	74.2	25.61	26.48
18	Gheyamdasht	74.2	45.04	73.32
19	Chahrdange	74.2	58.24	92.05
20	Rodehen	74.2	114.28	166.06
21	Golestan	74.2	16.22	14.20
22	Nasimshahr	74.2	27.42	27.76
23	Malard	74.2	20.82	18.06

Table 7. Iranian Gas Company cost model

Activities	Cost of activities
Sustaining	67,556,973,516
Main subscribers	22,063,999,407
Transportation	13,506,261,257
Engineering	12,011,891,617
Computer	2,135,399,310
Telecommunication	697,008,847
Measuring &distribution of gas	499,394,708
Total	118,413,328,662

80% indirect overhead { Sustaining, Main subscribers }

20% indirect overhead { Transportation, Engineering, Computer, Telecommunication, Measuring &distribution of gas }

Table 8. The analysis of the allocation of the indirect overhead to regions

Row	Regions	Indirect Overhead	
1	Karaj	28,735,072,635	
2	Pakdasht	11,745,367,432	
3	Varamin	10,814,242,910	
4	Eslamshar	8,242,049,347	
5	Shahriyar	7,433,833,655	80% Indirect
6	Fardis	5,550,306,883	
7	Nazaabad	4,846,620,943	
8	Gharchak	4,819,327,433	
9	Hashtgerd	4,423,988,286	
10	Chahardange	4,363,706,902	
11	Shahregids	4,076,828,473	
12	Pishva	3,991,557,873	
13	Robatkarim	3,234,874,982	
14	Damavand	2,532,943,923	
15	Eshtehard	2,493,669,073	20% Indirect Overhead
16	Vardavard	2,198,714,507	
17	Rodehen	1,694,872,895	
18	Nasimshahr	1,649,326,174	
19	Golestan	1,470,661,874	
20	Malard	1,372,749,530	
21	Ghiyamdasht	1,189,369,406	
22	Vavan	783,808,021	
23	Bagherabad	749,435,505	
	Sum	118,413,328,662	

Table 9. Analysis of allocating the cost of main subscribers and sustaining

	Regions	Indirect Overhead (Main Subscribers)	Indirect Overhead (Sustaining)	Regions
70% cost of main subscribers activity	Sakdasht	8,553,094,506	19,301,992,433	Karaj
	Chahrdange	3,073,768,338	7,795,035,406	Pakdasht
	Karaj	2,628,294,666	5,939,074,595	Varamin
	Gharchak	2,494,652,564	5,196,690,270	Eslamshahr
	Nazarabad	890,947,344	3,340,729,460	Shahriyar
	Eshtehard	846,399,977	2,969,537,297	Fardis
	Shahgods	668,210,508	2,969,537,297	Nazarabad
	Varamin	623,663,141	2,598,345,135	Gharchak
	Eslamshahr	445,473,672	2,227,152,973	Hashtgerd
	Fardis	400,926,305	2,227,152,973	Chahardange
	Pishva	356,378,938	1,484,768,649	Shahrgods
	Robatkarim	178,189,469	1,484,768,649	Pishva
	Varavard	178,189,469	1,484,768,649	Robatkarim
	Shahriyar	133,642,102	1,484,768,649	Damavad
	Hashtgerd	133,642,102	1,113,576,487	Eshtehard
	Damavand	89,094,734	1,113,576,487	Vardavard
	Rodehen	89,094,734	1,113,576,487	Rodehen
	Vavan	44,547,367	1,113,576,487	Nasimshahr
	Bagherabad	44,547,367	742,384,324	Golestan
	Gheyamdasht	44,547,367	742,384,324	Malard
	Golestan	44,547,367	371,192,162	Gheyamdasht
	Malard	44,547,367	371,192,162	Vavan
	Nasimshahr	0	371,192,162	Bagherabad
	Sum	22,006,399,407	67,556,973,516	Sum

Table10. Direct overhead cost of regions

Region	Direct Overhead	
Karaj	35,261,349,391	
Eslamshahr	10,973,641,432	60% Direct
Varamin	10,058,556,657	
Shahriyar	7,904,874,527	
Pakdasht	7,064,689,498	
Damavand	5,837,942,052	
Gharchak	4,311,379,402	
Nazarabad	4,210,894,392	
Shahrgods	4,205,979,077	
Hashtgerd	4,160,669,071	
Fardis	4,069,206,106	
Robatkarim	3,217,622,823	
Pishva	2,126,767,048	
Nasimshahr	1,482,235,723	
Rodehen	1,383,979,312	
Malard	1,131,989,986	
Vavan	1,005,137,925	
Eshtehard	966,087,288	
Vardavrd	878,271,904	40% Direct
Golestan	813,384,650	
Gheyamdasht	714,941,592	
Bagherabad	636,483,417	
Chahrdange	355,541,763	
Sum	112,771,625,036	

Table11. Cost of one cubic meter gas (COCMG) in regions

Regions	(COCMG)
Varamin	391.65
Vardavrd	333.20
Robatkarim	195.71
Eshtehard	190.87
Hashtgerd	179.07
Rodehen	166.06
Pishva	140.36
Shahriyar	136.14
Eslamshahr	126.03
Karaj	113.26
Gharchak	109.11
Vavan	107.55
Nazarabad	104.95
Sharegods	97.91
Chahrdange	92.05
Gheyamdasht	73.32
Pakdasht	59.05
Damavand	54.52
Fardis	40.50
Nasimshahr	27.76
Bagherabad	26.48
Malard	18.06
Golestan	14.20
Mean	85.12

Bank Productivity Analysis: An Empirical Evidence from Iranian Banking Industry

JEL Classification Codes: G21, D24, M2

AMROLAH AMINI (Ph.D)

Associate Professor, Allameh Tabatabaei University (ATU), Tehran, Iran.

aminij@atu.ac.ir

ALIREZA EMAMI

Master of Science, Tehran University, Tehran, Iran

memami@alumni.ut.ac.ir

MOSTAFA EMAMI*

Master of Science, Michigan Technological University (MTU)

memami@mtu.edu

*Corresponding Address

Applied Research and Technology Office, Michigan Technological University

1400 Townsend Dr, Houghton, MI 49931

Tel & Fax : +1-(816) 237-0018

E-mail: memami@mtu.edu

Bank Productivity Analysis: An Empirical Evidence from Iranian Banking Industry

Abstract

This paper explains the process of measuring and analyzing Bank Total Productivity (BTP) and the productivity changes in bank braches using Data Envelopment Analysis (DEA), Slack Based Measure (SBM) and Malmquiest Productivity Index (MPI) in Export Development Bank of Iran (EDBI). For this purpose, we have measured and analyzed the productivity growth in EDBI branches using MPI in the period of 1994-2005. The trend of efficiency scores' moving averages confirms improvement in BTP over the period of study. Moreover, the results show %1 and %2 on average improvement in the productivity of EDBI branches in period 2004 and 2005, respectively.

Key words: Bank Productivity, Data Envelopment Analysis, Slack Based Model, Malmquist Productivity Index, Decision Making Unit.

1. Introduction

Managerial accounting systems provide beneficial information to support managers' decision making and organizational performance evaluation process. One of the most important information that managerial accounting systems provide is about organizational productivity. In reality, measuring the productivity regards as one of the most important and difficult steps in productivity analysis process. In order to measure productivity, several methods have been introduced in literature.

One of the most famous non-parametric techniques in measuring the productivity of similar Decision Making Units (DMUs) is Data Envelopment Analysis (DEA). DEA is a mathematical programming that generates production function or efficient frontier using observed or available data. In addition to DEA, one can apply Malmquist Productivity Index (MPI) to measure firms' productivity growth.

This paper explains the process and the results of an empirical study that was conducted in one of the most leading Iranian banks named Export Development Bank of Iran (EDBI). The paper explains how to measure and analyze Bank Total Productivity (BTP) and productivity growth using DEA, Slack Based Measure (SBM) and Malmquiest Productivity Index (MPI). For this purpose, rest of the paper is organized as following. In the next section, we explain some related literature. Section 3 introduces two main research hypotheses. Research methodology is explained in section 4. Section 5 provides the results of empirical analysis. Finally, the paper ends with conclusions and final remarks.

2. Literature Review

Several researchers have focused on bank efficiency analysis. For example, Berger and Humphrey (1992) measure the efficiency in commercial banking. Berger and Humphrey (1997) investigate measuring efficiency of financial institutions. Berger and Mester (1997) in their paper titled "Inside the black box: What explains differences in the efficiencies of financial institutions?" profound the literature on financial institution efficiency. Rogers (1998) focuses on the nontraditional activities and the efficiency of US commercial banks. Altunbas et al. (2000) measures the efficiency and risk in Japanese banking. Laeven and Majnoni (2003) study on the loan loss provisioning and economic slowdowns.

Some researchers have applied DEA as a non-parametric technique in their productivity analysis. For example, Golany and Storbeck (1999) apply a multiperiod DEA to measure the efficiencies of selected branches of a large US bank over second quarter of 1992 to the third quarter of 1993. They develop budgeting and target-setting modules, within a DEA framework. Mukherjee et al. (2001) measure the productivity growth for 201 large US commercial banks in the period of 1984 to 1990 using DEA and MPI. They attempt to distinct the contributions of technical change, technical efficiency change, and scale change to productivity growth. Isik and Hassan (2003) study total factor productivity change in Turkish commercial bank. They utilize a DEA-type Malmquist total factor productivity change index and examine productivity growth, efficiency change, and technical progress in Turkish commercial banks during the deregulation of financial markets in Turkey. Halkos and Salamouris (2004) apply DEA in measuring the performance of the Greek banking sector. They study the efficiency of Greek banks and use a number of financial efficiency ratios for the time period 1997–1999. The ratios are return difference of interest bearing assets, return on average equity, profit or loss per employee, efficiency ratio, and net interest margin. Their model helps bank to compare the inefficient banks with the efficient ones. They suggest DEA as either an alternative or complement to ratio analysis for the evaluation of an organization's performance and find a positive relation between the size of total assets and the efficiency. They also argue that reducing the number of small banks due to mergers and acquisitions leads to increasing in efficiency and can not find systematic significant relationship between transfer of ownership and last period's performance.

Drakea et al. (2006) evaluates the relative technical efficiency of institutions operating in a market that have been significantly affected by environmental and market factors in recent years. They incorporate environmental factors into the efficiency analysis using SBM, incorporate the operating environment into a nonparametric measure of technical efficiency, and employ SBM in DEA.

As mentioned earlier, this paper aims to explain the process of measuring and analyzing BTP in one of Iranian leading banks and the productivity changes in its branches using DEA, SBM and MPI. Next section of the pape, introduces research hypotheses.

3. Research Hypotheses

This research aims to assess BTP over period 1994-2005 and bank branches' productivity growth over 2003-2005 using DEA model. To compare bank total productivity in 1994-2005, SBM is applied. Also, in order to compare bank branches efficiency scores and analyze their efficiency growth over the period of study, DEA model is applied.

In this research, two main hypotheses are defined as follows:

H1: BTP has improved over the periods of study (1994-2005).

H2: The average productivity growth of the branches has improved over the periods of study (2003-2005).

4. Research Methodology

Statistical population of this research includes EDBI and its all 28 branches over the country. Each branch of bank provides foreign currency services as well as regular banking activities.

BTP was calculated over 1994-2005. In order to measure branches productivity, we selected all branches that were active in period 2003-2005. Since two branches were established in the middle of 2004, then, 26 of 28 branches were empirically examined. The data and information for BTP are based on bank's audited financial statement. But, in order to analyze bank branches productivity growth, we have used bank documents, bank statistical reports and bank's branches' monthly balance reports over the period of 2003-2005.

To measure and assess BTP, assuming variable rate of return to scale, SBM full ranking model of super-efficiency was applied. SBM is a DEA model that directly uses slack variables (input surplus and output slack variables) and focuses on both inputs and outputs at the same time so that provides a Scalar for efficiency score. (Tone, 2001) We used SBM and assumed variable rate of return to scale because it was not possible for the bank to increase its productivity just by decreasing its inputs or by increasing outputs. Accordingly, we find SBM and variable rate of return suitable for this case.

Suppose $X = (x_{ij}) \in R^{m \times n}$ and $Y = (y_{rj}) \in R^{r \times n}$ denote input and output matrix for *n* DMUs, respectively. In this case, the Production Possibility Set (PPS) for these DMUs can be defined as $P = \{(x,y) | x \geq X\lambda, y \leq Y\lambda, \lambda \geq 0\}$ where λ is a non-negative vector in R^n and for each $DMU(x_o, y_o)$ we will have $x_o = X\lambda + s^-$, $y_o = Y\lambda - s^+$, and $s^+ \geq 0$ s^+ and s^- where $\lambda \geq 0$، $s^- \geq 0$، are slack variables imply to output shortfall and input surplus vectors, respectively. Using slack variable vectors and assuming $\Lambda = t\lambda$, $S^- = ts^-$, $S^+ = ts^+$, a linear programming SBM under variable rate of return to scale assumption can be formulated as following:

$$
\begin{aligned}
Minimize: \quad & \rho = t - (1/m)\sum_{i=1}^{m} S_i^- / x_{io} \\
subject\ to: \quad & 1 = t + (1/s)\sum_{r=1}^{s} S_r^+ / y_{ro} \\
& t\, x_o = X\Lambda + S^- \\
& t\, y_o = Y\Lambda - S^+ \\
& \sum_{j=1}^{n} \Lambda_j = 1 \\
& \Lambda \geq 0,\ S^- \geq 0,\ S^+ \geq 0,\ t > 0
\end{aligned} \quad (1)
$$

In SBM, $DMU(x_o, y_o)$ is efficient if $\rho^* = 1$. Also, for full ranking of all DMUs in SBM, we have to include DMUs that their efficiency score value are equal to 1 (Tone, 2002). Accordingly, full ranking linear programming model under variable rate of return to scale can be defined as following:

$$
\begin{aligned}
\tau^* = \min \tau = &\ \frac{1}{m}\sum_{i=1}^{m} \tilde{x}_i / x_{io} \\
subject\ to \quad & 1 = \frac{1}{s}\sum_{r=1}^{s} \tilde{y}_r / y_{ro} \\
& \tilde{x} \geq \sum_{j=1,\neq o}^{n} \Lambda_j x_j \\
& \tilde{y} \leq \sum_{j=1,\neq o}^{n} \Lambda_j y_j \\
& \sum \Lambda_j = 1 \\
& \tilde{x} \geq t\, x_o,\ \tilde{y} \leq t y_o,\ \tilde{y} \geq 0,\ \lambda \geq 0
\end{aligned} \quad (2)
$$

where $\tau^* \geq 1$.

In order to assess BTP using SBM, we have considered yearly performance of bank in period 1994-2005 as a distinct DMU. We have solved SBM for each DMU in each financial period by Lindo software. Then, a full ranking linear programming model has been formulated and solved for DMUs with efficiency score value 1. We also measured scale inefficiency and compared SBM results under both variable and constant rate of return to scale assumptions. To test H1 (first research hypothesis), we used the results of SBM under variable rate of return to scale.

In order to measure banks branches' efficiency scores, we measured MPI. This index measures DMUs efficiency changes over the periods and calculates a yearly efficiency of a DMU based on the data of that year respect to previous year production technology. MPI does not assume that a DMU behavior is an optimized behavior. Moreover, it uses non-parametric method of DEA (Rezitis and Anthony 2006).

If a DMU in period t (where t:=‹1‹ ... T) can produce M of y^t outputs using x^t inputs, in each period t, production technology and distance functions can be defined as $S^t = (x^t, y^t)$ and $D_o^t(x^t, y^t) = \inf\{\theta : (y^t/\theta) \in S^t\}, t = 1,...,T$, respectively. This equations show the maximum outputs that can be obtained with the technology of period t. If outputs vector locates on the technology frontier, the value of distance function for outputs, θ, will be one. MPI, using distance function for outputs, measures the changes in productivity between t and $t+1$ as follows:

$$M_O(x^{t+1}, y^{t+1}, x^t, y^t) = [M_O^t(x^{t+1}, y^{t+1}, x^t, y^t) \times M_O^{t+1}(x^{t+1}, y^{t+1}, x^t, y^t)]^{1/2} = \left[(D_O^t(x^{t+1}, y^{t+1})/D_O^t(x^t, y^t)) \times (D_O^{t+1}(x^{t+1}, y^{t+1})/D_O^{t+1}(x^t, y^t))\right]^{1/2} \quad (3)$$

When $M_0 > 1$, it means that the productivity is increased. MPI uses DEA to estimate the function. Solving four linear programming problems, we can generate the functions as $D_o^t(x^{t+1}, y^{t+1})$, kth. For example, distance function for the $D_o^{t+1}(x^t, y^t)$ and $D_o^t(x^{t+1}, y^{t+1})$, $D_o^{t+1}(x^{t+1}, y^{t+1})$ DMUs (k:1, 2, K) under constant rate of return to scale assumption can be calculated as following:

$$Max\ \theta^P = \left(D_o^t(x^{p,t}, y^{p,t})\right)^{-1}$$
subject to

$$\theta^P y_m^{p,t} \leq \sum_{k=1}^{K} z^{k,t} y_m^{k,t} \quad\quad m = 1,...., M \quad\quad (4)$$

$$\sum_{k=1}^{K} z^{k,t} x_n^{k,t} \leq x_n^{p,t} \quad\quad n = 1,....., N$$

$$z^{k,t} \geq 0 \quad\quad k = 1,......, K$$

In order to measure MPI for our case of study, first we have solved $D_o^t(x^{t+1}, y^{t+1})$, $D_o^{t+1}(x^{t+1}, y^{t+1})$, $D_o^t(x^{t+1}, y^{t+1})$ and $D_o^{t+1}(x^t, y^t)$ using EMS software and then the index was calculated for each period.

For selecting the inputs and outputs variables, the literature is reviewed. Some researchers suggested correlation technique. For this research, the following widely used inputs and outputs variables were selected:

- In SBM, number of employee, cost of doubtful liabilities, and main financing resources considered as input variables, and facilities amounts as output variable.
- In MPI, number of employees, administrative & salary costs, profit and fees paid considered as input variables, and fees received, facility donated, without cost deposits and cost consuming deposits as output variables.

5. The Results

Table 1 and 2 show the descriptive statistical results.

[Insert Table 1]

[Insert Table 2]

Using inputs and outputs data in Figure 1 and for each financial period, regular linear programming model of SBM and full ranking SBM for efficient DMUs under constant and variable rate of returns to scale assumptions were formulated. Table 3 presents the solutions over the period of study.

[Insert Table 3]

Figure 1 shows BTP trends under variable and constant rate of return to scale (VRRS and CRRS) assumptions over the period of study.

[Insert Figure 1]

As shown in Figure 1, there is a significant difference between two trends. This difference is called as scale inefficiency. Remind that first research hypothesis (H1) states that BTP has improved over the periods of study. The data on Figure 1 confirms H1. Moreover, to have a better conclusion, moving averages were calculated.

Table 4 provides results of calculations.

[Insert Table 4]

Remind that second research hypothesis (H2) indicates that the average productivity growth of the branches improved over the past three periods. To examine this research hypothesis, we have calculated MPI for the period 2003-2005. In other words, once we have measured this index and compared change in productivity between 2003 and 2004, and again it has been calculated for the years 2004 and 2005, respectively. Table 5 presents results of calculating MPI and rank of each branch in terms of its MPI values. According the data, average productivity growth of the branches in 2004 and 2005 are 1% and 2%, respectively.

[Insert Table 5]

Table 6 shows lower level and upper level of productivity growth in 2004 and 2005.

[Insert Table 6]

Since the bank uses a three level ranking system, in order to define the categories, we have divided the range of productivity growth to 3. Then, using this method of partitioning, we have positioned all branches in their proper groups in terms of their MPI value.

6. Conclusions and Final Remarks

This paper explained the process of measuring BTP and analyzing bank branches' productivity growth over the time using DEA, SBM and MPI. To explain the process more simply, empirical evidence of EDBI was provided. In this research, we have examined two main research hypotheses. These hypotheses stated that "BTP and its branches' average productivity have improved over the periods of study. Results of empirical examination show that both research hypotheses have been confirmed. The results show that in addition to increasing BTP, its branches productivity has improved on average %1 and %2 in 2004 and 2005, respectively. Moreover, in order to compare our reluts to the result obtained by current ranking system of the bank, we have provided a simple three level categorization framework.

References

Altunbas, Y Liu, M-H Molyneux, P and Seth, R (2000). Efficiency and risk in Japanese banking. *Journal of Banking and Finance,* 24(10), 1605–1628.

Berger, A and D Humphrey (1992). Measurement and efficiency issues in commercial banking. Chicago National Bureau of Economic Research, 245–296.

Berger, A and D Humphrey (1997). Efficiency of financial institutions: International survey and directions for future research. *European Journal Operational Reseach*, 98, 175–212.

Berger, A and L Mester (1997). Inside the black box: What explains differences in the efficiencies of financial institutions? *Journal of Banking and Finance,* 21, 895–947.

Drake, L Hall Maximilian, JB and R Simper (2006). The impact of macroeconomic and regulatory factors on bank efficiency: A non-parametric analysis of Hong Kong's banking system. *Journal of Banking and Finance,* 30(5), 1443–1466.

Golany, B and JE Storbeck (1999). A data envelopment analysis of the operational efficiencies of bank branches. *Interfacts*, 29(3), 14-26.

Halkos, GE and DS Salamouris (2004). Efficiency measurement of Greek commercial banks with the use of financial ratios: a data envelopment analysis approach. *Management Accounting Research,* 15(2), 201-224.

Isik, I and MK Hassan (2003). Fainancial deregulation and total factor productivity change: an empirical study of Turkish commercial bank. *Journal of Banking and Finance,* 27(8), 1455-1485.

Laeven, L and G Majnoni (2003). Loan loss provisioning and economic slowdowns: Too much, too late. *Journal of Financial Intermediation,* 12(2), 178–197.

Mukherjee, K Ray, SC and SM Miller (2001). Productivity growth in large US commercial banks. *Journal of Banking and Finance,* 25(5), 913-939.

Rezitis, AN (2006). Productivity growth in the Greek banking industry: a non parametric approach. *Journal of Applied Economics,* 9(1), 119-138.

Rogers, KE (1998). Nontraditional activities and the efficiency of US commercial banks. *Journal of Banking and Finance,* 22(4), 467–482.

Tone, K (2001). A slacks-based measure of efficiency in data envelopment analysis. *European Journal of Operational Research*, 130, 498- 509.

Tone, K (2002). A slacks-based measure of super-efficiency in data envelopment analysis. *European Journal of Operational Research*, 143(1), 32–41.

Table 1: Descriptive statistics of selected variables in SBM

Outputs	Inputs			
Facilities *Amounts	Cost of doubtful *Liabilities	Number of Employees	Main Financing *Resources	
10,128	175	895	11,888	Maximum
164	3	156	325	Minimum
2,823	40	578	3,655	Mean
3,294	51	234	3,827	Standard Deviation
* Numbers in million rials				

Table 2: Descriptive statistics of three years average of selected variables in SBM

Outputs				Inputs			
Cost Consuming Deposits *	Without Cost Deposits*	Facility *Donation	Fees *Received	Profit and *Fees paid	Administrative & *Salary Costs	Number of Employees	
352,503	1,726,815	3,484,583	38,479	27,584	6,783	85	Maximum
1,142	2,270	6,911	105	114	767	6	Minimum
27,420	99,589	239,892	3,070	2,140	1,513	14	Mean
68,073	333,355	684,385	7,648	5,334	1,167	15	Standard Deviation
* Numbers in million rials							

Table 3: Solution of SBM using linear programming

Years	Variable Return to Scale		Constant Return to Scale	
	τ^*	ρ^*	τ^*	ρ^*
1994		0.40	1.42	1.00
1995		0.28		0.75
1996		0.38		0.63
1997		0.38		0.59
1998		0.53	1.05	1.00
1999		0.47		0.56
2000		0.52		0.60
2001	1.21	1.00	1.21	1.00
2002		0.65		0.69
2003	1.04	1.00	1.04	1.00
2004	1.15	1.00	1.23	1.00
2005	1.08	1.00	1.10	1.00

Table 4: Moving average of efficiency scores for different durations

Duration of Moving Averages \ Periods	1	2	3	4	5	6	7	8	9	10	11
2 Years	1.08	0.69	0.61	0.82	0.81	0.58	0.90	0.93	0.85	1.14	1.17
3 Years	0.93	0.66	0.76	0.74	0.74	0.79	0.82	0.97	0.97	1.13	
4 Years	0.85	0.76	0.71	0.70	0.86	0.75	0.87	1.03	1.01		
5 Years	0.89	0.72	0.69	0.80	0.81	0.81	0.95	1.05			
6 Years	0.83	0.70	0.77	0.78	0.85	0.88	0.97				
7 Years	0.80	0.77	0.76	0.81	0.91	0.91					
8 Years	0.83	0.79	0.84	0.89	0.93						
9 Years	0.83	0.79	0.84	0.89							
10 Years	0.85	0.83	0.87								
11 Year	0.88	0.86									

Table 5: Results of MPI moving and grouping branches in terms of their productivity growth

2005 Comparing to 2004			2004 Comparing to 2003			
Rank of Branch in Terms of Its Productivity Growth	Productivity Situation	MPI	Rank of Branch in Terms of Its Productivity Growth	Productivity Situation	MPI	Branches
2	Stable	1.00	2	Stable	1.00	DMU1
1	Increased	2.30	3	Decreased	0.35	DMU2
2	Decreased	0.85	2	Decreased	0.97	DMU3

2	Increased	1.01	3	Decreased	0.77	DMU4
2	Decreased	0.92	2	Increased	1.16	DMU5
3	Decreased	0.79	2	Decreased	0.88	DMU6
2	Stable	1.00	2	Decreased	0.91	DMU7
2	Decreased	0.91	2	Decreased	0.96	DMU8
2	Stable	1.00	2	Stable	1.00	DMU9
2	Decreased	0.94	2	Decreased	0.86	DMU10
2	Increased	1.20	2	Increased	1.04	DMU11
3	Decreased	0.61	2	Increased	1.12	DMU12
2	Decreased	0.96	2	Increased	1.03	DMU13
1	Increased	1.46	2	Decreased	0.91	DMU14
2	Stable	1.00	2	Stable	1.00	DMU15
2	Decreased	0.94	2	Increased	1.06	DMU16
2	Increased	1.10	2	Increased	1.02	DMU17
2	Stable	1.00	2	Stable	1.00	DMU18
3	Decreased	0.89	1	Increased	1.75	DMU19
2	Decreased	0.97	2	Increased	1.03	DMU20
2	Decreased	0.84	2	Decreased	0.98	DMU21
2	Decreased	0.83	2	Decreased	0.87	DMU22
2	Stable	1.00	2	Increased	1.13	DMU23
2	Increased	1.07	2	Stable	1.00	DMU24
3	Decreased	0.61	2	Decreased	0.87	DMU25
1	Increased	1.32	2	Decreased	0.88	DMU26
-	Increased	1.02	-	Increased	1.01	Average

Table 6: Basic data for grouping branches based on MPI

Group Rank	2005		2004	
	Upper Level	Lower Level	Upper Level	Lower Level
Group 1	2.30	1.73	1.75	1.28
Group 2	1.73	1.17	1.28	0.82
Group 3	1.17	0.61	0.82	0.35

Figure 1: Comparing BTP trend under variable and constant return to scale (VRRS and CRRS) assumptions

In Figure 1:
- horizontal and vertical axis show the years and BTP values, respectively,
- BTP is abbreviation of Bank Total Productivity,
- VRRS and CRRS mean variable and constant return to scale, respectively.

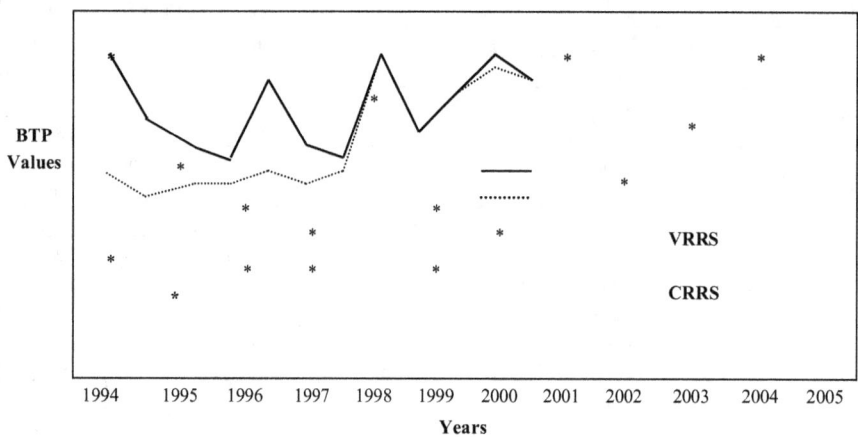

Figure 1: Comparing BTP trend under variable and constant return to scale (VRRS and CRRS) assumptions

Empirical Investigation of Factors Moderating IT–Performance Relationship in Developed and Developing Countries

AMROLAH AMINI (Ph.D)*

Associate Professor, Allameh Tabatabaei University (ATU), Tehran, Iran.

aminij@atu.ac.ir

ALIREZA EMAMI

Master of Science, Tehran University, Tehran, Iran

memami@alumni.ut.ac.ir

MOSTAFA EMAMI

Master of Science, Michigan Technological University (MTU)

memami@mtu.edu

*Corresponding Address

Applied Research and Technology Office, Michigan Technological University

1400 Townsend Dr, Houghton, MI 49931

Tel & Fax : +1-(816) 237-0018

E-mail: memami@mtu.edu

Empirical Investigation of Factors Moderating IT–Performance Relationship in Developed and Developing Countries

Abstract

This paper provides and tests a new conceptual model that offering an empirically based insight into the effects of IT-Performance moderators in developed and developing countries. Using data from 34 developed and 211 developing countries and applying Pearson Correlation Method and Structured Equation Model, we found that Economic, Business and Competition, Geographical, and Population factors with their interactions significantly moderate the relationship between IT diffusion and national level performance in both developed and developing countries. However, we found that National Health modertor variable significantly moderates the IT-performance relationship in developing but not in developed countrirs. Results of this research confirm fitness of the data with our proposed new model.

Key words: IT diffusion, national performance, developing countries, developed countries, structured equation model

1. Introduction

Most of researchers and development specialist believe that IT has a great impact on organizations performances and nations' developments. Although the amount of investment on IT has rapidly increased in recent years, however researchers are concern because of paradox in the results of IT. In other words, the application of IT to development goals has not always succeeded to date and there are many cases of partial or complete failure. [2][3] Accordingly, the main question of most researchers has now become how IT can be benefical for development and what factors affect on IT diffusion with national performance. Although literature introduces a numerous factors affecting IT investment and usage and shows various differences in these factors between developed and developing countries, however, there are a few empirical researches to study their effects on IT-Performance relationship in a systematic way.

The purpose of this paper is to develop and test a new conceptual model that offering an empirically based insight into the effects of IT-Performance moderators in developed and developing countries. For this purpose, the remainder of the paper structured as follows. The following section summarizes the literature. Section 3 provides the new conceptual model and research hypotheses. Section 4 describes data and methodology. Section 5 provides the empirical results. Finally, the paper ends with conclusions and final remarks.

2. The Literature

Brief review of the literature shows that there are numerous factors affecting IT usage and there are various differences in these factors between developed and developing countries. Tables 1 and 2 summarize factors moderating the relationship between IT and performance in general and in developed and developing countries.

Table 1: Most widely used variables in literature

Type of Variables	Factors	Measures
Independent Variable	*Information Technology Diffusion (Investments)*	• IT investment [7][13][21][35][36][40][43] • IT use at country level [12][16][21][29][35] • IT spending on hardware and software as percent of GDP [36] • Computer hardware imports and production [12]
Dependent Variable	*National Productivity Level*	• Productivity growth at the macroeconomic level [12][13][21][24] • Level of national wealth [35][40][43] • Technical progress [11][35]
Common Used General Moderator Variables	*Most widely-used, official-source development data from the World Bank and other international agencies*	• Total external debt to gross national income (Economic Indicator) • GDP (current US$) (billions) (Economic Indicator) • GNI per capita, Atlas method (current US$) (Economic Indicator) • Life expectancy at birth, total (years) (Social Indicator) • Population, total (millions) (Social Indicator) • Population growth (annual %)(Social Indicator) • Surface area (sq. km) (thousands) (Infrastructural &Natural Indicator)

Table 2: Factors affecting IT investment and diffusion

Factors	Factors
• Educational level [7][12][21][23][25][34][42]	• Cost of living and pricing [10]
• Professional and Training level [23][7][21][25]	• Technology accumulation [35]
• Perception of user toward IT [25]	• Lack of resources for technology investment [35]
• Commitment level [26]	• Infrastructures [12][21][29][35]
• Enterprise readiness [27]	• Skilled human resource [12][21][29][35]
• ICT readiness [27]	• Property rights protection [12][36]
• External Environment readiness [[27]	• Lack of clean water, inadequate housing and freedom [34][42]
• Human readiness [27]	• National culture and cross cultural differences [1][4][5][8][9][10][14][16][20][22][28][30][31][33][37][38][39][41]
• Information readiness [27]	• Organizational culture [17][19]
• Completeness assets [12][13][21][29][35][40][43]	• Business Ethics [30]
• Telecommunications networks [12][21][29][40][43][35]	• Language and translation problems [8]
• Skilled IT professionals [35][40][43]	• Culturally heterogeneous teams [6][15]
• Lack of resource for technology investments [34][35][40][42][43]	• Culture of bureaucracy and institutional fragmentation [32]
• Structure of economy [7][12][21][29][35][36][40][43]	• Poverty [35]
• Openness to external influence [12][13][35][40][43]	• Lack of infrastructure [35]
• Digital infrastructure [7][10][21]	• Inadequate education [35]
• Macro economy situation [10]	• Incorrect assumptions and policy makings [35]
• Ability to invest [10]	• Legal similarity [38]
• Knowledge citizens [10]	• Political context [38][42]
• Competitiveness [10]	
• Access to skilled workforce [10]	

As shown in Tables 1 and 2, there are huge number of factors moderating the relationship between IT diffusion and performance. In order to test their effects, we have categorized all factors into 5 general dimension; Economic Dimension, Business and Competition Dimension, Geographical and Infrastructural Dimension, Population, Gender and Literacy Dimension, and National Health Dimension. The main idea is that the relation between IT diffusion and national performance in developed and developing countries moderate by these five general factors (dimensions). We describe the conceptual model of this research in the next section.

3. The Model and Research Hypotheses

3.1 The Conceptual Model

In order to investigate the effects of moderator factors on the relationship between IT usage and country level performance, we developed the following general conceptual mode (Figure 1):

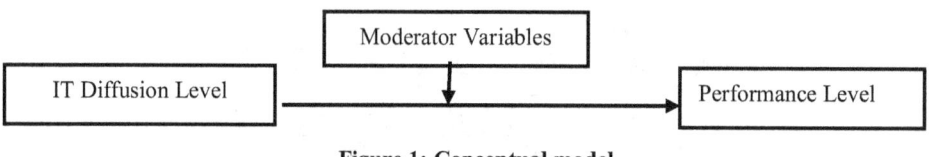

Figure 1: Conceptual model

Figure 2 shows the extended version of conceptual model.

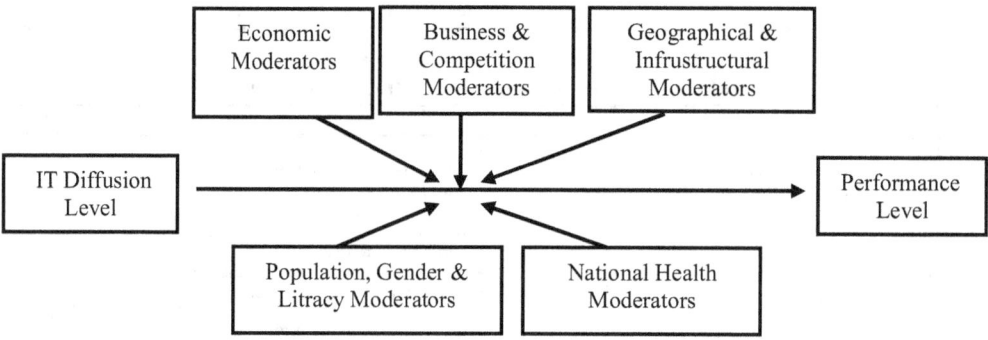

Figure 2: Extended version of the conceptual model

3.2 The Operational Model and Variables

In this section, we define independent, dependent and moderator variables and introduce the operational model of this research. The variables are as follows:

IT Diffusion Level (Independent Variables: X)

XTE1=Internet hosts country ranks

XTE2=Internet users country ranks

XTE3=Telephones-main lines in use country ranks

XTE4=Telephones-mobile cellular country ranks

XTE5=Television broadcast stations country ranks

Country level Performances (Dependent Variables:Y)

XEB4=Reserves of foreign exchange and gold country ranks

XEB1=Unemployment rate (%)country ranks

XEB6=Population below poverty line (%) country ranks

XEB13=Inflation rate(consumer prices)(%) country ranks

XEB18=GDP - per capita (PPP) country ranks

Economic Moderator Variables

XEB2=Stock of direct foreign investment - at home country ranks

XEB3=Stock of direct foreign investment - abroad country ranks

XEB7=Market value of publicly traded shares country ranks

XEB8=Labor force - by occupation–services (%) country ranks

XEB9=Labor force - by occupation–industry (%) country ranks

XEB11=Labor force country ranks

XEB12=Investment (gross fixed and % of GPD) country ranks

XEB15=Imports country ranks

XEB17=GDP - purchasing power parity country ranks

XEB20=GDP - composition by sector – services (%) country ranks

XEB23=Exports country ranks

XEB24=Economic aid - recipient country ranks

XEB25=Economic aid - donor country ranks

Business & Competition Moderators Variables

XDB2=Starting a business country ranks

XDB3=Dealing with licenses country ranks

XDB4=Employing workers country ranks

XDB5=Registering property country ranks

XDB6=Getting credit country ranks

XDB7=Protecting investors country ranks

XDB8=Paying taxes country ranks

XDB9=Trading across borders country ranks

XDB10=Enforcing contracts country ranks

XDB11=Closing a business country ranks

XDB12= Number of foreign companies listed in a country, country ranks

Geographical & Infrastructural Moderator Variables

XT1= Airports country ranks

XT2=Heliports country ranks

XT3=Merchant marine (ships) country ranks

XT4=Pipelines (km) country ranks

XT5=Railways (km) country ranks

XT6=Roadways (km) country ranks

XT7=Waterways (km) country ranks

XG1=Land Area - sq km country ranks

XG2=Total Area - sq km country ranks

National Health Moderators Variables

XP14=HIV/AIDS - people living with HIV/AIDS country ranks

XP17=Infant mortality rate – total (deaths/1,000 live births) country ranks

XP35=Total fertility rate (children born/woman) country ranks

XP11=Death Rate (deaths/1,000 population) country ranks

XP20=Life expectancy at birth – total (years) country ranks

Population, Gender & Literacy Moderators Variables

XP4=Age structure 15-64 years country ranks

XP10=Birth Rate (births/1,000 population) country ranks

XP26=Median age–total (years) country ranks

XP27=Net migration rate country ranks

XP28=Population country ranks

XP29=Population growth rate (%) country ranks

XP34=Sex ratio 15-64 years (male(s)/female) country ranks

XP23=Literacy–total (%) country ranks

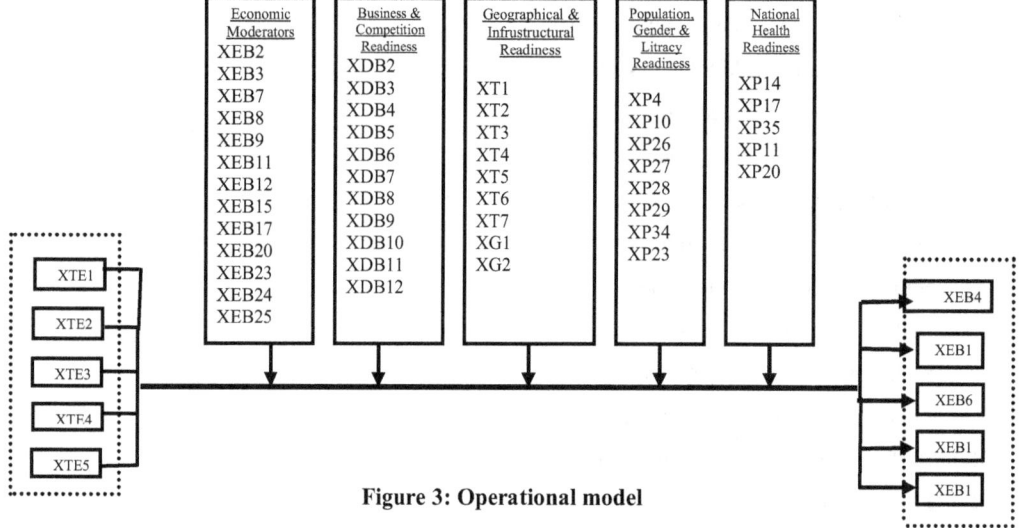

Figure 3: Operational model

3.3 The Research Hypotheses

This research examines following research hypotheses for developed and developing countries:

For developed countries:

H11a: (XTE1) correlates positively with (XEB4)

H12a: (XTE1) correlates negatively with (XEB1)

H13a: (XTE1) correlates negatively with (XEB6)

H14a: (XTE1) correlates negatively with (EXB13)

H15a: (XTE1) correlates positively with (XEB18)

H21a: (XTE2) correlates positively with (XEB4)

H22a: (XTE2) correlates negatively with (XEB1)

H23a: (XTE2) correlates negatively with (XEB6)

H24a: (XTE2) correlates negatively with (EXB13)

H25a: (XTE2) correlates positively with (XEB18)

H31a: (XTE3) correlates positively with (XEB4)

H32a: (XTE3) correlates negatively with (XEB1)

H33a: (XTE3) correlates negatively with (XEB6)

H34a: (XTE3) correlates negatively with (EXB13)

H35a: (XTE3) correlates positively with (XEB18)

H41a: (XTE4) correlates positively with (XEB4)

H42a: (XTE4) correlates negatively with (XEB1)

H43a: (XTE4) correlates negatively with (XEB6)

H44a: (XTE4) correlates negatively with (EXB13)

H45a: (XTE4) correlates positively with (XEB18)

H51a: (XTE5) correlates positively with (XEB4)

H52a: (XTE5) correlates negatively with (XEB1)

H53a: (XTE5) correlates negatively with (XEB6)

H54a: (XTE5) correlates negatively with (EXB13)

H55a: (XTE5) correlates positively with (XEB18)

H1am: Economic, Business and Competition, Geographical and Infrustructural, Population-Gender-Literacy, and National Health readiness factors moderate the relationships among (XTE1), (XTE2), (XTE3), (XTE4), and (XTE5) with (XEB4),(XEB1), (XEB6), (XEB13),and (XEB18) in developed courtiers.

For developing countries:

H11b: (XTE1) correlates positively with (XEB4)

H12b: (XTE1) correlates negatively with (XEB1)

H13b: (XTE1) correlates negatively with (XEB6)

H14b: (XTE1) correlates negatively with (EXB13)

H15b: (XTE1) correlates positively with (XEB18)

H21b: (XTE2) correlates positively with (XEB4)

H22b: (XTE2) correlates negatively with (XEB1)

H23b: (XTE2) correlates negatively with (XEB6)

H24b: (XTE2) correlates negatively with (EXB13)

H25b: (XTE2) correlates positively with (XEB18)

H31b: (XTE3) correlates positively with (XEB4)

H32b: (XTE3) correlates negatively with (XEB1)

H33b: (XTE3) correlates negatively with (XEB6)

H34b: (XTE3) correlates negatively with (EXB13)

H35b: (XTE3) correlates positively with (XEB18)

H41b: (XTE4) correlates positively with (XEB4)

H42b: (XTE4) correlates negatively with (XEB1)

H43b: (XTE4) correlates negatively with (XEB6)

H44b: (XTE4) correlates negatively with (EXB13)

H45b: (XTE4) correlates positively with (XEB18)

H51b: (XTE5) correlates positively with (XEB4)

H52b: (XTE5) correlates negatively with (XEB1)

H53b: (XTE5) correlates negatively with (XEB6)

H54b: (XTE5) correlates negatively with (EXB13)

H55b: (XTE5) correlates positively with (XEB18)

H1bm: Economic, Business and Competition, Geographica and Infrustructural, Population-Gender-Literacy, and National Health readiness factors signifcantly moderate the relationships among (XTE1),(XTE2), (XTE3), (XTE4), and (XTE5) with (XEB4),(XEB1), (XEB6), (XEB13),and (XEB18) in developing courtiers.

4. Data and Methodology

In this paper, we developed a conceptual model to investigate the effects of some key moderators on the relationship between the level of IT usage and national performance level in developed and developing countries. We used multiple measures to capture the independent, dependent and moderator variables.

In order to test the hypotheses, we divide the sample into developed and developing countries. Developed countries usually have economic systems based on continuous, self-sustaining economic growth in the tertiary and quaternary sectors and high standards of living. Countries not fitting this definition referred to as developing countries. Accordingly, in this research, developed countries are Andorra, Australia, Austria, Belgium, Canada, China, Denmark, Faroe Islands, Finland, France, Germany, Gibraltar, Greece, Hong Kong, Iceland, Ireland, Territories not administered by the Palestinian authority, Italy, Japan, Luxembourg, Malta, Netherlands, New Zealand, Norway, Portugal, Singapore, Slovenia, Spain, South Korea, Sweden, Switzerland, Taiwan, United Kingdom, and United States of America (n1=34). Countries not including in this list referred to as developing countries (n2=211).

The main part of data is based on a well-structured international database for year 2008 [44]. This website strategizes historical information in the Library of Congress, World Fact Books and some other major international databases such as UNCTAD, World Bank database, International Monetary Funds (IMF) database, as well as some other international geography, economic, social and cultural related organizations. In order to calculate rank of each country in terms of number of foreign companies listed in a country, we used final World Exchange database for 2007 [45].

In order to analyze the data and compare the results in developed and developing counties, we applied Pearson Correlation Test (SPSS Software) and Structured Equation Model LISREL Software). Pearson Correlation Test and Partial Pearson Correlation Test show how each moderator variable significantly moderate each pair of IT-performance variables. Since there are 5 independent and 5 dependent variables in this research, we provided the effects of each moderator variable on 25 possible relations between independent and dependent variables. The results for developed and developing countries are provided in Tables 4 and 5 of the next section. Moreover, in order to analyze the data in a systematic way, we used Structured Equation Model (LISREL Software). Results of LISREL let to assess the fitness of the data with the proposed new conceptual model and explain the interactions between moderator variables and the roles of each moderator variables on IT-Performance relationship in developed and developing countries.

5. The Empirical Results

5.1 Results of Pearson and Partial Correlation Tests

The first and second parts of Table 3 show results of Pearson Correlation tests for developed countries and developing countries, respectively.

Results of Pearson Correlation tests for developed countries show that:

Hypotheses H11a and H12a supported, but H13a, H14a and H15a not supported.

Hypotheses H21a, H22a, and H23a supported, but H24a, H25a not supported.

Hypotheses H31a, H32a, and H33a, but H34a and H35a not supported.

Hypotheses H41a, H42a, and H43a supported, but H44a and H45a not supported.

Hypotheses H51a and H52a supported, but H53a, H54a and H55a not supported.

Hypothesis H1am supported.

Results of Pearson Correlation tests for developing countries show that:

Hypotheses H11b, H13b, H14b and H15b supported, but H12b not supported.

Hypotheses H21b, H22b, H23b, H24b and H25b supported.

Hypotheses H31b, H32b, H33b, H34b and H35b supported.

Hypotheses H41b, H42b, H43b, H44b and H45b supported.

Hypotheses H51b, H54b and H55b supported, but H52b and H53b not supported.

Hypothesis H1bm supported.

Table 3 : Results of Pearson Correlation tests for developed and developing countries

Developed Cointries	XEB4			XEB1			XEB6			XEB13			XEB18		
	Correlation	Sig	N	Correlation	Sig	N	Correlation	Sig	N	Correlation	Sig	N	Correlation	Sig	N
XTE1	0.778**	0.000	34	0.343*	0.024	34	0.218	0.108	34	-0.195	0.135	34	-0.106	0.275	34
XTE2	0.867**	0.000	34	0.406**	0.009	34	0.376*	0.014	34	-0.201	0.127	34	-0.184	0.149	34
XTE3	0.858**	0.000	34	0.456**	0.003	34	0.356*	0.017	34	-0.189	0.142	34	-0.204	0.124	34
XTE4	0.850**	0.000	34	0.469**	0.003	34	0.383*	0.013	34	-0.197	0.132	34	-0.226	0.099	34
XTE5	0.680**	0.000	34	0.358*	0.019	34	0.169	0.169	34	-0.101	0.285	34	-0.268	0.063	34
XEB4	1	---	34	0.215	0.111	34	0.240	0.086	34	-0.362*	0.018	34	-0.222	0.104	34
XEB1				1	---	34	0.454**	0.003	34	-0.073	0.340	34	-0.364*	0.017	34
XEB6							1	---	34	0.031	0.431	34	-0.203	0.125	34
XEB13										1	---	34	-0.220	0.105	34

Developing Countries	XEB4			XEB1			XEB6			XEB13			XEB18		
	Correlation	Sig	N	Correlation	Sig	N	Correlation	Sig	N	Correlation	Sig	N	Correlation	Sig	N
XTE1	0.624**	0.000	211	0.054	0.219	211	0.114*	0.050	211	0.260**	0.000	211	0.375**	0.000	211
XTE2	0.847**	0.000	211	0.184**	0.004	211	0.318**	0.000	211	0.446**	0.000	211	0.230**	0.000	211
XTE3	0.849**	0.000	211	0.216**	0.001	211	0.277**	0.000	211	0.475**	0.000	211	0.292**	0.000	211
XTE4	0.866**	0.000	211	0.216**	0.001	211	0.368**	0.000	211	0.494**	0.000	211	0.171**	0.006	211
XTE5	0.720**	0.000	211	0.100	0.073	211	0.101	0.072	211	0.227**	0.000	211	0.222	0.001	211
XEB4			211	0.167**	0.007	211	0.148*	0.016	211	0.360**	0.000	211	0.299**	0.000	211
XEB1						211	0.244**	0.000	211	0.140*	0.021	211	0.065	0.173	211
XEB6									211	0.467**	0.000	211	-0.361**	0.000	211
XEB13												211	0.029	0.336	211

** Correlation is significant at the 0.01 level (1-tailed).

* Correlation is significant at the 0.05 level (1-tailed).

Tables 4 and 5 show the results of partial correlation for developed and developing countries, respectively.

Table 4: Results of partial correlation for developed countries

Hypotheses	Control Variable	Independent Variable	Dependent Variable	Correlation	Significance (1-tailed)	df n-2-m	Hypotheses	Control Variable	Independent Variable	Dependent Variable	Correlation	Significance (1-tailed)	df n-2-m
H11a*	EM*	XTE1	XEB4	0.189	0.146	31	H34a**	EM	XTE3	XEB13	-0.077	0.336	31
	BM	XTE1	XEB4	0.6	0.000	31		BM	XTE3	XEB13	-0.219	0.110	31
	GM	XTE1	XEB4	0.55	0.000	31		GM**	XTE3	XEB13	-0.371	0.017	31
	PM	XTE1	XEB4	0.498	0.002	31		PM**	XTE3	XEB13	-0.319	0.035	31
	NM	XTE1	XEB4	0.787	0.000	31		NM	XTE3	XEB13	-0.189	0.146	31
H12a*	EM*	XTE1	XEB1	-0.214	0.116	31	H35a**	EM	XTE3	XEB18	0.006	0.486	31
	BM	XTE1	XEB1	0.470	0.003	31		BM**	XTE3	XEB18	-0.580	0.000	31
	GM*	XTE1	XEB1	0.068	0.354	31		GM	XTE3	XEB18	0.001	0.498	31
	PM*	XTE1	XEB1	0.212	0.118	31		PM	XTE3	XEB18	-0.212	0.118	31
	NM*	XTE1	XEB1	0.224	0.105	31		NM	XTE3	XEB18	-0.150	0.202	31
H13a**	EM**	XTE1	XEB6	-0.310	0.040	31	H41a*	EM	XTE4	XEB4	0.369	0.017	31
	BM	XTE1	XEB6	0.174	0.166	31		BM	XTE4	XEB4	0.747	0.000	31
	GM	XTE1	XEB6	-0.017	0.463	31		GM	XTE4	XEB4	0.715	0.000	31
	PM	XTE1	XEB6	-0.075	0.340	31		PM	XTE4	XEB4	0.673	0.000	31
	NM	XTE1	XEB6	0.149	0.205	31		NM	XTE4	XEB4	0.882	0.000	31
H14a**	EM	XTE1	XEB13	-0.082	0.324	31	H42a*	EM*	XTE4	XEB1	-0.029	0.436	31
	BM	XTE1	XEB13	-0.242	0.088	31		BM	XTE4	XEB1	0.588	0.000	31
	GM**	XTE1	XEB13	-0.343	0.026	31		GM*	XTE4	XEB1	0.289	0.051	31
	PM**	XTE1	XEB13	-0.313	0.038	31		PM	XTE4	XEB1	0.445	0.005	31
	NM	XTE1	XEB13	-0.194	0.140	31		NM	XTE4	XEB1	0.344	0.025	31
H15a**	EM	XTE1	XEB18	0.172	0.170	31	H43a*	EM*	XTE4	XEB6	-0.020	0.456	31
	BM**	XTE1	XEB18	-0.497	0.002	31		BM	XTE4	XEB6	0.390	0.012	31
	GM	XTE1	XEB18	0.147	0.207	31		GM*	XTE4	XEB6	0.270	0.064	31
	PM	XTE1	XEB18	-0.034	0.425	31		PM*	XTE4	XEB6	0.227	0.102	31
	NM	XTE1	XEB18	-0.051	0.389	31		NM	XTE4	XEB6	0.319	0.035	31
H21a*	EM	XTE2	XEB4	0.495	0.002	31	H44a**	EM	XTE4	XEB13	-0.109	0.273	31
	BM	XTE2	XEB4	0.767	0.000	31		BM	XTE4	XEB13	-0.223	0.106	31
	GM	XTE2	XEB4	0.768	0.000	31		GM**	XTE4	XEB13	-0.391	0.012	31
	PM	XTE2	XEB4	0.717	0.000	31		PM**	XTE4	XEB13	-0.324	0.033	31
	NM	XTE2	XEB4	0.894	0.000	31		NM	XTE4	XEB13	-0.200	0.133	31
H22a*	EM	XTE2	XEB1	-0.338	0.027	31	H45a**	EM	XTE4	XEB18	-0.102	0.286	31
	BM	XTE2	XEB1	0.543	0.001	31		BM**	XTE4	XEB18	-0.574	0.000	31
	GM*	XTE2	XEB1	0.159	0.188	31		GM	XTE4	XEB18	-0.040	0.413	31
	PM	XTE2	XEB1	0.337	0.027	31		PM	XTE4	XEB18	-0.248	0.082	31
	NM*	XTE2	XEB1	0.276	0.060	31		NM	XTE4	XEB18	-0.171	0.170	31
H23a*	EM*	XTE2	XEB6	-0.055	0.381	31	H51a*	EM*	XTE5	XEB4	0.276	0.060	31
	BM	XTE2	XEB6	0.398	0.011	31		BM	XTE5	XEB4	0.593	0.000	31
	GM*	XTE2	XEB6	0.260	0.072	31		GM*	XTE5	XEB4	0.265	0.068	31
	PM*	XTE2	XEB6	0.212	0.118	31		PM	XTE5	XEB4	0.420	0.007	31
	NM	XTE2	XEB6	0.313	0.038	31		NM	XTE5	XEB4	0.755	0.000	31
H24a**	EM	XTE2	XEB13	-0.126	0.243	31	H52a*	EM*	XTE5	XEB1	0.036	0.421	31
	BM	XTE2	XEB13	-0.243	0.087	31		BM	XTE5	XEB1	0.378	0.015	31
	GM**	XTE2	XEB13	-0.425	0.007	31		GM*	XTE5	XEB1	0.045	0.402	31
	PM**	XTE2	XEB13	-0.349	0.023	31		PM*	XTE5	XEB1	0.245	0.084	31
	NM	XTE2	XEB13	-0.203	0.129	31		NM*	XTE5	XEB1	0.114	0.263	31
H25a**	EM	XTE2	XEB18	0.085	0.318	31	H53a**	EM	XTE5	XEB6	-0.157	0.192	31
	BM**	XTE2	XEB18	-0.581	0.000	31		BM	XTE5	XEB6	0.125	0.245	31
	GM	XTE2	XEB18	0.052	0.386	31		GM	XTE5	XEB6	-0.182	0.155	31
	PM	XTE2	XEB18	-0.179	0.160	31		PM	XTE5	XEB6	-0.047	0.397	31
	NM	XTE2	XEB18	-0.128	0.240	31		NM	XTE5	XEB6	0.030	0.433	31
H31a*	EM	XTE3	XEB4	0.445	0.005	31	H54a**	EM	XTE5	XEB13	0.030	0.435	31
	BM	XTE3	XEB4	0.754	0.000	31		BM	XTE5	XEB13	-0.092	0.306	31
	GM	XTE3	XEB4	0.561	0.000	31		GM	XTE5	XEB13	-0.245	0.085	31
	PM	XTE3	XEB4	0.693	0.000	31		PM	XTE5	XEB13	-0.117	0.259	31
	NM	XTE3	XEB4	0.882	0.000	31		NM	XTE5	XEB13	-0.098	0.294	31
H32a*	EM*	XTE3	XEB1	-0.123	0.247	31	H55a**	EM	XTE5	XEB18	-0.175	0.165	31
	BM	XTE3	XEB1	0.595	0.000	31		BM**	XTE5	XEB18	-0.448	0.004	31
	GM*	XTE3	XEB1	0.265	0.068	31		GM	XTE5	XEB18	-0.114	0.264	31
	PM	XTE3	XEB1	0.429	0.006	31		PM	XTE5	XEB18	-0.262	0.070	31
	NM	XTE3	XEB1	0.342	0.026	31		NM	XTE5	XEB18	-0.205	0.126	31
H33a*	EM*	XTE3	XEB6	-0.138	0.222	31							
	BM	XTE3	XEB6	0.375	0.016	31							
	GM*	XTE3	XEB6	0.235	0.094	31							
	PM*	XTE3	XEB6	0.192	0.142	31							
	NM	XTE3	XEB6	0.303	0.043	31							

** A variable that moderates the relation between independent and dependent variables. By controlling this variable, an insignificant relationship becomes significant.
* A variable that moderates the relationship between independent and dependent variables. By controlling this variable a significant relationship becomes insignificant.

Table 5: Results of partial correlation for developing countries

Hypothesis	Control Variable	Independent Variable	Dependent Variable	Correlation	Significance (1-tailed)	df n-2-m	Hypothesis	Control Variable	Independent Variable	Dependent Variable	Correlation	Significance (1-tailed)	df n-2-m
H11b*	EM*	XTE1	XEB4	0.091	0.096	208	H34b*	EM*	XTE3	XEB13	0.032	0.322	208
	BM	XTE1	XEB4	0.491	0.000	208		BM	XTE3	XEB13	0.328	0.000	208
	GM	XTE1	XEB4	0.391	0.000	208		GM	XTE3	XEB13	0.185	0.004	208
	PM	XTE1	XEB4	0.426	0.000	208		PM	XTE3	XEB13	0.245	0.000	208
	NM	XTE1	XEB4	0.606	0.000	208		NM	XTE3	XEB13	0.371	0.000	208
H12b**	EM**	XTE1	XEB1	-0.148	0.016	208	H35b*	EM*	XTE3	XEB18	0.075	0.140	208
	BM	XTE1	XEB1	-0.051	0.231	208		BM	XTE3	XEB18	0.308	0.000	208
	GM	XTE1	XEB1	-0.034	0.312	208		GM	XTE3	XEB18	0.460	0.000	208
	PM	XTE1	XEB1	-0.095	0.086	208		PM*	XTE3	XEB18	-0.089	0.099	208
	NM	XTE1	XEB1	0.018	0.396	208		NM	XTE3	XEB18	0.330	0.000	208
H13b*	EM	XTE1	XEB6	-0.165	0.008	208	H41b*	EM	XTE4	XEB4	0.313	0.000	208
	BM*	XTE1	XEB6	-0.050	0.234	208		BM	XTE4	XEB4	0.815	0.000	208
	GM*	XTE1	XEB6	-0.107	0.061	208		GM	XTE4	XEB4	0.651	0.000	208
	PM*	XTE1	XEB6	0.006	0.465	208		PM	XTE4	XEB4	0.785	0.000	208
	NM*	XTE1	XEB6	-0.008	0.457	208		NM	XTE4	XEB4	0.877	0.000	208
H14b*	EM	XTE1	XEB13	-0.125	0.036	208	H42b*	EM*	XTE4	XEB1	-0.007	0.459	208
	BM*	XTE1	XEB13	0.072	0.151	208		BM	XTE4	XEB1	0.131	0.029	208
	GM*	XTE1	XEB13	0.001	0.495	208		GM	XTE4	XEB1	0.162	0.009	208
	PM*	XTE1	XEB13	0.001	0.494	208		PM*	XTE4	XEB1	0.096	0.083	208
	NM	XTE1	XEB13	0.187	0.003	208		NM	XTE4	XEB1	0.152	0.014	208
H15b*	EM	XTE1	XEB18	0.258	0.000	208	H43b*	EM	XTE4	XEB6	0.174	0.006	208
	BM	XTE1	XEB18	0.395	0.000	208		BM	XTE4	XEB6	0.244	0.000	208
	GM	XTE1	XEB18	0.444	0.000	208		GM	XTE4	XEB6	0.124	0.036	208
	PM	XTE1	XEB18	0.137	0.024	208		PM	XTE4	XEB6	0.329	0.000	208
	NM	XTE1	XEB18	0.394	0.000	208		NM	XTE4	XEB6	0.132	0.028	208
H21b*	EM	XTE2	XEB4	0.244	0.000	208	H44b*	EM*	XTE4	XEB13	0.098	0.079	208
	BM	XTE2	XEB4	0.787	0.000	208		BM	XTE4	XEB13	0.349	0.000	208
	GM	XTE2	XEB4	0.624	0.000	208		GM	XTE4	XEB13	0.198	0.002	208
	PM	XTE2	XEB4	0.752	0.000	208		PM	XTE4	XEB13	0.300	0.000	208
	NM	XTE2	XEB4	0.843	0.000	208		NM	XTE4	XEB13	0.338	0.000	208
H22b*	EM*	XTE2	XEB1	-0.084	0.114	208	H45b*	EM	XTE4	XEB18	-0.300	0.000	208
	BM*	XTE2	XEB1	0.091	0.095	208		BM	XTE4	XEB18	0.161	0.010	208
	GM*	XTE2	XEB1	0.107	0.062	208		GM	XTE4	XEB18	0.302	0.000	208
	PM*	XTE2	XEB1	0.052	0.226	208		PM	XTE4	XEB18	-0.208	0.001	208
	NM	XTE2	XEB1	0.126	0.034	208		NM	XTE4	XEB18	0.221	0.001	208
H23b*	EM*	XTE2	XEB6	0.028	0.341	208	H51b*	EM	XTE5	XEB4	0.307	0.000	208
	BM	XTE2	XEB6	0.179	0.005	208		BM	XTE5	XEB4	0.637	0.000	208
	GM*	XTE2	XEB6	0.055	0.055	208		GM	XTE5	XEB4	0.474	0.000	208
	PM	XTE2	XEB6	0.263	0.000	208		PM	XTE5	XEB4	0.601	0.000	208
	NM	XTE2	XEB6	0.117	0.046	208		NM	XTE5	XEB4	0.720	0.000	208
H24b*	EM*	XTE2	XEB13	-0.39	0.288	208	H52b**	EM	XTE5	XEB1	-0.092	0.091	208
	BM	XTE2	XEB13	0.284	0.000	208		BM	XTE5	XEB1	0.016	0.406	208
	GM	XTE2	XEB13	0.130	0.030	208		GM	XTE5	XEB1	0.005	0.471	208
	PM	XTE2	XEB13	0.227	0.000	208		PM	XTE5	XEB1	-0.017	0.404	208
	NM	XTE2	XEB13	0.312	0.000	208		NM	XTE5	XEB1	0.084	0.114	208
H25b*	EM*	XTE2	XEB18	-0.094	0.088	208	H53b**	EM**	XTE5	XEB6	-0.201	0.002	208
	BM	XTE2	XEB18	0.235	0.000	208		BM	XTE5	XEB6	-0.043	0.266	208
	GM	XTE2	XEB18	0.366	0.000	208		GM**	XTE5	XEB6	-0.183	0.004	208
	PM	XTE2	XEB18	-0.126	0.034	208		PM	XTE5	XEB6	0.005	0.471	208
	NM	XTE2	XEB18	0.273	0.000	208		NM	XTE5	XEB6	0.049	0.239	208
H31b*	EM	XTE3	XEB4	0.216	0.001	208	H54b*	EM	XTE5	XEB13	-0.200	0.002	208
	BM	XTE3	XEB4	0.790	0.000	208		BM*	XTE5	XEB13	0.057	0.204	208
	GM	XTE3	XEB4	0.632	0.000	208		GM	XTE5	XEB13	-0.114	0.050	208
	PM	XTE3	XEB4	0.754	0.000	208		PM*	XTE5	XEB13	-0.003	0.482	208
	NM	XTE3	XEB4	0.841	0.000	208		NM	XTE5	XEB13	0.205	0.001	208
H32b*	EM*	XTE3	XEB1	-0.004	0.479	208	H55b*	EM*	XTE5	XEB18	0.031	0.326	208
	BM	XTE3	XEB1	0.134	0.026	208		BM	XTE5	XEB18	0.214	0.001	208
	GM	XTE3	XEB1	0.158	0.011	208		GM	XTE5	XEB18	0.286	0.000	208
	PM*	XTE3	XEB1	0.082	0.117	208		PM*	XTE5	XEB18	-0.031	0.329	208
	NM	XTE3	XEB1	0.168	0.008	208		NM	XTE5	XEB18	0.229	0.000	208
H33b*	EM*	XTE3	XEB6	-0.110	0.056	208							
	BM	XTE3	XEB6	0.132	0.028	208							
	GM*	XTE3	XEB6	-0.12	0.429	208							
	PM	XTE3	XEB6	0.208	0.001	208							
	NM*	XTE3	XEB6	0.097	0.081	208							

** A variable that moderates the relation between independent and dependent variables. By controlling this variable, an insignificant relationship becomes significant.
* A variable that moderates the relationship between independent and dependent variables. By controlling this variable, a significant relationship becomes insignificant.

5.2 Results of Structured Equation Models (LISREL)

5.2.1. Results of LISREL for developed countries

Figure [4] shows results of LISREL for developed countries. Let define the variables as follows:
ITDIFFUS: IT Diffusion level
PERFORMA: National Performance level
ECONOMIC: Economic Moderator (EM)
BUSINESS: Business & Competition Moderator (BM)
GEOGRAPH: Geographical & Infrastructure Moderator (GM)
POPULATI: Population, Gender and Literacy Moderator (PM)
NATIONAL: National Health Moderator (NM)

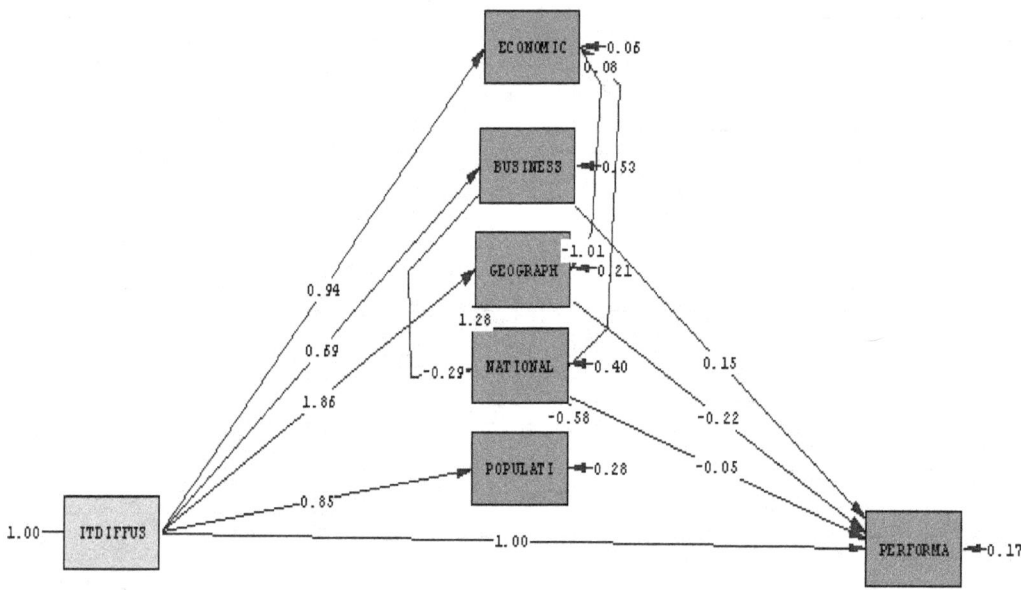

Chi-Square=13.41, df=8, P-value=0.09865, RMSEA=0.057

Figure 4: LISREL for developed countrie

As shown in Figure [4], the structure of the hypothetical model for interactions between IT diffusion, moderating factors and performance level in developed countries was supported for chi- square statistics ($\chi2$=13.41 with 8 degree of freedom, p=0.09865). The Goodness of Fit Index (GFI) of the model was 0.98. The additional index values for the model were 1.00 for the Comparative Fit Index (CFI). These statistics suggest a good fit. The RMSEA was 0.057 (95% CIS 0.0; 0.094) with a p-value (for test of close fit RMSEA<0.05) of 0.36. These global goodness of fit statistics suggesting an acceptable fit of the data with the model. The path coefficient estimates were statistically significant with t-values from 2.86 to 43.42, indicating that the variables were linked to the model (a t-value of 1.96 or higher at the significance level of 0.05). Only t-value between National Health moderator (NATIONAL) and Performance level (PERFORMA) is less than 2, and therefore this relation is insignificant.

As shown in the above figure, IT diffusion affects on the moderator factors (ECONOMIC, BUSINESS, GEOGRAPH, POPULATI, and NATIONAL). The moderator factors in turn with their interactions affect on the Performance Level (PERFORMA). The Measurement Equations for the modelare as follows:

ECONOMIC = 0.18*NATIONAL + 0.57*ITDIFFUS, Errorvar.= 38.44, R^2 = 0.94

p-values: (0.064)   (0.013)   (4.57)

t-values: 2.73   43.42   8.41

BUSINESS = 0.78*ITDIFFUS, Errorvar.= 1107.23, R^2 = 0.47

p-values: (0.057)   (108.31)

t-values: 13.65   10.22

GEOGRAPH = - 1.56*ECONOMIC + 1.73*ITDIFFUS, Errorvar.= 296.36, R^2 = 0.79

p-values: (0.28)   (0.17)   (30.60)

t-values: -5.59   10.41   9.69

NATIONAL = -0.069*BUSINESS+ 0.37*GEOGRAPH - 0.65*POPULATI, Errorvar.= 47.69, R^2= 0.60

p-values: (0.014)   (0.023)   (0.080)   (4.70)

t-values: -4.99   16.20   -8.06   10.15

POPULATI = 0.20*ITDIFFUS, Errorvar.= 26.72, R^2 = 0.72

p-values: (0.0089)   (2.61)

t-values: 23.08   10.22

PERFORMA= 0.034*BUSINESS - 0.060*GEOGRAPH + 0.26*ITDIFFUS, Errorvar.= 18.98, R^2 = 0.83

p-values: (0.0094)   (0.021)   (0.017)   (1.86)

t-values: 3.63   -2.86   14.93   10.22

5.2.2. Results of LISREL for developing countries

Figure [5] shows results of LISREL for developking countries.

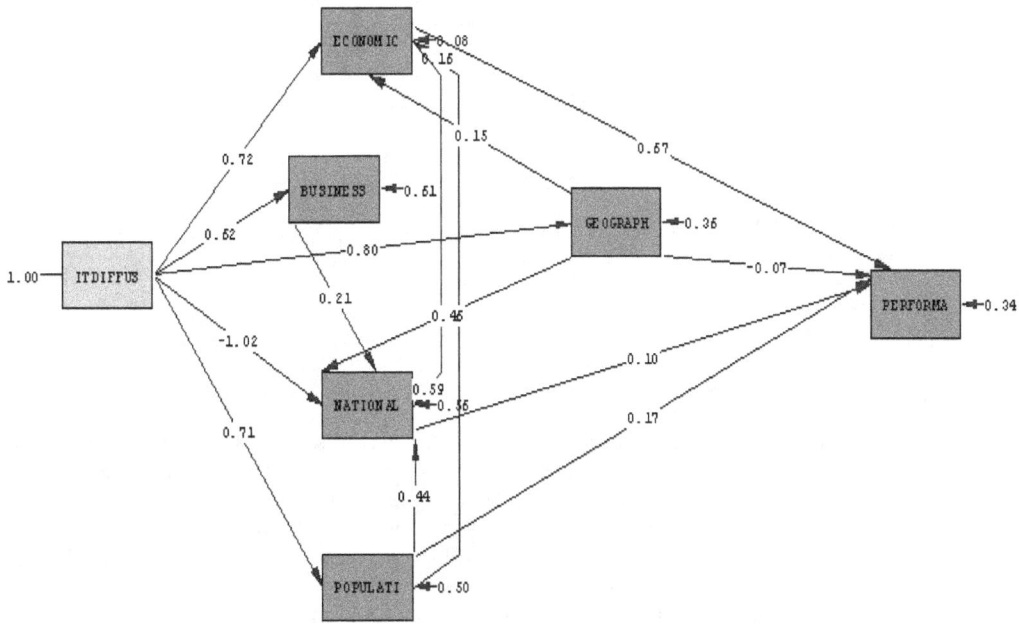

Chi-Square=4.35, df=6, P-value=0.62943, RMSEA=0.000

Figure 5: LISREL for developing countrie

As shown in Figure [5], the structure of the hypothetical model for interactions between IT diffusion, moderating factors and performance level in developing countries was supported for chi-square statistics ($\chi2$=4.35 with 6 degree of freedom, p=0.62943). The Goodness of Fit Index (GFI) of the model was 0.99. The additional index values for the model were 1.00 for the Comparative Fit Index (CFI). These statistics suggest a good fit. The RMSEA was 0.00 (95% CIS 0.0; 0.075) with a p-value (for test of close fit

RMSEA<0.05) of 0.84. These global goodness of fit statistics suggesting an acceptable fit of the data with the model. The path coefficient estimates were statistically significant with t-values from 2.08 to 19.26, indicating that the variables were linked to the model (a t-value of 1.96 or higher at the significance level of 0.05). Only t-value of the between Geographical & Infrastructure Readiness (GeographiReadi) and Performance level (Performance) is less than 2, and therefore this relation is insignificant.

As shown in Figure 5, IT diffusion affects on the moderator factors (ECONOMIC, BUSINESS, GEOGRAPH, POPULATI, and NATIONAL). The moderator factors in turn with their interactions affect on the Performance Level (PERFORMA). The Measurement Equations for the model is as follow:

ECONOMIC = 0.12*GEOGRAPH + 0.23*POPULATI + 0.44*ITDIFFUS, Errorvar.= 64.22, R^2 = 0.92

p-values: (0.027)   (0.041)   (0.023)   (6.28)
t-values: 4.65   5.72   19.26   10.22

BUSINESS = 0.52*ITDIFFUS, Errorvar.= 964.31, R^2 = 0.39

p-values: (0.045)   (94.33)
t-values: 11.56   10.22

GEOGRAPH = 0.58*ITDIFFUS, Errorvar.= 427.00, R^2 = 0.64

p-values: (0.030)   (41.77)
t-values: 19.25   10.22

NATIONAL = 0.72*ECONOMIC + 0.19*BUSINESS + 0.47*GEOGRAPH + 0.81*POPULATI - 0.76*ITDIFFUS, Errorvar.= 695.39, R^2 = 0.44

p-values: (0.23) (0.059) (0.093) (0.15) (0.13) (68.03)
t-values: 3.17   3.21   5.11   5.55   -5.89   10.22

POPULATI = 0.29*ITDIFFUS, Errorvar.= 182.30, R^2 = 0.50

p-values: (0.020)   (17.83)
t-values: 14.56   10.22

PERFORMA= 0.52*ECONOMIC + 0.065*NATIONAL + 0.19*POPULATI, Errorvar.= 166.92, R^2 = 0.66

p-values: (0.067) (0.031) (0.076) (16.33)
t-values: 7.65   2.08   2.58   10.22

6. Conclusions and Final Remarks

This paper provides a new conceptual model and offering an empirically based insight into the effects of IT-Performance moderators in developed and developing countries. In order to test the model, we used data from 34 developed and 211 developing countries and applied both Pearson Correlation and Structured Equation Model. Pearson correlation and partial correlation results show how each of moderator variables moderates IT-performance relation in developed and developing countries. However, as a general conclusion from structured equation models, we found that four moderator variables ((ECONOMIC, BUSINESS, GEOGRAPH, and POPULATI) with their interactions significantly moderate the relationship between IT diffusion and national level performance in both developed and developing countries. Moreover, we found that NATIONAL modertor variable significantly moderates the IT-performance relationship in developing but not in developed countrirs. Results of this research confirm fitness of the data with our proposed new model and clearly explain the roles of each moderator variables on IT-Performance relationship in developed and developing countries.

References

Adam, M., and Myers, M. Have You Got Anything to Declare? Neo-colonialism, Information Systems, and the Imposition of Customs and Duties in a Third World Country, 2003, In Organizational Information

Systems in the Context of Globalization, M. Korpela, R. Montealegre, and A. Poulymenakou (eds.), Kluwer Academic Publishers, Boston, 2003: 101-116.

Adkinson, W. F., Lenard, T. M., and Pickford, M. J. The Digital Economy Fact Book, 6th Ed., Washington D.C., The Progress and Freedom Foundation, 2004.

Avgerou, C., and Walsham, G. Information Technology in Context: Studies from the Perspective of Developing Countries, Ashgate Publishing, Aldershot, UK, 2000.

Avgerou, C. The Link Between ICT and Economic Growth in the Discourse of Development, in Organizational InformationSystems in the Context of Globalization, M. Korpela, R. Montealegre, and A. Poulymenakou (eds.), Kluwer Academic Publishers, Boston, 2003: 373-386.

Awasthi, V. N. Chow, C. W. and Wu, A. Cross-cultural Differences in the Behavioral Consequences of Imposing Performance Evaluation and Reward Systems: An Experimental Investigation, International Journal of Accounting, 36(3), 2001: 291-309.

Bada, A. O. Local Adaptation to Global Trends: A Study of an IT-Based Organizational Change Program in a Nigerian Bank," The Information Society, 18(2), 2002: 77-86.

Barrell, R. and Pain, N. Foreign Direct Investment, Technological Change and Economic Growth within Europe, Economic Journal, 107(445), 1997: 1770–1786.

Brett, J. M. Tinsiey, C. H. Janssens, M. Barsness Z. I. and Lytle A. L. New Approaches to the Study of Culture in Industrial/Organizational Psychology, In Eariey P.C., Erez M (Eds.), New Perspectives on Intemationai Industrial/Organizational Ssychology, San Francisco: New Lexington Press, 1997.

Brewster, C. Different Paradigms in Strategic HRM: Questions Raised by Comparative Research, in Wright, P. Dyer, L. Boudreau, J. and Milkovich, G. (eds) Research in Personnel and HRM. Supplement 4, Greenwich, CT: JAI Press, 1999.

Bui, T. X. Sankaran, S. and Sebastian I. M. A Framework for Measuring National Readiness, International Journal of Electronic Business, 1(1), 2003: 3-22.

Coe, D.T. Helpman, E. and Hoffmaister, A. W. North-south R & D Spillovers, The Economic Journal, 107(440), 1997: 134–149.

Caselli, F. and Coleman II, W. J. Cross-country Technology Diffusion: The Case of Computers, The American Economic Review, 91(2), 2001.

Dewan, S., and Kraemer, K.L. Information Technology and Productivity: Evidence from Country-level Data, Management Science 46, 4, 2000: 548–562.

Dowling, P. J. Welch, D. E. and Schuler, R. S. International Human Resource Management. Cincinnati, OH: South-Westem, 1999.

Dunkel, A. and Meierewert, S. Culture Standards and Their Impact on Teamwork–An Empirical Analysis of Austrian, German, Hungarian and Spanish Culture Differences, Journal for East European Management Studies, 2, 2004: 147-174.

Fang, X. and Rau, P-L. P. Culture Differences in Design of Portal Sites, Ergonomics, 46(1-3), 2003: 242-254.

Gerhart, B. and Fang, M. National Culture and Human Resource Management: Assumptions and Evidence, International Journal of Human Management, 16(6), 2005: 971-986.

Herscovitch, L. and Meyer, J. P. Commitment to Organizational Change: Extension of a Three Component Model, Journal of Applied Psychology, 87, 2002: 474–487.

Hofstede, G. Neuijen, B. Ohayv, D. D. and Sanders, G. Measuring Organizational Cultures: A Qualitative and Quantitative Study across Twenty Cases, Administrative Science Quarterly, 35(2), 1990: 286-316.

Hofstede, G. Cultural Consequences: Comparing Values, Behaviors, Institutions, and Organizations across Nations, Second Edition, Sage Publication Inc., Thousand Oaks, California, USA, 2001.

Kraemer, K. L. and Dedrick, J. Payoffs from Investment in Information Technology: Lessons from Asia-Pacific Region, World Development, 22, 1994: 1921–1931.

Liu, W., and Westrup, C. ICTs and Organizational Control across Cultures: The Case of a UK Multinational Operating in China, in Organizational Information Systems in the Context of Globalization, M. Korpela, R. Montealegre, and A. Poulymenakou (eds.), Kluwer Academic Publishers, Boston, 2003: 155-168.

Macome, E. On the Implementation of an Information System in the Mozambican Context: The EDM Case, in Organizational Information Systems in the Context of Globalization, M. Korpela, R. Montealegre, and A. Poulymenakou (eds.), Kluwer Academic Publishers, Boston, 2003: 169-184.

Madon, S. The Internet and Socio-Economic Development: Exploring the Interaction, Information Technology and People, 13(2), 2000: 85-101.

Mahmood Adam, M. A. and Swanberg, D. L. Factors Effecting Information Technology Usage: A Meta-Analysis of the Empirical Literature, Journal of Organizational Computing and Electronic Commerce, 11(2), 2001: 107-130.

Meyer, J. P. Srinivas, E. S. Lal, J. B. and Topolnytsky, L. Employee Commitment and Support for an Organizational Change: Test of the Three-component Model inTwo Cultures, Journal of Occupational and Organizational Psychology, 80, 2007: 185–211.

Mutula, S. M. and Brakel P. V. An evaluation of E-readiness Assessment Tools with Respect to Information Access: Towards an Integrated Information Rich Tool, International Journal of Information Management, 26(3), 2006: 212–223.

Pothukuchi, V. Damanpour, F. Choi, J. Chen, C. C. and Park, S. H. National and Organizational Culture Differences and International Joint Venture Performance, Journal of International Business Studies, 32(2), 2002: 243-265.

Robison, K. K. and Crenshaw, E. M. Post-industrial Transformations and Cyber-space: A Cross-national Analysis of Internet Development, Social Science Research, 31, 2002: 334–363.

Rossouw, G. J. Business Ethics in Developing Countries, Business Ethics Quarterely, 4(1), 1994: 43-51.

Ryan, A. M. Chang, D. Ployhart, R. E. and Slade, L. A. Employee Attitude Surveys in a Multinational Organization: Considering Language and Culture in Assessing Measurement Equivalence, Personnel Psychology, 52, 1999: 37-58.

Saad, M. and Zawdie, G. From Technology Transfer to the Emergence of a Triple Helix Culture: The Experience of Algeria in Innovation and Technological Capability Development, Technology Analysis and Strategic Management, 17(1), 2005: 89–103.

Salter, S. B. and Sharp, D. J. Agency Effects and Escalation of Commitment Do Small National Culture Differences Matter? International Journal of Accounting, 36(1), 2001: 33-45.

Sen, A. Development as Freedom, Oxford University Press, Oxford, UK, 1999.

Shih, E. Kraemer, K. L. and Dedrick, J. IT Diffusion in Developing Countries, Communications of the ACM, 51(2), February 2008: 43-48.

Shih, E. Kraemer, K. L. and Dedrick, J. Research Note: Determinants of Country-level Investment in Information Technology, Management Science, 53(3), 2007: 521–528.

Shoib, G. M., and Nandhakumar, J. Cross-Cultural IS Adoption in Multinational Corporations: A Study of Rationality, in Organizational Information Systems in the Context of Globalization, M. Korpela, R. Montealegre, and A. Poulymenakou (eds.), Kluwer Academic Publishers, Boston, 2003:435-454.

Silva, L., and Figueroa, E. B. Institutional Intervention and the Expansion of ICTs in Latin America: The Case of Chile, Information Technology and People, 15(1), 2002: pp. 8-25.

Spony, G. The Development of a Work-value Model Assessing the Cumulative Impact of Individual and Cultural Differences on Managers' Work-value Systems: Empirical Evidence from French and British Managers, International Journal of Human Resource Management, 14(4), 2003: 658-679.

United Nations Development Program (UNDP) Human Development Report 2001: Making New Technologies Work for Human Development, Oxford University Press, New York, 2001.

Walsham, G. Cross-Cultural Software Production and Use: A Structurational Analysis, MIS Quarterly, (26:4), 2002: pp. 359-380.

Walsham, G. Robey, D. Sahay, S. Forwadr: Special issue on Information Systems in Developing Countries, MIS Quarterly, 31(2), 2007: 317-326.

World Bank Group, Information and Communication Technologies: A World Bank Group Strategy, Washington D.C., 2002.

Internet Sources:

http://www.theodora.com/wfb

http://www.world-exchange.org

Cover Sheet

Employees' Social Status in Iranian Public & Governmental Organizations: The Effects of Individual, Organizational & Social Factors

AMROLAH AMINI (Ph.D)

Associate Professor, Allameh Tabatabaei University (ATU), Tehran, Iran.

aminij@atu.ac.ir

ALIREZA EMAMI

Master of Science , Tehran University, Tehran, Iran

memami@alumni.ut.ac.ir

MOSTAFA EMAMI*

Master of Science, Michigan Technological University (MTU)

memami@mtu.edu

*Corresponding Address

Applied Research and Technology Office, Michigan Technological University

1400 Townsend Dr, Houghton, MI 49931

Tel & Fax : +1-(816) 237-0018

E-mail: memami@mtu.edu

Employees' Social Status in Iranian Public & Governmental Organizations:
The Effect of Individual, Organizational & Social Factors

Abstract

Employees' social status has great influences on employees' satisfaction and organizational performance. In spite of several researches on employees' social status in literature, unfortunately, very few studies have been focused on employees' status in public and governmental organizations, especially with regard to different provinces across a country. The purpose of this study is to determine the elements and the effects of individual, organizational, and social factors on the employees' social status in Iranian public and governmental organizations. Then, a conceptual model was developed and tested by Path Analysis Method using LISREL. In order to test the model, 5000 questionnaires were distributed among 30 randomly selected Iranian public and governmental organizations. The results have some useful implications for public policy makers and top management.

Key words

Public and governmental organizations

Employees' social status

Individual factors

Organizational factors

Social factors

1. Introduction

Employees have several formal and informal communications and interactions with their organizations as well as with their family member and people in the society. When an individual, namely employee, interacts and communicates within a society, an organization, and different groups, he/she will get an special rank or value. The rank or value of an employee shows the reflection of his/her status.

According to the literature, social status has great influences on employees' satisfaction, self-employment, social power and economic value. Also, job status congruence is positively associated with job satisfaction, organizational commitment, employee retention, as well as in-role and extra-role performance. It is also well known that employee satisfaction, in turns, was positively related to customer satisfaction, customer loyalty, customers' retention and finally to organizational performance.

Because of the effects of employees' social status on organizational performance, especially in public and governmental organizations, this research was implemented in Iran. The aim of this study is to determine the effects and the elements of factors which impact on employees' social status and their relations in Iranian public and governmental organizations at the national level–that is, from a perspective which explicitly includes individual as well as organizational and social components in an explanation of status.

Iran, as a large country in the West of Asia, is divided into several provinces which most of them have their own social, economical and cultural conditions and characteristics. Unfortunately, very few studies have been focused on employees' social status in public and governmental organizations, especially with regard to different provinces across the country. Previous studies showed that cultural, economical, and social situation differences will impact on people social status in different regions (e.g., Ball & Eckel 1998, Fang & Sidanius 1998, Mansfield et al., 1999, and Fredrickson & Jun-chih 1992). Results of this research have some useful implications for public policy makers and top management.

Next section of the paper explains the literature. A conceptual model is provided in section 3. The materials and methods including questionnaire development, data collection and analysis are explained in section 4. Section 5 provides the empirical results. Final section of the paper provides conclusions and final remarks.

2. The Literature Review

Zelditch (1972) believed that *status* is a unit of social system because it is the most elementary component of social system which has been studied by sociologists. Furthermore, Vechio (1992) believes that status is a situation which an individual obtains within a group. Accordingly, when the subject of status is an employee, in fact several issues should be considered including: a)the kind of relation that society makes with an employee, b)a combination of employee's personality and occupation, and c)the attitude of people in society about employees' status.

Regarding the *individual status* it should be noted that an individual will get his/her status characteristics in two ways. Those characteristics are born with him/her (such as family name, race and wealth) and those characteristics can be obtained and achieved by an individual (such as by education and job-title). Therefore, many characteristics contribute to demonstrate an individual's status. Koslowsky and Schwarzwald cited in Staheski (1995) that individuals who were perceived as higher status used a greater variety of influence than those perceived as lower status did. According to Rosenthal (1987), those having high status are naturally more desirable. These individuals' status has some bearing on how he/she ranks occupations. This should reflect the characteristics of the work performed in it rather than the status characteristics of its incumbents. To Hodge (1981), prestige scores can be used for studying status, since prestige scores are independent of the characteristics of an occupation's incumbents.

Nicholson (1995) separated the status term into three types: social, organizational and occupational prestige. *Social status* refers to standing of a person in general society, *organizational status* indicates the position one holds in an organizational setting, and *occupational prestige* is the importance of an occupation to society.

Social status is a value that a group determines for a given social role and social status of a job can be defined as the value that a society determines for job. Regarding the social status, it should be mentioned that many studies have focused and examined this issue in various ways (e.g., Dong & Weisfeld 1996, Fang & Sidanius 1998, Fredrickson & Jun-chih 1992, Kuentzel & Heberlein 1997, and Stevens & Featherman 1981). Most of these studies have explored the ways that social status relates to or influences on other factors such as satisfaction, self-employment, social power and economic value. According to Deephouse (1995), social status is a concept with descriptive and evaluative aspects. The descriptive aspect of status refers to the position of social entity in a social system based on a set of relevant dimensions mostly associated with roles (e.g., president of an organization). The evaluative aspect is a ranking of a social entity in terms of the values of a social system when the president of an organization is regarded important in both the organization and society.

Accordingly, Waldron (1998) in study of *organizational status* indicates that status refers to two interrelated concepts; creation of status, and the striving for the achievement of high-status ranking. The first emphasizes on the rankings or orderings of individuals in group within an organizational context. Waldron continued that it is important to distinguish between status rankings in organizational context and the formalized position obtained through organizational chart and title. The striving to achieve high status ranking within organizational context is obtained through both "dominance" and "prestige". To Woldron, organizational status is the multitude of symbols that individuals use to demonstrate and manipulate their status such as the use of doors to limit access to oneself, nearness to windows, the use of furnishings and space, the use of job title, and so on.

Study of Lee and Tidd (2002) showed that a match or congruence between worker preferences and organizational staffing practices would be associated with positive employee attitudes and behaviors. Results of their study indicate that work status congruence is positively associated with job satisfaction, organizational commitment, employee retention, as well as in-role and extra-role performance.

Creed and Saporta (2003) studied on the subject of unmet expectations and the effect of status inconsistency on quitting and internal job changing. Manoux et al. (2003) studied subjective social status, its determinants and its association with measures of ill-health in the Whitehall II study. Results of their study indicate that subjective status is a strong predictor of ill-health, and that education, occupation and income do not explain this relationship fully for all the health measures examined. The results support multidimensional nature of both social inequality and health. Multiple regression shows subjective status to be determined by occupational position, education, household income, satisfaction with standard of living, and feeling of financial security regarding the future.

Vough et al. (2005) studied the effects of nonstandard work status on work group processes and outcomes. Lawler (2005) believes that status differentials generate corresponding differences in performance expectations which, in turn, produce behaviors that affirm performance expectations. Rosette and Thompson (2005) argue that in many organizational settings, status hierarchies result in the conferral of privileges that are based on achievement. However, status may result in the bestowal of privileges that are unearned. These unearned privileges are often awarded based on ascribed characteristics, but are perceived to be achieved. These misattributions occur because acknowledging that one has benefited from unearned advantages that are awarded in a meritocracy can be threatening to a person's self-identity. They propose that by studying unearned privileges in an organizational settings, a more accurate assessment of status hierarchies may result.

Stephanie and Webber (2006) studied the relationship among job satisfaction, affective commitment, service-oriented organizational citizenship behaviors (OCBs), customer satisfaction, and customer loyalty. They found that employee satisfaction was positively related to service-oriented OCBs, customer satisfaction, and customer loyalty, whereas affective commitment was not related to these outcomes. The extent to which the predictor variables interacted with one another and the role of employment status on these relationships was also explored. According to literature:

- Employees' social status relates to or influences on employees' satisfaction, self-employment, social power and economic value.
- Work status congruence is positively associated with job satisfaction, organizational commitment, employee retention, as well as in-role and extra-role performance.
- Employee satisfaction, in turns, was positively related to customer satisfaction and loyalty.
- Subjective status itself determines by occupational position, education, household income, satisfaction with standard of living, and feeling of financial security regarding the future.
- Social status relates to employee's satisfaction, prestige, dominance, ill-health, variety of influence, income/salary and organizational performance.

- Match or congruence between worker performance and organizational staffing practice relates to employee's attitudes and social status.

3. The Conceptual Model

According to the literature and the Iranian academic professors, top managers and experts' opinions, three following key research questions were considered:

1. What elements/ factors strongly effect on employees' social status?
2. What kind of relationships there are among the effective factors/elements?
3. How these factors finally affect on employees' social status?

A large number of researches have been reported in literature to answer these questions. These researches introduce several classifications of the elements/factors effects on employees' social status. In our study, based on results of the panel of Iranian academic professors, top managers and experts, three classes of factors (Individual, organizational and social factors) were recognized.

Accordingly, the main research hypothesis can be defined as:

H1: Individual, organizational, and social factors meaningfully effecting on employees' social status in public and governmental organizations.

Figure 1 indicates a graphical explanation of the main research hypothesis.

[Insert Figure 1 near hear]

To answer the first question, we reviewed the literature. To answer the second and third questions, we applied Path Analysis Technique using LISREL software. The results are provided in section 5. Next section explains the research materials and methodology.

4. Research Materials and Methodology

4.1 Questionnaire Development:

By reviewing the literature, 57 elements regarding individual factor, 36 elements regarding organization factor, and 41elements regarding social factor were identified. To reduce the number of influence elements and to determine the most important ones, the following steps were taken:

- First a panel of three groups was formed including 26 high distinguished academic professors from five universities, 35 outstanding top managers identified from a list that was provided by the Management and Planning Organization (MPO) of Iran, and 32 experts and consultants from different public and governmental organizations.

- Second, a scheduled interview with above persons was made to explain the purpose of research and the format of completing the developed questionnaire. The interviewees were asked to score each item with regard to individual, organizational, and social status' factors, separately.

- Third, the data was collected and classified, the mean and standard divination values for all elements were calculated, a t-test and Friedman test were applied to determine the most important elements of individual, organizational, and social factors. Finally, 28 individual elements, 24 organizational elements, and 18 social elements effecting on employees' social status were finalized.

- Forth, based on the results of the third step, a questionnaire for studying and measuring the employees' status in Iranian public and governmental organizations was developed. To test the validity of the questionnaire, Delphi method was applied. Also, to test the reliability of the questionnaire, a pilot study was conducted and 65 employees from 4 different organizations were randomly selected. The results showed an acceptable level of Cronbach's Alpha Coefficient (0.95). Finally, ten most effective elements for each of individual, social and organizational factors were finalized for the purpose of path analysis.

4.2 Data Collection:

To collect data from employees in Iranian public and governmental organizations across the country, the following steps were taken:

1. First, based on cultural, social, and administrative similarities, all provinces were classified into 6 regions. According to the classification, one province from each region was chosen randomly.

2. To select the organizations randomly, based on the categorization of MPO of Iran, first all organizations were classified into 5 categories. Then, one organization from each category (totally 30 organizations) was selected randomly.

3. Third, number of employees in each randomly selected organization was counted and the random statistical sampling method was used to identify the total sample size. Then, the statistical method was used to identify portion of each organization/category from the allocated sample size to each province.

4. Finally, 5000 questionnaires were distributed among randomly selected organizations' managers, supervisors, and employees in the 6 provinces. From 5000 questionnaire, 3972 questionnaires were returned. The total response rate was 79.4%.

5. Experimental Results

With respect to responses from the selected Iranian organizations across the country, Friedman test using SPSS[1] was applied to determine the most important elements of individual, organizational, and social factors. Tables 1, 2, and 3 demonstrate ten highly ranked individual elements, ten highly ranked organizational elements, and ten highly ranked social elements effecting on employees' social status and their related ranks.

[Insert Table 1 near hear]

[Insert Table 2 near hear]

[Insert Table 3 near hear]

Since the elements of individual, organizational and social factors are not independent and have interactions with each others, we studied these interactions and relations by Path Analysis method using LISREL[2] 8.53 software. Structural equation modeling was used to test the model and to estimate the standardized path coefficients. Structural equations of LISREL help researchers to know the relative power of the relations between variables.

---

[1] Statistical Package for Social Sciences, version 13
[2] The name LISREL is an acronym for "Linear Structural relations". The latest student version of the LISREL is available on the URL: http://www.ssicentral.com/lisrel/new.html

Figure 2 demonstrates hypothesized model of cause and effects that study the relations among individual, organizational and social factors and employees' social status in Iranian public and governmental organizations.

[Insert Figure 2 near hear]

At first, the hypothesized measurement model was assessed for its significance and overall fit. The goodness of fit of the hypothesized measurement model was assessed using such indicators as $\chi 2$, the goodness of fit index (GFI), the adjusted goodness of fit index (AGFI), and the comparative fit index (CFI). The measurement model is considered to have satisfactory fit if it meets the following criteria: insignificant $\chi 2$ (the smaller $\chi 2$, the better the model fit), GFI above 0.90, AGFI above 0.80, and CFI above 0.90 (Jo¨reskog & So¨rbom, 1989; Lee and Xia, 2005). Furthermore, RMSEA[1] which describes the discrepancy between the proposed model and the population covariance matrix, is considered to be lower than the recommended cut-off value of 0.08 (Hong and Zhu, 2006).

The structure of the hypothetical measurement model was supported by chi-square statistics ($\chi 2$=29411.79 with 0 degree of freedom, p=1.00). The RMSEA was 0.0 (95% CIS[2] 0.0; 0.0) with a p-value (for test of close fit RMSEA<0.05) of 1.00. These global goodness of fit statistics suggest an acceptable fit of the data with the model (see figure 1). The path coefficient estimates were statistically significant with t-values from 12.33 to 37.76, indicating that the variables were linked to the model (a t-value of 1.96 or higher at the significance level of 0.05). In other words, employees' social status is affected 0.65 by individual, 0.90 by organizational, and 0.77 by social factors.

Figures 3, 4 and 5 demonstrate the relations and interactions among individual, organizational and social factors influence, on employees' social status in Iranian public and governmental organizations. The hypothetical model that demonstrates the relationships and interactions among the element of individual factor is shown in Figure 3.

[Insert Figure 3 near hear]

---

[1] Root Mean Square Error of Approximation (RMSEA)
[2] Confidence Intervals

The structure of the hypothetical model for interactions of individual items was supported by chi square statistics ($\chi 2=1.01$ with 1 degree of freedom, $p=0.31$). The GFI for the individual model was 1.0. The additional index values for the model were 1.00 for the CFI. These statistics suggest a good fit. The RMSEA was 0.0018 (95% CIS 0.0; 0.042) with a p-value (for test of close fit RMSEA<0.05) of 0.98. These global goodness of fit statistics suggesting an acceptable fit of the data within the model. The path coefficient estimates were statistically significant with t-values from 2.12 to 20.69, indicating that the variables were linked to the model (a t-value of 1.96 or higher at the significance level of 0.05). Table 4 shows the structural equations, the path coefficients, their t-values and P-values of the model of individual factors.

[Insert Table 4 near hear]

As shown in Table 4, the JSAT and JSEC had no statistically significant relationship with EM. Remaining path coefficients were found to be statistically significant. Also, figure 3 summarizes ten most effective elements of individual factors as follows; 1)Distinguished Professionality (DP), 2)Incumbent's Mental Health (IMH), 3)Employees Morality (EM), 4)Job Security (JSEC), 5)Individuals' Job-Interested (IJI), 6)Self-Confidence (SC), 7)Incentive for High Quality Work (IFHQM), 8)Incumbents' Self-Esteem (ISE), 9)Fitness of Job With Incumbent's Talent (FJIT), and 10)Job Satisfaction (JSAT). The results imply that DP, IMH, IJI, FJIT and JS have meaningful interactions with each others and with EM, ISE, SC, JS, IFHQW.

The hypothetical model that explains the relations and interactions among the elements of organizational factor is shown in Figure 4.

[Insert Figure 4 near hear]

The structure of the hypothetical model for interactions of organizational items was supported by chi square statistics ($\chi 2=2.31$ with 1 degree of freedom, p=0.13). The GFI for the individual model was 1.0. The additional index values for the model were 1.00 for the CFI. These statistics suggest a good fit. The RMSEA was 0.018 (95% CIS 0.0; 0.050) with a p-value (for test of close fit RMSEA<0.05) of 0.95. These global goodness of fit statistics suggesting an acceptable fit of the data within the model. The path coefficient estimates were statistically significant with t-values from 2.97 to 16.32, indicating that the variables were linked to the model (a t-value of 1.96 or higher at the significance level of 0.05). Table 5 explains the structural equations, the path coefficients, the t-values and p-values of the model of organizational factors.

[Insert Table 5 near hear]

As shown in Table 5, only the element of M had no statistically significant relationship with HSP. Remaining path coefficients were found to be statistically significant. In addition, figure 4 shows that ten effective elements of organizational factor are 1) Managers' Consideration to Employees' High Performance (MCEHP), 2) Fair and Consistence Criteria to Promote Employees (FCCPE), 3) Job Security (JSEC), 4) Appropriate Management Style with Regard to Organizational Conditions (AMSROC), 5) Providing Facilities to Improve Educational Level (PFIEL), 6) Meritocracy (M), 7 Respecting Incumbents' Skills (RIS), 8) High Salary Payment (HSP), 9) Decision Making Participation by Employees (DMPE), and 10) Proper Job Position within Organization (PJPO). The results also imply that M, FCCPE, JSEC, RIS and PFIEL have meaningful interactions with each others and with AMSROC, MCEHP, DMPE, PJPO, HSP.

The hypothetical model that demonstrates the relationships and interactions among the elements of social factor is shown in Figure 5.

[Insert Figure 5 near hear]

The structure of the hypothetical model for interactions of social items was supported by chi square statistics ($\chi 2=3.35$ with 6 degree of freedom, p== 0.76). The GFI for the individual model was 1.0. The additional index values for the model were 1.00 for the CFI. These statistics suggest a good fit. The RMSEA was 0.0 (95% CIS 0.0; 0.042) with a p-value (for test of close fit RMSEA<0.05) of 1.00. These global goodness of fit statistics suggesting an acceptable fit of the data within the model. The path coefficient estimates were statistically significant with t-values from 2.86 to 37.64, indicating that the variables were linked to the model (a t-value of 1.96 or higher at the significance level of 0.05). Table 6 demonstrates the structural equations, the path coefficients, the t-values and p-values of the model of social factors.

[Insert Table 6 near hear]

In Table 6, all path coefficients were found to be statistically significant. As shown in figure 5, ten effective elements of organizational factor are 1)Good Behavior of Incumbent with Others (GBIO), 2)Positive Attitude of Society to Public Organization (PASPO), 3)Positive Reputation of Organization's Performance (PROP), 4)Reputation and Interesting Job (RIJ), 5)High Salary of Public Organizations' Employees (HSPOE), 6)Employee's Care to Religion and Ethic Ordinance (ECREO), 7)Employee's Reputation of Their High Job Performance (ERHJP), 8)Providing Welfare – Entertainment Facilities to Employee's Family (PW), 9)Social Acceptance of Job (SAJ), and 10) Having Professional Job (HPJ). The results also imply that RIJ, GBIO, HPJ, ERHJP, HSPOE and ECREO have meaningful interactions with each others and with PASPO, PROP, SAJ, PW.

6. Conclusions and Final Remarks

It is well known that employees' social status has a great influence on employees' satisfaction, organizational commitment, employees' retention, as well as in-role and extra-role performance. Employees' satisfaction, in turns, is positively related to customer satisfaction, customer loyalty, customers' retention and organizational performance. Then, determining the factors and the elements effecting on employees' social status is regarded an important and interesting subject of research around the world.

In literature, very few studies have been focused on employees' status in public and governmental organizations especially with regard to different regions across the countries. It is well known that cultural, economical, and social situation differences will impact on people status in different regions. The purpose of this study was to determine and examine the employees' social status in Iranian public and governmental organizations in terms of the individual, organizational, and social factors.

Results of the statistical tests clearly reveal the complexity and multidimensionality of the nature of employees' social status. Morever, the results of Path Analysis show that there are meaningful interactions among the factors effecting on employees' social status and among their elements. Results of this research imply that:

- Distinguished Professionality (DP), Incumbent's Mental Health (IMH), Individuals' Job-Interested (IJI), Fitness of Job With Incumbent's Talent (FJIT) and Job Satisfaction (JSAT) have meaningful interactions with each others and with Employees Morality (EM), Incumbents' Self-Esteem (ISE), Self-Confidence (SC), Job Security (JS), Incentive for High Quality Work (IFHQW).

- Meritocracy (M), Fair and Consistence Criteria to Promote Employees (FCCPE), Job Security (JSEC), Respecting Incumbents Skills (RIS) and Providing Facilities to Improve Educational Level (PFIEL) have meaningful interactions with each others and with Appropriate Management Style with Regard to Organizational Conditions (AMSROC), Managers' Consideration to Employees' High Performance(MCEHP), Decision Making Participation by Employees (DMPE), Proper Job Position within Organization (PJPO), High Salary Payment (HSP).

- Reputation and Interesting Job (RIJ), Good Behavior of Incumbent with Others (GBIO), Having Professional Job (HPJ), Employee's Reputation of Their High Job Performance (ERHJP), High Salary of Public Organizations' Employees (HSPOE) and Employee's Care to Religion and Ethic Ordinance (ECREO) have meaningful interactions with each others and with Positive Attitude of Society to Public Organization (PASPO), Positive Reputation of Organization's Performance (PROP), Social Acceptance of Job (SAJ), Providing Welfare (PW) – Entertainment Facilities to Employee's Family.

The authors believe that the results of this research brings about useful implications for policy makers and top managers of the public and governmental organizations in order to formulate their future employees' social status improvement programs more effective and efficient.

References

Ball, S. and Eckel, C. C. 1998. 'The Economic Value of Status', Journal of Socio-economics. 27: 495-515.

Douglas, C. and Saporta I. 2003. 'Unmet Expectations: the Effect of Status Inconsistency on Quitting and Internal Job Changing', Research in Social Stratification and Mobility, 20: 285-323.

Deephouse, D. L. 1995. 'Status in N. Nicholson, Dictionary of Organizational Behavior', Blackwell Publisher, London.

Dong, Q. and Weisfeld, G. 1996. 'Correlates of Social Status among Chinese Adolescents', Journal of Cross-Cultural Psychology, 27: 476-494.

Fang, C. Y. and Sidanius, J. 1998. 'Romance across the Social Status Continuum', Journal of Cross-Cultural Psychology. 29: 290-306.

Fredrickson, R. H. and Jun-Chih, G. .1992. 'Social Status Ranking of Occupations in the People's Republic of China, Taiwan, and the United State', Career Development Quarterly. 40: 351-361.

Hodge, R. W. 1981. 'The Measurement of Occupational Status', Social Science Research, 10: 396-415.

Hong, Weiyin, and Zhu K. 2006. 'Migrating to Internet-based E-commerce: Factors Affecting E-commerce Adoption and Migration at the Firm Level', Information & Management, 43, pp. 204–221.

Joreskog, KG, and Sorbom, D. 1989. LISREL7: A Guide to the Program and Applications. SPSS Inc., Chicago, IL.

Kuentzel, W. F. and Heberlein, T. A. 1997. 'Social Status, Self-development, and the Process Leisure Specialization', Journal of Leisure Research, 29: 300-320.

Lawler, E. J. 2005. 'Role of Status in Group Processes', Research on Managing Groups and Teams, 7: 315-325.

Lee, H. and Tidd, 2002. 'The Relationship between Work Status Congruence and Work-related Attitudes and Behaviors', Journal of Applied Psychology, 87(5): 903-915

Lee, Gwanhoo, and Weidong, Xia. 2005. 'The Ability of Information Systems Development Project Teams to Respond to Business and Technology Changes: A Study of Flexibility Measures', European Journal of Information Systems, 14, pp.75–92.

Mansfield, C. J., Wilson, J. L., Kobrinski, E. J., and Mitchell, J. 1999. American Journal of Public Health, 89: 893-899.

Singh, M. Adlerb, N. E., and Marmota, M. G. 2003. 'Subjective Social Status: Its Determinants and Its Association with Measures of Ill-health in the Whitehall II Study', Social Science & Medicine. 56(6):.1321-1333.

Nicholson, N. 1995. 'Dictionary of Organizational Behavior, (Eds.) Blackwell Publisher, London.

Shelby R. and Thompson, L. 2005. 'The Camouflage Effect: Separating Achieved Status and Unearned Privilege in Organizations', Research on Managing Groups and Teams, 7: 259-281.

Rosenthal, N. H. 1989. 'More than Wages at Issue in Job Quality Debate', Monthly Labor Review, 4: 8.

Stahelski, A. J. and Paynton, C. F. 1995. 'The Effect of Status Cues on Choices of Social Power and Influence Strategies', Journal of Social Psychology, 135: 553-561.

Stephanie C. P. and Webber, S. S. 2006. 'Effects of Service Provider Attitudes and Employment Status on Citizenship Behaviors and Customers' Attitudes and Loyalty Behavior', Journal of Applied Psychology, 91(2): 365-378.

Stevens, G. and Featherman, D. L. 1981. 'A Revised Socioeconomic Index of Occupational Status', Social Science Research, 10: 364-395.

Vecchio, R. P. 1992. Organizational Behavior, 2nd Ed.

Heather C. V., Broschak, J. P. and Northcraft, G. B. 2005. 'Here Today, Gone Tomorrow? Effects of Nonstandard Work Status on Work Group Processes and Outcomes', Research on Managing Groups and Teams, 7: 229-257.

Waldron, D. A. 1998. 'Status in Organizations: Where Evolutionary Theory Ranks', Managerial and Decision Economics, 19: 505-520.

Zelditch, M. 1972. 'International Encyclopedia of the Social Science', 15, Macmillan Co. & the Free Press.

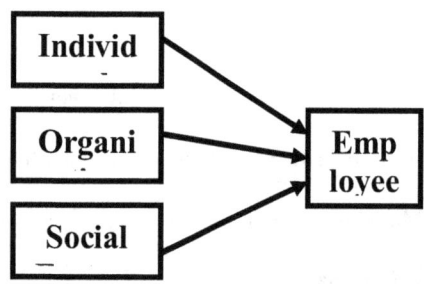

FIGURE 1. Graphical explanation of the research hypothesis

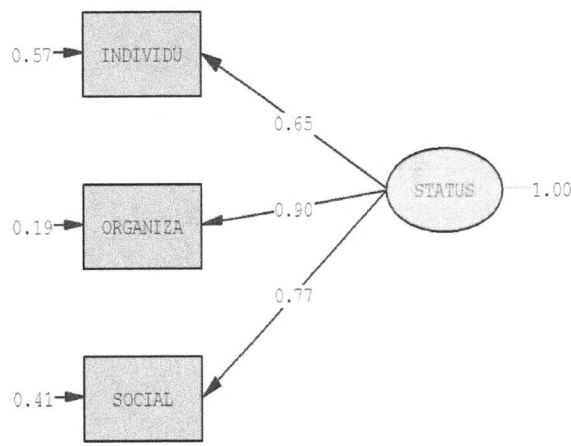

Chi-Square=29411.79, df=0, P-value=1.00000, RMSEA=0.000

FIGURE 2. Factors that affecting on employees social status in Iranian public and governmental organizations

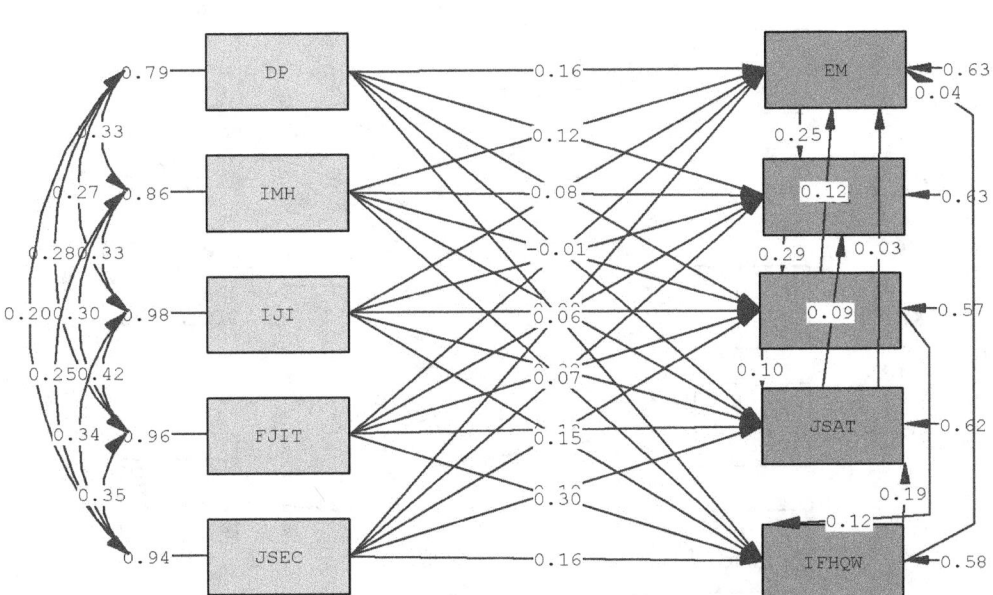

Chi-Square=1.01, df=1, P-value=0.31433, RMSEA=0.002

FIGURE 3. Individual effective factors relations and interactions

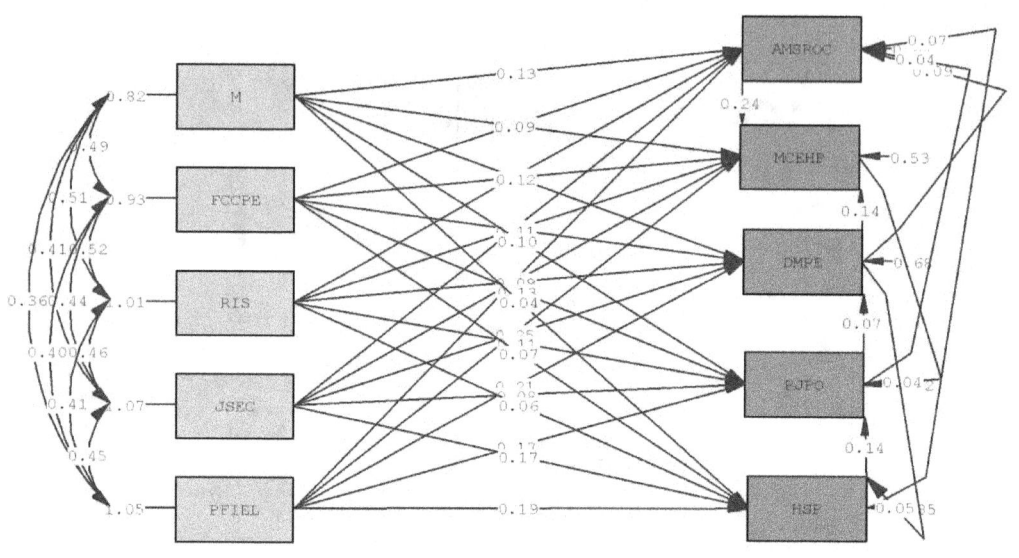

Chi-Square=2.31, df=1, P-value=0.13, RMSEA=0.018
FIGURE 4. Organizational effective factors relations and interactions

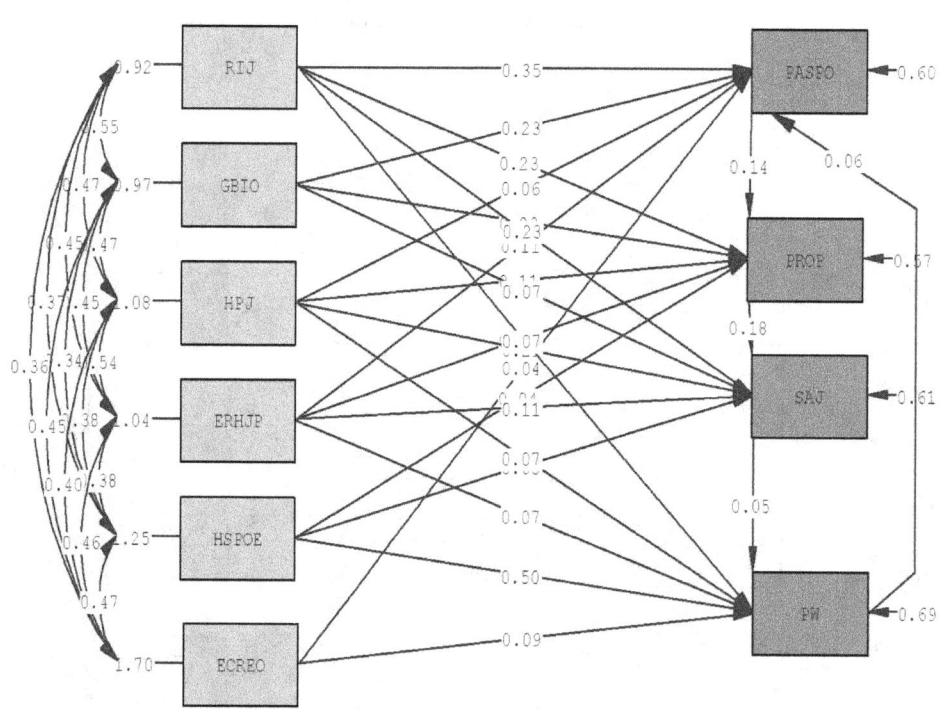

Chi-Square=3.35, df=6, P-value=0.76382, RMSEA=0.000
FIGURE 5. Social effective factors relations and interactions

TABLE 1. The Most Effective Individual Items Affecting on Employees' Social Status

Rank	Effective Individual Factors	Abbreviation	Rank Mean	Score Mean
1	Distinguished Professionality	(DP)	17.41	4.52
2	Incumbent's Mental Health	(IMH)	16.51	4.45
3	Employees Morality	(EM)	16.29	4.39
4	Job Security	(JSEC)	15.57	4.34
5	Individuals' Job-Interested	(IJI)	15.53	4.33
6	Self-Confidence	(SC)	15.50	4.33
7	Incentive for High Quality Work	(IFHQW)	15.42	4.35
8	Incumbents' Self-Esteem	(ISE)	15.36	4.35
9	Fitness of Job With Incumbent's Talent	(FJIT)	15.09	4.31
10	Job Satisfaction	(JSAT)	14.98	4.30

TABLE 2. The Most Effective Organizational Items Affecting on Employees' Social Status

Rank	Effective Organizational Variables on Employees' Status	Abbreviation	Rank Mean	Score Mean
1	Managers' Consideration to Employees' High Performance	(MCEHP)	14.03	4.37
2	Fair and Consistence Criteria to Promote Employees	(FCCPE)	13.86	4.35
3	Job Security	(JSEC)	13.84	4.36
4	Appropriate Management Style with Regard to Organizational Conditions	(AMSROC)	13.63	4.36
5	Providing Facilities to Improve Educational Level	(PFIEL)	13.44	4.30
6	Meritocracy	(M)	13.39	4.29
7	Respecting Incumbents' Skills	(RIS)	13.31	4.29
8	High Salary Payment	(HSP)	13.27	4.29
9	Decision Making Participation by Employees	(DMPE)	13.20	4.31
10	Proper Job Position within Organization	(PJPO)	13.06	4.26

TABLE 3. The Most Effective Social Items Affecting on Employees' Social Status

Rank	Effective Social Variables on Employees' Status	Abbreviation	Rank Mean	Score Mean
1	Good Behavior of Incumbent with Others	(GBIO)	10.52	4.36
2	Positive Attitude of Society to Public Organization	(PASPO)	10.38	4.37

3	Positive Reputation of Organization's Performance	(PROP)	10.31	4.40
4	Reputation and Interesting Job	(RIJ)	10.27	4.39
5	High Salary of Public Organizations' Employees	(HSPOE)	9.99	4.29
6	Employee's Care to Religion and Ethic Ordinance	(ECREO)	9.95	4.23
7	Employee's Reputation of Their High Job Performance	(ERHJP)	9.88	4.24
8	Providing Welfare – Entertainment Facilities to Employee's Family	(PW)	9.84	4.21
9	Social Acceptance of Job	(SAJ)	9.82	4.27
10	Having Professional Job	(HPJ)	9.71	4.25

TABLE 4. The structural equations, the path coefficients, the t-values and p-values of the model of Individual Factors (n= 3971)

EM= 0.12*SC + 0.026*JSAT + 0.036*IFHQW + 0.16*DP + 0.32*IMH + 0.11*IJI + 0.043*FJIT +0.023*JSEC,	Errorvar.= 0.63, R^2 = 0.33
P-Values: (0.017) (0.016) (0.017) (0.016) (0.016) (0.016) (0.016) (0.015) (0.014)	
T-Values: 6.87 1.61 2.12 9.74 19.55 6.94 2.65 1.52 44.24	
ISE = 0.25*EM + 0.089*JSAT + 0.12*DP + 0.15*IMH + 0.087*IJI + 0.086*FJIT + 0.072*JSEC,	Errorvar.= 0.63, R^2 = 0.35
P-Values: (0.016) (0.016) (0.016) (0.017) (0.016) (0.016) (0.015) (0.014)	
T-Values: 15.42 5.42 7.26 9.12 5.28 5.52 4.90 44.41	
SC = 0.29*ISE + 0.077*DP + 0.12*IMH + 0.13*IJI + 0.11*FJIT + 0.082*JSEC,	Errorvar.= 0.57 R^2 = 0.35
P-Values: (0.015) (0.015) (0.015) (0.015) (0.015) (0.014) (0.013)	
T-Values: 19.25 4.99 7.87 8.85 7.27 5.90 44.45	
JSAT = 0.098*SC + 0.19*IFHQW – 0.013*DP + 0.087*IMH + 0.32*IJI + 0.13*FJIT + 0.097*JSEC,	Errorvar.= 0.62 R^2 = 0.40
P-Values: (0.017) (0.016) (0.016) (0.016) (0.015) (0.016) (0.015) (0.014)	
T-Values: 5.94 11.24 -0.84 5.49 20.69 7.86 6.57 44.49	
IFHQW = 0.12*SC + 0.057*DP + 0.065*IMH + 0.15*IJI + 0.30*FJIT + 0.16*JSEC,	Errorvar.= 0.58, R^2 = 0.37
P-Values: (0.015) (0.015) (0.015) (0.015) (0.015) (0.014) (0.013)	
T-Values: 7.62 3.67 4.25 9.97 20.63 11.67 44.52	

TABLE 5. The structural equations, the path coefficients, the t-values and p-values of the model of Organizational Factors (n= 3970)

AMSROC = 0.091*DMPE + 0.041*PJPO + 0.067*HSP + 0.13*M + 0.17*FCCPE + 0.11*RIS + 0.15*JSEC + 0.10*PFIEL,	Errorvar.= 0.64, R^2= 0.37
P-Values: (0.015) (0.014) (0.014) (0.019) (0.017) (0.017) (0.016) (0.015) (0.014)	
P-Values: 5.96 2.97 4.81 6.97 9.85 6.63 9.38 6.86 44.14	
MCEHP = 0.24*AMSROC + 0.14*DMPE + 0.091*M + 0.12*FCCPE + 0.12*RIS + 0.17*JSEC + 0.062*PFIEL,	Errorvar.= 0.53, R^2= 0.48
P-Values: (0.014) (0.014) (0.017) (0.016) (0.015) (0.014) (0.014) (0.012)	
T-Values: 16.32 9.99 5.36 7.58 7.91 11.68 4.55 44.52	
DMPE = 0.075*PJPO + 0.12*M + 0.11*FCCPE + 0.088*RIS + 0.25*JSEC + 0.21*PFIEL,	Errorvar.= 0.68, R^2=0.37
P-Values: (0.014) (0.019) (0.018) (0.017) (0.016) (0.015) (0.015)	
T-Values: 5.37 6.31 6.04 5.10 16.31 13.81 44.51	
PJPO = 0.042*MCEHP + 0.14*HSP + 0.096*M + 0.13*FCCPE + 0.11*RIS + 0.080*JSEC +0.17*PFIEL,	Errorvar.= 0.92, R^2== 0.24
P-Values: (0.021) (0.017) (0.022) (0.021) (0.020) (0.019) (0.018) (0.021)	
T-Values: 1.98 8.38 4.28 6.01 5.47 4.23 9.33 44.48	
HSP = 0.054*DMPE + 0.041*M + 0.073*FCCPE + 0.057*RIS + 0.17*JSEC + 0.19*PFIEL,	Errorvar.= 0.85 , R^2 = 0.19
P-Values: (0.018) (0.021) (0.020) (0.019) (0.018) (0.017) (0.019)	
T-Values: 3.00 1.93 3.67 2.98 9.72 11.24 44.51	

TABLE 6. The structural equations, the path coefficients, the t-values and p-values of the model of Social Factors (n= 3970)

PASPO= 0.058*PW + 0.35*RIJ + 0.23*GBIO + 0.056*HPJ + 0.11*ERHJP + 0.044*ECREO,	Errorvar.= 0.60, R^2= 0.42
P-Values: (0.013) (0.017) (0.017) (0.015) (0.015) (0.011) (0.014)	
T-Values: 4.55 20.61 14.03 3.78 7.04 4.15 44.51	
PROP = 0.14*PASPO + 0.23*RIJ + 0.23*GBIO + 0.11*HPJ + 0.12*ERHJP + 0.044*HSPOE,	Errorvar.= 0.57 , R^2= 0.44
P-Values: (0.015) (0.017) (0.016) (0.015) (0.015) (0.012) (0.013)	
T-Values: 8.78 13.21 13.97 7.65 8.23 3.69 44.51	
SAJ = 0.18*PROP + 0.23*RIJ + 0.068*GBIO + 0.21*HPJ + 0.11*ERHJP + 0.046*HSPOE,	Errorvar.= 0.61 , R^2= 0.42
P-Values: (0.016) (0.018) (0.017) (0.015) (0.015) (0.012) (0.014)	
T-Values: 11.19 13.28 4.03 14.15 7.51 3.75 44.51	
PW = 0.047*SAJ + 0.074*RIJ + 0.075*HPJ + 0.072*ERHJP + 0.50*HSPOE + 0.087*ECREO,	Errorvar.= 0.69 , R^2= 0.43
P-Values: (0.017) (0.017) (0.016) (0.016) (0.013) (0.011) (0.015)	
P-Values: 2.86 4.24 4.60 4.44 37.64 7.76 44.51	

Evaluating the comparative effectiveness of staff In-service trainings on improving the service quality(before and after the In-service trainings)

AMROLAH AMINI (Ph.D)

Associate Professor, Allameh Tabatabaei University (ATU), Tehran, Iran.

aminij@atu.ac.ir

ALIREZA EMAMI

Master of Science , Tehran University, Tehran, Iran

memami@alumni.ut.ac.ir

MOSTAFA EMAMI*

Master of Science, Michigan Technological University (MTU)

memami@mtu.edu

*Corresponding Address

Applied Research and Technology Office, Michigan Technological University

1400 Townsend Dr, Houghton, MI 49931

Tel & Fax : +1-(816) 237-0018

E-mail: memami@mtu.edu

Evaluating the comparative effectiveness of staff In-service trainings on improving the service quality (before and after the In-service trainings)

Abstract

The present study has been conducted with the aim of examining the effectiveness of staff in-service trainings on improving the service quality in Islamic Azad University, Aliabad Katoul Branch. The statistical sample of this study has comprised 66 unit personnel who have been selected by simple random sampling. The method of study is applied based on the aim and survey based on the descriptive method. Data collection tools of questionnaire have been based on the closed answer with the Likert range. After data collection the distance estimation method of success ratio (p) has been used for employees in order to analyze data and the nonparametric chi-square for the managers. The statistical model of difference between two correlated ratios has been used in order to evaluate the effect of performance before and after the training course. The results indicated that the personnel have considered the In-service training positive and effective on improving and promoting the service quality at university.

Keywords: Staff In-service training; improving and promoting the service quality; effectiveness of training

1. Introduction

The manpower training is the most prominent appearance of investment in the institutions and organizations for their employees. Through this training, people in organizations acquire the needed abilities, develop their capabilities, and learn the skills needed for organizations. Implementing such a program requires a financial investment and allocation of necessary funds and the question about which managers are sometimes concerned is whether implementing the training programs is effective or not? And if it is necessary to implement these programs and there are experiences which indicate that they are effective, how they can be implemented in a specific organization, achieve the intended goals, ensure the accuracy of performances more than before, and thus increase the confidence in the effectiveness of trainings? In fact, one of the scientific strategies for achieving this goal is responding to the considered above questions, achieving and planning all stages of in-service training including assessment, designing and implementation, measuring and assessing its effectiveness. Planning leads various activities toward a specific purpose and focuses the resources in line with achieving the determined target. Therefore, the additional and unnecessary activities will be eliminated, additional costs be reduced, and the economic efficiency and efficient use of time be done.

The more the personnel knowledge and skills in the organization are coordinate with the community needs, developments and technology changes, the more the individual is successful in the organization.

Improving the human resources is one of the important managers' responsibilities and includes the activities which are carried out in order to promote the employees' awareness, increase the knowledge, create the employees' skills, and provide the better services. In-service training in one of the method for human resources improvement and includes all job trainings which are given to them in order to improve the quality of their performance (Girrs, 1998) In-service training is the only factor for saving a system from the personnel routine job. By in-service training, the staff occupational knowledge will be acquirable and the future of system will be guaranteed to be in success and achieving the noble goals of university.

Therefore, the main goals of this study is to understand and evaluate whether the University staff in-service trainings can promote and improve the service quality at university, and identifying the scientific and applied strategies for enhancing the effectiveness of staff in-service trainings. The conceptual framework is as follows.

1.1. Research Conceptual Framework and Model

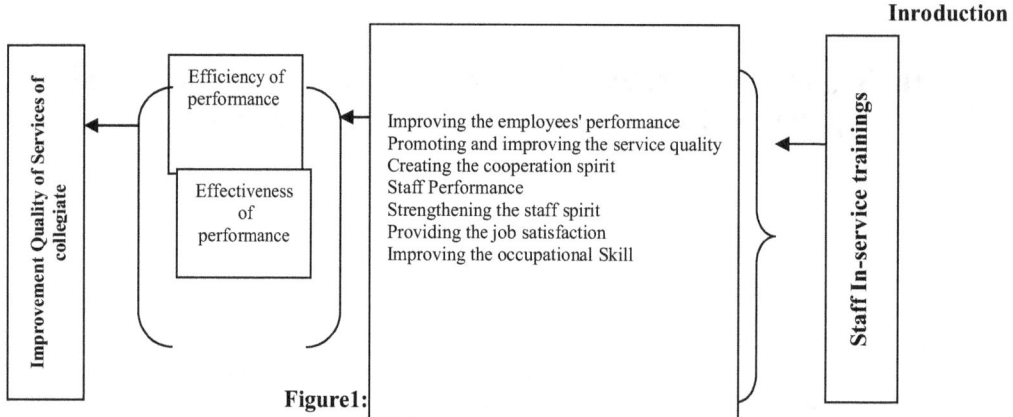

Figure1:

2- Review of theoretical principles and literature and theoretical principles

2.1. In-Service training

John F. May defines the in-service training as follows: The in-service training is the systematic and continuous improvement of employees' knowledge, skills and behaviors which help them for achieving their own and their organization welfare. Pear and Gutter have considered the in-service training as the systematic effort which its main purpose is to coordinate and align the individuals' desires, interests and future needs, with the needs and goals of organization in terms of what is expected from people. Goldstien defines the in-service training as a systematic process of acquiring the skills, rules, concepts or attitudes which lead to improved performance in the workplace. In-Service training differs from the on-the-job training. In-Service training has a broader concept than the on-the-job training and refers to all trainings which people pass during the service in the organization, and even in the wider consideration for their retirement period, while the on-the-job training refers to those trainings under which the individual can be familiar with the methods, and implementing techniques during a specific job. In other words, the job in-service training is one of the in-service training methods which have the practical and scientific nature (Peters, 1997, p. 16).

2.2. Necessity for staff training

In general, factors which have made the training essential are as follows:
1 - Increasing technological advances and changes; 2 - Increasing the organizational complexities; 3 - Personal requirements; 4 - Globalization of competition and job; 5- job changing, relocation and modification; 6 - Staff promotion; 7 - Growing momentum in all fields

Along with more complex jobs, the importance of staff training has also been increased. When jobs were simple they could be easily learned, and the technical changes had no effect on them, therefore the employees have little need to increase or change their skills, but accelerated changes which recently have been occurred in the sophisticated and developed communities have increased the pressure on the organizations.

Type of needed jobs and skills to do these businesses in the current situation indicates the need for training. Therefore, the organization managers should take the resources for training into account in order to always have the efficient and informed human resources.

The list below contains the benefits which the job training can have for the organization and staff:
1- It leads to profitability.
2 – It strengthens the honesty and trust among the employees and managers.
3 – It allows the organizational progress within the organization.
4 - It reduces the costs.
5 – It leads to the better decision-making.
6 - It improves the occupational skills.
7 – It improves the relationships between the subordinate and individual.
8 – It helps to increase the productivity and work quality.
9 – It reduce s the conflicts.
10 - It leads to the progress, growth and responsibility in the individuals. (Tousi, p. 246)

2.3. Staff Training Process

According to Table 1, which its details is specified in the educational process, the staff training process is discussed and evaluated:

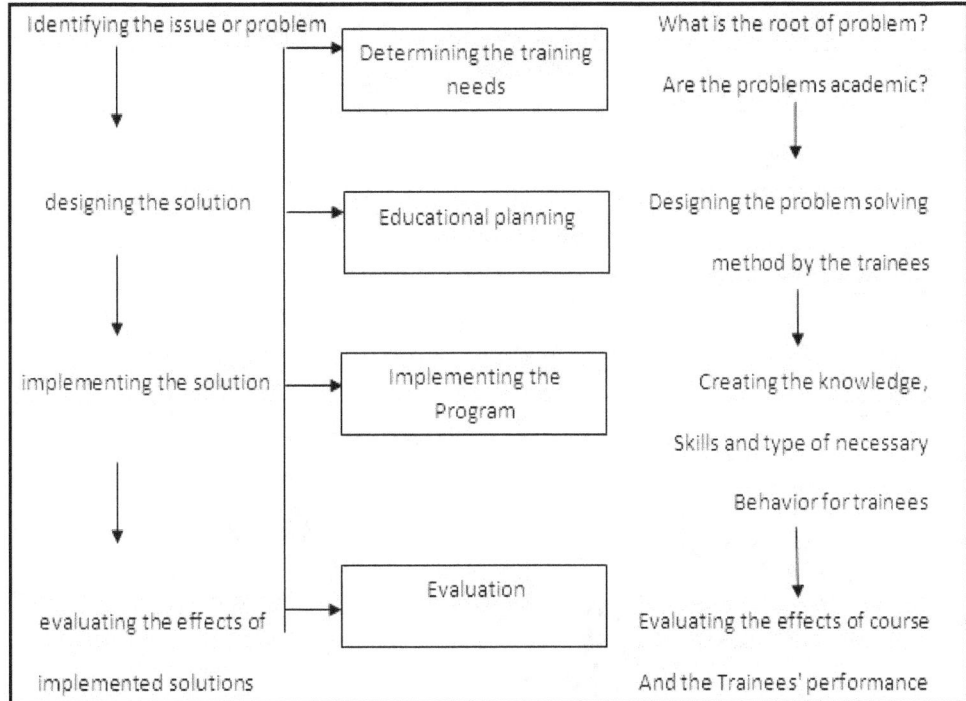

Figure 2. The process of staff training (Abtahi, 1373, p. 118)

Job trainings consist of new perceptions of vital factors in an individual's professional career. Therefore, the job trainings enable people to benefit from the basic insight and skills which are necessary for understanding the techniques and sciences of their own profession and their effectiveness in their social life. The organizational professions content planners should understand the job requirements properly through the job analysis, and based on it prepare people for the job training by the regular programs.

2.4. Various stages of training planning

Various stages of training planning are presented in Figure 3, so we describe them briefly:

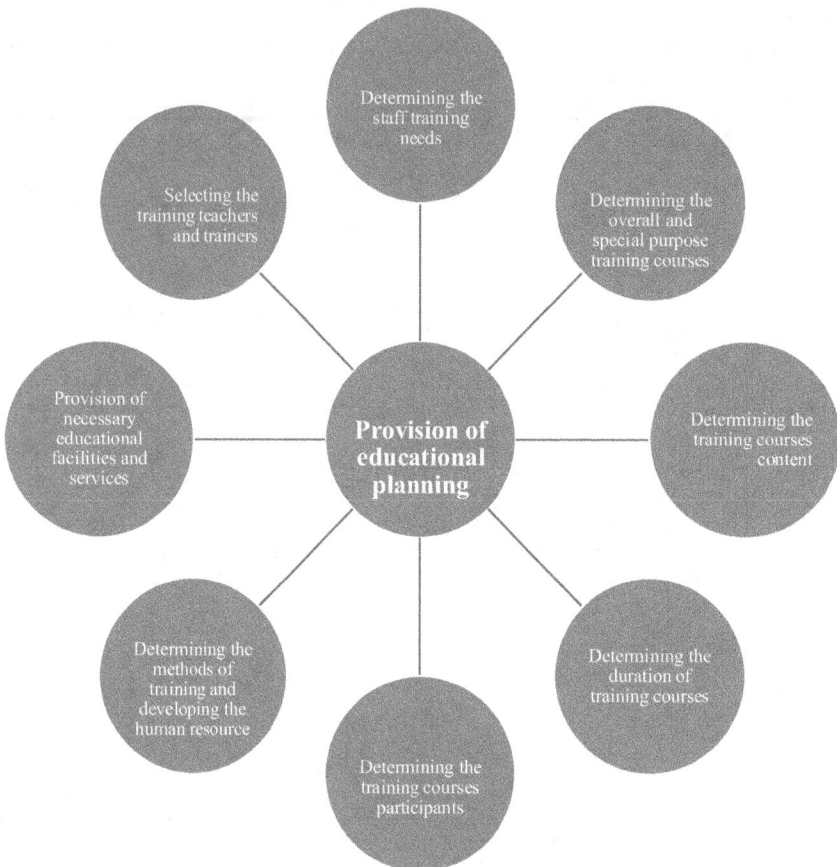

Figure 3 - Various stages of training planning (Abtahi, 1373, p. 123)

2.5. Determining the overall and special training purposes
The first essential step in the planning and especially in the training planning is determining the overall and special training purposes.
Determining the overall training purposes in the educational process is done after the purposes analysis and the organizational responsibilities and before determining the special purposes of training programs and their implementation. The special training purposes are determined in the framework of overall purposes of organization and according to the educational needs.

2.6. Determining the content
Determining the content of training programs should always be about the overall and special goals of programs; because if it is not regarded, not only the program is not implemented, but also the education, as a mean for eliminating the deficiencies and ultimately for achieving the organizational goals, will lose its safe and proper way. Another factor which should be considered in determining the content of training programs is the survey of program participants and it should be carried out.

2.7. Determining the duration of program
Managers, experts and officials in the training programs should consider the necessary and enough time in order to achieve the training goals, so that if the duration of a training course is considered shorter than the reasonable time, our educational goals will not be accomplished, and if the duration exceeds the reasonable time, participants will became tired during the program.

2.8. Determining the participants characteristics
Even if the educational unit and the officials are optimistic, they should accept this fact that they cannot educate all individuals, who need to train, in a certain time due to limited financial and human resources. Therefore, the most logical way is following the priority, and first educating those who need more than others. If the number of

people, who need to be educated, is the same in terms of priority and educating all individuals in a range of time is impossible, the needed individuals should be selected and invited to attend the course by the help of direct supervisor. This can be done by sending the specific forms.

The managers, experts or training officials' task requires that a group should be invited as the participants in the training program. They are selected by particular points and indicators and in general the maximum efficiency is obtained from the course.

2.9. Determining the training methods

The program success largely depends on the method(s) which are selected for providing the determined content; on the other hand, the administrators, educational planners and experts cannot select and apply the method(s), which they have identified their effectiveness, without comprehensive evaluation of training planning.

2.10. Skills training

As Pereda and Berrocal (1999, 2001) and García (2003) show, skills training is based on the use of active, participative methodologies. The most important skills training techniques include 'real-life work experience'or, in their absence, 'simulations' (e.g. role-playing, business games and outdoor training), which promote experiential learning and modelling (ob-serving more experienced work colleagues, or watching videos), which in turn foster learning by observation and social learning. The context of on-site work is ideal for developing skills as it provides a real work setting in which the skills required by a given job must be put into practice.

Skills training is based on practice and 'action', and on-site work expe-rience therefore offers a unique opportunity to develop skills as students are enabled to 'experiment', 'try out', 'apply', 'test', 'acquire' and/or 'extin-guish' skills (behaviours) in a real work setting.(E.R.Talavera and J.C.Pérez-González,2007,pp.83-109).

2.11. Workplace training

On-site training played no systematic part in vocational training [For-mación Profesional] (FP II) in Spain until the 1980s. This was when an em-phasis began to be placed on vocational training, and an atmosphere of closer and more active collaboration between entrepreneurs and educa-tional institutions first emerged (Martínez, 2002, p. 46). In substantive terms,the establishment of on-site training (Formación en Centros de Trabajo,FCT) arose out of Article 34.2 of the Organic Act 1/1990 of 3 October on the General Organisation of the Education System (Ley Orgánica 1/1990de 3 de octubre, de Ordenación General del Sistema Educativo , LOGSE),which sought to promote learning in the workplace and in the classroom. Today, this system of alternating classroom and workplace training has fortunately become widespread in vocational training in Spain. It may be partly because of this that vocational training qualifications, which were once much less highly regarded, have gained greater social acceptance in Spain in the last few decades. .(E.R.Talavera and J.C.Pérez-González,2007,pp.83-109).

Moreover, according to figures from the Ministry of Education and the Eurydice report for 2005, the last few years have seen an increase in the number of Spanish students studying vocational training, although many fewer than those opting for the Bachilleratoand going to university (approx-imately 38 % as compared with 62 %). However, la formación professional tiene un mayor potencial de inserción laboral que la universitaria (vocation-al training has greater potential than a university education for enabling peo-ple to enter the labour market) (Informe Infoempleo, 2005, p. 24).

Like Sobrado and Romero (2002), we believe that practical work and on-site training are both key elements of vocational integration guidance and an excellent opportunity for developing personal and key competen-cies. When students and recent graduates of vocational training and high-er education take part in on-site training, they have a chance to learn from experience, although it has to be remembered that experience in itself in-volves no learning nor is it educational. For the experience of on-site train-ing to become a genuine learning process, it must boast at least three char-acteristics (Álvarez Rojo et al., 2000):

a) integrating well planned and coherent experiences with skills to be de-veloped;
b) promoting reflection over experience;
c) facilitating the integration of experience through self-assessment, the analysis of consequences, and the promotion of transference to other situations.

Initial Specialised Vocational Training (Formación Profesional Inicial Específica) in Spain aims to fulfil these three requirements by promoting on-site training through FCT modules. Spanish legislation on the subject currently differentiates between four separate blocks of training, or 'Pro-fessional Modules' (Modelos Profesionales) (MECD, 2003b, p. 5):

a) professional modules linked to a unit of skill, and consisting of specif-ic, professional skills training designed to enable students to acquire
the professional behaviours set out in the unit of skill;
b) a basic, or transversal, module consisting of knowledge of a particu-lar technical field, and on which a number of course's specific modules are based;

c) a Training and Vocational Integration Module (Módulo de Formación y Orientación Laboral, FOL), a training package aimed at providing stu-dents with more comprehensive preparation for entering the labour mar-ket and developing appropriately in the world of work;

d) an On-site Training Module (Módulo de Formación en Centros de Tra-bajo , FCT), which seeks to consolidate and complement students' pro-fessional skills acquired in the educational establishment through the performance of productive activities at the workplace.

Training in the workplace (FCT) corresponds to the on-site training mod-ule in Initial/Regulated Specialist Vocational Training (Formación Profe-sional Inicial/Reglada Específica); it lasts between 10 and 20 weeks, approximately 25% of the total workload for each qualification. La caracterís-tica más relevante de esta formación es que se desarrolla en un ámbito productivo real (la empresa), donde los alumnos podrán desempeñar las actividadesy funciones propias de los distintos puestos de trabajo de una profesión, conocer la organización de los procesos productivos o de ser-vicios y de las relaciones laborales, siempre orientados y asesorados por los Tutores del Centro Educativo y del Centro de Trabajo [The key fea-ture of this training is that it takes place in a genuine productive setting (theenterprise) where students may perform the real activities and functions of the jobs in a profession, and learn about the organisation of the productive processes or services and of employment relations, with constant guid-ance and advice from tutors in the educational establishment and the work-place] (MECD, 2003b, p. 6; MEC, 1994).

The aim of workplace training is to promote the vocational training of students in three areas (MECD, 2004): theoretical-cognitive (knowledge), practical (technical skill) and attitudinal (social attitudes and skills). Under this system, the development of socio-emotional skills only appears to be represented by the third area, where some attitudes are inter-mingled with certain socio-emotional skills. .(E.R.Talavera and J.C.Pérez-González,2007,pp.83-109).

.Customer's perception of quality:

Quality of a particular service is *whatever the customer perceives it to be.* Service quality as perceived by the customer may differ from the quality of the service actually delivered. Services are subjectively experienced processes where production and consumption activities take place simultaneously. Interactions, including a series of moments of truth between the customer and the service provider occur. Such buyer-seller interactions or service encounters have a critical impact on the perceived service. The Nordic Model, originated by Christian Gronroos and developed by others, adopts a disconfirmation of expectations approach. This claims that customers have certain expectations of service performance with which they compare their actual experience. If the expectations are met, this is confirmation; if they are over performed, this is positive disconfirmation; if they are underperformed this is negative disconfirmation. According to Gronroos (1984), the quality of service as perceived by customers has two dimensions; a *technical or outcome dimension* and a *functional or process-related dimension.*

What customers receive in their interaction with a firm is clearly important to them and their quality evaluation. This is one quality dimension, the *Technical Quality of the outcome* of the service production process. However, as there are numerous interactions between the service provider and customers, including various series of moments of truth, the technical quality dimension will not count for the total quality which the customer perceives he has received. The customer will also be influenced by the way in which technical quality- the outcome of the process is transferred to him and this will have an impact on the process experience. Examples include the accessibility of ATM, a website, appearance and behavior of waiting staff, how service employees perform their task, what they say and how they do it. Interestingly, other customers simultaneously consuming the same or similar services may influence the way in which customers will perceive a service. Thus, the consumer is also influenced by **how** he receives the service and how he experiences the simultaneous production and consumption process. This is the second quality dimension, the *Functional Quality of the process*, closely related to how the moments of truth of the service encounters themselves and are taken care of and how the service provider functions. Illustrated in **figure 1**, there are the two basic quality dimensions, namely, **What** the customer receives and **How** the customer receives it; the technical result or outcome of the process (technical quality) and the functional dimension of the process (functional quality. An organization's image is an important variable that positively or negatively influences marketing activities. Image is considered to have the ability to influence customers' perception of the goods and services offered (Zeithaml and Bitner, 1996).Thus, image will have an impact on customers' buying behaviour. Image is considered to influence customers' minds through the combined effects of advertising, public relations, physical image, word-of-mouth, and their actual experiences with the goods and services (Normann, 1991). Similarly, Grönroos (1983), using numerous researches on service organizations, found that service quality was the single most important determinant of image. Thus, a customer's experience with the products and services is considered to be the most important factor that influences his mind in regard to image. For instance, if the service provider shares a positive or favorable image in the minds of the customers, minor mistakes will probably be overlooked or forgiven. However, if the image is negative, the impact of any mistake will often be considerably greater than it otherwise would be. This entire combination shall lead to total quality.

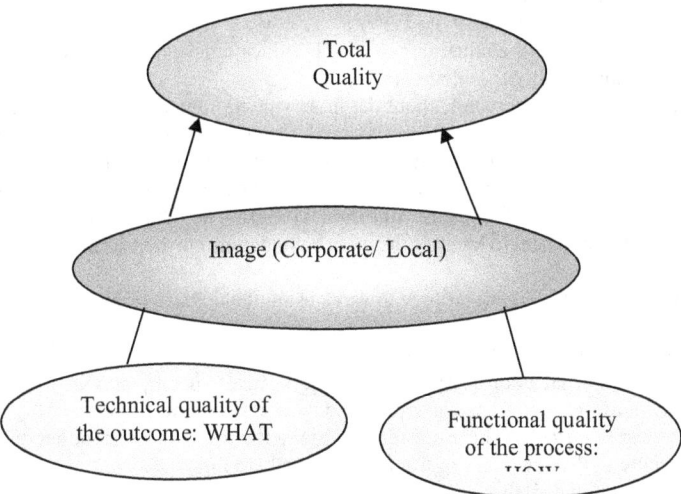

Figure 4: Two service quality dimensions

(Gronroos, 2001)

2.13. Research Background

Kasmaki and Mellander (1999) has indicated in a research on Sweden corporations about the in-service training that these periods could reduce the production costs and working hazards markedly, however these results are obtained from the industrial companies and institutions.

Mulholland (2001) has indicated that 90 percent of in-service trainings in the United States are effective, but since they are not transferred appropriately to the personnel, 90 million dollars are wasted in the United States each year. The main cited reasons for lack of effectiveness of these training include:

The inappropriateness of In-service training courses with the staff occupational areas, and lack of transferring to the personnel to staff and so creating the staff anxiety and pressure due to the fast transferring of skills to the employees.

Jarvis believes that in most countries, the professional formulation and implementation of continuing education are taken into account and constantly growing. And developing the staff talent and abilities now is considered as an integral part of their job.

Emamjomeh and Saeedi Rezvani also have expressed that the main essence of in-service training is to increase the staff efficiency and creating the appropriateness with the workplace through the "problem-solving" and as a result, increasing the services provided by the staff.

Anna Craft (1997) has expressed that the In-service trainings increase the employees' valuable feeling and job satisfaction.

Wei-toi-tai (2006) expresses: the main goal of any training institutional program is that it can replace a new set of knowledge, skills, and attitudes. Due to the importance of organizations in meeting the community needs, experts have greatly emphasized on continuing the in-service trainings. For example, Jennifer Good says that: The opportunities for professional development should be are available for teachers (staff) throughout the occupational life.

One of the important effects of organizational trainings is the identification of organizational functions. The in-service training needs to explain the organizational functions for the staff in that organization. As David Donaell expresses: The quality of training the staff determines the full or partial recognition of tasks which an organization should perform.

Tang Chan Huang (2001) writes: "If the need assessment is not performed, the organization will not be ensured that the appropriate training is provided for the staff". Huang has indicated in his research report that there is a direct relationship between the needs assessment and the efficacy of training at the significant level.

Gllessman and Pogh (1989) began a study through educating subjects in the various educational places with this aim that the portion of training could be determined for achieving the teaching skills. Educating the teaching methods was done by the film and it was concluded that the training, as a requirement for changing the skills, need to be understood. Also, it was proposed that the practice continuation is effective in acquiring the desirable skills. Ballot and Taymaz (2001) has indicated in a research carried out in France from 1986 to 1992 that the productivity in the industry field has increased due to the increased trained staff. In other words, by increasing the trained staff to one percent, the productivity will be increased two percent. Other studies are also monitoring these results. And from the perspective that the in-service trainings have a significant positive effect on the productivity and staff wage growth, perhaps for this reason the developing and developed countries use the in-service trainings as a tool for increasing the employees' wages / (Margvis, 1999).

Tyler (1930) has written in his famous evaluation model: The educational evaluation is to determine to what extent the aims of training program have been implemented.

Dunkin (1998) has concluded in his research about the in-service trainings that the short-term in-service training courses will enhance the teachers' skills and professional attitudes. In addition, it will enhance the teachers' awareness of creating the new and better teaching method, so they will do their tasks better.

Sabar (2000) has concluded that the school personnel especially the teachers are faced with the problems in assessment and evaluation activities of students' educational progress and the classroom management; and the in-service training system will help them to identify the main path, determine their limitations and sources, and select the solutions for these problems.

Aithon (2000) has concluded that the staff attitude towards using the modern teaching methods can be changed by holding the in-service training courses.

Valcke (2007) has concluded that the Information and Communication Technology (ICT) policy of schools is well developed, and there is a partial coordination among the policies, needs, and in-service training about the awareness of actual ways for managing the classroom and new teaching methods.

Carol (2007) in his research suggested the areas for improving the teachers' educational quality in the in-service training courses especially in the new ways of teaching and evaluation.

Rahmani Morid (1384) concluded that the teachers' greatest need is for the methods of strengthening the educational motivation and new strategies of teaching and the least need is for the evaluation methods.

Kazemi Asfeh (1386) has concluded that the familiarizing the teachers with the management and leadership techniques in the class is the first priority, and the need for familiarizing them with the creating educational motivation techniques and the modern teaching methods and also familiarizing with the creativity techniques creation are the next priorities.

3. Research Methodology

The presented research is applied in terms of aim of study, and descriptive based on the implementing method, but the dominant method in this study is survey. The researcher's aim of conducting this study is the visual, regular, and actual description of features of a position or subject. In these kinds of research, the researcher tries to identify what there is and introduce the barriers to achieving the planned targets. Moreover, the survey method is used for being aware of trained staff attitudes and their managers about the assessment of in-service training effectiveness. In the first step, researcher has examined the records and documents at the Islamic Azad University and gathered the necessary information about the performance of training unit in terms of training activities (in the time period considered in this study) and evaluated them in connection with the organizational goals. In the second step, the researcher analyzed the employees and managers' view bout the data obtaining activities, all data, and collected by available information which are obtained through the questionnaires.

3.1. Data collection tools

Due to the different stages of research, data collection methods are also different. As mentioned in the research methodology, part of this study evaluates the quality of implementing the educational activities in line with the organizational goals. Therefore, the data collection techniques include:

1- Referring to the information and statistics available at the Islamic Azad University of Aliabad Katoul Branch archive which is separated annually.

2- Identifying the qualitative and quantitative defined objectives for each year through the directions, regulations, and circulars.

3- Using the closed questions questionnaire for evaluating the target community opinions towards the organizational behavior and quality of implementing the training activities.

4- Utilizing the interviews in order to increase the accuracy in the archival investigations and questioning as well as complementing the research process especially in preparing and compiling the questionnaire.

3.2. Statistical population, sample size, sampling and data analysis method

The statistical population of this study consists of all formal, contractual, and experimental employees at Islamic Azad University of Aliabad Katoul Branch during the years 1384-1388, those who took part in the in-service training courses of university unit, and they were evaluated by the senior, intermediate, and executive managers. The formal, contractual, and experimental employees, who have passed at least 100 hours of training course in the mentioned years, have been considered as the experimental group. The descriptive statistical methods (frequency table, percentage frequency) have been used for analyzing the study data. In order to analyze data, the paired T-comparison test and the statistical model of test for differences between two correlated ratios, have been used.

3.3. Determination of validity and reliability of research tools

The content validity has been used in the present study in order to determine the validity of questionnaire. The content validity refers to this subject that to what extend the sample questions used in a test sample can represent the total community and the considered content or subject can be obtained (Seif, 1382, p. 419). Thus, the researcher has defined the key words in order to understand the questions more and applied them in the questionnaire; at the same time, the necessary descriptions about the questions have been available for the in-service trained ones.

The reliability of test means the stability of measuring at different times. Reliability of a measuring tool mainly refers to the accuracy of obtained results. About the reliability, more than 10% of samples were provided for the employees and managers in order to check the validity, and after collecting, their validities were calculated by Spss software for Cronbach's alpha; in addition, the values obtained for employees with 81%, which represented of the high validity of questionnaires, were obtained and the reliability coefficient was acceptable.

4. Research Findings

4.1. First Hypothesis Test:

First hypothesis: Staff In-service trainings have been effective on improving the staff performance in the Islamic Azad University.

Data table of first hypothesis in the form of frequency before the participation and attendance in the poor training data

	Good	Weak	
A + B=33	22B	11A	Good
C + D	26D	6C	After the participation and attendance of poor performance

Data table in the form of ratio before the participation and attendance at the training courses

	Good	Weak	
$P_1= 0.51$	0.34 b	0.17 a	Good performance
$q_1= 0.49$	0.40 d	0.09 c	After the participation and attendance of weak performance
1	$P_2= 0.74$	$q_2 = 0.26$	

The contravention of Hypothesis was claimed: The staff In-service trainings have not had a positive effect on improving the performance.

$H_0 = P_2 \leq P_1$
$H_1 = P_2 \geq P_1$

Claimed Hypothesis: Staff in-service trainings have had the positive effects on performance improvement; $H_1 = P_2 \leq P_1$

Test criterion: $Z = \dfrac{P_2 - P_1}{\sqrt[2]{\dfrac{a+d}{n}}} = \dfrac{0.74 + 0.51}{\sqrt{\dfrac{0.17 + 0.40}{65}}} = \dfrac{0.23}{0.0936} = 2.46 \Rightarrow Z = 2.46$

Error rate:	Value:
α=1-c=1-0.095=0/05	α=1-c=1-0.095=0/05
Z_α=Z	$Z_\alpha = Z_{0.05} = 1.65$
Value:	
α=1-c=1-0.095=0/05	
$Z_\alpha = Z_{0.05} = 1.65$	

Because the test criterion of test statistic is greater than the critical value of table, the difference between two ratios of employees' performance before and after the in-service training is probably significant at the 95% level in terms of statistics. In other words, with reliability 95 percent, it can be expressed that the staff participation and attendance at in-service training courses has a positive effect on improving the performance of their organization.

4.2. Second Hypothesis Test:

Second Hypothesis: Staff In-service trainings have been effective on improving the service quality in the Islamic Azad University.

Data table of second hypothesis in the form of frequency before the participation and attendance in the in-service training data

	Good	Weak	
A + B=33	24B	8A	Good
C + D=32	30D	2C	After the participation and attendance of weak performance
n = 64	B + D=54	A + C=10	

Data table of second hypothesis in the form of ratio (%) before the participation and attendance at the in-service training courses

	Good	Weak	
P_1= 0.50	0.37b	0.13a	Good performance
q_1 =0.50	0.47d	0.03c	After the participation and attendance of weak performance
	P_2 =0.84	q_2 = 0.16	

The contravention of Hypothesis was claimed: The staff In-service trainings have not had an effect on improving the service quality of university.

$H_0 = P_2 \leq P_1$
$H_1 = P_2 \geq P_1$

Claimed Hypothesis: Staff in-service trainings have had the positive effects on improving the service quality of university ; $H_1 = P_2 \geq P_1$

Test criterion: $\quad Z = \dfrac{P_2 - P_1}{\sqrt{\dfrac{a+d}{n}}} = \dfrac{0.84 + 0.50}{\sqrt{\dfrac{0.13+0.47}{65}}} = \dfrac{0.34}{0.031} = 10.97 \Rightarrow Z = 10.97$

Error rate:	Value:
α=1-c=1-0.095=0/05	α=1-c=1-0.095=0/05
$Z_α$=z	$Z_α$=$Z_{0.05}$=1.65
Value:	
α=1-c=1-0.095=0/05	
$Z_α$=$Z_{0.05}$=1.65	

Because the test criterion of test statistic is greater than the critical value of table, the difference between two ratios of performance related to the service quality before and after the participation and attendance in the in-service training courses is significant in terms of statistics. In other words, with reliability 95 percent, it can be expressed that the staff in-service training has a positive effect on improving the service quality at university.

4.3. Third Hypothesis Test

Third hypothesis: Staff In-service trainings have been effective on creating the cooperation and collaboration spirit among the staff.

Data table in the form of frequency before the participation and attendance in the in-service training data

	Good	Weak	
A + B=33	24B	9A	Good
C + D=32	28D	4C	After the participation and attendance of poor performance

Data table in the form of ratio (%) before the participation and attendance at the in-service training courses

	Good	Weak	
P_1= 0.59	0.37 b	0.14 a	Good performance
q_1 =0.41	0.43 d	0.06 c	After the participation and attendance of weak performance

| | | P=1 | $P_2 = 0.80$ | $q_2 = 0.20$ | |

The contravention of Hypothesis was claimed: The staff In-service trainings have not had a positive effect on creating the cooperation and collaboration spirit among the staff.

$H_0 = P_2 \leq P_1$

$H_1 = P_2 \geq P_1$

Claimed Hypothesis: Staff in-service trainings have had the positive effects on creating the cooperation and collaboration spirit among the staff; $H_1 = P_2 \geq P_1$

Test criterion: $Z = \dfrac{P_2 - P_1}{\sqrt[2]{\dfrac{a+d}{n}}} = \dfrac{0.80 + 0.59}{\sqrt{\dfrac{0.14 + 0.43}{65}}} = \dfrac{0.21}{0.0304} = 6.91 \Rightarrow Z = 6.91$

Error rate:	Value:
α=1-c=1-0.095=0/05	α=1-c=1-0.095=0/05
$z_α = z$	$Z_α = Z_{0.05} = 1.65$
Value:	
α=1-c=1-0.095=0/05	
$Z_α = Z_{0.05} = 1.65$	

Because the test criterion of test statistic is greater than the critical value of table, the difference between two ratios of cooperation and collaboration spirit among staff before and after the in-service training courses is probably significant at the 95% level. In other words, with reliability 95 percent, it can be expressed that the staff participation and attendance at in-service training courses has a positive effect on creating the cooperation and collaboration spirit among staff.

4.4. Fourth Hypothesis Test

Fourth Hypothesis: Staff In-service trainings have been effective on staff efficiency.

Data table in the form of frequency before the participation and attendance in the in-service training data.

	Good	Weak	
A + B=32	24 B	8 A	Good
C + D=33	28 D	5 C	After the participation and attendance of poor performance

Data table in the form of ratio (%) before the participation and attendance at the training courses

	Good	Weak	
P_1= 0.49	0.37 b	0.12 a	Good performance
q_1= 0.49	0.43 d	0.08 c	After the participation and attendance of weak performance
1	$P_2 = 0.80$	$q_2 = 0.20$	

The contravention of Hypothesis was claimed: The staff In-service trainings have not had a positive effect on staff efficiency.

$H_0 = P_2 \leq P_1$

$H_1 = P_2 \geq P_1$

Claimed Hypothesis: Staff in-service trainings have had the positive effects on the staff efficiency; $H_1 = P_2 \geq P_1$

Test criterion: $Z = \dfrac{P_2 - P_1}{\sqrt[2]{\dfrac{a+d}{n}}} = \dfrac{0.80 + 0.49}{\sqrt{\dfrac{0.13 + 0.47}{65}}} = \dfrac{0.31}{\sqrt[2]{0.008461}} = \dfrac{31}{0.092} = 3.37 \Rightarrow Z = 3.37$

Error rate:	Value:
α=1-c=1-0.095=0/05	α=1-c=1-0.095=0/05
$z_α = z$	$Z_α = Z_{0.05} = 1.65$
Value:	
α=1-c=1-0.095=0/05	
$Z_α = Z_{0.05} = 1.65$	

Because the test criterion of test statistic is greater than the critical value of table, the difference between two ratios of staff efficiency before and after the employees' participation and attendance at the in-service training courses is statistically significant. In other words, with reliability 95 percent, it can be expressed that the staff in-service training staff has a positive effect on improving and increasing the staff efficiency.

4.5. Fifth Hypothesis Test

Fifth Hypothesis: Staff In-service trainings have been effective on strengthening the staff spirit.

Data table in the form of frequency before the participation and attendance in the in-service training data

	Good	Weak	
A + B=33	22B	10A	Good
C + D=32	10D	6C	After the participation and attendance of poor performance
n =65	B+D=49	A+C=16	

Data table in the form of ratio (%) before the participation and attendance at the in-service training courses

	Good	Weak	
P_1= 0.51	0.35 b	0.15 a	Good performance
q_1 =0.49	0.40 d	0.10 c	After the participation and attendance of weak performance
1	P_2 = 0.75	q_2 = 0.25	

The contravention of Hypothesis was claimed: The staff In-service trainings have not had any effects on strengthening the staff spirit.

$H_0 = P_2 \leq P_1$
$H_1 = P_2 \geq P_1$

Claimed Hypothesis: Staff in-service trainings have had the positive effects on strengthening the staff spirit; $H_1 = P_2 \geq P_1$

Test criterion: $$Z = \frac{P_2 - P_1}{\sqrt[2]{\frac{a+d}{n}}} = \frac{0.75 + 0.50}{\sqrt{\frac{0.15 + 0.40}{65}}} = \frac{31}{0.092} = 2.72 \Rightarrow Z = 2.72$$

Error rate:	Value:
α=1-c=1-0.095=0/05	α=1-c=1-0.095=0/05
Z_α=Z	Z_α=$Z_{0.05}$=1.65
Value:	
α=1-c=1-0.095=0/05	
Z_α=$Z_{0.05}$=1.65	

Because the test criterion of test statistic is greater than the critical value of table, the difference between two ratios of employees' spirit before and after the participation and attendance at the in-service training courses is significant at the reliability 95%. In other words, it can be expressed that the staff in-service training has a positive effect on strengthening and improving the staff spirit.

4.6. Sixth Hypothesis Test

Sixth Hypothesis: Staff In-service trainings have been effective on creating the staff job satisfaction.

Data table in the form of frequency before the participation and attendance in the in-service training data

	Good	Weak	
A + B=32	21B	11A	Good
C + D=33	27D	6C	After the participation and attendance of poor performance
n =65	B+D=48	A+C=17	

Data table in the form of ratio (%) before the participation and attendance at in-service training courses

	Good	Weak	
P_1= 0.49	0.32 b	0.17 a	Good performance
q_1 =0.51	0.42 d	0.09 c	After the participation and attendance of weak performance
1	P_2 = 0.74	q_2 = 0.26	

The contravention of Hypothesis was claimed: The staff In-service trainings have not had any effects on creating the staff satisfaction.

$H_0 = P_2 \leq P_1$
$H_1 = P_2 \geq P_1$

Claimed Hypothesis: Staff in-service trainings have had the effects on creating the staff satisfaction; $H_1 = P_2 \geq P_1$

Test criterion: $Z = \dfrac{P_2 - P_1}{\sqrt[2]{\dfrac{a+d}{n}}} = \dfrac{0.74 + 0.49}{\sqrt{\dfrac{0.17 + 0.42}{65}}} = \dfrac{0.25}{0.00953} = 2.62 \Rightarrow Z = 2.62$

Error rate:	Value:
α=1-c=1-0.095=0/05	α=1-c=1-0.095=0/05
$Z_\alpha = Z$	$Z_\alpha = Z_{0.05} = 1.65$
Value:	
α=1-c=1-0.095=0/05	
$Z_\alpha = Z_{0.05} = 1.65$	

Because the test criterion of test statistic is greater than the critical value of table, the difference between two ratios of creating the staff job satisfaction before and after the participation and attendance at in-service training courses is statistically significant. In other words, with reliability 95 percent, it can be expressed that the staff in-service training has a positive effect on creating the staff job satisfaction.

4.7. Seventh Hypothesis Test

Seventh Hypothesis: Staff In-service trainings have been effective on improving the staff occupational skill.

Data table in the form of frequency before the participation and attendance in the in-service training data

	Good	Weak	
A + B=31	22B	9A	Good
C + D=31	24D	6C	After the participation and attendance of poor performance
n =62	B+D=46	A+C=16	

Data table in the form of ratio (%) before the participation and attendance at the training courses

	Good	Weak	
$P_1 = 0.50$	0.35 b	0.15 a	Good performance
$q_1 = 0.50$	0.39 d	0.11 c	After the participation and attendance of weak performance
1	$P_2 = 0.76$	$q_2 = 0.26$	

The contravention of Hypothesis was claimed: The staff In-service trainings have not had any effects on improving the staff occupational skill.

$H_0 = P_2 \leq P_1$
$H_1 = P_2 \geq P_1$

Claimed Hypothesis: Staff in-service trainings have had the effect on improving the staff occupational skill; $H_1 = P_2 \geq P_1$

Test criterion: $Z = \dfrac{P_2 - P_1}{\sqrt[2]{\dfrac{a+d}{n}}} = \dfrac{0.76 + 0.50}{\sqrt{\dfrac{0.15 + 0.39}{65}}} = \dfrac{0.26}{0.0093} = 2.62 \Rightarrow Z = 2.79$

Error rate:	Value:
α=1-c=1-0.095=0/05	α=1-c=1-0.095=0/05
$Z_\alpha = Z$	$Z_\alpha = Z_{0.05} = 1.65$
Value:	
α=1-c=1-0.095=0/05	
$Z_\alpha = Z_{0.05} = 1.65$	

Because the test criterion of test statistic is greater than the critical value of table, the difference between two ratios of improving the staff occupational skill before and after the participation and attendance at in-service training courses is statistically significant. In other words, with reliability 95 percent, it can be expressed that the staff in-service training has a positive effect on improving the staff occupational skill.

5. Discussion and Conclusion

- The results of theoretical (library) studies of research in line with the conducted studies about the subject of research including the concept of assessing the staff in-service training, effectiveness of education, and role of training in developing the staff skill and… are the points which can improve the effectiveness and quality of providing the services for the customers at Islamic Azad University if necessary. Therefore, the staff in-service training is one of the most basic ways in order to avoid wasting the resources of organization. In this field, the staff continuous in-service training should be done with the specialized and non-specialized courses, and this should be included at employees' different levels. Therefore, achieving the technical and scientific skill and information needed for improving the effectiveness of organization on one hand, and the field for staff occupational improvement on the other hand are the main objectives of staff in-service training at university. It should be noted that the staff in-service training can not only cause the effectiveness in the organization, but it also depends on the compliance with the criteria which can enhance the satisfaction and effectiveness of organization by the fair wages and salary system, using the system of reward and punishment appropriately, and the workplace conditions.

Data analysis results have indicated that the employees' needs for in-service training have been positive in two groups of employees and managers, and this is consistent with the results obtained by Aithon (2000). He concluded in his research that the staff in-service training has had a positive effect in New Zealand.

Moreover, the results suggest that the staff in-service training has enhanced and improved the quality of effectiveness at university, and this is consistent with the results obtained by Aithon (2000). Aithon concluded that the staff in-service training in New Zealand has had a positive effect on efficiency and quality of services provided by teachers.

The results of research have indicated that the staff in-service training has had a positive effect on improving the staff occupational skills, and this is consistent with the results obtained by Dunkin (1998). In this regard, he concluded that the staff short-term in-service training courses have increased the teachers' professional skill and attitude. In addition, managers believe that passing the staff training courses can enhance the cooperation and coordination spirit among the staff. They also believe that passing the staff training courses will increase the employees' efficiency, enhance the staff morale, and meet the staff job satisfaction; and these results are consistent with the findings of most of the internal and external studies which are conducted about the subject of research.

References:

Abtahi, Seyed Hossein,.(1373)."Training and developing the human resources", Educational Planning and Development Institute publication.

Abtahi, Seyed Mohammad Hassan, (1375), "Human Resources Management", Payame Nour Institute publication.

Bazzaz - Jazayeri, Seyed Ahmad, "Staff training as a known necessity in the public and industrial organizations", Tehran: State Management Training Center (1373).

Álvarez Rojo, V. et al. ,.(2000)."Propuestas del profesorado bien evaluado para po-tenciar el aprendizaje de los estudiantes . Seville: University of Seville,.

Elvira Repetto Talavera and Juan Carlos Pérez-González . (2007). Training in socio-emotional skills throughon-site training (1),. European journal of vocational training – No 40 – 2007/1 – ISSN 1977-0219,pp.83-109.

Informe Infoempleo. Oferta y Demanda de Empleo Cualificado en España .Madrid: Círculo de Progreso, S.L.

Pereda, S.; Berrocal, F.: Gestión de Recursos Humanos por Competen-cias . Madrid: Editorial Centro de Estudios Ramón Areces, 1999.

Pereda, S.; Berrocal, F. ,.(2001)."Técnicas de gestión de recursos humanos poR competencias. Madrid: Editorial Centro de Estudios Ramón Areces,.

Tyler, Ralph, (1930), "Principles of curriculum and education", translated by: Taghipour, Zahir.

Rahmani, Morid, (1384), "Needs assessment of teachers' in-service training courses at primary school in Izeh County", MA. Thesis, Islamic Azad University of Khorasegan Branch.

Seif, Ali Akbar, (1380), "Training Psychology (Learning and Teaching Psychology)", Agah publication, Sixth Edition.

Kazemi Asfeh, Zohreh, (1386), "Evaluating the female teachers' training needs at primary school in the in-service training courses in Isfahan city", MA thesis, Islamic Azad University of Khorasegan Branch.

Tousi, Mohammad Ali, (1379), "Staff training articles Collections", Vol. 2, State Management Training Center, Tehran.

Aithon.j.e (2000).in service tranning for teacher in school in organizations(3rd)New Jersey: Prentice Hall.p.6.

Ballot, G, and tayma2 , E.(2001) Effect of Quastions during the teaching of students. Retrieved from http://novelschoomanagement.com

Carol p. Demands FD (2007)Continuous quality improvement:Integration best practice in to teacher educationThe Journal of educational Management , Vol:211, No.9 pp:2-4.

Craft, Anna (1997) national policy quielines for staff development national Association of state universities and Land-Grant colleges. Extension committee on organization and policy.

Donnell, David and Thomas N. Garavan (1997) view point: Linking training policy and practice to organizational Goals journal of European industrial training, vol.21,pp.301-309

Dunkin.m(1998), E).in service education of teacher in teacing.encylopedia of teacher education michel.hdunkin of pxford pergaman..

Gillrs DA (1998) Nursing management : a system apporoach.3rd ed. Philadelphia: WB saunders co

Glessman, David; pugh, Richard. Paper presented at annual meeting of thnorth Central association conceptual variable as predictors of change in teaching skills Chicago: 1989.

Good. Jennifer(2003) Innovation stakeholders in Determining professional Development Center Atterdonce policies. The International journal of Educational management, vol.12,pp.14-18.

Gronroos, C. (1984), "A service quality model and its marketing implications", European Journal of Marketing, 18, 36-44 .

Gronroos, C. (1983), "Strategic Management and Marketing in the Service Sector", Report No. 83-104, Marketing Science Institute, Cambridge, MA.

Gronroos, C. (2001), Service Management and Marketing, 2nd edition, Chichester: John Wiley & Sons Ltd

Gronroos, C. (1983), "Strategic Management and Marketing in the Service Sector", Sweden and Chartwell-Bratt: Bromley Student Litteratu ab Lund.

Huang, Tuny chun(zool) the Relation of Traning practices and organizational performance in small and medium size Enterprises, Journal of Education Traning. Vol 43.No8/9 pp.437-444

kazmaki, & mellander. (1990) Evalvating fire traning effect on perporment & labuorder and Applied , economic letters. 6,pp431-437.

marquis , H.M.(1991). Formal traning, on the job traning and allocation of time joucna of macroeconomics. Vol.21.No.7 pp.423-44.

mulholland , (2001). A metho dological approach to supporting organizational learning Human-corputer studies. Vol55, pp.337-367.

MEC. Formación Profesional. Formación en Centros de Trabajo (FCT).Madrid: MEC, Spanish Directorate-General of Regulated VocationalTraining and Educational Promotion, 1994.

MECD. Formación en centros de trabajo. Guías prácticas para tutores (CD-ROM). Madrid: MECD and Chambers of Commerce, 2003a.

MECD. Formación Profesional. Titulaciones(CD-ROM). Madrid: MECD,2003b.

MECD. Manual de formación en centros de trabajo. Guía para el tutor de empresa [2004]. Downloaded from the Internet (03/05/04):http://wwwn.mec.es/educa/formacion-profesional/index.html.

Martínez, Mª J. Historia de la Formación Profesional en España. De la ley de 1955 a los Programas Nacionales de Formación Profesional. Va-lencia: Publicaciones de la Universidad de Valencia (PUV).

Martínez, D. ,.(1373)."2001 Evolución del Concepto de Trabajo Emocional: dimensiones,antecedentes y consecuencias. Una revisión teórica. Revista de Psi-cología del Trabajo y de las Organizaciones, , Vol. 17 (2), p. 131-153.

Peters, L. at . a (1997) encyclopedia of Human Resource management, Blachwell pubishers, ltd.

sabar P(2000), curriculum Development at School level.http.//www.findarticales . com..

Normann, R.(1991), "Service Management Strategy and Leadership in Service Businesses", Chichester: John Wiley & Sons Ltd.

Subcommittee on personnel training and Development. Fort valley, Ga. Cooperative Extension, Fort Valley state college.

Valcke.m.. (2007). ict, teacher E Training,:Evaluation of the curriculum and training approach .

wei- Tao ti (2005) Effects of training framing, General self –Efficacy and Traning motivation of tranees, Traning Effectiveness. Personnel review. Vol.35na.1.2006pp.51-65.

Zeithaml, V. A., & Binter, M.J. (1996), "Service Marketing", New York: The McGraw-Hill Companies, INC.

Factors Moderate IT Diffusion-Performance Relationship in Developing and Developed Countries: An Empirical Evidence

AMROLAH AMINI (Ph.D)

Associate Professor, Allameh Tabatabaei University (ATU), Tehran, Iran.

aminij@atu.ac.ir

ALIREZA EMAMI

Master of Science, Tehran University, Tehran, Iran

memami@alumni.ut.ac.ir

MOSTAFA EMAMI*

Master of Science, Michigan Technological University (MTU)

memami@mtu.edu

*Corresponding Address

Applied Research and Technology Office, Michigan Technological University

1400 Townsend Dr, Houghton, MI 49931

Tel & Fax : +1-(816) 237-0018

E-mail: memami@mtu.edu

Factors Moderate IT Diffusion-Performance Relationship in Developing and Developed Countries: An Empirical Evidence

Abstract

According to the literature, there is a paradox in IT results and significant difference between developed and developing countries in the IT diffusion. Consequently, one of the most important questions of development researchers is now what factors affecting the relation between IT and national development in developed and developing countries. This paper determines and classifies factors affecting the relation between IT diffusion and nations' performance in developed and developing countries. Moreover, in order to facilitate future empirical studies on developed and developing countries, a general conceptual model, some key potential research hypotheses, and a new calculation methodology are provided.

Key words: IT diffusion, Conceptual model, Developing countries, Developed countries

1. Introduction

Most of researchers and development specialist believe that information technology (IT) has a great impact on organizations performance and nations' developments. On the other hand, the amount of investments on IT has rapidly increased in recent years. [3] In spite of positive viewpoints about the effects of IT on organizational and national performances, some researchers are concern. In other words, they question about the positive relationship between IT investments and the performance. Accordingly, their main question about IT is "does IT investments improve the performance?" There is huge number of papers in literature to answer this question and explain the relation between IT and national performance and development. However, the results show a Paradox in the results. [8][12][15][16][17][22]

[29][33][35][39][45][59] General speaking, the application of IT to development goals has not always succeeded to date and there are many cases of partial or complete failure. [4]

Respecting the paradox in the results of IT, the researchers find it more useful to answer a new question of "what factors influence IT usage?" In other words, the main question has now become not whether, but how IT can be benefial for development and what factors affect its disfusion. Although the literature introduces a numerous number of factors that affecting IT usage and shows various differences in these factors between developed and developing countries, however, there are few general conceptual models to identify, classify and quantify the factors in a systematic way.

This research aims to achieve three following objectives; 1)review the literature and determine factors affecting IT usage, 2)introduce some main measures and ndicators that quantify the factors, and 3)provide a generic conceptual model that facilitate future studies on IT diffusion in developed and developing countries. It focuses on the differences between developed and developing countries in IT usage and emphasis on developing countries because they have the majority of the world's population, contain millions of people who lack access to resources such as clean water, adequate housing, education, and freedom to choices their own lives. [54][65] For this purpose, the remainder of the paper is structurized as follows. Tthe following section explains a brief review of literature. Section 3 provides a framework to classify affecting factors and measures. Section 4 describes the conceptual model, the research potential hypotheses, and the computational methodology for future empirical analysis. Finally, the paper ends with conclusions and final remarks.

2. Review of the Literature

Two main questions on IT usage are "what factors influence IT usage?" and "are there any significant differences in these factors between developed and developing countries?" To answer these questions several researches have been conducted. For example, Mahmood Adam and Swanberg attempt to determine organizational factors affecting IT usage using a meta-analysis of empirical literature. They provide a combined model of IT usage and IT effectiveness. In this model, IT effectiveness is a function of IT usage and IT usage, in turn, consists of four main factors, organizational IT application, organization characteristics, individual characteristics, and perceived benefits. Results of their meta-analysis confirm a strong and significant positive relation between the perception of ease of use and the perceived usefulness of an IT system to the actual amount of usage. [42]

Mutula and Brakel propose an assessment tool for evaluating e-readiness at organizational level. Their proposed model includes five main components of enterprise readiness, ICT readiness, external environment readiness, human resource readiness, and information readiness. They define 29 measures for enterprise readiness, 19 measures for human resource readiness, 21 measure for information readiness, 22 measures for ICT readiness, and finally 21 measures for environment readiness component (totally 112 measures). [46]

Meyer, Srinivas, Lal and Topolnytsky study the relations between the commitment components and behavioral support for a change using Herscovitch and Meyer's three-component model (affective, normative and continuance commitments) of commitment to an organizationa. They found a considerable support for the relations between commitment and support predicted by the model. However, they also found evidence for potential culture differences. [30][43]

Although there is a widespread belief in potential value of IT and its supportive roles in human and nations' economic development, however there is significant differences between developed and developing countries in the use of IT. Several researches have been conducted to determine factors affecting the differences in IT usage between developed and developing countries. For example, Barrel and Pain, and Kraemer and Dedrick determine factors influencing the level of IT investment. They find that IT investment is associated with diffusion of telecommunications, infrastructure, education levels, technical skills, and the percent of the economy in services industries. [10][11][36]

Dewan and Kraemer compare developed and developing countries and find a significant positive relationship between IT investment and productivity growth at the macroeconomic level in developed countries, but not in developing countries. [23] Moreover, Madon examined the use of the Internet in sectors such as health and education, and in domains such as economic productivity and sustainable development. [41]

Caselli and Coleman findings show association between computer hardware imports, an indicator of IT investment, with educational attainment, openness to imports and property rights protection. [20]

Some researches and international documents confirm the effect of the availability of complementary assets such as telecommunications networks and skilled IT professionals and their drives for IT investments. [55][62][66] Although the studies show that IT investment is correlated with the level of national wealth, other factors such as resources for technology investments, structure of the economy, and openness to external influences have been shown to be significant as well.

Bui, Sankaran and Sebastian propose a framework to evaluate the IT e-readiness of a nation based on eight factors of digital infrastructure, macro economy, ability to invest, knowledgeable citizens, competitiveness, access to skilled workforce, culture, and cost of living and pricing. They identify 52 measures to quantify these eight factors and provide a simple algorithm to calculate an overall e-readiness index for a country. Finally, they provide benchmarking e-readiness using a 5-point scale diagram. [18]

Caselli and Coleman, Kraemer and Dedrick, and Robinson and Crenshaw point out structure of the economy (such as size of country's services sector because of existing significant positive association between the size of a country's services sector and IT investment) as important affecting factor. [20][36][48] They also believe that inadequate complementary assets such as telecommunications networks and/or infrastructures and skilled human resources (SHR) are also important in increasing differences in IT usage between developed and developing countries. They emphasis on SHR because it has less opposition to social changes associated with adoption of new technologies and empirical studies strongly support the association between education levels and IT use at the country level.

Dewan and Kraemer show that marginal impact of complementary assets is greater in developing countries, which are still in the process of creating adequate levels of such assets than developed countries and openness to external influences, foreign trade especially Foreign Direct Investment FDI, as an indicator, facilitates the diffusion of managerial and technical knowledge across borders. [23] In addition, Coe, Helpman and Hoffmaister, and Shih, Kraemer and Dedrick find that FDI has a positive impact on technical progress in the host country. [19][55]

Shih, Kraemer and Dedrick found a negative relationship between IT investment and interest rates, but significant positive relationships between investment, openness to trade, and tele-communications infrastructure. When they include interaction effects between national income levels and country variables, they find that the impacts of interest rates, size of the financial sector, teledensity, and intellectual property rights are strongest in shaping IT investment for developed countries. In contrast, they find that the impact of openness to trade is greater for developing countries, as is the size of government and education levels. [56]

Hanafizadeh, Khodabakhshi and Hanafizadeh provide a set of recommendations for e-business development in developing countries. They test the recommendations by study of case of Iran. Based on benchmarking 19 countries and 4 regions, 339 recommendations for e-business development are determined and finally using content analysis, 36 of 339 recommendations were selected and categorized into four groups of human resource, security, e-infrastructure, and policies and plans. They also provide a national survey to test the recommendations that fit with Iran internal situations. Finally, they ranked the recommendations based on pundits' opinions. [28]

Shih, Kraemer and Dedrick consider poverty, lack of infrastructure, inadequate education, policy making based on incorrect assumptions about IT usage, low level of IT investment to achieve measurable productivity gains, technology accumulation (evolutionary process of continuous innovation and imitation), and lack of resources for technology investments (because of credit, loan and capital gathering problems and operating in more ill-developed and not matured monetary and stock markets) as important issues make differences between developed and developing countries. [55]

In addition to earlier mentioned economic and business, social and infrastructural issues, there is also a long history for the cultural issues and their effects on the differences between developed and developing countries. Although there is a general agreement on the effects on culture on the differences in IT usage and governance between developed and developing countries, however each research in literature has its own angle of view. It should be mind that there are two major areas for cultural studies: organizational culture and national culture. [61] The following researches are some evidence of cultural effects.

Hofstede, Neuijen, Ohayv and Sanders study the relationships between organizational culture and organizational characteristics. They gathered data on organizational cultures in twenty units from ten different organizations in Denmark and the Netherlands. Based on gathered data on organizational cultures in twenty units from ten different organizations in Denmark and the Netherlands, they study the relationships between organizational culture and organizational characteristics. [31]

According to Rossouw, business ethics, as an integral part of business culture, has a much larger extent become part of the business culture in developed countries than in developing countries. Rossouw provides an explanation for the fact that business ethics is fighting an uphill battle in becoming part of the business culture in developing countries. Although cultural factors in developing countries set limits to organizational effectiveness, variations in effectiveness nevertheless do exist within countries. [49]

Ryan, Chang, Ployhart and Slade study the cross-cultural equivalence of a multinational employee opinion using multiple-groups covariance structure analysis in four countries (U.S. and Australia, Mexico and Spain). [50] Conceptual equivalence occurs when a construct can be meaningfully discussed in each culture and has a similar meaning across cultures. [13] Cultural and linguistic influences were considered by assessing equivalence across two pairs of countries having the same language but different cultures (U.S. and Australia, Mexico and Spain) and across countries differing in culture and language (U.S. and Mexico). The measure was equivalent across U.S. and Australian samples only. One cause source of lack of invariance was translation problems.

Brewster and Dowling, Welch and Schuler identify national culture as one of five variables that 'moderate (i.e. either diminish or accentuate) differences between domestic and international human resource management. [14][24] These include differences in the centrality of markets, institutions, regulations, collective bargaining, and labor-force characteristics. Hofstede study cultural consequences comparing values, behaviors, institutions, and organizations across nations. [32]

Awasthi, Chow, and Wu examine the effects of national cultural differences on the behavioral consequences of imposing performance evaluation and reward systems (PERS). They conclude that two cultural dimensions (individualism versus collectivism and power distance) can modify employees' decisions and satisfaction under imposed performance evaluation and rewards aimed at modifying their work-related behavior. US nationals had significantly lower satisfaction under imposed rather than self-selected performance evaluation and reward structures, while Chinese counterparts did not have a similar adverse reaction. Their results were consistent with prior Anglo-American-based research that the significantly affects employee behavior. They suggest that thier finding may not be directly generalizable to employees whose national cultures differ from those of Anglo-Americans. [6][34]

Salter and Sharp investigate the effects of national culture on management control systems and performance. Results of their study show that even apparently small cultural differences, such as that between the USA and Canada, can be particularly troublesome. In fact, their study explores the effect of an apparently small difference in national culture on the ability of agency theory to explain escalation of commitment to failing projects in two countries with significant cross-border investment, i.e., USA and Canada. They found that the effect of adverse selection conditions was significantly stronger among managers from the more individualist USA and that more experienced managers were less likely to escalate commitment. [52]

Pothukuchi, Damanpour, Choi, Chen and Park examined the effects of national and organizational cultural differences on international joint venture performance. They found that negative effects from cultural distance stems from organizational culture than from national culture. In other words, their study shows the importance of organizational culture similarity for joint venture (JV) success. They found that distance in the open (with a better communication climate) versus closed system dimension negatively affects all measures of International JV performance. The results suggest that while JVs have little control over each other's national culture, they could nevertheless engage in shaping similar organizational practices. [44][47]

Silva and Figueroa discusse how to promote the use of IT in the context of Chile. They discuss that SIS can fail to become institutionalized in a developing country despite adequate planning, strong leadership, and knowledgeable IS professionals. They state some factors including core values and beliefs, political time, the distribution of power, formal organizational structure, and control systems prevent achieving to the developmental goals. [58]

Bada explained a longitudinal case study of radical organizational change related to the computerization and networking of branches in the Nigerian banking sector. He implies that cultural homogeneity is not becoming the norm; it is needed to understand and value local practices. [7]

Walsham dealt with cross-cultural issues in software production and use, drawing on secondary data from two case studies, including that of a joint Jamaican/Indian software team. [64]

Spony examined an analytical model, which enables the operationalization of cultural concepts related to the work context at both the individual and cultural levels of analyses. The model was empirically tested using with a population of French and British managers from two different sectors, bank/insurance and pharmaceutical/ healthcare organizations. They have tyried to control the impact of organizational culture differences. The final four work-value scales (self-enhancement, individual dynamics, consideradon for others and group dynamics) elicited through five-step analysis successfully achieved the purpose of the model's development. [60]

Fang and Rau examined the effects of cultural differences between the Chinese and the US people in terms of the perceived usability and search performance of World Wide Web portal sites. They found significant differences of satisfaction and steps in performing some tasks between Chinese and American. The results also provided more detailed insights into the cultural differences among countries' users. Results of their study indicate that the cultural differences have significant impact on users' perception and usage of the same portal Website. Their studies provided important insights in designing portal sites for different users with different cultures. [26]

Avgerou show the complex dynamics of the link between IT and development. She discuss that an effective action requires involvement and collaboration between industry, government, and international organizations. [5]

Adam and Myers using case study of the Maldives customs service addressed the challenge of culturally inappropriate impositions of IT. [1]

Shoib and Nandhakumar used two case studies to argue that multiple forms of rationality exist in any context and that national culture is only one aspect of actors' sense-making activities. They suggest need to the notion of culture rather than seeing it as a fixed entity. [57]

Liu and Westrup examined a case study of coordination and control between the United Kingdom and China in a multinational corporation. They discuss that IT-enabled coordination is only effective when linked with other approaches such as the use of expatriates and face-to-face contacts. These studies emphasize the crucial importance of IT in cross-cultural working in the contemporaryworld. [38]

Dunkel and Meierewert examined the impact of different cultural standards on the processes and performances of Austrian, Spanish, German and Hungarian task groups using 201 qualitative interviews. They concluded that culturally heterogeneous teams have more potential for conflicts, thus, resulting in more challenges for the team members. [25]

Saad and Zawdie reveal the need for both technology transfer and the development of the triple helix culture in developing countries. They believe that the business incubation system as an aspect of the triple helix model of innovation in which universities, industry, government and non-government organizations feature as principal actors in the national innovation system. The culture of bureaucracy and institutional fragmentation has been major factors militating against initiatives for technological capability development; and the conventional technology transfer practice has reinforced this culture. They beleive that a major policy initiative is needed in developing countries to put the national system of innovation in place and remove the constraints on the development of the triple helix culture. [51]

Gerhart and Fang studied the national culture and human resource management. Their study implies that although countries can be differ in many ways (e.g. institutional and regulatory environment, labor-force characteristics such as education), a dominant focuses of the international management literature is on national differences in culture, especially culture values. They conclude that while national culture difference can be important, their role needs to be put in the context of other important contextual factors, including organizational culture. [27]

Some researchers consider local adaptation and new technologies as important factor as well as cultural factors. For example, Sayed and Westrup study the case of Egypt and explains the role of a specific IT, Enterprise Resource Planning (ERP) systems networks in country development. [53] Some researchers study the local adaptation and cultivation of IT. Macome shows that the local context was crucial in the implementation process and that it was essential to involve local stakeholders in the entire process. [40] D'Mello was also concerned with local adaptation related to new ICTs she addressed the adaptation of people in the context of global software outsourcing and argued that adaptation has produced a new breed of knowledge workers in the software industry in countries such as India from where she drew her field data. [21]

As Walsham, Robey, and Sahay state, IT disffusion consequences emerge from a complex set of processes over a significant period. It needs involving a wide range of actors and institutions. IT has no deterministic effects on development because it has being applied to complex social issues. In other words, social influences are crucially important to the trajectory of any technology-based project. [65] Accordingly, the studies on the developing countries and the potential role of IT to support their development emphasis on a complex set of factors such as social, political, and cultural contexts. According to Walsham, Robey and Sahay, we need to conduct more researchers to consider geographical spread, NGOs roles as important intermediaries in IT related development, and different level of analysis such as individuals, groups, organizations, industry sectors, societies, and international organizations. [63] Work at the community level also promises to contribute to an understanding of IT in marginalized groups in developed countries. [37] Research is also needed on society-wide critical issues (such as HIV/AIDS or gender) in developing countries. Gender studies received more attentions in IT research, but there is little work as yet which addresses the role of women in connection with IT in developing countries. [2][65]

3. Factors Affecting IT Diffusion

Brief review of the literature shows that there are a numerous number of factors affecting IT usage and there are various differences in these factors between developed and developing countries. Tables 1, 2 and 3 will sammurize and classfify the most important factors that affecting the relation between IT and performance and make difference between developed and developing countries. These Tables facilitate answering to the main question of "what factors affecting IT diffusion and create differences between developed and developing countries?"

Table 1: Most widely used variables in literature

Type of Variables	Factors	Measures
Independent Variable	ITechnology Diffusion (Investments)	• IT investment [11][23][36][55][56][62][66] • IT use at country level [20][26][36][48][55] • IT spending on hardware and software as percent of GDP [56] • Computer hardware imports and production [20]
Dependent Variable	National Productivity Level	• Productivity growth at the macroeconomic level [20][23][36][41] • Level of national wealth [55][62][66] • Technical progress [19][55]
Common Used General Moderator Variables	Most widely-used, official-source development data from the World Bank and other international agencies	• Total external debt to gross national income (Economic Indicator) • GDP (current US$) (billions) (Economic Indicator) • GNI per capita, Atlas method (current US$) (Economic Indicator) • Life expectancy at birth, total (years) (Social Indicator) • Population, total (millions) (Social Indicator) • Population growth (annual %)(Social Indicator) • Surface area (sq. km) (thousands) (Infrastructural &Natural Indicator)

Table 2: Factors affecting IT diffusion

Factors	Factors
• Educational level [11][20][36][42][54][65]	• Cost of living and pricing [18]
• Professional and Training level [11][36][42]	• Techmology accumulation [55]
• Perception of user toward IT [42]	• Lack of resources fortechnology investment [55]
• Commitement level [43]	• Infrastructures [20][36][48][55]
• Enterprice readiness [46]	• Skilled human resource [20][36][48][55]
• ICT readiness [46]	• Proterty rights protection [20][56]
• External Environmen readiness [[46]	• Lack of clean water, inadequate housing and freedom [54][65]
• Human readiness [46]	• National culture and cross cultural differences [1][5][6][13][14][18][24][26][32][38][47][49][50][52][57][58][60][64]
• Information readiness [46]	
• Completeness assets [20][23][36][48][55][62][66]	
• Telecommunications networks [20][36][48][62][66][55]	• Organizational culture [27][31]
• Skilled IT professionals [55][62][66]	• Business Ethics [49]
• Lack of resourece for technology investments [54][55][62][65][66]	• Language and translation problems [13]
	• Culturally heterogeneous teams [7][25]
• Structure of economy [11][20][36][48][55][56][62][66]	• Culture of bureaucracy and institutional fragmentation [51]
• Openness to external influence [20][23][55][62][66]	• Poverty [55]
• Digital infrastructure [11][18][36]	• Lack of infrastructure [55]
• Macro econy situation [18]	• Inadequate educaton [55]
• Ability to invest [18]	• Incorrect assumptions and policy makings [55]
• Knowledge citizens [18]	• Legal similarity [58]
• Competitiveness [18]	• Political context [58][65]
• Access to skilled workforce [18]	

Table 3: Moderator variables/factors and their measures classification

Moderator Variables	Factors	Measures/Indicators	
Economic & Business Moderator Variable	Globalization and International Trade	<ul><li>Merchandise exports (current US$) (millions)</li><li>Merchandise imports (current US$) (millions)</li><li>Merchandise trade (% of GDP)</li><li>Trade Balance (</li><li>Trade (% of GDP)</li><li>Tariff & Non-tariff Barriers</li><li>Net financial flows</li></ul>	<ul><li>International tourism, receipts (current US$)</li><li>International tourism, number of departures</li><li>International tourism, number of arrivals</li><li>Bank and trade-related lending (PPG + PNG) (NFL, current US$) (millions)</li><li>Private capital flows, total (BoP, current US$)</li><li>Foreign direct investment, net inflows (BoP, current US$) (millions)</li><li>Foreign direct investment, net inflows (% of GDP)</li></ul>
	Macroeconomics Situation	<ul><li>GDP (current US$) (millions)</li><li>GDP growth (annual %)</li><li>GDP per capita, Shih, Kraemer and Dedrick (2007)</li><li>GDP - real growth rate(%)</li><li>GNI, Atlas method (current US$) (millions)</li><li>GNI per capita, Atlas method (current US$)</li><li>Budget expenditures</li><li>Budget-capital (%)</li><li>Budget deficit</li><li>Current account balance</li><li>Industrial production growth rate (%)</li><li>Investment (gross fixed)(% of GDP)</li><li>Industry, value added (current US$) (millions)</li><li>Adequate Regulations & Supervision of Financial Institutions</li></ul>	<ul><li>Soundness of Banks</li><li>Local Competition</li><li>Regulatory Framework</li><li>Government Effectiveness</li><li>Political Stability</li><li>Rule of Law and Control of Corruption</li><li>Industry, value added (% of GDP)</li><li>Cereal yield (kg per hectare)</li><li>Economic growth in the following periods (EGF)</li><li>Size of the financial sector</li><li>Interest rates</li><li>Wealth (GNP), economic growth in the past periods (EGP)</li><li>Structure of the economy such as size of country's services sector</li><li>Protection of Property Rights</li></ul>	<ul><li>Agriculture, value added (% of GNI)</li><li>Total debt service (% of GNI)</li><li>Total debt service (% of exports of goods, services and income)</li><li>Current account balance (% of GDP)</li><li>Exports of goods and services (% of GDP)</li><li>GNI per capita, PPP (current international $)</li><li>Inflation, GDP deflator (annual %)</li><li>Gross capital formation (current US$) (millions)</li><li>Gross capital formation (% of GDP)</li><li>Services, etc., value added (% of GDP)</li><li>Imports of goods and services (% of GDP)</li><li>Industry, value added (annual % growth)</li><li>The size of government</li><li>Cash surplus/deficit (% of GDP)</li></ul>
	Labor and Employment	<ul><li>Labor force, female (% of total labor force)</li><li>Labor force, total (millions)</li><li>Labor force with primary education (% of total)</li><li>Worker remittances and compensation of employees, received (US$)</li></ul>	<ul><li>Employment in industry (% of total employment)</li><li>Employment in services (% of total employment)</li><li>Labor force - by occupation – in agriculture,</li><li>Employees, agriculture, male (% of male employment)</li></ul>	<ul><li>Population ages 15-64, total (millions)</li><li>Unemployment, total (% of total labor force)</li><li>Employees, agriculture, female (% of female employment)</li></ul>
	Private and Public Sectors	<ul><li>Domestic credit to private sector (% of GDP)</li><li>GFCF, private sector (% of GDP)</li><li>Private Sector Spending on R&D</li><li>Credits made to the private sector as percent of GDP</li></ul>	<ul><li>Global Fund for Community Foundations GFCF, public sector (current LCU)</li><li>Public sector long-term debt of public sector LDOD (current US$)</li><li>Privatization transactions values by country, region or sector**</li></ul>	<ul><li>Claims on private sector (annual growth as % of M2)</li><li>PNG, total private nonguaranteed L-T debt service (TDS, current US$)</li><li>Expense (% of GDP)</li><li>Revenue, excluding grants (% of GDP)</li></ul>
	States, Markets & Competitiveness	<ul><li>Total Expenditure for R&D as % of GNI</li><li>Stocks traded, total value (% of GDP)</li><li>Market capitalization of listed companies (% of GDP)</li><li>Market capitalization (% of GDP)</li><li>Inward foreign direct investment as percent of GDP</li><li>Intellectual property rights</li><li>Property rights protection</li></ul>	<ul><li>Composite ICRG Risk Rating</li><li>Availability of Venture Capital</li><li>Openness to external Influences, foreign trade specially Foreign Direct Investment FDI as % of GDP</li><li>openness to imports/trades trade as percent of GDP</li><li>Values of AIDA or official development aid activities by Country*****</li></ul>	<ul><li>Time required to start a business (days)</li><li>Easiness of Doing Business (rank) ***</li><li>Admin. Burden for Start-Ups a business (rank)</li><li>Military expenditure (% of GDP)</li><li>Entrepreneurship among Managers</li><li>High-technology exports (% of manufactured exports)</li><li>Tenders and procurement opportunities worldwide or Tenders and consulting opportunities worldwide*</li></ul>
	Poverty, Debts & Aids	<ul><li>Cost of Living and Pricing</li><li>International Cost of Living Indices</li><li>Income share held by lowest 10% and 20%</li><li>Poverty gap at $1 and $2 a day (PPP) (%)</li><li>Poverty headcount ratio at $1 and $2 a day (PPP) (% of population)</li><li>Malnutrition prevalence, weight for age (% of children under 5)</li><li>PPP conversion factor to official exchange rate ratio</li><li>Purchasing power parity conversion factor (LCU per international $)</li><li>Inflation Rate–CPI in %</li><li>GDP per capita (PPP)</li><li>Poverty index</li></ul>	<ul><li>Food production index (1999-2001 = 100)</li><li>Homeownership Rates</li><li>Population below poverty line(%)</li><li>Reserves of foreign exchange and gold</li><li>GDP - composition by sector – agriculture, industry and services</li><li>Inflation rate(consumer prices) (%)</li><li>Household income or consumption by percentage share – highest 10%</li><li>Present value of debt (% of GNI)</li><li>Total debt service (TDS, current US$) (millions)</li><li>Total debt service, total long-term (TDS, current US$) (millions)</li><li>Long-term debt (DOD, current US$) (millions)</li><li>Present value of debt (current US$) (millions)</li></ul>	<ul><li>External debt (% of exports of goods and services)</li><li>External debt (% of GNI)</li><li>External debt, total (DOD, current US$) (millions)</li><li>Economic aid - donor</li><li>Economic aid - recipient</li><li>Official development assistance and official aid (current US$) (millions)</li><li>Aid per capita (current US$)</li><li>Aid (% of GNI)****</li><li>Aid (% of gross capital formation)</li><li>Aid (% of imports of goods and services)</li><li>Short-term debt (% of total external debt)</li><li>Lending interest rate (%)</li></ul>

Table 3: Moderator variables factors and measures classification (continued)

Moderator Variables	Factors		Measures/Indicators
Infrastructural and Natural Moderator Variable	Geographical	• Roads, total network (thousands km) • Vehicles (per 1,000 people) • Airports, Heliports • Merchant marine (ships) • Pipelines (km) • Railways (km) • Roadways (km) • Computers per 1,000 People • Television broadcast stations • Internet Hosts per 10,000 People • Internet users per 10,000 People • Households with television (%) • Waterways(km) Oil and Gas proved reserves • Passenger cars (per 1,000 people) • Price basket for internet • Fixed line and mobile phone subscribers (per 1,000 people) • International Telecommunications • Total Investments in Telecommunications • Telecommunication equipment (Export) (US$) • Telecommunication equipment (Import) (US$) • % of households with a telephone	• Residential monthly telephone subscription (US$) • Business telephone monthly subscription Business telephone monthly subscription (US$) • Mobile cellular monthly subscription • Mobile cellular monthly subscription (US$) • Price of a 3-minute fixed telephone local call (peak rate) • Price of a 3-minute fixed telephone local call (peak rate – US$) • Mobile cellular - price of 3-minute local call (peak) • Mobile cellular - price of 3-minute local call (peak – US$) • Mobile cellular - price of 3-minute local call (off-peak) • Mobile cellular - price of 3-minute local call (off-peak – US$) • Price of a 3-minute fixed telephone local call (off-peak rate) • Price of a 3-minute fixed telephone local call (off-peak rate – US$) • Households Mobile cellular telephone subscribers - (Post-paid + Pre-paid) • Mobile cellular telephone subscribers (Digital) • Mobile cellular telephone subscribers –prepaid subscribers • POP Coverage of mobile cellular network (population, in %) • Staff (Total full-time telecommunications staff) • Staff (Female telecommunications staff) • Mobile communications staff • Revenue from fixed telephone service • Revenue from fixed telephone service (US$) • Revenue from mobile communication • Revenue from mobile communication (US$) • Total revenue from all telecommunication services • Total revenue from all telecommunication services (US$) • Total annual investment in telecom • Total annual investment in telecom (US$) • Fixed telephone service investment • Fixed telephone service investment (US$) • Mobile communication investment • Mobile communication investment (US$) • Main (fixed) telephone lines per 100 inhabitants • Mobile cellular telephone subscribers per 100 inhabitants • Total telephone subscribers (fixed + mobile) per 100 inhabitants • Public payphones per 1000 inhabitants	• % of homes with Internet • Total fixed broadband Internet subscribers • International Internet Bandwidth (Mbps) • Personal computers • % of homes with a Personal Computer • Personal computers per 100 inhabitants • Internet users per 100 inhabitants • Total fixed broadband Internet subscribers per 100 inhabitants • Total (fixed) Internet subscribers per 100 inhabitants • International Internet Bandwidth per inhabitant (bit(s) • Schools connected to internet (%) • Broadband subscribers (per 1000 people) • International voice traffic (minutes per person) • Daily newspapers (per 1,000 people) • Telephone mainlines (per 1,000 people) • Technology Assessment Index • Patent Applications Granted • Computer Processing Power (% of total worldwide MIPS) • E-Government Index • Freedom on the Internet • ICT Expenditure as % of GDP • International internet bandwidth bits (per capita) • Internet services per million people • Permanent cropland (% of land area) • Arable land (% of land area) • Land use - arable land(%) • Land use - permanent crops(%) • Electricity - consumption(kWh) • Electricity - exports (kWh) • Electricity - imports (kWh) • Electricity - production(kWh) • Natural gas and oil consumption, production, exports, imports • Electric power consumption (kWh per capita) Coastline • Elevation extremes – highest point • Elevation extremes – lowest point • Irrigated land • Land boundaries - km • Surface area (sq. km) • Forest area (sq. km) • Agricultural land (% of land area) • Land and water area sq km • Total Area - sq.km • CO2 emissions (kt) (thousands) • CO2 emissions (metric tons per capita) • Improved water source, rural (% of rural population with access) • Improved water source, urban (% of urban population with access) • Improved water source (% of population with access) • Improved sanitation facilities, urban (% of urban population with access) • Land area (sq. km) (thousands) • Organic water pollutant (BOD) emissions (kg per day) • Energy use (kg of oil equivalent per capita) • Energy imports, net (% of energy use)
	Environmental		
	General Infrastructural	• Public payphones • Main (fixed) telephone lines in operation • Main (fixed) telephone lines in largest city • Total telephone subscribers (fixed + mobile) • % automatic main lines • % digital main lines • % residential main lines • % of main lines in urban areas • Total capacity of local public switching exchanges • International telephone circuits • Waiting list for main (fixed) lines		
	ICT Infrastructural	• Number of local (fixed) telephone (calls) • Number of local (fixed) telephone (minutes) • Number of national (fixed) long distance telephone (calls) • Number of national (fixed) long distance telephone (minutes) • Total national (fixed) telephone traffic (calls) • Total national (fixed) telephone traffic (minutes) • International outgoing fixed telephone traffic (calls) • International incoming fixed telephone traffic (calls) • International incoming fixed telephone traffic (minutes) • International outgoing fixed telephone traffic (minutes) • %of telephone faults cleared by next working day • Faults per 100 main (fixed) lines per year • Residential telephone connection charge • Residential telephone connection charge (US$) • Business telephone connection charge • Business telephone connection charge (US$) • Mobile cellular connection charge • Mobile cellular connection charge (US$) • Residential monthly telephone subscription	• Radio sets • Radio equipped households • % of households with a radio • Television receivers • Television receivers per 100 inhabitants • Cable television subscribers • Television equipped households • % of households with a television • Home satellite antennas • ISDN subscribers • SDN Channels • Estimated Internet users • Total (fixed) Internet subscribers • Cable modem Internet subscribers • Dial-up Internet subscribers • DSL Internet subscribers	

Table 3: Moderator variables factors and measures classfification (continued)

Moderator Variables	Factors	Measures	
Cultural & Educational Moderator Variable	**Cultural (Education /Literacy)**	• Expenditure per student, primary (% of GDP per capita) • Public Spending on Education • Literacy rate, adult total (% of people ages 15 and above) • Literacy rate, adult female (% of females ages 15 and above) • Literacy rate, adult male (% of males ages 15 and above) • Persistence to grade 5, total (% of cohort) • Pupil-teacher ratio, primary • School enrollment, primary (% gross) • School enrollment, primary, female (% gross) • School enrollment, primary, male (% gross) • Primary completion rate, total (% of relevant age group) • School enrollment, tertiary (% gross) • School enrollment, tertiary, female (% gross)	• School enrollment, secondary (% gross) • Adult Literacy Rate • Tertiary Enrollment • 8th Grade Achievement in Science • MGMT Education Locally Available in first-class Business Schools • Flexibility of People to Adapt to New Challenges • Tertiary Science & Engineering Enrollment • University Education Meets the Needs of Competitive Economy • Well Educated People Do not Emigrate Abroad • Extent of Staff Trainings • Research Collaboration Companies/Universities • Technical Papers per Million Population • Labor force with tertiary education (% of total) • Business ethics as an integral part of business culture • Educational level measured by tertiary school enrollment as percent of relevant age group • skilled human resources
Social & Demographical Moderator Variable	**Social Development** **Gender and Population** **Health** **Rural and Urban Development**	• Proportion of seats held by women in national parliament (%) • Ratio of girls to boys in primary and secondary education (%) • Mortality rate, under-5 (per 1,000) • Mortality rate, infant (per 1,000 live births) • Health expenditure per capita (current US$) • Health expenditure, total (% of GDP) • Hospital beds (per 1,000 people) • Immunization, DPT (% of children ages 12-23 months) • Immunization, measles (% of children ages 12-23 months) • Malnutrition prevalence, weight for age (% of children under 5) • Mortality rate, under-5 (per 1,000) • Physicians (per 1,000 people) • Prevalence of HIV, total (% of population ages 15-49) • Death rate (birth/1000 population) • Gender, and even age • Fertilizer consumption (metric tons) (thousands) • Land under cereal production (hectares) • Agricultural machinery, tractors per 100 sq. km of arable land • Rural population density (rural population per sq. km of arable land) • Population in the largest city (% of urban population)	• Population in urban agglomerations > 1 million (% of total population) • Poverty headcount ratio at urban poverty line (% of urban population) • Urban population • Urban population (% of total) • Latitude (LAT) • Organizational size (ORS) • Relatives organizational size (ROS) • Population size (POP) • Population growth (PGR) • Population density (PDN) • Population, total (millions) • Population, female • Population, female (% of total) • Population growth (annual %) • Population density (people per sq. km) • Births attended by skilled health staff (% of total) • Age dependency ratio (dependents to working-age population) • Fertility rate, total (births per woman) • Age structure in terms of ages (0-14, 15-64, 65 and over) and the gender (male and female) (%) • Life expectancy at birth, female (years) • Life expectancy at birth, male (years) • Life expectancy at birth, total (years) • Occupation

http://web.worldbank.org
http://www.dgmarket.com
http://rru.worldbank.org
http://www.doingbusiness.org
http://www.unctad.org/wir
http://aida.developmentgateway.org/aida/AidaAbout.do
http://www.imf.org/external/data.htm#data
http://www.itu.int/ITU-D/icteye/Indicators/Indicators.aspx

4.2. Research Hypotheses

H11a	(XTE1) correlates positively with (XEB4)	H11b	(XTE1) correlates positively with (XEB4)
H12a	(XTE1) correlates negatively with (XEB1)	H12b	(XTE1) correlates negatively with (XEB1)
H13a	(XTE1) correlates negatively with (XEB6)	H13b	(XTE1) correlates negatively with (XEB6)
H14a	(XTE1) correlates negatively with (EXB13)	H14b	(XTE1) correlates negatively with (EXB13)
H15a	(XTE1) correlates positively with (XEB18)	H15b	(XTE1) correlates positively with (XEB18)
H21a	(XTE2) correlates positively with (XEB4)	H21b	(XTE2) correlates positively with (XEB4)
H22a	(XTE2) correlates negatively with (XEB1)	H22b	(XTE2) correlates negatively with (XEB1)
H23a	(XTE2) correlates negatively with (XEB6)	H23b	(XTE2) correlates negatively with (XEB6)
H24a	(XTE2) correlates negatively with (EXB13)	H24b	(XTE2) correlates negatively with (EXB13)
H25a	(XTE2) correlates positively with (XEB18)	H25b	(XTE2) correlates positively with (XEB18)
H31a	(XTE3) correlates positively with (XEB4)	H31b	(XTE3) correlates positively with (XEB4)
H32a	(XTE3) correlates negatively with (XEB1)	H32b	(XTE3) correlates negatively with (XEB1)
H33a	(XTE3) correlates negatively with (XEB6)	H33b	(XTE3) correlates negatively with (XEB6)
H34a	(XTE3) correlates negatively with (EXB13)	H34b	(XTE3) correlates negatively with (EXB13)
H35a	(XTE3) correlates positively with (XEB18)	H35b	(XTE3) correlates positively with (XEB18)
H41a	(XTE4) correlates positively with (XEB4)	H41b	(XTE4) correlates positively with (XEB4)
H42a	(XTE4) correlates negatively with (XEB1)	H42b	(XTE4) correlates negatively with (XEB1)
H43a	(XTE4) correlates negatively with (XEB6)	H43b	(XTE4) correlates negatively with (XEB6)
H44a	(XTE4) correlates negatively with (EXB13)	H44b	(XTE4) correlates negatively with (EXB13)
H45a	(XTE4) correlates positively with (XEB18)	H45b	(XTE4) correlates positively with (XEB18)
H51a	(XTE5) correlates positively with (XEB4)	H51b	(XTE5) correlates positively with (XEB4)
H52a	(XTE5) correlates negatively with (XEB1)	H52b	(XTE5) correlates negatively with (XEB1)
H53a	(XTE5) correlates negatively with (XEB6)	H53b	(XTE5) correlates negatively with (XEB6)
H54a	(XTE5) correlates negatively with (EXB13)	H54b	(XTE5) correlates negatively with (EXB13)
H55a	(XTE5) correlates positively with (XEB18)	H55b	(XTE5) correlates positively with (XEB18)
H1am	Each of Economic, Business & Competition, Geographica & Infrustructural, Population-Gender-Literacy, and National Health readiness measures moderates the set of relations among (XTE1),(XTE2), (XTE3), (XTE4), and (XTE5) with (XEB4),(XEB1), (XEB6), (XEB13),and (XEB18) in *developed coutries*.		
H1bm	Each of Economic, Business & Competition, Geographica & Infrustructural, Population-Gender-Literacy, and National Health readiness measures moderates the set of relations among (XTE1),(XTE2), (XTE3), (XTE4), and (XTE5) with (XEB4),(XEB1), (XEB6), (XEB13),and (XEB18) in *developing coutries*.		
H1m	Each of Economic, Business & Competition, Geographica & Infrustructural, Population-Gender-Literacy, and National Health readiness measures *differently* moderates the set of relations among (XTE1),(XTE2), (XTE3), (XTE4), and (XTE5) with (XEB4),(XEB1), (XEB6), (XEB13),and (XEB18) in *developed and developing coutries*.		

4.3 The methodology

4.4 The Results

5. Summary and Conclusions

References

1. Adam, M., and Myers, M. Have You Got Anything to Declare? Neo-colonialism, Information Systems, and the Imposition of Customs and Duties in a Third World Country, 2003, In Organizational Information Systems in the Context of Globalization, M. Korpela, R. Montealegre, and A. Poulymenakou (eds.), Kluwer Academic Publishers, Boston, 2003: 101-116.
2. Adam, A., Howcroft, D., and Richardson, H. A Decade of Neglect: Reflecting on the Gender and IS Field," New Technology, Work and Employment, 19(3), 2005: 222-240.
3. Adkinson, W. F., Lenard, T. M., and Pickford, M. J. The Digital Economy Fact Book, 6th Ed., Washington D.C., The Progress and Freedom Foundation, 2004.
4. Avgerou, C., and Walsham, G. Information Technology in Context: Studies from the Perspective of Developing Countries, Ashgate Publishing, Aldershot, UK, 2000.
5. Avgerou, C. The Link Between ICT and Economic Growth in the Discourse of Development, in Organizational InformationSystems in the Context of Globalization, M. Korpela, R. Montealegre, and A. Poulymenakou (eds.), Kluwer Academic Publishers, Boston, 2003: 373-386.
6. Awasthi, V. N. Chow, C. W. and Wu, A. Cross-cultural Differences in the Behavioral Consequences of Imposing Performance Evaluation and Reward Systems: An Experimental Investigation, International Journal of Accounting, 36(3), 2001: 291-309.
7. Bada, A. O. Local Adaptation to Global Trends: A Study of an IT-Based Organizational Change Program in a Nigerian Bank," The Information Society, 18(2), 2002: 77-86.
8. Bakos Y. The Productivity Payoff of Computers, a Review of Computer Revolution: An Economic Perspective, Daniel E. Sichel Science, 52(3), 1998.
9. Baron, R. M. and Kenny, D. A. The Moderator-Mediator Variable Distinction in Social Psychological Research: Conceptual, Strategic, and Statistical Considerations, Journal of Personality and Social Psychology, 51(6), 1986: 1173-1182.
10. Bem, D. J. Belifes, Attitudes, and Human Affairs, Belmont, CA: Brook/Cole, 1970.
11. Barrell, R. and Pain, N. Foreign Direct Investment, Technological Change and Economic Growth within Europe, Economic Journal, 107(445), 1997: 1770–1786.

12. Bharadwaj Anandhi S., Sundar G. Bharadwaj, Benn R. Konsynski Information Technology Effects on Firm Performance as Measured by Tobin's Q. Management Science, 45(6), 1999.
13. Brett, J. M. Tinsiey, C. H. Janssens, M. Barsness Z. I. and Lytle A. L. New Approaches to the Study of Culture in Industrial/Organizational Psychology, In Eariey P.C., Erez M (Eds.), New Perspectives on Intemationai Industrial/Organizational Ssychology, San Francisco: New Lexington Press, 1997.
14. Brewster, C. Different Paradigms in Strategic HRM: Questions Raised by Comparative Research, in Wright, P. Dyer, L. Boudreau, J. and Milkovich, G. (eds) Research in Personnel and HRM. Supplement 4, Greenwich, CT: JAI Press, 1999.
15. Brynjolfsson, E. The Productivity Paradox of Information Technology, Communications of ACM, 36(12), 1993.
16. Brynjolfsson E. and Hitt, L. M. Paradox Lost? Firm Level Evidence on the Returns to Information Technology Spending, Management Science, 42(4), 1996.
17. Brynjolfsson E. and Yang, S. Information Technology and Productivity: A Review of the Literature, Advances in Computers, Academic Press, 43, 1996.
18. Bui, T. X. Sankaran, S. and Sebastian I. M. A Framework for Measuring National Readiness, International Journal of Electronic Business, 1(1), 2003: 3-22.
19. Coe, D.T. Helpman, E. and Hoffmaister, A. W. North-south R & D Spillovers, The Economic Journal, 107(440), 1997: 134–149.
20. Caselli, F. and Coleman II, W. J. Cross-country Technology Diffusion: The Case of Computers, The American Economic Review, 91(2), 2001.
21. D'Mello, M. Thinking Local, Acting Global: An Analysis of Identity Related Issues in a GSO in India, Research in Progress paper presented at the IFIP 9.4/8.2 Joint Conference on Organizational Information Systems in the Context of Globalization, 2003.
22. Dowlatshahi Shad and Cao Qing The Relationships among Virtual Enterprise, Information Technology and Business Performance in Sgile Manufacturing: An Industry Perspective, European Journal of Operational Research, 174 (2), 2006.
23. Dewan, S., and Kraemer, K.L. Information Technology and Productivity: Evidence from Country-level Data, Management Science 46, 4, 2000: 548–562.

24. Dowling, P. J. Welch, D. E. and Schuler, R. S. International Human Resource Management. Cincinnati, OH: South-Westem, 1999.
25. Dunkel, A. and Meierewert, S. Culture Standards and Their Impact on Teamwork– An Empirical Analysis of Austrian, German, Hungarian and Spanish Culture Differences, Journal for East European Management Studies, 2, 2004: 147-174.
26. Fang, X. and Rau, P-L. P. Culture Differences in Design of Portal Sites, Ergonomics, 46(1-3), 2003: 242-254.
27. Gerhart, B. and Fang, M. National Culture and Human Resource Management: Assumptions and Evidence, International Journal of Human Management, 16(6), 2005: 971-986.
28. Hanafizadeh, P. Khodabakhshi, M. and Hanafizadeh, M. R. Recommendations for E-business Development in Developing Countries: A Case Study of Iran, European and Mediterranean Conference on Information Systems 2008 (EMCIS 2008), May 25-26 2008, Dubai, UEA.
29. Huang, Shi-Ming, Qu Chin-Shyh, Chen Chyi-Miaw, Lin Binshan An Empirical Study of Relationship between IT Investment and Firms Performance: A Resource–based Perspective, European Journal of Operational Research, 173(3), 2006.
30. Herscovitch, L. and Meyer, J. P. Commitment to Organizational Change: Extension of a Three Component Model, Journal of Applied Psychology, 87, 2002: 474–487.
31. Hofstede, G. Neuijen, B. Ohayv, D. D. and Sanders, G. Measuring Organizational Cultures: A Qualitative and Quantitative Study across Twenty Cases, Administrative Science Quarterly, 35(2), 1990: 286-316.
32. Hofstede, G. Cultural Consequences: Comparing Values, Behaviors, Institutions, and Organizations across Nations, Second Edition, Sage Publication Inc., Thousand Oaks, California, USA, 2001.
33. Kennerley, M. and Andy, N. Evaluating the Impact of Information Technology on Business Performance, Presented at the Fifth International Conference of the European Operations Management Association, Trinity College, Dublin, Ireland, 1998.
34. Kluckhohn, C. Values and Value-orientation in Theory of Action: An Exploration in Definition and Classification, in T. Parsons & E. A. Shils (Eds.), Toward a General Theory of Action, Cambridge, MA, Harvard University Press, 1967.

35. Kohli Rajiv and Sarv Devaraj Measuring Information Technology Payoff: A Meta-Analysis of Structural Variables in Firm-Level Empirical Research, Information Systems Research, 14(2), 2003.

36. Kraemer, K. L. and Dedrick, J. Payoffs from Investment in Information Technology: Lessons from Asia-Pacific Region, World Development, 22, 1994: 1921–1931.

37. Kvasny, L. Cultural (Re) Production of Digital Inequality in a US Community Technology Initiative, Information, Communication & Society, 9(2), 2006: 160-181.

38. Liu, W., and Westrup, C. ICTs and Organizational Control across Cultures: The Case of a UK Multinational Operating in China, in Organizational Information Systems in the Context of Globalization, M. Korpela, R. Montealegre, and A. Poulymenakou (eds.), Kluwer Academic Publishers, Boston, 2003: 155-168.

39. Lubbe, S. Parker, G. and Hoard, A. The Profit Impact of IT Investment, Journal of Information Technology, 10, 1995: 44-51.

40. Macome, E. On the Implementation of an Information System in the Mozambican Context: The EDM Case, in Organizational Information Systems in the Context of Globalization, M. Korpela, R. Montealegre, and A. Poulymenakou (eds.), Kluwer Academic Publishers, Boston, 2003: 169-184.

41. Madon, S. The Internet and Socio-Economic Development: Exploring the Interaction, Information Technology and People, 13(2), 2000: 85-101.

42. Mahmood Adam, M. A. and Swanberg, D. L. Factors Effecting Information Technology Usage: A Meta-Analysis of the Empirical Literature, Journal of Organizational Computing and Electronic Commerce, 11(2), 2001: 107-130.

43. Meyer, J. P. Srinivas, E. S. Lal, J. B. and Topolnytsky, L. Employee Commitment and Support for an Organizational Change: Test of the Three-component Model inTwo Cultures, Journal of Occupational and Organizational Psychology, 80, 2007: 185–211.

44. Milne, R. S. Mechanistic and Organic Models of Public Administration in Developing Countries, Administrative Science Quarterely, 1970: 57-67.

45. Motohashi K. Firm Level Analysis of Information Network Use and Productivity in Japan, Comparative Analysis of Enterprise Data (CAED) Conference, London, 2003.

46. Mutula, S. M. and Brakel P. V. An evaluation of E-readiness Assessment Tools with Respect to Information Access: Towards an Integrated Information Rich Tool, International Journal of Information Management, 26(3), 2006: 212–223.

47. Pothukuchi, V. Damanpour, F. Choi, J. Chen, C. C. and Park, S. H. National and Organizational Culture Differences and International Joint Venture Performance, Journal of International Business Studies, 32(2), 2002: 243-265.

48. Robison, K. K. and Crenshaw, E. M. Post-industrial Transformations and Cyber-space: A Cross-national Analysis of Internet Development, Social Science Research, 31, 2002: 334–363.

49. Rossouw, G. J. Business Ethics in Developing Countries, Business Ethics Quarterely, 4(1), 1994: 43-51.

50. Ryan, A. M. Chang, D. Ployhart, R. E. and Slade, L. A. Employee Attitude Surveys in a Multinational Organization: Considering Language and Culture in Assessing Measurement Equivalence, Personnel Psychology, 52, 1999: 37-58.

51. Saad, M. and Zawdie, G. From Technology Transfer to the Emergence of a Triple Helix Culture: The Experience of Algeria in Innovation and Technological Capability Development, Technology Analysis and Strategic Management, 17(1), 2005: 89–103.

52. Salter, S. B. and Sharp, D. J. Agency Effects and Escalation of Commitment Do Small National Culture Differences Matter? International Journal of Accounting, 36(1), 2001: 33-45.

53. Sayed, E. H., and Westrup, C. Egypt and ICTs Bring National Initiatives, Global Actors and Local Companies Together, Information Technology and People (16:1), 2003: 93-110.

54. Sen, A. Development as Freedom, Oxford University Press, Oxford, UK, 1999.

55. Shih, E. Kraemer, K. L. and Dedrick, J. IT Diffusion in Developing Countries, Communications of the ACM, 51(2), February 2008: 43-48.

56. Shih, E. Kraemer, K. L. and Dedrick, J. Research Note: Determinants of Country-level Investment in Information Technology, Management Science, 53(3), 2007: 521–528.

57. Shoib, G. M., and Nandhakumar, J. Cross-Cultural IS Adoption in Multinational Corporations: A Study of Rationality, in Organizational Information Systems in the

Context of Globalization, M. Korpela, R. Montealegre, and A. Poulymenakou (eds.), Kluwer Academic Publishers, Boston, 2003:435-454.

58. Silva, L., and Figueroa, E. B. Institutional Intervention and the Expansion of ICTs in Latin America: The Case of Chile, Information Technology and People, 15(1), 2002: pp. 8-25.

59. Smith Howard, L. Bullers, W. I. and Piland, N. F. Does Information Technology Make Difference in Healthcare Organization Performance? Hospital Topics: Research and Perspectives on Healthcare, 78(2), 2000.

60. Spony, G. The Development of a Work-value Model Assessing the Cumulative Impact of Individual and Cultural Differences on Managers' Work-value Systems: Empirical Evidence from French and British Managers, International Journal of Human Resource Management, 14(4), 2003: 658-679.

61. Trice, H. M. and J. M. Beyer The Cultures of Work Organizations, Englewood Cliffs, NJ: Prentice Hall, 1993.

62. United Nations Development Program (UNDP) Human Development Report 2001: Making New Technologies Work for Human Development, Oxford University Press, New York, 2001.

63. Walsham, G. Making a World of Difference: IT in a Global Context, Wiley, Chichester, UK, 2001.

64. Walsham, G. Cross-Cultural Software Production and Use: A Structurational Analysis, MIS Quarterly, (26:4), 2002: pp. 359-380.

65. Walsham, G. Robey, D. Sahay, S. Forwadr: Special issue on Information Systems in Developing Countries, MIS Quarterly, 31(2), 2007: 317-326.

66. World Bank Group, Information and Communication Technologies: A World Bank Group Strategy, Washington D.C., 2002.

H11a	Supported	H11b	Supported
H12a	Supported	H12b	Not Supported
H13a	Not Supported	H13b	Supported
H14a	Not Supported	H14b	Supported
H15a	Not Supported	H15b	Supported
H21a	Supported	H21b	Supported
H22a	Supported	H22b	Supported
H23a	Supported	H23b	Supported
H24a	Not Supported	H24b	Supported
H25a	Not Supported	H25b	Supported
H31a	Supported	H31b	Supported
H32a	Supported	H32b	Supported
H33a	Supported	H33b	Supported
H34a	Not Supported	H34b	Supported
H35a	Not Supported	H35b	Supported
H41a	Supported	H41b	Supported
H42a	Supported	H42b	Supported
H43a	Supported	H43b	Supported
H44a	Not Supported	H44b	Supported
H45a	Not Supported	H45b	Supported
H51a	Supported	H51b	Supported
H52a	Supported	H52b	Not Supported
H53a	Not Supported	H53b	Not Supported
H54a	Not Supported	H54b	Supported
H55a	Not Supported	H55b	Supported
H1am	Supported	H1bm	Supported

Fuzzy Partitioning and Its Application to Reservoir Operation Problem (A Multistage Approach Using Markov Chain)

AMROLAH AMINI (Ph.D)

Associate Professor, Allameh Tabatabaei University (ATU), Tehran, Iran.

aminij@atu.ac.ir

ALIREZA EMAMI

Master of Science, Tehran University, Tehran, Iran

memami@alumni.ut.ac.ir

MOSTAFA EMAMI*

Master of Science, Michigan Technological University (MTU)

memami@mtu.edu

*Corresponding Address

Applied Research and Technology Office, Michigan Technological University

1400 Townsend Dr, Houghton, MI 49931

Tel & Fax : +1-(816) 237-0018

E-mail: memami@mtu.edu

Abstract

This paper investigates mathematical models on reservoir operation problem and provides a fuzzy model based on the Markov Chain time series for Karkheh dam in Iran. Based on fuzzy partitioning of monthly streamflows, that are calculated by time series, a Markovian forecasting model is developed. A deterministic and a stochastic dynamic programming model are formulated for the problem. The goals are formulated with weighting priorities and the optimal reservoir operation is determined. Using the results of an example and historical data, the performance of the dam is simulated. Results of the simulation clearly show that the proposed stochastic fuzzy model outperforms the deterministic model.

Key words: Fuzzy partitioning, Dynamic programming, Markov chain time series, Reservoir operation.

1. Introduction

After word war II, several mathematical techniques are developed to determine the optimal utilization of reservoirs. Introducing sequential programming algorithm by Little in 50's and developing dynamic programming models facilitated the process of modeling for the operation of reservoirs [7,5]. The aim of designing such kind of models is to determine an optimal policy for a limited or even unlimited period of time. **Nearly, all of the optimization methods classified as either deterministic or stochastic. Deterministic methods use "perfect foresight" of future inflows, while the stochastic methods incorporate stochastic models of inflows directly in the optimization process and consider multiple scenarios. Most of these methods were developed based on control theory such as deterministic feedback control and OR (such as deterministic/stochastic dynamic/linear programming, mixed integer programming and multiobjective programming [3.** Most of researches used the average historical monthly stream flows and analyzed them by ARIMA models or Markov Chains.

Because of limited number of historical data for given month over several years, classified historical data and its frequency distribution can not represent the actual behavior of streamflow's. This problem is more serious when the new data for updating a grouped frequency distribution locates on the border of a group. Consequently, the parameters of new frequency distributions are meaningfully different from the samples.

This paper applies fuzzy partitioning in place of classical frequency distribution. Using historical data, a deterministic and a stochastic model for Karkheh reservoir are developed.

2. Fuzzy Partitioning and Markovian Models

Fuzzy sets theory is a powerful tool for more realistic analysis of the behavior of the human and the nature. Fuzzy theory changes the classic logical mathematical structure to a structure with logical continuous values [6]. The idea of fuzzy partitioning stems from fuzzy sets theory. A fuzzy partition includes a given number of fuzzy sets. Each set in turn includes individual elements. These type of fuzzy sets named extreme profiles. For each element related to each extreme profile, there are a number of grades of membership. Based on the definitions of Manton, Woodbury, and Tolley, fuzzy partitioning has the following features [4]:

- For each element in a fuzzy set, there is a Grade of Membership score (denoted as g_{ik}) that represents the degree to which the element i belongs to the jth sets.

  - In order to have a fuzzy partition with k fuzzy sets (extreme profiles) over the set including all elements of i, the following terms should be valid:

$$g_{ik} \geq 0 \quad for\,each\,element\,of\,i\,and\,fuzzy\,set\,k \qquad (1)$$

$$\sum_k g_{ik} = 1 \quad for\,each\,element\,of\,i\,\,and\,\,overall\,fuzzy\,sets \qquad (2)$$

$g_{ik} = 0$ denotes the ith element is not a member of the kth fuzzy set, $g_{ik} = 1$ denotes complete membership of the ith element in the kth fuzzy set, and $0 < g_{ik} < 1$ denotes a relative membership of the ith element in the kth fuzzy set. If $g_{ik} = 0\ or\ 1$, we have a partition that is introduced in classical sets theory.

There are several applications for partitioning in mathematics. In classical statistics, partitioning idea is used to form a grouped frequency when a lot of data or observations exists. In practice, frequency of a group of data obtains by counting the elements of that group in order to estimate population parameters. In statistics based on the fuzzy partitioning, this estimations can be implemented by using grades of membership. The advantage of this kind of frequency calculation is its better representation of the effects of the real data that are located on the borders of groups. Comparing to the classical frequency distribution and specially for a small size of samples, fuzzy frequency distribution is smoother.

Suppose X_n denotes the elements of time series for monthly streamflows. Then, all observations for the j th month of a year can be defined as

$$A_j = \{X_i \mid i = 12m + j \;\; m = 1, 2, ...\} \qquad (3)$$

If all observations for the jth month locate between interval $\left[X_{j\,min}, X_{j\,max}\right]$, the interval can be divided into a number of cross groups. The membership function of each element relative to each group can be shown as figure 1:

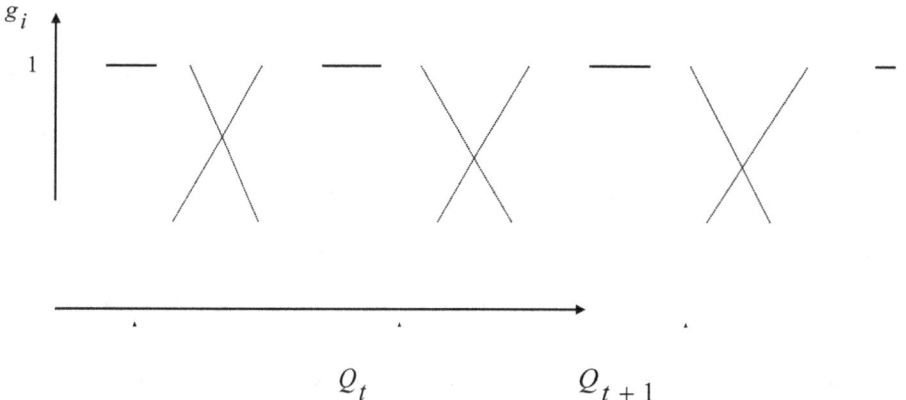

Figure 1: Grade of membership of observations for overlapped groups

The fuzzy statistical model developed by Manton, Woodbury, and Tolley considers five assumptions [4]. The fourth and the fifth assumptions are:

- **Assumption 4**: The probability of a response l for the jth question by the individual with kth extreme profile is λ_{kjl} (where $\lambda_{kjl} \geq 0$ and $\sum_i \lambda_{kjl} = 1$. It is supposed that at least one, possibly theoretical, individual exists in the kth profile).

- **Assumption 5**: The probability of a response of level l to the jth question by individual i, conditional on the g_{ik} scores, is given by the bilinear form $P_{ijl} = \sum_k \lambda_{kjl} g_{ik}$.

If the question be "does the element belong to *jth* extreme profile?" and it has two possible answers "yes" or "not", then for "yes", $\lambda_{kjl} \neq 0 = 1$ where $k = j$. Therefor, the probability "the *ith* element being a member of *jth* extreme profile" will be $P_{ijl} = g_{ij}$. Partitioning all sets of A_J (the historical data for *jth* month), time series for streamflows can be considered as Markov chain and it would be possible to calculate point estimation of transition probabilities. These are similar to typical conditional probabilities used in reservoir operation models.

For time series X_n, consider fuzzy partition A_j with related fuzzy sets A_{jk}. Let transition probability from partition A_{jk} to partition $A_{(j+1)l}$ be P^j_{kl}. If we select a element of A_J, X_i, randomly and $X_{i+1} \in A_{(j+1)}$ be the next historical data, then

$$P(X_i \in A_{jk}) = g_{ik} \text{ and } P(X_{i+1} \in A_{(j+1)l}) = g_{(j+1)l} \quad (5)$$
$$P(X_i \in A_{jk}, X_{i+1} \in A_{(j+1)l}) = g_{ik} g_{(j+1)l} \quad (6)$$

where g_{ik} and $g_{(j+1)l}$ denote the grades of membership for elements X_i and X_{i+1} of extreme profiles A_{jk} and $A_{(j+1)l}$. Point estimation of transition probability from *k*th level of *jth* month to *l*th level of $(j+1)$, P^j_{kl}, can be estimated as:

$$P^j_{kl} = P(A_{(j+1)l} | A_{jk}) = \frac{P(A_{(j+1)l} \cap A_{jk})}{P(A_{jk})} = \frac{E(P(X_i \in A_{jk}, X_{i+1} \in A_{(j+1)l}))}{E(P(X_i \in A_{jk}))}$$
$$= \frac{\left(\sum_i g_{(j+1)l} g_{ik}\right)/N}{\left(\sum_i g_{ik}\right)/N} = \frac{\sum_i g_{ik} g_{(j+1)l}}{\sum_i g_{ik}} \quad (7)$$

It should be reminder that in the above equation the sum is over all elements (*i's*). Now, it is possible to calculate conditional probabilities and apply them to the model.

3. The Model

Karkheh river stem from the western mountains of Iran. After going through Khouzestan province, it ends at Hourolazim area. The objectives of Karkheh reservoir, that is in the west of Andimeshk city, are:

- To prepare about 3.3 billions cubic meter water for about 320000 hectare farm lands.
- Power (energy) generation about 934 gigabits (400 megawatt).
- To control the destructive flood water.
- To prepare the required water for about 40000 hectare and transferring it by tunnel to the Dasht-e Abbas lands.

Historical streamflow data exist for 40 years. They range from 20 to 1320 cubic meter. Analyzing data, it concluded that the streamflows consist of two components as follows:

$$Q_t = S_t + X_t \qquad (8)$$

where Q_t, S_t and X_t denote natural streamflows, the average of streamflows for a given month over 40 years, and the deviations from the averages, respectively. Time series analysis shows that X_t has a tail of self-coefficient as shown in figure 2 and based on Box-Pierce test, a process of AR(1), Markov process is suited for it.

Figure 2: tail of self-coefficient

By estimating least square errors in terms of parameters, the regress process will be as $X_t = 0.57715 X_{t-1}$. Thus, using grouped data, it would be possible to define time series by Markov chain. For each month over years and based on the fuzzy partitioning, we can classify data as follows:

$$g_{ik} = \begin{cases} \dfrac{X_i - (100k - 120)}{40} & (100k - 120) < X_i < (100k - 80) \\ 1 & (100k - 80) \leq X_i \leq (100k - 20) \\ \dfrac{(100k + 20) - X_i}{40} & (100k - 20) \leq X_i \leq (100k + 20) \end{cases} \quad (9)$$

Based on the definitions, the length of each class is 140 units and there are 40 units overlap for each pair of classes. Each data belongs at least to one class and maximum to two classes (with a grade of membership value greater than 0). Transitional probabilities between different classes and for sequential months can be calculated by $\dfrac{\sum_i g_{ik} g_{(j+1)i}}{\sum_i g_{ik}}$

. The sequential structure for the reservoir operation model can be shown as follow:

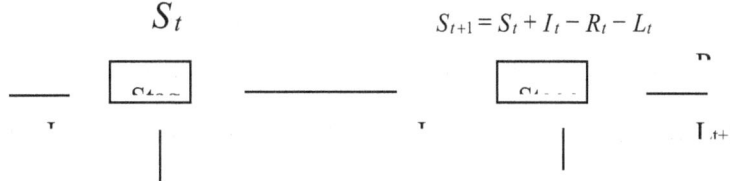

The relations and the constraints are as follows:
1. the upper and the lower limits for the volume of water in reservoir are

$$S_{Min} \leq S_t \leq S_{Max} \quad (10)$$

2. the continuity equation that expresses changes in the volume of water in reservoir is

$$S_{t+1} = S_t + I_t - R_t - L_t \quad (11)$$

3. empty space that should always exist in reservoir in order to control probable destructive flood water in the future is

$$S_t \leq S_{t\,Max} - S_{con} \quad (12)$$

4. the relation for the power and the energy in power station where $H > H_{Min}$ is

$$K = \dfrac{9.81 \times Q H \varepsilon}{3600} \quad (13)$$

Respect to the objectives, priorities, and constraints, a cost function with several components and different weights can be defined[3]. In cost function, R_{t1} and R_{t2} denote the released volume of water to the lands at the lower section of the dam to the

Dasht-e Abbas lands, respectively. When the water level is higher than minimum, required water flows through tunnel and otherwise the flow stops. I_t and L_t denote the imported and steaming water to and from the lake that is at the back of the dam. In order to avoid flooding water at the lower lands, constraint $R_{t1} \leq R_{Max}$ is added and in order to avoid flooding water in 11th and 12th months of Iran (middle of February-middle of march) constraints $S_t \leq S_{Max} - S_{control}$ is added and

$$F_1(t) = \begin{cases} M^3 \times Min\{(R_{Max} - R_{t1}), 0\} + 0.1 \times M^3 \times Min\{(S_{Max} - S_{control} - S_t), 0\} & if\ t = 11,12 \\ M^3 \times Min\{(R_{Max} - R_{t1}), 0\} & otherwise \end{cases}$$

0.1 is based on the probability of having a flood water. If the required space in reservoir is not enough to control it, the costs will be huge. R_{Max} is the maximum volume that can be directed to the river per month (1000 cubic meter per second and 2.592 billions cubic meter per month). $S_{Max} = 7.5$ billion cubic meters. Since the biggest number of streamflows over last 40 years is 1311 cubic meters per second and in order to control the water that is more than 1000 cubic meter per second, $S_{control} = 75$ million cubic meters are determined. To supply enough water for lower lands $R_{t1} \geq Q_{t1}$ and for Dasht-e Abbas, $R_{t2} = Q_{t2}$ if $H_t > H_{Min}$. Also

$$F_2(t) = \begin{cases} M^2 \times Min\{(R_{t1} - Q_{t1}), 0\} - M^2 \times R_{t2} & if\ H_t < H_{Min} \\ M^2 \times Min\{(R_{t1} - Q_{t1}), 0\} & otherwise \end{cases}$$

where Q_{t1}, Q_{t2} denote the required water for the lower lands and for Dasht-e Abbas. To prevent extinguishing in power station and to utilize full capacity, we defined $H_t > H_{Min}$, $H_t R_{t1} \geq (H_t \times R_{t1})_{Min}$ and

$$F_3(t) = \begin{cases} -M \times R_{operate} & if\ H_t < H_{Min} \\ M \times R_{operate} \times Min\left\{\left(\frac{H_t \times R_{t1}}{(H_t \times R_{t1})_{Min}} - 1\right), 0\right\} & otherwise \end{cases}$$

where H_t and H_{Min} denote the height from turbine to water level and the height from the minimum allowed level to turbine. R_{opeate} is the minimum volume of water required for the operation of turbine, that is about 150 cubic meter per second.

Finally, the total costs function can be formulated by sum of the above mentioned costs:
$$F(t) = F_1(t) + F_2(t) + F_3(t)$$
In addition, the continuity equation of reservoir is
$$S_{t+1} = S_t + I_t - R_{t1} - R_{t2} - L_t(S_t)$$
In dynamic model for reservoir operation, the state of the system in each stage is determined by the volume of water in reservoir at the beginning of the month, (S_t), and the average streamflow of the latest month, (I_{t-1}). Volume of water is separated into 50 stages and the average streamflow for the latest month is partitioned as shown in figure 1.

Using the forecasting relation and having streamflows for the latest month in deterministic case, the streamflows for a given period in the future can be estimated. Solving the model, the optimal policy for current stage can be determined. The regress relation for deterministic dynamic model is :

$$f_n^*(S_n) = Opt_i \{c(S_n, X_{ni}) + f_{n+1}^*(S_{n+1})\}$$

where

S_n: the position of stage n,
X_{ni}: various decisions in stage n (released water)
$c(S_n, X_{ni})$: the additional costs of stage n because of making decision X_{ni}
f^*: minimum costs from the current stage to the next stages.

Supposing $S_{12} = S_0$ as annual equilibrium performance equation, we analyzed the deterministic dynamic model to obtain the optimal policies $TG(j, S_t, I_{t-1})$ for the first state of $0(S_t, I_{t-1})$ and the jth month. For stochastic model, the backward method with infinite stages is used so that the optimal policy for each month over years be only depended on the first state (S_t, I_{t-1}). The recursive relation for stochastic dynamic model can be explained as

$$f_t^*(S_t, I_{t-1}) = Opti_{st} \left\{ \sum_k Pr(I_t = ik \mid I_{t-1} = it_{-1}) \left[c(S_t, I_t) + f_{t+1}^*(S_{t+1}, I_t) \right] \right\}$$

In this model, we used conditional probability for a given streamflow. It is also assumed that the streamflow for current month is unknown. For sample problem, the latest relation is applied in order to determine optimal policies in terms of the first state, (S_t, I_{t-1}) and each month in the form of $TG(j, S_t, I_{t-1})$ [1].

Pair comparison of results of deterministic and stochastic models is implemented for four possible situations and for different months, separately. The results are as table 1. Measurement unit is 10 cubic meter per second. In table 1, S denotes the result of the stochastic model is meaningfully less than the deterministic model and D means the result of the deterministic model is meaningfully less than the stochastic model. The results show that except for 12th month, stochastic model proposed less released water for lower lands. In 12th month, only for the situation with huge volume of water, it suggested more released water for lower lands.

Table 1. d1, d2, d3, d4 denote the deviations for four situations. $\left(\frac{1}{3}S\,Max < S_t < \frac{2}{3}S\,Max\right)$ is for the normal situation of the reservoir, $\left(S_t < \frac{1}{3}S\,Max\right)$ is for the situation that reservoir is relatively empty, and $\left(S_t > \frac{2}{3}S\,Max\right)$ when reservoir is relatively full. CI1, Ci2, CI3, CI4 are confidence intervals, separately.

4. Simulating of the Performance

Having the historical data and the proposal policies that are suggested by two models, it is possible to simulate the performance of the reservoir respect to each of two model frameworks. Supposing equilibrium situation as first state, the results are

1. figure 3 shows changes in volume of water in reservoir. In figure 3, the scale for volume of reservoir is million cubic meters per month and the goals for supplied volume of required water and supplied level of power generation are not scaled because they are expressed by ratios. It is clear that for years that the average streamflow's are less than 178 cubic meters per second, for a relatively long period we have a low water situation. Comparing to the deterministic model, the stochastic model provides fewer number of months in which the water of the reservoir are less than the minimum level (1100 millions cubic meter). Because of inadequacy of water in

reservoir, the stochastic model for 0.39% of months and the deterministic model for 2.09% of months could not supply considered policies successfully.

2. figure 3 shows the degree of success in supplying water to lower lands. This degree is equal to 1 when the volume of released water is greater than the required volume and otherwise it is equal to the ratio of released volume to the required volume. The result shows that the stochastic model outperforms deterministic model in terms of supplying required water to lower lands. The degree of success is 95.67% for the stochastic model and 94.40% for the deterministic model. In stochastic model, lack of water for Dasht-e Abbas is about 44 months. This number for the deterministic model is 76 months.

3. goal achievement degree for the power generation objective is as figure 3. The rates are 78.3% and 77.1% for the stochastic and the deterministic models, respectively.

4. both of the models are successful in controlling flood water. However, the stochastic model for 2 months and the deterministic model for 7 months could not satisfy the volume of water that is required to control flood water.

5. the last section of figure 4 explains the damages creates by implementing each of the models over 40 years. It is estimated by costs equation. The results show the better results of the stochastic model.

For the defuzzification, if membership degree of the last streamflow for both of conjoining partitions are greater than zero, then the weighted average of the optimal policies for two stages (with weights g_{ij}) would be the optimal policy[2].

Figure 3: Simulation of system performance over 40 years

5. Summary and Final Remarks

This paper provides a fuzzy model based on the Markov Chain time series for Karkheh dam in Iran. Using fuzzy partitioning of monthly streamflows, a Markovian forecasting model is developed. A deterministic and a stochastic dynamic programming model formulated for the problem. The goals formulated by weighting priorities and the optimal utilization policy for reservoir operation are determined. Using the results of the historical data, performance of the dam is simulated. The results of simulation clearly show that the proposed stochastic fuzzy model outperforms the deterministic model.

References

1] Goulter, I.C. and T.F. Tai, " Practical Implication in the Use of Stochastic Dynamic Programming for Reservoir Operation", *Water Resource Bulletin*, **21(1)** (1985).

2] Hellendar T. C., "Defuzzification in Fuzzy Controllers. *Journal of Intelligent & Fuzzy Systems*, **1** (1993).

3] Liang, Q., J.E. Johnson, and Y.S. Yu," A Comparison of two Methods for Multi-objective Optimization for Reservoir Operation", *Water Resources Research* **32(2)** (1996).

4] Loucks, D.P, J.R. Stedinger, and D.A. Haith: *Water Resource Systems Planning and Analysis*.

5] Manton, K.G., M.A. Woodbury, and H.D. Tolley, " *Statistical Applications Using Fuzzy Sets",* (John Wiley and Sons Inc, 1994).

6] Russ, C., JR Philbrick. and Peter K. Kitanidis, " Limitation of Deterministic Optimization Applied to Reservoir Operations ", *Journal of Water Resource Planning and Management*, Vol. 125, No. 3, May/June 1999

7] Srinivasan, K., T.R. Neelakantan, P. Shyam and C. Nagarajukumar,"Mixed Integer Programming Model for Reservoir Performance Optimization", *Journal of Water Resource Planning and Management,* Vol. 125, No. 5, September/October 1999.

8] Yakowitz, S.," Dynamic Programming Applications in Water Resources", *Water*

Resources Research, **18(4)** (1982).

9] Zimmermann H.J., " Fuzzy Set Theory and Its Applications", (Kluwer-Nijhoff
   Publishing, U.S.A. 1984).

Data for correlation (Figure 1):

```
R  1 = 0.578314  R  2 = 0.344063  R  3 = 0.185205  R  4 = 0.120522
R  5 = 0.071443  R  6 = 0.064037  R  7 = 0.067507  R  8 = 0.074338
R  9 = 0.066849  R 10 = 0.025816  R 11 =-0.003563  R 12 =-0.015977
R 13 =-0.024574  R 14 =-0.029448  R 15 =-0.024639  R 16 = 0.004657
R 17 =-0.001900  R 18 = 0.005806  R 19 = 0.004404  R 20 = 0.018125
R 21 = 0.028357  R 22 = 0.056226  R 23 = 0.049984  R 24 = 0.086548
R 25 = 0.056058  R 26 =-0.009630  R 27 = 0.012722  R 28 = 0.011476
R 29 = 0.011090  R 30 =-0.004914  R 31 =-0.001412  R 32 =-0.006618
R 33 =-0.026942  R 34 =-0.044355  R 35 = 0.020685  R 36 = 0.069586
R 37 = 0.078238  R 38 = 0.077716  R 39 = 0.061032  R 40 = 0.036512
R 41 = 0.032298  R 42 = 0.020875  R 43 = 0.032662  R 44 = 0.051041
R 45 = 0.085626  R 46 = 0.038821  R 47 = 0.006151  R 48 =-0.044925
R 49 =-0.002385  R 50 = 0.036220  R 51 = 0.004164  R 52 = 0.014925
R 53 = 0.005398  R 54 = 0.003371  R 55 =-0.012587  R 56 = 0.032650
R 57 = 0.060729  R 58 = 0.077244  R 59 = 0.060658  R 60 = 0.117916
R 61 = 0.067077  R 62 = 0.092546  R 63 = 0.029697  R 64 = 0.040126
R 65 = 0.029309  R 66 = 0.032343  R 67 = 0.024963  R 68 = 0.042004
R 69 = 0.092632  R 70 = 0.130166  R 71 = 0.165116  R 72 = 0.126487
R 73 = 0.061133  R 74 = 0.023336  R 75 = 0.001024  R 76 =-0.013698
R 77 =-0.016145  R 78 =-0.000277  R 79 = 0.018572  R 80 = 0.047485
R 81 = 0.053345  R 82 = 0.067391  R 83 = 0.011743  R 84 = 0.005877
R 85 = 0.022665  R 86 = 0.023131  R 87 = 0.062286  R 88 = 0.043864
R 89 = 0.035629  R 90 =-0.000174  R 91 =-0.010657  R 92 =-0.002439
R 93 = 0.006555  R 94 =-0.041644  R 95 =-0.006200  R 96 =-0.046677
R 97 =-0.080152  R 98 =-0.054018  R 99 =-0.055997  R100 =-0.034990
```

Data for deterministic dynamic programming model:

```
S_ 1_ 2= 5771.2  OP=1.0  OV=0  REL=1.000  EL=0.000  DAB=0.0  COST=  1944.000
S_ 1_ 3= 5580.9  OP=1.0  OV=0  REL=1.000  EL=1.000  DAB=0.0  COST=     0.000
S_ 1_ 4= 5234.7  OP=1.0  OV=0  REL=1.000  EL=1.000  DAB=0.0  COST=     0.000
S_ 1_ 5= 4880.2  OP=1.0  OV=0  REL=1.000  EL=1.000  DAB=0.0  COST=    45.000
S_ 1_ 6= 4489.8  OP=1.0  OV=0  REL=1.000  EL=1.000  DAB=0.0  COST=    75.000
S_ 1_ 7= 4276.4  OP=1.0  OV=0  REL=1.000  EL=1.000  DAB=0.0  COST=   105.000
S_ 1_ 8= 4087.7  OP=1.0  OV=0  REL=1.000  EL=1.000  DAB=0.0  COST=   135.000
S_ 1_ 9= 4036.3  OP=1.0  OV=0  REL=1.000  EL=1.000  DAB=0.0  COST=   135.000
S_ 1_10= 4037.1  OP=1.0  OV=0  REL=1.000  EL=1.000  DAB=0.0  COST=   150.000
S_ 1_11= 3955.0  OP=1.0  OV=0  REL=1.000  EL=1.000  DAB=0.0  COST=   150.000
S_ 1_12= 3946.6  OP=1.0  OV=0  REL=1.000  EL=1.000  DAB=0.0  COST=   150.000
S_ 2_ 1= 4153.3  OP=1.0  OV=0  REL=1.000  EL=1.000  DAB=0.0  COST=   135.000
```

```
S_  2_  2=  4419.5   OP=1.0   OV=0   REL=1.000   EL=1.000   DAB=0.0   COST=       120.000
S_  2_  3=  4318.1   OP=1.0   OV=0   REL=1.000   EL=1.000   DAB=0.0   COST=       105.000
S_  2_  4=  3976.6   OP=1.0   OV=0   REL=1.000   EL=1.000   DAB=0.0   COST=       135.000
S_  2_  5=  3618.5   OP=1.0   OV=0   REL=1.000   EL=1.000   DAB=0.0   COST=       165.000
S_  2_  6=  3247.7   OP=1.0   OV=0   REL=1.000   EL=1.000   DAB=0.0   COST=       210.000
S_  2_  7=  3006.2   OP=1.0   OV=0   REL=1.000   EL=1.000   DAB=0.0   COST=       240.000
S_  2_  8=  2708.1   OP=1.0   OV=0   REL=1.000   EL=1.000   DAB=0.0   COST=       255.000
S_  2_  9=  2529.3   OP=1.0   OV=0   REL=1.000   EL=1.000   DAB=0.0   COST=       285.000
S_  2_10=  2581.4   OP=1.0   OV=0   REL=1.000   EL=1.000   DAB=0.0   COST=       285.000
S_  2_11=  2578.9   OP=1.0   OV=0   REL=1.000   EL=1.000   DAB=0.0   COST=       285.000
S_  2_12=  2744.9   OP=1.0   OV=0   REL=1.000   EL=1.000   DAB=0.0   COST=       285.000
S_  3_  1=  3137.9   OP=1.0   OV=0   REL=1.000   EL=1.000   DAB=0.0   COST=       255.000
S_  3_  2=  3449.7   OP=1.0   OV=0   REL=1.000   EL=1.000   DAB=0.0   COST=       210.000
S_  3_  3=  3250.5   OP=1.0   OV=0   REL=1.000   EL=1.000   DAB=0.0   COST=       210.000
S_  3_  4=  2972.4   OP=1.0   OV=0   REL=1.000   EL=1.000   DAB=0.0   COST=       240.000
S_  3_  5=  2672.7   OP=1.0   OV=0   REL=1.000   EL=1.000   DAB=0.0   COST=       270.000
S_  3_  6=  2281.8   OP=1.0   OV=0   REL=1.000   EL=1.000   DAB=0.0   COST=       300.000
S_  3_  7=  2016.5   OP=1.0   OV=0   REL=1.000   EL=1.000   DAB=0.0   COST=       330.000
S_  3_  8=  1676.9   OP=1.0   OV=0   REL=1.000   EL=1.000   DAB=0.0   COST=       360.000
S_  3_  9=  1412.6   OP=1.0   OV=0   REL=1.000   EL=0.096   DAB=0.0   COST=       577.572
S_  3_10=  1267.5   OP=1.0   OV=0   REL=1.000   EL=0.288   DAB=0.0   COST=       980.451
S_  3_11=  1242.7   OP=1.0   OV=0   REL=1.000   EL=0.461   DAB=0.0   COST=      1316.712
S_  3_12=  1661.2   OP=1.0   OV=0   REL=1.000   EL=0.262   DAB=0.0   COST=       915.251
S_  4_  1=  2755.9   OP=1.0   OV=0   REL=1.000   EL=1.000   DAB=0.0   COST=       330.000
S_  4_  2=  4431.6   OP=1.0   OV=0   REL=1.000   EL=1.000   DAB=0.0   COST=       180.000
S_  4_  3=  4948.3   OP=1.0   OV=0   REL=1.000   EL=1.000   DAB=0.0   COST=        75.000
S_  4_  4=  4754.6   OP=1.0   OV=0   REL=1.000   EL=1.000   DAB=0.0   COST=        60.000
S_  4_  5=  4508.5   OP=1.0   OV=0   REL=1.000   EL=1.000   DAB=0.0   COST=        75.000
S_  4_  6=  4196.4   OP=1.0   OV=0   REL=1.000   EL=1.000   DAB=0.0   COST=       105.000
S_  4_  7=  4031.9   OP=1.0   OV=0   REL=1.000   EL=1.000   DAB=0.0   COST=       135.000
S_  4_  8=  3977.2   OP=1.0   OV=0   REL=1.000   EL=1.000   DAB=0.0   COST=       150.000
S_  4_  9=  4211.1   OP=1.0   OV=0   REL=1.000   EL=1.000   DAB=0.0   COST=       135.000
S_  4_10=  4235.6   OP=1.0   OV=0   REL=1.000   EL=1.000   DAB=0.0   COST=       120.000
S_  4_11=  4421.5   OP=1.0   OV=0   REL=1.000   EL=1.000   DAB=0.0   COST=       120.000
S_  4_12=  4690.1   OP=1.0   OV=0   REL=1.000   EL=1.000   DAB=0.0   COST=        90.000
S_  5_  1=  4810.0   OP=1.0   OV=0   REL=1.000   EL=1.000   DAB=0.0   COST=        75.000
S_  5_  2=  4628.3   OP=1.0   OV=0   REL=1.000   EL=1.000   DAB=0.0   COST=        75.000
S_  5_  3=  4410.1   OP=1.0   OV=0   REL=1.000   EL=1.000   DAB=0.0   COST=        90.000
S_  5_  4=  4010.6   OP=1.0   OV=0   REL=1.000   EL=1.000   DAB=0.0   COST=       120.000
S_  5_  5=  3603.3   OP=1.0   OV=0   REL=1.000   EL=1.000   DAB=0.0   COST=       165.000
S_  5_  6=  3200.8   OP=1.0   OV=0   REL=1.000   EL=1.000   DAB=0.0   COST=       210.000
S_  5_  7=  2939.1   OP=1.0   OV=0   REL=1.000   EL=1.000   DAB=0.0   COST=       240.000
S_  5_  8=  2608.8   OP=1.0   OV=0   REL=1.000   EL=1.000   DAB=0.0   COST=       270.000
S_  5_  9=  2627.6   OP=1.0   OV=0   REL=1.000   EL=1.000   DAB=0.0   COST=       285.000
S_  5_10=  2519.5   OP=1.0   OV=0   REL=1.000   EL=1.000   DAB=0.0   COST=       285.000
S_  5_11=  2370.3   OP=1.0   OV=0   REL=1.000   EL=1.000   DAB=0.0   COST=       300.000
S_  5_12=  2318.8   OP=1.0   OV=0   REL=1.000   EL=1.000   DAB=0.0   COST=       315.000
S_  6_  1=  3507.7   OP=1.0   OV=0   REL=1.000   EL=1.000   DAB=0.0   COST=       255.000
S_  6_  2=  3799.0   OP=1.0   OV=0   REL=1.000   EL=1.000   DAB=0.0   COST=       180.000
S_  6_  3=  3680.2   OP=1.0   OV=0   REL=1.000   EL=1.000   DAB=0.0   COST=       165.000
S_  6_  4=  3372.5   OP=1.0   OV=0   REL=1.000   EL=1.000   DAB=0.0   COST=       195.000
S_  6_  5=  3057.7   OP=1.0   OV=0   REL=1.000   EL=1.000   DAB=0.0   COST=       225.000
S_  6_  6=  2660.3   OP=1.0   OV=0   REL=1.000   EL=1.000   DAB=0.0   COST=       255.000
S_  6_  7=  2397.8   OP=1.0   OV=0   REL=1.000   EL=1.000   DAB=0.0   COST=       300.000
S_  6_  8=  2086.6   OP=1.0   OV=0   REL=1.000   EL=1.000   DAB=0.0   COST=       330.000
S_  6_  9=  1855.5   OP=1.0   OV=0   REL=1.000   EL=0.054   DAB=0.0   COST=       450.427
S_  6_10=  1758.7   OP=1.0   OV=0   REL=1.000   EL=1.000   DAB=0.0   COST=       360.000
S_  6_11=  1552.9   OP=1.0   OV=0   REL=1.000   EL=0.021   DAB=0.0   COST=       416.203
S_  6_12=  1325.7   OP=1.0   OV=0   REL=1.000   EL=0.115   DAB=0.0   COST=       627.844
S_  7_  1=  1174.6   OP=1.0   OV=0   REL=1.000   EL=1.000   DAB=0.0   COST=       420.000
S_  7_  2=  1223.8   OP=1.0   OV=0   REL=0.181   EL=0.195   DAB=0.0   COST=      7694.631
S_  7_  3=   997.2   OP=1.0   OV=0   REL=1.000   EL=0.195   DAB=0.0   COST=       814.911
S_  7_  4=   658.2   OP=1.0   OV=0   REL=1.000   EL=0.000   DAB=0.0   COST=      2409.000
S_  7_  5=   382.3   OP=1.0   OV=0   REL=0.019   EL=0.000   DAB=1.0   COST=      6378.840
S_  7_  6=   110.5   OP=1.0   OV=0   REL=0.100   EL=0.000   DAB=1.0   COST=      9959.880
S_  7_  7=     0.0   OP=0.8   OV=0   REL=0.285   EL=0.000   DAB=1.0   COST=     13389.279
S_  7_  8=     0.0   OP=0.2   OV=0   REL=0.753   EL=0.000   DAB=1.0   COST=     19461.600
S_  7_  9=     0.0   OP=0.8   OV=0   REL=1.000   EL=0.000   DAB=1.0   COST=      3598.560
S_  7_10=   107.1   OP=1.0   OV=0   REL=1.000   EL=0.000   DAB=1.0   COST=      2872.800
S_  7_11=   849.9   OP=1.0   OV=0   REL=1.000   EL=0.000   DAB=1.0   COST=      3890.520
S_  7_12=   830.8   OP=1.0   OV=0   REL=1.000   EL=0.000   DAB=0.0   COST=      2409.000
S_  8_  1=   972.9   OP=1.0   OV=0   REL=1.000   EL=0.000   DAB=0.0   COST=      2394.000
S_  8_  2=  1496.2   OP=1.0   OV=0   REL=1.000   EL=0.000   DAB=0.0   COST=      2364.000
S_  8_  3=  1309.4   OP=1.0   OV=0   REL=1.000   EL=1.000   DAB=0.0   COST=       405.000
```

```
S_  8_  4=   981.4  OP=1.0  OV=0  REL=1.000  EL=1.000  DAB=0.0  COST=    435.000
S_  8_  5=   631.3  OP=1.0  OV=0  REL=1.000  EL=0.000  DAB=0.0  COST=   2409.000
S_  8_  6=   304.3  OP=1.0  OV=0  REL=1.000  EL=0.000  DAB=1.0  COST=   5886.360
S_  8_  7=   102.5  OP=1.0  OV=0  REL=1.000  EL=0.000  DAB=1.0  COST=   4879.560
S_  8_  8=     0.0  OP=0.7  OV=0  REL=0.133  EL=0.000  DAB=1.0  COST=   6957.922
S_  8_  9=     0.0  OP=0.8  OV=0  REL=1.000  EL=0.000  DAB=1.0  COST=   3598.560
S_  8_10=   108.6  OP=1.0  OV=0  REL=1.000  EL=0.000  DAB=1.0  COST=   2872.800
S_  8_11=   257.0  OP=1.0  OV=0  REL=1.000  EL=0.000  DAB=1.0  COST=   3920.520
S_  8_12=   299.4  OP=1.0  OV=0  REL=1.000  EL=0.000  DAB=1.0  COST=   3998.280
S_  9_  1=   175.4  OP=1.0  OV=0  REL=1.000  EL=0.000  DAB=1.0  COST=   5138.760
S_  9_  2=   414.7  OP=1.0  OV=0  REL=0.045  EL=0.000  DAB=1.0  COST=   7367.880
S_  9_  3=   289.4  OP=1.0  OV=0  REL=1.000  EL=0.000  DAB=1.0  COST=   5953.200
S_  9_  4=   341.5  OP=1.0  OV=0  REL=0.793  EL=0.000  DAB=1.0  COST=  36357.360
S_  9_  5=    94.8  OP=1.0  OV=0  REL=0.019  EL=0.000  DAB=1.0  COST=   6408.840
S_  9_  6=    52.5  OP=1.0  OV=0  REL=0.614  EL=0.000  DAB=1.0  COST=  30710.880
S_  9_  7=     0.0  OP=0.7  OV=0  REL=0.401  EL=0.000  DAB=1.0  COST=  16830.456
S_  9_  8=     0.0  OP=0.4  OV=0  REL=0.557  EL=0.000  DAB=1.0  COST=  15495.840
S_  9_  9=     0.0  OP=0.3  OV=0  REL=0.562  EL=0.000  DAB=1.0  COST=  11348.640
S_  9_10=     0.0  OP=0.8  OV=0  REL=1.000  EL=0.000  DAB=1.0  COST=   2872.800
S_  9_11=   215.9  OP=1.0  OV=0  REL=1.000  EL=0.000  DAB=1.0  COST=   3935.520
S_  9_12=   215.0  OP=1.0  OV=0  REL=1.000  EL=0.000  DAB=1.0  COST=   3998.280
S_ 10_  1=   609.8  OP=1.0  OV=0  REL=1.000  EL=0.000  DAB=0.0  COST=   5123.760
S_ 10_  2=  1558.6  OP=1.0  OV=0  REL=0.045  EL=0.000  DAB=0.0  COST=   4089.720
S_ 10_  3=  1779.5  OP=1.0  OV=0  REL=1.000  EL=0.000  DAB=0.0  COST=   2319.000
S_ 10_  4=  1531.4  OP=1.0  OV=0  REL=1.000  EL=1.000  DAB=0.0  COST=    375.000
S_ 10_  5=  1267.5  OP=1.0  OV=0  REL=1.000  EL=1.000  DAB=0.0  COST=    405.000
S_ 10_  6=   921.3  OP=1.0  OV=0  REL=1.000  EL=1.000  DAB=0.0  COST=    435.000
S_ 10_  7=   751.3  OP=1.0  OV=0  REL=1.000  EL=0.000  DAB=1.0  COST=   4819.560
S_ 10_  8=   625.8  OP=1.0  OV=0  REL=1.000  EL=0.000  DAB=1.0  COST=   4212.480
S_ 10_  9=   600.3  OP=1.0  OV=0  REL=1.000  EL=0.000  DAB=1.0  COST=   3538.560
S_ 10_10=   521.2  OP=1.0  OV=0  REL=1.000  EL=0.000  DAB=1.0  COST=   2827.800
S_ 10_11=   538.7  OP=1.0  OV=0  REL=1.000  EL=0.000  DAB=1.0  COST=   3890.520
S_ 10_12=   640.2  OP=1.0  OV=0  REL=1.000  EL=0.000  DAB=1.0  COST=   3968.280
S_ 11_  1=   667.6  OP=1.0  OV=0  REL=1.000  EL=0.000  DAB=0.0  COST=   2424.000
S_ 11_  2=   608.1  OP=1.0  OV=0  REL=0.045  EL=0.000  DAB=1.0  COST=   7322.880
S_ 11_  3=   441.1  OP=1.0  OV=0  REL=0.026  EL=0.000  DAB=1.0  COST=   6741.720
S_ 11_  4=   153.1  OP=1.0  OV=0  REL=1.000  EL=0.000  DAB=1.0  COST=   6616.200
S_ 11_  5=    87.7  OP=1.0  OV=0  REL=0.580  EL=0.000  DAB=1.0  COST=  27159.840
S_ 11_  6=    23.8  OP=1.0  OV=0  REL=0.614  EL=0.000  DAB=1.0  COST=  30710.880
S_ 11_  7=     0.0  OP=0.5  OV=0  REL=0.568  EL=0.000  DAB=1.0  COST=  21796.231
S_ 11_  8=     0.0  OP=0.1  OV=0  REL=0.891  EL=0.000  DAB=1.0  COST=  22235.040
S_ 11_  9=     0.0  OP=0.9  OV=0  REL=1.000  EL=0.000  DAB=1.0  COST=   3598.560
S_ 11_10=   244.7  OP=1.0  OV=0  REL=1.000  EL=0.000  DAB=1.0  COST=   2872.800
S_ 11_11=   596.3  OP=1.0  OV=0  REL=1.000  EL=0.000  DAB=1.0  COST=   3905.520
S_ 11_12=   812.0  OP=1.0  OV=0  REL=1.000  EL=0.000  DAB=0.0  COST=   2424.000
S_ 12_  1=   929.6  OP=1.0  OV=0  REL=1.000  EL=0.000  DAB=0.0  COST=   2409.000
S_ 12_  2=  1118.2  OP=1.0  OV=0  REL=1.000  EL=0.000  DAB=0.0  COST=   2394.000
S_ 12_  3=   969.9  OP=1.0  OV=0  REL=1.000  EL=0.000  DAB=0.0  COST=   2379.000
S_ 12_  4=   662.8  OP=1.0  OV=0  REL=1.000  EL=0.000  DAB=0.0  COST=   2409.000
S_ 12_  5=   402.5  OP=1.0  OV=0  REL=0.019  EL=0.000  DAB=1.0  COST=   6378.840
S_ 12_  6=   137.4  OP=1.0  OV=0  REL=0.100  EL=0.000  DAB=1.0  COST=   9959.880
S_ 12_  7=     7.2  OP=1.0  OV=0  REL=0.130  EL=0.000  DAB=1.0  COST=   8756.640
S_ 12_  8=    30.8  OP=1.0  OV=0  REL=1.000  EL=0.000  DAB=1.0  COST=   4272.480
S_ 12_  9=     0.0  OP=0.9  OV=0  REL=1.000  EL=0.000  DAB=1.0  COST=   3598.560
S_ 12_10=     0.0  OP=0.4  OV=0  REL=0.394  EL=0.000  DAB=1.0  COST=   8627.040
S_ 12_11=   431.7  OP=1.0  OV=0  REL=1.000  EL=0.000  DAB=1.0  COST=   3920.520
S_ 12_12=   716.4  OP=1.0  OV=0  REL=1.000  EL=0.000  DAB=1.0  COST=   3968.280
S_ 13_  1=   868.2  OP=1.0  OV=0  REL=1.000  EL=0.000  DAB=0.0  COST=   2409.000
S_ 13_  2=   945.4  OP=1.0  OV=0  REL=0.045  EL=0.000  DAB=0.0  COST=   4104.720
S_ 13_  3=   765.9  OP=1.0  OV=0  REL=1.000  EL=0.000  DAB=0.0  COST=   2409.000
S_ 13_  4=   485.6  OP=1.0  OV=0  REL=1.000  EL=0.000  DAB=1.0  COST=   6571.200
S_ 13_  5=   224.5  OP=1.0  OV=0  REL=0.019  EL=0.000  DAB=1.0  COST=   6393.840
S_ 13_  6=     8.5  OP=1.0  OV=0  REL=0.229  EL=0.000  DAB=1.0  COST=  15158.880
S_ 13_  7=     0.0  OP=0.7  OV=0  REL=0.417  EL=0.000  DAB=1.0  COST=  17320.550
S_ 13_  8=     0.0  OP=0.4  OV=0  REL=0.487  EL=0.000  DAB=1.0  COST=  14096.160
S_ 13_  9=     0.0  OP=0.2  OV=0  REL=0.729  EL=0.000  DAB=1.0  COST=  13655.520
S_ 13_10=     0.0  OP=0.3  OV=0  REL=0.575  EL=0.000  DAB=1.0  COST=  11270.880
S_ 13_11=     0.0  OP=0.6  OV=0  REL=0.092  EL=0.000  DAB=1.0  COST=   5283.360
S_ 13_12=     0.0  OP=0.9  OV=0  REL=1.000  EL=0.000  DAB=1.0  COST=   4013.280
S_ 14_  1=     0.0  OP=0.7  OV=0  REL=0.291  EL=0.000  DAB=1.0  COST=  16299.360
S_ 14_  2=   142.7  OP=1.0  OV=0  REL=0.454  EL=0.000  DAB=1.0  COST=  22934.880
S_ 14_  3=   280.6  OP=1.0  OV=0  REL=0.664  EL=0.000  DAB=1.0  COST=  26470.920
S_ 14_  4=   274.9  OP=1.0  OV=0  REL=0.721  EL=0.000  DAB=1.0  COST=  33689.640
S_ 14_  5=   200.1  OP=1.0  OV=0  REL=0.580  EL=0.000  DAB=1.0  COST=  27144.840
```

```
S_14_  6=      0.0  OP=0.9  OV=0  REL=0.301  EL=0.000  DAB=1.0  COST=   18061.492
S_14_  7=      0.0  OP=0.4  OV=0  REL=0.667  EL=0.000  DAB=1.0  COST=   24749.280
S_14_  8=      0.0  OP=0.3  OV=0  REL=0.618  EL=0.000  DAB=1.0  COST=   16740.000
S_14_  9=     81.3  OP=1.0  OV=0  REL=1.000  EL=0.000  DAB=1.0  COST=    3598.560
S_14_ 10=     47.9  OP=1.0  OV=0  REL=1.000  EL=0.000  DAB=1.0  COST=    2872.800
S_14_ 11=     85.2  OP=1.0  OV=0  REL=1.000  EL=0.000  DAB=1.0  COST=    3935.520
S_14_ 12=    339.8  OP=1.0  OV=0  REL=1.000  EL=0.000  DAB=1.0  COST=    3998.280
S_15_  1=    619.2  OP=1.0  OV=0  REL=1.000  EL=0.000  DAB=1.0  COST=    5108.760
S_15_  2=   1357.0  OP=1.0  OV=0  REL=0.045  EL=0.000  DAB=0.0  COST=    4104.720
S_15_  3=   1556.7  OP=1.0  OV=0  REL=1.000  EL=0.000  DAB=0.0  COST=    2349.000
S_15_  4=   1283.2  OP=1.0  OV=0  REL=1.000  EL=1.000  DAB=0.0  COST=     405.000
S_15_  5=   1013.9  OP=1.0  OV=0  REL=0.019  EL=0.032  DAB=0.0  COST=    1197.970
S_15_  6=    649.7  OP=1.0  OV=0  REL=1.000  EL=0.000  DAB=0.0  COST=    2409.000
S_15_  7=    464.8  OP=1.0  OV=0  REL=1.000  EL=0.000  DAB=1.0  COST=    4849.560
S_15_  8=    444.1  OP=1.0  OV=0  REL=1.000  EL=0.000  DAB=1.0  COST=    4227.480
S_15_  9=    565.8  OP=1.0  OV=0  REL=1.000  EL=0.000  DAB=1.0  COST=    3553.560
S_15_ 10=   1001.3  OP=1.0  OV=0  REL=1.000  EL=0.000  DAB=0.0  COST=    2409.000
S_15_ 11=   2274.4  OP=1.0  OV=0  REL=1.000  EL=0.000  DAB=0.0  COST=    2334.000
S_15_ 12=   3720.0  OP=1.0  OV=0  REL=1.000  EL=0.075  DAB=0.0  COST=     385.386
S_16_  1=   6549.3  OP=1.0  OV=0  REL=1.000  EL=1.000  DAB=0.0  COST=      30.000
S_16_  2=   7500.0  OP=1.0  OV=0  REL=1.000  EL=1.000  DAB=0.0  COST=       0.000
S_16_  3=   7223.1  OP=1.0  OV=0  REL=1.000  EL=1.000  DAB=0.0  COST=       0.000
S_16_  4=   7136.4  OP=1.0  OV=0  REL=1.000  EL=1.000  DAB=0.0  COST=       0.000
S_16_  5=   6914.2  OP=1.0  OV=0  REL=1.000  EL=1.000  DAB=0.0  COST=       0.000
S_16_  6=   6644.5  OP=1.0  OV=0  REL=1.000  EL=1.000  DAB=0.0  COST=       0.000
S_16_  7=   6497.1  OP=1.0  OV=0  REL=1.000  EL=1.000  DAB=0.0  COST=       0.000
S_16_  8=   6445.9  OP=1.0  OV=0  REL=1.000  EL=1.000  DAB=0.0  COST=       0.000
S_16_  9=   6312.9  OP=1.0  OV=0  REL=1.000  EL=1.000  DAB=0.0  COST=       0.000
S_16_ 10=   6377.8  OP=1.0  OV=0  REL=1.000  EL=1.000  DAB=0.0  COST=       0.000
S_16_ 11=   6533.0  OP=1.0  OV=0  REL=1.000  EL=1.000  DAB=0.0  COST=       0.000
S_16_ 12=   6625.5  OP=1.0  OV=0  REL=1.000  EL=1.000  DAB=0.0  COST=       0.000
S_17_  1=   6609.2  OP=1.0  OV=0  REL=1.000  EL=1.000  DAB=0.0  COST=       0.000
S_17_  2=   6738.5  OP=1.0  OV=0  REL=1.000  EL=1.000  DAB=0.0  COST=       0.000
S_17_  3=   6484.7  OP=1.0  OV=0  REL=1.000  EL=1.000  DAB=0.0  COST=       0.000
S_17_  4=   6095.4  OP=1.0  OV=0  REL=1.000  EL=1.000  DAB=0.0  COST=       0.000
S_17_  5=   5705.0  OP=1.0  OV=0  REL=1.000  EL=1.000  DAB=0.0  COST=       0.000
S_17_  6=   5291.2  OP=1.0  OV=0  REL=1.000  EL=1.000  DAB=0.0  COST=       0.000
S_17_  7=   5036.0  OP=1.0  OV=0  REL=1.000  EL=1.000  DAB=0.0  COST=      30.000
S_17_  8=   4767.7  OP=1.0  OV=0  REL=1.000  EL=1.000  DAB=0.0  COST=      60.000
S_17_  9=   4619.7  OP=1.0  OV=0  REL=1.000  EL=1.000  DAB=0.0  COST=      75.000
S_17_ 10=   4378.4  OP=1.0  OV=0  REL=1.000  EL=1.000  DAB=0.0  COST=      90.000
S_17_ 11=   4225.1  OP=1.0  OV=0  REL=1.000  EL=1.000  DAB=0.0  COST=     120.000
S_17_ 12=   4372.3  OP=1.0  OV=0  REL=1.000  EL=0.032  DAB=0.0  COST=     182.351
S_18_  1=   5560.3  OP=1.0  OV=0  REL=1.000  EL=1.000  DAB=0.0  COST=      45.000
S_18_  2=   6192.0  OP=1.0  OV=0  REL=1.000  EL=1.000  DAB=0.0  COST=       0.000
S_18_  3=   6072.8  OP=1.0  OV=0  REL=1.000  EL=1.000  DAB=0.0  COST=       0.000
S_18_  4=   5738.0  OP=1.0  OV=0  REL=1.000  EL=1.000  DAB=0.0  COST=       0.000
S_18_  5=   5391.2  OP=1.0  OV=0  REL=1.000  EL=1.000  DAB=0.0  COST=       0.000
S_18_  6=   4992.6  OP=1.0  OV=0  REL=1.000  EL=1.000  DAB=0.0  COST=      30.000
S_18_  7=   4752.4  OP=1.0  OV=0  REL=1.000  EL=1.000  DAB=0.0  COST=      60.000
S_18_  8=   4648.6  OP=1.0  OV=0  REL=1.000  EL=1.000  DAB=0.0  COST=      75.000
S_18_  9=   4686.7  OP=1.0  OV=0  REL=1.000  EL=1.000  DAB=0.0  COST=      75.000
S_18_ 10=   4671.2  OP=1.0  OV=0  REL=1.000  EL=1.000  DAB=0.0  COST=      75.000
S_18_ 11=   4751.7  OP=1.0  OV=0  REL=1.000  EL=1.000  DAB=0.0  COST=      75.000
S_18_ 12=   5420.6  OP=1.0  OV=0  REL=1.000  EL=1.000  DAB=0.0  COST=      45.000
S_19_  1=   7500.0  OP=1.0  OV=0  REL=1.000  EL=1.000  DAB=0.0  COST=       0.000
S_19_  2=   7500.0  OP=1.0  OV=0  REL=1.000  EL=1.000  DAB=0.0  COST=       0.000
S_19_  3=   7500.0  OP=1.0  OV=0  REL=1.000  EL=1.000  DAB=0.0  COST=       0.000
S_19_  4=   7329.3  OP=1.0  OV=0  REL=1.000  EL=1.000  DAB=0.0  COST=       0.000
S_19_  5=   7061.0  OP=1.0  OV=0  REL=1.000  EL=1.000  DAB=0.0  COST=       0.000
S_19_  6=   6763.5  OP=1.0  OV=0  REL=1.000  EL=1.000  DAB=0.0  COST=       0.000
S_19_  7=   6599.9  OP=1.0  OV=0  REL=1.000  EL=1.000  DAB=0.0  COST=       0.000
S_19_  8=   6529.1  OP=1.0  OV=0  REL=1.000  EL=1.000  DAB=0.0  COST=       0.000
S_19_  9=   6677.3  OP=1.0  OV=0  REL=1.000  EL=1.000  DAB=0.0  COST=       0.000
S_19_ 10=   6700.4  OP=1.0  OV=0  REL=1.000  EL=1.000  DAB=0.0  COST=       0.000
S_19_ 11=   6850.0  OP=1.0  OV=0  REL=1.000  EL=1.000  DAB=0.0  COST=       0.000
S_19_ 12=   7228.9  OP=1.0  OV=0  REL=1.000  EL=1.000  DAB=0.0  COST=  150000.000
S_20_  1=   6617.2  OP=1.0  OV=0  REL=1.000  EL=1.000  DAB=0.0  COST=       0.000
S_20_  2=   6535.5  OP=1.0  OV=0  REL=1.000  EL=1.000  DAB=0.0  COST=       0.000
S_20_  3=   6253.0  OP=1.0  OV=0  REL=1.000  EL=1.000  DAB=0.0  COST=       0.000
S_20_  4=   5861.0  OP=1.0  OV=0  REL=1.000  EL=1.000  DAB=0.0  COST=       0.000
S_20_  5=   5475.7  OP=1.0  OV=0  REL=1.000  EL=1.000  DAB=0.0  COST=       0.000
S_20_  6=   5058.3  OP=1.0  OV=0  REL=1.000  EL=1.000  DAB=0.0  COST=      15.000
S_20_  7=   4810.4  OP=1.0  OV=0  REL=1.000  EL=1.000  DAB=0.0  COST=      45.000
```

```
S_20_ 8=  4545.1  OP=1.0  OV=0  REL=1.000  EL=1.000  DAB=0.0  COST=      75.000
S_20_ 9=  4297.1  OP=1.0  OV=0  REL=1.000  EL=1.000  DAB=0.0  COST=     105.000
S_20_10=  4204.7  OP=1.0  OV=0  REL=1.000  EL=1.000  DAB=0.0  COST=     120.000
S_20_11=  4337.0  OP=1.0  OV=0  REL=1.000  EL=1.000  DAB=0.0  COST=     120.000
S_20_12=  5835.2  OP=1.0  OV=0  REL=1.000  EL=1.000  DAB=0.0  COST=      45.000
S_21_ 1=  7500.0  OP=1.0  OV=0  REL=1.000  EL=1.000  DAB=0.0  COST=       0.000
S_21_ 2=  7362.9  OP=1.0  OV=0  REL=1.000  EL=1.000  DAB=0.0  COST=       0.000
S_21_ 3=  7431.8  OP=1.0  OV=0  REL=1.000  EL=1.000  DAB=0.0  COST=       0.000
S_21_ 4=  7252.8  OP=1.0  OV=0  REL=1.000  EL=1.000  DAB=0.0  COST=       0.000
S_21_ 5=  7019.5  OP=1.0  OV=0  REL=1.000  EL=1.000  DAB=0.0  COST=       0.000
S_21_ 6=  6744.5  OP=1.0  OV=0  REL=1.000  EL=1.000  DAB=0.0  COST=       0.000
S_21_ 7=  6596.5  OP=1.0  OV=0  REL=1.000  EL=1.000  DAB=0.0  COST=       0.000
S_21_ 8=  6433.4  OP=1.0  OV=0  REL=1.000  EL=1.000  DAB=0.0  COST=       0.000
S_21_ 9=  6512.7  OP=1.0  OV=0  REL=1.000  EL=1.000  DAB=0.0  COST=       0.000
S_21_10=  6709.4  OP=1.0  OV=0  REL=1.000  EL=1.000  DAB=0.0  COST=       0.000
S_21_11=  6971.0  OP=1.0  OV=0  REL=1.000  EL=0.004  DAB=0.0  COST=       7.588
S_21_12=  7500.0  OP=1.0  OV=0  REL=1.000  EL=1.000  DAB=0.0  COST=  450000.000
S_22_ 1=  7083.8  OP=1.0  OV=0  REL=1.000  EL=1.000  DAB=0.0  COST=       0.000
S_22_ 2=  7500.0  OP=1.0  OV=0  REL=1.000  EL=1.000  DAB=0.0  COST=       0.000
S_22_ 3=  7444.4  OP=1.0  OV=0  REL=1.000  EL=1.000  DAB=0.0  COST=       0.000
S_22_ 4=  7118.7  OP=1.0  OV=0  REL=1.000  EL=1.000  DAB=0.0  COST=       0.000
S_22_ 5=  6744.5  OP=1.0  OV=0  REL=1.000  EL=1.000  DAB=0.0  COST=       0.000
S_22_ 6=  6355.4  OP=1.0  OV=0  REL=1.000  EL=1.000  DAB=0.0  COST=       0.000
S_22_ 7=  6148.4  OP=1.0  OV=0  REL=1.000  EL=1.000  DAB=0.0  COST=       0.000
S_22_ 8=  5963.8  OP=1.0  OV=0  REL=1.000  EL=1.000  DAB=0.0  COST=       0.000
S_22_ 9=  5856.9  OP=1.0  OV=0  REL=1.000  EL=1.000  DAB=0.0  COST=       0.000
S_22_10=  6190.4  OP=1.0  OV=0  REL=1.000  EL=1.000  DAB=0.0  COST=       0.000
S_22_11=  7067.8  OP=1.0  OV=0  REL=1.000  EL=1.000  DAB=0.0  COST=       0.000
S_22_12=  6873.7  OP=1.0  OV=0  REL=1.000  EL=1.000  DAB=0.0  COST=  150000.000
S_23_ 1=  7500.0  OP=1.0  OV=0  REL=1.000  EL=1.000  DAB=0.0  COST=       0.000
S_23_ 2=  7500.0  OP=1.0  OV=0  REL=1.000  EL=1.000  DAB=0.0  COST=       0.000
S_23_ 3=  7500.0  OP=1.0  OV=0  REL=1.000  EL=1.000  DAB=0.0  COST=       0.000
S_23_ 4=  7279.5  OP=1.0  OV=0  REL=1.000  EL=1.000  DAB=0.0  COST=       0.000
S_23_ 5=  6984.0  OP=1.0  OV=0  REL=1.000  EL=1.000  DAB=0.0  COST=       0.000
S_23_ 6=  6676.9  OP=1.0  OV=0  REL=1.000  EL=1.000  DAB=0.0  COST=       0.000
S_23_ 7=  6502.2  OP=1.0  OV=0  REL=1.000  EL=1.000  DAB=0.0  COST=       0.000
S_23_ 8=  6363.6  OP=1.0  OV=0  REL=1.000  EL=1.000  DAB=0.0  COST=       0.000
S_23_ 9=  6276.2  OP=1.0  OV=0  REL=1.000  EL=1.000  DAB=0.0  COST=       0.000
S_23_10=  6292.3  OP=1.0  OV=0  REL=1.000  EL=1.000  DAB=0.0  COST=       0.000
S_23_11=  6367.1  OP=1.0  OV=0  REL=1.000  EL=1.000  DAB=0.0  COST=       0.000
S_23_12=  6628.6  OP=1.0  OV=0  REL=1.000  EL=1.000  DAB=0.0  COST=       0.000
S_24_ 1=  6933.8  OP=1.0  OV=0  REL=1.000  EL=1.000  DAB=0.0  COST=       0.000
S_24_ 2=  6829.6  OP=1.0  OV=0  REL=1.000  EL=1.000  DAB=0.0  COST=       0.000
S_24_ 3=  6619.4  OP=1.0  OV=0  REL=1.000  EL=1.000  DAB=0.0  COST=       0.000
S_24_ 4=  6227.2  OP=1.0  OV=0  REL=1.000  EL=1.000  DAB=0.0  COST=       0.000
S_24_ 5=  5843.8  OP=1.0  OV=0  REL=1.000  EL=1.000  DAB=0.0  COST=       0.000
S_24_ 6=  5433.0  OP=1.0  OV=0  REL=1.000  EL=1.000  DAB=0.0  COST=       0.000
S_24_ 7=  5186.7  OP=1.0  OV=0  REL=1.000  EL=1.000  DAB=0.0  COST=      15.000
S_24_ 8=  5192.4  OP=1.0  OV=0  REL=1.000  EL=1.000  DAB=0.0  COST=      30.000
S_24_ 9=  5454.4  OP=1.0  OV=0  REL=1.000  EL=1.000  DAB=0.0  COST=      15.000
S_24_10=  5673.9  OP=1.0  OV=0  REL=1.000  EL=1.000  DAB=0.0  COST=       0.000
S_24_11=  5811.8  OP=1.0  OV=0  REL=1.000  EL=1.000  DAB=0.0  COST=       0.000
S_24_12=  6466.8  OP=1.0  OV=0  REL=1.000  EL=1.000  DAB=0.0  COST=       0.000
S_25_ 1=  6633.5  OP=1.0  OV=0  REL=1.000  EL=1.000  DAB=0.0  COST=       0.000
S_25_ 2=  6462.4  OP=1.0  OV=0  REL=1.000  EL=1.000  DAB=0.0  COST=       0.000
S_25_ 3=  6189.0  OP=1.0  OV=0  REL=1.000  EL=1.000  DAB=0.0  COST=       0.000
S_25_ 4=  5812.6  OP=1.0  OV=0  REL=1.000  EL=1.000  DAB=0.0  COST=       0.000
S_25_ 5=  5426.2  OP=1.0  OV=0  REL=1.000  EL=1.000  DAB=0.0  COST=       0.000
S_25_ 6=  5031.0  OP=1.0  OV=0  REL=1.000  EL=1.000  DAB=0.0  COST=      30.000
S_25_ 7=  4794.1  OP=1.0  OV=0  REL=1.000  EL=1.000  DAB=0.0  COST=      60.000
S_25_ 8=  4530.6  OP=1.0  OV=0  REL=1.000  EL=1.000  DAB=0.0  COST=      75.000
S_25_ 9=  5003.4  OP=1.0  OV=0  REL=1.000  EL=1.000  DAB=0.0  COST=      75.000
S_25_10=  5153.3  OP=1.0  OV=0  REL=1.000  EL=0.004  DAB=0.0  COST=      52.254
S_25_11=  5795.3  OP=1.0  OV=0  REL=1.000  EL=1.000  DAB=0.0  COST=       0.000
S_25_12=  5944.9  OP=1.0  OV=0  REL=1.000  EL=1.000  DAB=0.0  COST=       0.000
S_26_ 1=  6269.2  OP=1.0  OV=0  REL=1.000  EL=1.000  DAB=0.0  COST=       0.000
S_26_ 2=  6268.2  OP=1.0  OV=0  REL=1.000  EL=1.000  DAB=0.0  COST=       0.000
S_26_ 3=  6146.4  OP=1.0  OV=0  REL=1.000  EL=1.000  DAB=0.0  COST=       0.000
S_26_ 4=  5892.3  OP=1.0  OV=0  REL=1.000  EL=1.000  DAB=0.0  COST=       0.000
S_26_ 5=  5622.6  OP=1.0  OV=0  REL=1.000  EL=1.000  DAB=0.0  COST=       0.000
S_26_ 6=  5334.7  OP=1.0  OV=0  REL=1.000  EL=1.000  DAB=0.0  COST=       0.000
S_26_ 7=  5169.3  OP=1.0  OV=0  REL=1.000  EL=1.000  DAB=0.0  COST=      15.000
S_26_ 8=  4971.2  OP=1.0  OV=0  REL=1.000  EL=1.000  DAB=0.0  COST=      45.000
S_26_ 9=  4889.8  OP=1.0  OV=0  REL=1.000  EL=1.000  DAB=0.0  COST=      60.000
```

```
S_26_10=  5078.8  OP=1.0  OV=0  REL=1.000  EL=1.000  DAB=0.0  COST=     45.000
S_26_11=  5607.0  OP=1.0  OV=0  REL=1.000  EL=1.000  DAB=0.0  COST=     15.000
S_26_12=  6652.1  OP=1.0  OV=0  REL=1.000  EL=1.000  DAB=0.0  COST=      0.000
S_27_ 1=  7500.0  OP=1.0  OV=0  REL=1.000  EL=1.000  DAB=0.0  COST=      0.000
S_27_ 2=  7088.0  OP=1.0  OV=0  REL=1.000  EL=1.000  DAB=0.0  COST=      0.000
S_27_ 3=  7009.6  OP=1.0  OV=0  REL=1.000  EL=1.000  DAB=0.0  COST=      0.000
S_27_ 4=  6741.1  OP=1.0  OV=0  REL=1.000  EL=1.000  DAB=0.0  COST=      0.000
S_27_ 5=  6416.2  OP=1.0  OV=0  REL=1.000  EL=1.000  DAB=0.0  COST=      0.000
S_27_ 6=  6084.1  OP=1.0  OV=0  REL=1.000  EL=1.000  DAB=0.0  COST=      0.000
S_27_ 7=  5874.4  OP=1.0  OV=0  REL=1.000  EL=1.000  DAB=0.0  COST=      0.000
S_27_ 8=  5710.6  OP=1.0  OV=0  REL=1.000  EL=1.000  DAB=0.0  COST=      0.000
S_27_ 9=  5663.8  OP=1.0  OV=0  REL=1.000  EL=1.000  DAB=0.0  COST=      0.000
S_27_10=  5792.2  OP=1.0  OV=0  REL=1.000  EL=1.000  DAB=0.0  COST=      0.000
S_27_11=  6217.6  OP=1.0  OV=0  REL=1.000  EL=1.000  DAB=0.0  COST=      0.000
S_27_12=  6971.7  OP=1.0  OV=0  REL=1.000  EL=1.000  DAB=0.0  COST=      0.000
S_28_ 1=  7293.9  OP=1.0  OV=0  REL=1.000  EL=1.000  DAB=0.0  COST=      0.000
S_28_ 2=  7257.2  OP=1.0  OV=0  REL=1.000  EL=1.000  DAB=0.0  COST=      0.000
S_28_ 3=  7148.0  OP=1.0  OV=0  REL=1.000  EL=1.000  DAB=0.0  COST=      0.000
S_28_ 4=  6842.1  OP=1.0  OV=0  REL=1.000  EL=1.000  DAB=0.0  COST=      0.000
S_28_ 5=  6499.8  OP=1.0  OV=0  REL=1.000  EL=1.000  DAB=0.0  COST=      0.000
S_28_ 6=  6154.3  OP=1.0  OV=0  REL=1.000  EL=1.000  DAB=0.0  COST=      0.000
S_28_ 7=  5990.2  OP=1.0  OV=0  REL=1.000  EL=1.000  DAB=0.0  COST=      0.000
S_28_ 8=  5830.8  OP=1.0  OV=0  REL=1.000  EL=1.000  DAB=0.0  COST=      0.000
S_28_ 9=  5680.4  OP=1.0  OV=0  REL=1.000  EL=1.000  DAB=0.0  COST=      0.000
S_28_10=  5711.8  OP=1.0  OV=0  REL=1.000  EL=1.000  DAB=0.0  COST=      0.000
S_28_11=  5733.8  OP=1.0  OV=0  REL=1.000  EL=1.000  DAB=0.0  COST=      0.000
S_28_12=  6107.2  OP=1.0  OV=0  REL=1.000  EL=1.000  DAB=0.0  COST=      0.000
S_29_ 1=  6990.0  OP=1.0  OV=0  REL=1.000  EL=1.000  DAB=0.0  COST=      0.000
S_29_ 2=  7360.6  OP=1.0  OV=0  REL=1.000  EL=1.000  DAB=0.0  COST=      0.000
S_29_ 3=  7235.1  OP=1.0  OV=0  REL=1.000  EL=1.000  DAB=0.0  COST=      0.000
S_29_ 4=  6895.9  OP=1.0  OV=0  REL=1.000  EL=1.000  DAB=0.0  COST=      0.000
S_29_ 5=  6535.0  OP=1.0  OV=0  REL=1.000  EL=1.000  DAB=0.0  COST=      0.000
S_29_ 6=  6163.8  OP=1.0  OV=0  REL=1.000  EL=1.000  DAB=0.0  COST=      0.000
S_29_ 7=  5923.2  OP=1.0  OV=0  REL=1.000  EL=1.000  DAB=0.0  COST=      0.000
S_29_ 8=  5952.1  OP=1.0  OV=0  REL=1.000  EL=1.000  DAB=0.0  COST=      0.000
S_29_ 9=  5977.4  OP=1.0  OV=0  REL=1.000  EL=1.000  DAB=0.0  COST=      0.000
S_29_10=  6044.7  OP=1.0  OV=0  REL=1.000  EL=1.000  DAB=0.0  COST=      0.000
S_29_11=  6175.2  OP=1.0  OV=0  REL=1.000  EL=1.000  DAB=0.0  COST=      0.000
S_29_12=  6498.9  OP=1.0  OV=0  REL=1.000  EL=1.000  DAB=0.0  COST=      0.000
S_30_ 1=  7123.6  OP=1.0  OV=0  REL=1.000  EL=1.000  DAB=0.0  COST=      0.000
S_30_ 2=  7276.7  OP=1.0  OV=0  REL=1.000  EL=1.000  DAB=0.0  COST=      0.000
S_30_ 3=  7184.3  OP=1.0  OV=0  REL=1.000  EL=1.000  DAB=0.0  COST=      0.000
S_30_ 4=  6838.5  OP=1.0  OV=0  REL=1.000  EL=1.000  DAB=0.0  COST=      0.000
S_30_ 5=  6473.5  OP=1.0  OV=0  REL=1.000  EL=1.000  DAB=0.0  COST=      0.000
S_30_ 6=  6112.6  OP=1.0  OV=0  REL=1.000  EL=1.000  DAB=0.0  COST=      0.000
S_30_ 7=  5875.9  OP=1.0  OV=0  REL=1.000  EL=1.000  DAB=0.0  COST=      0.000
S_30_ 8=  5649.1  OP=1.0  OV=0  REL=1.000  EL=1.000  DAB=0.0  COST=      0.000
S_30_ 9=  5612.7  OP=1.0  OV=0  REL=1.000  EL=1.000  DAB=0.0  COST=      0.000
S_30_10=  5603.6  OP=1.0  OV=0  REL=1.000  EL=1.000  DAB=0.0  COST=      0.000
S_30_11=  5495.0  OP=1.0  OV=0  REL=1.000  EL=1.000  DAB=0.0  COST=      0.000
S_30_12=  5346.7  OP=1.0  OV=0  REL=1.000  EL=1.000  DAB=0.0  COST=      0.000
S_31_ 1=  5400.2  OP=1.0  OV=0  REL=1.000  EL=1.000  DAB=0.0  COST=     15.000
S_31_ 2=  5317.4  OP=1.0  OV=0  REL=1.000  EL=1.000  DAB=0.0  COST=     15.000
S_31_ 3=  5101.4  OP=1.0  OV=0  REL=1.000  EL=1.000  DAB=0.0  COST=     30.000
S_31_ 4=  4667.9  OP=1.0  OV=0  REL=1.000  EL=1.000  DAB=0.0  COST=     60.000
S_31_ 5=  4263.1  OP=1.0  OV=0  REL=1.000  EL=1.000  DAB=0.0  COST=    105.000
S_31_ 6=  3843.8  OP=1.0  OV=0  REL=1.000  EL=1.000  DAB=0.0  COST=    135.000
S_31_ 7=  3555.7  OP=1.0  OV=0  REL=1.000  EL=1.000  DAB=0.0  COST=    180.000
S_31_ 8=  3432.0  OP=1.0  OV=0  REL=1.000  EL=1.000  DAB=0.0  COST=    195.000
S_31_ 9=  3908.1  OP=1.0  OV=0  REL=1.000  EL=1.000  DAB=0.0  COST=    180.000
S_31_10=  4117.1  OP=1.0  OV=0  REL=1.000  EL=1.000  DAB=0.0  COST=    150.000
S_31_11=  4574.2  OP=1.0  OV=0  REL=1.000  EL=1.000  DAB=0.0  COST=    105.000
S_31_12=  4772.4  OP=1.0  OV=0  REL=1.000  EL=1.000  DAB=0.0  COST=     75.000
S_32_ 1=  5471.1  OP=1.0  OV=0  REL=1.000  EL=1.000  DAB=0.0  COST=     30.000
S_32_ 2=  5608.9  OP=1.0  OV=0  REL=1.000  EL=1.000  DAB=0.0  COST=      0.000
S_32_ 3=  5421.4  OP=1.0  OV=0  REL=1.000  EL=1.000  DAB=0.0  COST=      0.000
S_32_ 4=  5062.2  OP=1.0  OV=0  REL=1.000  EL=1.000  DAB=0.0  COST=     15.000
S_32_ 5=  4686.3  OP=1.0  OV=0  REL=1.000  EL=1.000  DAB=0.0  COST=     60.000
S_32_ 6=  4280.0  OP=1.0  OV=0  REL=1.000  EL=1.000  DAB=0.0  COST=     90.000
S_32_ 7=  4008.0  OP=1.0  OV=0  REL=1.000  EL=1.000  DAB=0.0  COST=    135.000
S_32_ 8=  3763.0  OP=1.0  OV=0  REL=1.000  EL=1.000  DAB=0.0  COST=    165.000
S_32_ 9=  3826.6  OP=1.0  OV=0  REL=1.000  EL=1.000  DAB=0.0  COST=    165.000
S_32_10=  3752.6  OP=1.0  OV=0  REL=1.000  EL=1.000  DAB=0.0  COST=    165.000
S_32_11=  3985.0  OP=1.0  OV=0  REL=1.000  EL=1.000  DAB=0.0  COST=    165.000
```

```
S_32_12= 4234.4  OP=1.0  OV=0  REL=1.000  EL=1.000  DAB=0.0  COST=    135.000
S_33_ 1= 4566.8  OP=1.0  OV=0  REL=1.000  EL=1.000  DAB=0.0  COST=    105.000
S_33_ 2= 5544.4  OP=1.0  OV=0  REL=1.000  EL=1.000  DAB=0.0  COST=     45.000
S_33_ 3= 5541.8  OP=1.0  OV=0  REL=1.000  EL=1.000  DAB=0.0  COST=      0.000
S_33_ 4= 5185.1  OP=1.0  OV=0  REL=1.000  EL=1.000  DAB=0.0  COST=     15.000
S_33_ 5= 4825.9  OP=1.0  OV=0  REL=1.000  EL=1.000  DAB=0.0  COST=     45.000
S_33_ 6= 4441.3  OP=1.0  OV=0  REL=1.000  EL=1.000  DAB=0.0  COST=     75.000
S_33_ 7= 4171.9  OP=1.0  OV=0  REL=1.000  EL=1.000  DAB=0.0  COST=    120.000
S_33_ 8= 4019.2  OP=1.0  OV=0  REL=1.000  EL=1.000  DAB=0.0  COST=    135.000
S_33_ 9= 4151.8  OP=1.0  OV=0  REL=1.000  EL=1.000  DAB=0.0  COST=    135.000
S_33_10= 4084.2  OP=1.0  OV=0  REL=1.000  EL=1.000  DAB=0.0  COST=    135.000
S_33_11= 4013.3  OP=1.0  OV=0  REL=1.000  EL=1.000  DAB=0.0  COST=    135.000
S_33_12= 4911.3  OP=1.0  OV=0  REL=1.000  EL=1.000  DAB=0.0  COST=    105.000
S_34_ 1= 5650.6  OP=1.0  OV=0  REL=1.000  EL=1.000  DAB=0.0  COST=     15.000
S_34_ 2= 5828.3  OP=1.0  OV=0  REL=1.000  EL=1.000  DAB=0.0  COST=      0.000
S_34_ 3= 5616.4  OP=1.0  OV=0  REL=1.000  EL=1.000  DAB=0.0  COST=      0.000
S_34_ 4= 5249.5  OP=1.0  OV=0  REL=1.000  EL=1.000  DAB=0.0  COST=      0.000
S_34_ 5= 4874.2  OP=1.0  OV=0  REL=1.000  EL=1.000  DAB=0.0  COST=     45.000
S_34_ 6= 4463.2  OP=1.0  OV=0  REL=1.000  EL=1.000  DAB=0.0  COST=     75.000
S_34_ 7= 4195.0  OP=1.0  OV=0  REL=1.000  EL=1.000  DAB=0.0  COST=    120.000
S_34_ 8= 4435.6  OP=1.0  OV=0  REL=1.000  EL=1.000  DAB=0.0  COST=    120.000
S_34_ 9= 4402.5  OP=1.0  OV=0  REL=1.000  EL=1.000  DAB=0.0  COST=    105.000
S_34_10= 5032.4  OP=1.0  OV=0  REL=1.000  EL=1.000  DAB=0.0  COST=     75.000
S_34_11= 5416.1  OP=1.0  OV=0  REL=1.000  EL=1.000  DAB=0.0  COST=     30.000
S_34_12= 7451.3  OP=1.0  OV=0  REL=1.000  EL=1.000  DAB=0.0  COST=      0.000
S_35_ 1= 6697.5  OP=1.0  OV=0  REL=1.000  EL=1.000  DAB=0.0  COST=      0.000
S_35_ 2= 7191.4  OP=1.0  OV=0  REL=1.000  EL=1.000  DAB=0.0  COST=      0.000
S_35_ 3= 7077.0  OP=1.0  OV=0  REL=1.000  EL=1.000  DAB=0.0  COST=      0.000
S_35_ 4= 6793.4  OP=1.0  OV=0  REL=1.000  EL=1.000  DAB=0.0  COST=      0.000
S_35_ 5= 6480.2  OP=1.0  OV=0  REL=1.000  EL=1.000  DAB=0.0  COST=      0.000
S_35_ 6= 6151.5  OP=1.0  OV=0  REL=1.000  EL=1.000  DAB=0.0  COST=      0.000
S_35_ 7= 5942.5  OP=1.0  OV=0  REL=1.000  EL=1.000  DAB=0.0  COST=      0.000
S_35_ 8= 5759.0  OP=1.0  OV=0  REL=1.000  EL=1.000  DAB=0.0  COST=      0.000
S_35_ 9= 5591.5  OP=1.0  OV=0  REL=1.000  EL=1.000  DAB=0.0  COST=      0.000
S_35_10= 5590.2  OP=1.0  OV=0  REL=1.000  EL=1.000  DAB=0.0  COST=      0.000
S_35_11= 5504.1  OP=1.0  OV=0  REL=1.000  EL=1.000  DAB=0.0  COST=      0.000
S_35_12= 6316.2  OP=1.0  OV=0  REL=1.000  EL=1.000  DAB=0.0  COST=      0.000
S_36_ 1= 7183.4  OP=1.0  OV=0  REL=1.000  EL=1.000  DAB=0.0  COST=      0.000
S_36_ 2= 7142.7  OP=1.0  OV=0  REL=1.000  EL=1.000  DAB=0.0  COST=      0.000
S_36_ 3= 6936.8  OP=1.0  OV=0  REL=1.000  EL=1.000  DAB=0.0  COST=      0.000
S_36_ 4= 6583.8  OP=1.0  OV=0  REL=1.000  EL=1.000  DAB=0.0  COST=      0.000
S_36_ 5= 6203.6  OP=1.0  OV=0  REL=1.000  EL=1.000  DAB=0.0  COST=      0.000
S_36_ 6= 5824.5  OP=1.0  OV=0  REL=1.000  EL=1.000  DAB=0.0  COST=      0.000
S_36_ 7= 5582.1  OP=1.0  OV=0  REL=1.000  EL=1.000  DAB=0.0  COST=      0.000
S_36_ 8= 5437.8  OP=1.0  OV=0  REL=1.000  EL=1.000  DAB=0.0  COST=      0.000
S_36_ 9= 5718.6  OP=1.0  OV=0  REL=1.000  EL=1.000  DAB=0.0  COST=      0.000
S_36_10= 5758.6  OP=1.0  OV=0  REL=1.000  EL=1.000  DAB=0.0  COST=      0.000
S_36_11= 5830.4  OP=1.0  OV=0  REL=1.000  EL=1.000  DAB=0.0  COST=      0.000
S_36_12= 6245.7  OP=1.0  OV=0  REL=1.000  EL=1.000  DAB=0.0  COST=      0.000
S_37_ 1= 6931.8  OP=1.0  OV=0  REL=1.000  EL=1.000  DAB=0.0  COST=      0.000
S_37_ 2= 6941.0  OP=1.0  OV=0  REL=1.000  EL=1.000  DAB=0.0  COST=      0.000
S_37_ 3= 6699.1  OP=1.0  OV=0  REL=1.000  EL=1.000  DAB=0.0  COST=      0.000
S_37_ 4= 6332.0  OP=1.0  OV=0  REL=1.000  EL=1.000  DAB=0.0  COST=      0.000
S_37_ 5= 5947.7  OP=1.0  OV=0  REL=1.000  EL=1.000  DAB=0.0  COST=      0.000
S_37_ 6= 5526.4  OP=1.0  OV=0  REL=1.000  EL=1.000  DAB=0.0  COST=      0.000
S_37_ 7= 5268.7  OP=1.0  OV=0  REL=1.000  EL=1.000  DAB=0.0  COST=      0.000
S_37_ 8= 5050.7  OP=1.0  OV=0  REL=1.000  EL=1.000  DAB=0.0  COST=     30.000
S_37_ 9= 4804.7  OP=1.0  OV=0  REL=1.000  EL=1.000  DAB=0.0  COST=     60.000
S_37_10= 4659.6  OP=1.0  OV=0  REL=1.000  EL=1.000  DAB=0.0  COST=     75.000
S_37_11= 4499.4  OP=1.0  OV=0  REL=1.000  EL=1.000  DAB=0.0  COST=     90.000
S_37_12= 4894.3  OP=1.0  OV=0  REL=1.000  EL=0.013  DAB=0.0  COST=    100.620
S_38_ 1= 5129.5  OP=1.0  OV=0  REL=1.000  EL=1.000  DAB=0.0  COST=     45.000
S_38_ 2= 4989.4  OP=1.0  OV=0  REL=1.000  EL=1.000  DAB=0.0  COST=     45.000
S_38_ 3= 4773.4  OP=1.0  OV=0  REL=1.000  EL=1.000  DAB=0.0  COST=     60.000
S_38_ 4= 4353.6  OP=1.0  OV=0  REL=1.000  EL=1.000  DAB=0.0  COST=     90.000
S_38_ 5= 3949.7  OP=1.0  OV=0  REL=1.000  EL=1.000  DAB=0.0  COST=    135.000
S_38_ 6= 3523.4  OP=1.0  OV=0  REL=1.000  EL=1.000  DAB=0.0  COST=    165.000
S_38_ 7= 3262.8  OP=1.0  OV=0  REL=1.000  EL=1.000  DAB=0.0  COST=    210.000
S_38_ 8= 2923.2  OP=1.0  OV=0  REL=1.000  EL=1.000  DAB=0.0  COST=    240.000
S_38_ 9= 3222.0  OP=1.0  OV=0  REL=1.000  EL=1.000  DAB=0.0  COST=    240.000
S_38_10= 3167.2  OP=1.0  OV=0  REL=1.000  EL=1.000  DAB=0.0  COST=    225.000
S_38_11= 3144.8  OP=1.0  OV=0  REL=1.000  EL=1.000  DAB=0.0  COST=    225.000
S_38_12= 4177.3  OP=1.0  OV=0  REL=1.000  EL=1.000  DAB=0.0  COST=    180.000
S_39_ 1= 5799.2  OP=1.0  OV=0  REL=1.000  EL=1.000  DAB=0.0  COST=     45.000
```

```
S_39_ 2= 7497.1  OP=1.0  OV=0  REL=1.000  EL=1.000  DAB=0.0  COST=      0.000
S_39_ 3= 6943.8  OP=1.0  OV=0  REL=1.000  EL=1.000  DAB=0.0  COST=      0.000
S_39_ 4= 6723.3  OP=1.0  OV=0  REL=1.000  EL=1.000  DAB=0.0  COST=      0.000
S_39_ 5= 6433.4  OP=1.0  OV=0  REL=1.000  EL=1.000  DAB=0.0  COST=      0.000
S_39_ 6= 6113.3  OP=1.0  OV=0  REL=1.000  EL=1.000  DAB=0.0  COST=      0.000
S_39_ 7= 5920.9  OP=1.0  OV=0  REL=1.000  EL=1.000  DAB=0.0  COST=      0.000
S_39_ 8= 5785.6  OP=1.0  OV=0  REL=1.000  EL=1.000  DAB=0.0  COST=      0.000
S_39_ 9= 6138.5  OP=1.0  OV=0  REL=1.000  EL=1.000  DAB=0.0  COST=      0.000
S_39_10= 6810.1  OP=1.0  OV=0  REL=1.000  EL=1.000  DAB=0.0  COST=      0.000
S_39_11= 7373.7  OP=1.0  OV=0  REL=1.000  EL=1.000  DAB=0.0  COST= 300000.000
S_39_12= 7500.0  OP=1.0  OV=0  REL=1.000  EL=1.000  DAB=0.0  COST= 600000.000
S_40_ 1= 7108.7  OP=1.0  OV=0  REL=1.000  EL=1.000  DAB=0.0  COST=      0.000
S_40_ 2= 7500.0  OP=1.0  OV=0  REL=1.000  EL=1.000  DAB=0.0  COST=      0.000
S_40_ 3= 7500.0  OP=1.0  OV=0  REL=1.000  EL=1.000  DAB=0.0  COST=      0.000
S_40_ 4= 7252.8  OP=1.0  OV=0  REL=1.000  EL=1.000  DAB=0.0  COST=      0.000
S_40_ 5= 6958.6  OP=1.0  OV=0  REL=1.000  EL=1.000  DAB=0.0  COST=      0.000
S_40_ 6= 6641.4  OP=1.0  OV=0  REL=1.000  EL=1.000  DAB=0.0  COST=      0.000
S_40_ 7= 6446.6  OP=1.0  OV=0  REL=1.000  EL=1.000  DAB=0.0  COST=      0.000
S_40_ 8= 6406.0  OP=1.0  OV=0  REL=1.000  EL=1.000  DAB=0.0  COST=      0.000
S_40_ 9= 6579.1  OP=1.0  OV=0  REL=1.000  EL=1.000  DAB=0.0  COST=      0.000
S_40_10= 6967.7  OP=1.0  OV=0  REL=1.000  EL=1.000  DAB=0.0  COST=      0.000
S_40_11= 7500.0  OP=1.0  OV=0  REL=1.000  EL=1.000  DAB=0.0  COST= 600000.000
S_40_12= 7399.3  OP=1.0  OV=0  REL=1.000  EL=1.000  DAB=0.0  COST= 600000.000
S_41_ 1= 7049.5  OP=1.0  OV=0  REL=1.000  EL=1.000  DAB=0.0  COST=      0.000
S_41_ 2= 7065.8  OP=1.0  OV=0  REL=1.000  EL=1.000  DAB=0.0  COST=      0.000
S_41_ 3= 6841.0  OP=1.0  OV=0  REL=1.000  EL=1.000  DAB=0.0  COST=      0.000
S_41_ 4= 6471.5  OP=1.0  OV=0  REL=1.000  EL=1.000  DAB=0.0  COST=      0.000
S_41_ 5= 6086.4  OP=1.0  OV=0  REL=1.000  EL=1.000  DAB=0.0  COST=      0.000
S_41_ 6= 5701.1  OP=1.0  OV=0  REL=1.000  EL=1.000  DAB=0.0  COST=      0.000
```

Data for stochastic dynamic programming model:
```
S_ 1_ 2= 5822.4  OP=1.0  OV=0  REL=1.000  EL=0.000  DAB=0.0  COST=   1944.000
S_ 1_ 3= 5709.1  OP=1.0  OV=0  REL=1.000  EL=1.000  DAB=0.0  COST=      0.000
S_ 1_ 4= 5413.7  OP=1.0  OV=0  REL=1.000  EL=1.000  DAB=0.0  COST=      0.000
S_ 1_ 5= 5109.1  OP=1.0  OV=0  REL=1.000  EL=1.000  DAB=0.0  COST=     15.000
S_ 1_ 6= 4768.9  OP=1.0  OV=0  REL=1.000  EL=1.000  DAB=0.0  COST=     45.000
S_ 1_ 7= 4605.9  OP=1.0  OV=0  REL=1.000  EL=1.000  DAB=0.0  COST=     75.000
S_ 1_ 8= 4467.5  OP=1.0  OV=0  REL=1.000  EL=0.103  DAB=0.0  COST=    290.929
S_ 1_ 9= 4441.4  OP=1.0  OV=0  REL=1.000  EL=1.000  DAB=0.0  COST=    105.000
S_ 1_10= 4493.5  OP=1.0  OV=0  REL=1.000  EL=1.000  DAB=0.0  COST=    105.000
S_ 1_11= 4462.5  OP=1.0  OV=0  REL=1.000  EL=1.000  DAB=0.0  COST=    105.000
S_ 1_12= 4504.8  OP=1.0  OV=0  REL=1.000  EL=1.000  DAB=0.0  COST=    105.000
S_ 2_ 1= 4735.9  OP=1.0  OV=0  REL=1.000  EL=1.000  DAB=0.0  COST=     90.000
S_ 2_ 2= 5050.9  OP=1.0  OV=0  REL=1.000  EL=1.000  DAB=0.0  COST=     60.000
S_ 2_ 3= 4971.6  OP=1.0  OV=0  REL=1.000  EL=1.000  DAB=0.0  COST=     45.000
S_ 2_ 4= 4703.0  OP=1.0  OV=0  REL=1.000  EL=1.000  DAB=0.0  COST=     60.000
S_ 2_ 5= 4418.2  OP=1.0  OV=0  REL=1.000  EL=1.000  DAB=0.0  COST=     90.000
S_ 2_ 6= 4093.7  OP=1.0  OV=0  REL=1.000  EL=1.000  DAB=0.0  COST=    120.000
S_ 2_ 7= 3899.4  OP=1.0  OV=0  REL=1.000  EL=1.000  DAB=0.0  COST=    150.000
S_ 2_ 8= 3727.5  OP=1.0  OV=0  REL=1.000  EL=0.147  DAB=0.0  COST=    451.079
S_ 2_ 9= 3676.2  OP=1.0  OV=0  REL=1.000  EL=0.345  DAB=0.0  COST=    850.998
S_ 2_10= 3881.9  OP=1.0  OV=0  REL=1.000  EL=0.354  DAB=0.0  COST=    852.360
S_ 2_11= 3928.9  OP=1.0  OV=0  REL=1.000  EL=1.000  DAB=0.0  COST=    150.000
S_ 2_12= 4143.4  OP=1.0  OV=0  REL=1.000  EL=1.000  DAB=0.0  COST=    150.000
S_ 3_ 1= 4556.7  OP=1.0  OV=0  REL=1.000  EL=1.000  DAB=0.0  COST=    105.000
S_ 3_ 2= 4939.3  OP=1.0  OV=0  REL=1.000  EL=1.000  DAB=0.0  COST=     75.000
S_ 3_ 3= 4822.7  OP=1.0  OV=0  REL=1.000  EL=1.000  DAB=0.0  COST=     60.000
S_ 3_ 4= 4533.2  OP=1.0  OV=0  REL=1.000  EL=1.000  DAB=0.0  COST=     75.000
S_ 3_ 5= 4222.2  OP=1.0  OV=0  REL=1.000  EL=1.000  DAB=0.0  COST=    105.000
S_ 3_ 6= 3873.2  OP=1.0  OV=0  REL=1.000  EL=1.000  DAB=0.0  COST=    135.000
S_ 3_ 7= 3650.7  OP=1.0  OV=0  REL=1.000  EL=1.000  DAB=0.0  COST=    165.000
S_ 3_ 8= 3435.0  OP=1.0  OV=0  REL=1.000  EL=0.158  DAB=0.0  COST=    502.283
S_ 3_ 9= 3296.5  OP=1.0  OV=0  REL=1.000  EL=0.362  DAB=0.0  COST=    913.852
S_ 3_10= 3225.9  OP=1.0  OV=0  REL=1.000  EL=0.370  DAB=0.0  COST=    945.214
S_ 3_11= 3224.2  OP=1.0  OV=0  REL=1.000  EL=0.379  DAB=0.0  COST=    961.706
S_ 3_12= 3637.4  OP=1.0  OV=0  REL=1.000  EL=0.024  DAB=0.0  COST=    256.824
S_ 4_ 1= 4750.3  OP=1.0  OV=0  REL=1.000  EL=1.000  DAB=0.0  COST=    120.000
S_ 4_ 2= 6493.9  OP=1.0  OV=0  REL=1.000  EL=1.000  DAB=0.0  COST=      0.000
S_ 4_ 3= 7076.3  OP=1.0  OV=0  REL=1.000  EL=1.000  DAB=0.0  COST=      0.000
S_ 4_ 4= 6947.7  OP=1.0  OV=0  REL=1.000  EL=1.000  DAB=0.0  COST=      0.000
```

```
S_ 4_ 5= 6741.0  OP=1.0  OV=0  REL=1.000  EL=1.000  DAB=0.0  COST=      0.000
S_ 4_ 6= 6468.6  OP=1.0  OV=0  REL=1.000  EL=1.000  DAB=0.0  COST=      0.000
S_ 4_ 7= 6345.4  OP=1.0  OV=0  REL=1.000  EL=1.000  DAB=0.0  COST=      0.000
S_ 4_ 8= 6387.0  OP=1.0  OV=0  REL=1.000  EL=1.000  DAB=0.0  COST=      0.000
S_ 4_ 9= 6668.4  OP=1.0  OV=0  REL=1.000  EL=1.000  DAB=0.0  COST=      0.000
S_ 4_10= 6767.4  OP=1.0  OV=0  REL=1.000  EL=1.000  DAB=0.0  COST=      0.000
S_ 4_11= 6262.5  OP=1.0  OV=0  REL=1.000  EL=1.000  DAB=0.0  COST=      0.000
S_ 4_12= 5724.1  OP=1.0  OV=0  REL=1.000  EL=1.000  DAB=0.0  COST=      0.000
S_ 5_ 1= 5866.4  OP=1.0  OV=0  REL=1.000  EL=1.000  DAB=0.0  COST=      0.000
S_ 5_ 2= 5731.4  OP=1.0  OV=0  REL=1.000  EL=1.000  DAB=0.0  COST=      0.000
S_ 5_ 3= 5532.6  OP=1.0  OV=0  REL=1.000  EL=1.000  DAB=0.0  COST=      0.000
S_ 5_ 4= 5204.0  OP=1.0  OV=0  REL=1.000  EL=1.000  DAB=0.0  COST=     15.000
S_ 5_ 5= 4867.1  OP=1.0  OV=0  REL=1.000  EL=1.000  DAB=0.0  COST=     45.000
S_ 5_ 6= 4508.4  OP=1.0  OV=0  REL=1.000  EL=1.000  DAB=0.0  COST=     75.000
S_ 5_ 7= 4291.6  OP=1.0  OV=0  REL=1.000  EL=1.000  DAB=0.0  COST=    105.000
S_ 5_ 8= 4086.3  OP=1.0  OV=0  REL=1.000  EL=0.120  DAB=0.0  COST=    368.987
S_ 5_ 9= 4127.9  OP=1.0  OV=0  REL=1.000  EL=1.000  DAB=0.0  COST=    135.000
S_ 5_10= 4069.4  OP=1.0  OV=0  REL=1.000  EL=1.000  DAB=0.0  COST=    135.000
S_ 5_11= 3969.4  OP=1.0  OV=0  REL=1.000  EL=1.000  DAB=0.0  COST=    150.000
S_ 5_12= 3965.7  OP=1.0  OV=0  REL=1.000  EL=1.000  DAB=0.0  COST=    150.000
S_ 6_ 1= 5174.5  OP=1.0  OV=0  REL=1.000  EL=1.000  DAB=0.0  COST=     90.000
S_ 6_ 2= 5509.2  OP=1.0  OV=0  REL=1.000  EL=1.000  DAB=0.0  COST=     15.000
S_ 6_ 3= 5406.4  OP=1.0  OV=0  REL=1.000  EL=1.000  DAB=0.0  COST=      0.000
S_ 6_ 4= 5086.6  OP=1.0  OV=0  REL=1.000  EL=1.000  DAB=0.0  COST=     15.000
S_ 6_ 5= 4760.8  OP=1.0  OV=0  REL=1.000  EL=1.000  DAB=0.0  COST=     60.000
S_ 6_ 6= 4405.3  OP=1.0  OV=0  REL=1.000  EL=1.000  DAB=0.0  COST=     90.000
S_ 6_ 7= 4185.4  OP=1.0  OV=0  REL=1.000  EL=1.000  DAB=0.0  COST=    120.000
S_ 6_ 8= 3997.2  OP=1.0  OV=0  REL=1.000  EL=0.129  DAB=0.0  COST=    385.516
S_ 6_ 9= 3891.6  OP=1.0  OV=0  REL=1.000  EL=0.329  DAB=0.0  COST=    789.702
S_ 6_10= 3947.1  OP=1.0  OV=0  REL=1.000  EL=0.337  DAB=0.0  COST=    804.506
S_ 6_11= 3789.2  OP=1.0  OV=0  REL=1.000  EL=1.000  DAB=0.0  COST=    165.000
S_ 6_12= 3584.3  OP=1.0  OV=0  REL=1.000  EL=1.000  DAB=0.0  COST=    180.000
S_ 7_ 1= 3450.1  OP=1.0  OV=0  REL=1.000  EL=1.000  DAB=0.0  COST=    195.000
S_ 7_ 2= 3409.4  OP=1.0  OV=0  REL=1.000  EL=1.000  DAB=0.0  COST=    210.000
S_ 7_ 3= 3166.1  OP=1.0  OV=0  REL=1.000  EL=1.000  DAB=0.0  COST=    210.000
S_ 7_ 4= 2808.4  OP=1.0  OV=0  REL=1.000  EL=1.000  DAB=0.0  COST=    240.000
S_ 7_ 5= 2455.7  OP=1.0  OV=0  REL=1.000  EL=1.000  DAB=0.0  COST=    285.000
S_ 7_ 6= 2079.5  OP=1.0  OV=0  REL=1.000  EL=1.000  DAB=0.0  COST=    315.000
S_ 7_ 7= 1829.5  OP=1.0  OV=0  REL=1.000  EL=0.034  DAB=0.0  COST=    411.692
S_ 7_ 8= 1618.1  OP=1.0  OV=0  REL=1.000  EL=0.306  DAB=0.0  COST=    969.121
S_ 7_ 9= 1564.1  OP=1.0  OV=0  REL=1.000  EL=0.487  DAB=0.0  COST=   1337.466
S_ 7_10= 1699.6  OP=1.0  OV=0  REL=1.000  EL=0.530  DAB=0.0  COST=   1419.474
S_ 7_11= 2450.1  OP=1.0  OV=0  REL=1.000  EL=0.502  DAB=0.0  COST=   1320.516
S_ 7_12= 2522.8  OP=1.0  OV=0  REL=1.000  EL=0.176  DAB=0.0  COST=    641.394
S_ 8_ 1= 2683.5  OP=1.0  OV=0  REL=1.000  EL=1.000  DAB=0.0  COST=    285.000
S_ 8_ 2= 3197.0  OP=1.0  OV=0  REL=1.000  EL=1.000  DAB=0.0  COST=    255.000
S_ 8_ 3= 3100.9  OP=1.0  OV=0  REL=1.000  EL=1.000  DAB=0.0  COST=    225.000
S_ 8_ 4= 2810.4  OP=1.0  OV=0  REL=1.000  EL=1.000  DAB=0.0  COST=    255.000
S_ 8_ 5= 2496.9  OP=1.0  OV=0  REL=1.000  EL=1.000  DAB=0.0  COST=    285.000
S_ 8_ 6= 2146.6  OP=1.0  OV=0  REL=1.000  EL=1.000  DAB=0.0  COST=    315.000
S_ 8_ 7= 1932.9  OP=1.0  OV=0  REL=1.000  EL=0.034  DAB=0.0  COST=    411.692
S_ 8_ 8= 1743.4  OP=1.0  OV=0  REL=1.000  EL=0.306  DAB=0.0  COST=    954.121
S_ 8_ 9= 1685.3  OP=1.0  OV=0  REL=1.000  EL=0.473  DAB=0.0  COST=   1294.417
S_ 8_10= 1821.2  OP=1.0  OV=0  REL=1.000  EL=0.513  DAB=0.0  COST=   1373.005
S_ 8_11= 1976.7  OP=1.0  OV=0  REL=1.000  EL=0.487  DAB=0.0  COST=   1307.466
S_ 8_12= 1997.2  OP=1.0  OV=0  REL=1.000  EL=0.172  DAB=0.0  COST=    678.941
S_ 9_ 1= 1837.4  OP=1.0  OV=0  REL=1.000  EL=1.000  DAB=0.0  COST=    360.000
S_ 9_ 2= 2005.9  OP=1.0  OV=0  REL=1.000  EL=1.000  DAB=0.0  COST=    360.000
S_ 9_ 3= 1831.1  OP=1.0  OV=0  REL=1.000  EL=0.096  DAB=0.0  COST=    547.572
S_ 9_ 4= 1516.8  OP=1.0  OV=0  REL=1.000  EL=1.000  DAB=0.0  COST=    375.000
S_ 9_ 5= 1276.6  OP=1.0  OV=0  REL=0.159  EL=0.121  DAB=0.0  COST=   6524.497
S_ 9_ 6=  929.4  OP=1.0  OV=0  REL=1.000  EL=1.000  DAB=0.0  COST=    435.000
S_ 9_ 7=  735.5  OP=1.0  OV=0  REL=1.000  EL=0.000  DAB=1.0  COST=   4819.560
S_ 9_ 8=  612.6  OP=1.0  OV=0  REL=1.000  EL=0.000  DAB=1.0  COST=   4212.480
S_ 9_ 9=  515.0  OP=1.0  OV=0  REL=1.000  EL=0.000  DAB=1.0  COST=   3553.560
S_ 9_10=  527.4  OP=1.0  OV=0  REL=1.000  EL=0.000  DAB=1.0  COST=   2827.800
S_ 9_11=  793.1  OP=1.0  OV=0  REL=1.000  EL=0.000  DAB=1.0  COST=   3875.520
S_ 9_12=  815.6  OP=1.0  OV=0  REL=1.000  EL=0.000  DAB=1.0  COST=   3938.280
S_10_ 1= 1180.1  OP=1.0  OV=0  REL=1.000  EL=0.000  DAB=0.0  COST=   2394.000
S_10_ 2= 2099.8  OP=1.0  OV=0  REL=1.000  EL=0.000  DAB=0.0  COST=   2334.000
S_10_ 3= 2317.2  OP=1.0  OV=0  REL=1.000  EL=0.075  DAB=0.0  COST=    475.386
S_10_ 4= 2091.3  OP=1.0  OV=0  REL=1.000  EL=1.000  DAB=0.0  COST=    330.000
S_10_ 5= 1822.4  OP=1.0  OV=0  REL=1.000  EL=1.000  DAB=0.0  COST=    345.000
S_10_ 6= 1497.2  OP=1.0  OV=0  REL=1.000  EL=1.000  DAB=0.0  COST=    375.000
```

```
S_10_ 7= 1272.7  OP=1.0  OV=0  REL=1.000  EL=0.048  DAB=0.0  COST=     498.295
S_10_ 8= 1152.1  OP=1.0  OV=0  REL=1.000  EL=0.447  DAB=0.0  COST=    1289.217
S_10_ 9= 1114.0  OP=1.0  OV=0  REL=1.000  EL=0.531  DAB=0.0  COST=    1466.615
S_10_10= 1081.5  OP=1.0  OV=0  REL=1.000  EL=0.000  DAB=0.0  COST=    2379.000
S_10_11= 1108.8  OP=1.0  OV=0  REL=1.000  EL=0.000  DAB=0.0  COST=    2379.000
S_10_12= 1192.6  OP=1.0  OV=0  REL=1.000  EL=0.000  DAB=0.0  COST=    2379.000
S_11_ 1= 1261.9  OP=1.0  OV=0  REL=1.000  EL=0.000  DAB=0.0  COST=    2364.000
S_11_ 2= 1139.7  OP=1.0  OV=0  REL=1.000  EL=1.000  DAB=0.0  COST=     420.000
S_11_ 3=  922.6  OP=1.0  OV=0  REL=1.000  EL=0.195  DAB=0.0  COST=     829.911
S_11_ 4=  653.4  OP=1.0  OV=0  REL=0.033  EL=0.000  DAB=1.0  COST=    7800.360
S_11_ 5=  374.4  OP=1.0  OV=0  REL=0.019  EL=0.000  DAB=1.0  COST=    6378.840
S_11_ 6=  101.0  OP=1.0  OV=0  REL=0.100  EL=0.000  DAB=1.0  COST=    9959.880
S_11_ 7=    0.0  OP=1.0  OV=0  REL=0.308  EL=0.000  DAB=1.0  COST=   14077.199
S_11_ 8=    0.0  OP=0.2  OV=0  REL=0.891  EL=0.000  DAB=1.0  COST=   22235.040
S_11_ 9=   82.3  OP=1.0  OV=0  REL=0.436  EL=0.000  DAB=1.0  COST=    9612.000
S_11_10=  482.0  OP=1.0  OV=0  REL=0.645  EL=0.000  DAB=1.0  COST=   12266.760
S_11_11=  884.6  OP=1.0  OV=0  REL=1.000  EL=0.000  DAB=1.0  COST=    3875.520
S_11_12= 1125.0  OP=1.0  OV=0  REL=1.000  EL=0.000  DAB=0.0  COST=    2394.000
S_12_ 1= 1266.8  OP=1.0  OV=0  REL=1.000  EL=0.000  DAB=0.0  COST=    2379.000
S_12_ 2= 1452.1  OP=1.0  OV=0  REL=1.000  EL=0.000  DAB=0.0  COST=    2349.000
S_12_ 3= 1301.1  OP=1.0  OV=0  REL=1.000  EL=0.171  DAB=0.0  COST=     736.826
S_12_ 4=  990.8  OP=1.0  OV=0  REL=1.000  EL=1.000  DAB=0.0  COST=     435.000
S_12_ 5=  694.8  OP=1.0  OV=0  REL=0.019  EL=0.000  DAB=0.0  COST=    3108.840
S_12_ 6=  426.3  OP=1.0  OV=0  REL=0.100  EL=0.000  DAB=1.0  COST=    9929.880
S_12_ 7=  241.0  OP=1.0  OV=0  REL=1.000  EL=0.000  DAB=1.0  COST=    4864.560
S_12_ 8=  289.2  OP=1.0  OV=0  REL=1.000  EL=0.000  DAB=1.0  COST=    4257.480
S_12_ 9=  262.2  OP=1.0  OV=0  REL=1.000  EL=0.000  DAB=1.0  COST=    3583.560
S_12_10=  194.1  OP=1.0  OV=0  REL=1.000  EL=0.000  DAB=1.0  COST=    2857.800
S_12_11=  677.1  OP=1.0  OV=0  REL=1.000  EL=0.000  DAB=1.0  COST=    3905.520
S_12_12=  928.5  OP=1.0  OV=0  REL=1.000  EL=0.000  DAB=0.0  COST=    2409.000
S_13_ 1= 1105.4  OP=1.0  OV=0  REL=1.000  EL=0.000  DAB=0.0  COST=    2394.000
S_13_ 2= 1155.4  OP=1.0  OV=0  REL=1.000  EL=0.000  DAB=0.0  COST=    2379.000
S_13_ 3=  972.9  OP=1.0  OV=0  REL=1.000  EL=0.000  DAB=0.0  COST=    2379.000
S_13_ 4=  716.8  OP=1.0  OV=0  REL=0.033  EL=0.000  DAB=1.0  COST=    7800.360
S_13_ 5=  454.0  OP=1.0  OV=0  REL=0.019  EL=0.000  DAB=1.0  COST=    6378.840
S_13_ 6=  182.2  OP=1.0  OV=0  REL=0.100  EL=0.000  DAB=1.0  COST=    9944.880
S_13_ 7=  136.5  OP=1.0  OV=0  REL=0.304  EL=0.000  DAB=1.0  COST=   13925.640
S_13_ 8=  135.1  OP=1.0  OV=0  REL=0.486  EL=0.000  DAB=1.0  COST=   14070.240
S_13_ 9=   94.1  OP=1.0  OV=0  REL=0.436  EL=0.000  DAB=1.0  COST=    9612.000
S_13_10=  103.7  OP=1.0  OV=0  REL=0.645  EL=0.000  DAB=1.0  COST=   12281.760
S_13_11=  185.0  OP=1.0  OV=0  REL=0.648  EL=0.000  DAB=1.0  COST=   13474.080
S_13_12=  238.8  OP=1.0  OV=0  REL=0.185  EL=0.000  DAB=1.0  COST=    8689.800
S_14_ 1=  197.0  OP=1.0  OV=0  REL=0.188  EL=0.000  DAB=1.0  COST=   12344.520
S_14_ 2=  260.0  OP=1.0  OV=0  REL=0.250  EL=0.000  DAB=1.0  COST=   15143.880
S_14_ 3=  294.2  OP=1.0  OV=0  REL=0.328  EL=0.000  DAB=1.0  COST=   16102.920
S_14_ 4=  287.7  OP=1.0  OV=0  REL=0.719  EL=0.000  DAB=1.0  COST=   33598.920
S_14_ 5=  161.0  OP=1.0  OV=0  REL=0.439  EL=0.000  DAB=1.0  COST=   21960.840
S_14_ 6=    0.0  OP=0.7  OV=0  REL=0.398  EL=0.000  DAB=1.0  COST=   21971.320
S_14_ 7=    0.0  OP=0.5  OV=0  REL=0.667  EL=0.000  DAB=1.0  COST=   24749.280
S_14_ 8=    0.0  OP=0.7  OV=0  REL=0.618  EL=0.000  DAB=1.0  COST=   16740.000
S_14_ 9=  184.9  OP=1.0  OV=0  REL=0.436  EL=0.000  DAB=1.0  COST=    9612.000
S_14_10=  202.9  OP=1.0  OV=0  REL=1.000  EL=0.000  DAB=1.0  COST=    2857.800
S_14_11=  291.4  OP=1.0  OV=0  REL=1.000  EL=0.000  DAB=1.0  COST=    3920.520
S_14_12=  622.5  OP=1.0  OV=0  REL=0.185  EL=0.000  DAB=1.0  COST=    8659.800
S_15_ 1=  873.3  OP=1.0  OV=0  REL=1.000  EL=0.000  DAB=0.0  COST=    2409.000
S_15_ 2= 1582.9  OP=1.0  OV=0  REL=1.000  EL=0.000  DAB=0.0  COST=    2364.000
S_15_ 3= 1754.1  OP=1.0  OV=0  REL=1.000  EL=0.061  DAB=0.0  COST=     494.229
S_15_ 4= 1505.2  OP=1.0  OV=0  REL=1.000  EL=1.000  DAB=0.0  COST=     390.000
S_15_ 5= 1284.9  OP=1.0  OV=0  REL=0.159  EL=0.146  DAB=0.0  COST=    6572.581
S_15_ 6=  943.9  OP=1.0  OV=0  REL=1.000  EL=1.000  DAB=0.0  COST=     435.000
S_15_ 7=  756.4  OP=1.0  OV=0  REL=1.000  EL=0.000  DAB=1.0  COST=    4819.560
S_15_ 8=  760.0  OP=1.0  OV=0  REL=1.000  EL=0.000  DAB=1.0  COST=    4197.480
S_15_ 9=  929.7  OP=1.0  OV=0  REL=0.039  EL=0.000  DAB=1.0  COST=    4067.880
S_15_10= 1416.3  OP=1.0  OV=0  REL=1.000  EL=0.000  DAB=0.0  COST=    2379.000
S_15_11= 2819.1  OP=1.0  OV=0  REL=1.000  EL=0.000  DAB=0.0  COST=    2274.000
S_15_12= 4315.4  OP=1.0  OV=0  REL=1.000  EL=0.133  DAB=0.0  COST=     453.641
S_16_ 1= 7168.6  OP=1.0  OV=0  REL=1.000  EL=1.000  DAB=0.0  COST=       0.000
S_16_ 2= 7500.0  OP=1.0  OV=0  REL=1.000  EL=1.000  DAB=0.0  COST=       0.000
S_16_ 3= 7500.0  OP=1.0  OV=0  REL=1.000  EL=1.000  DAB=0.0  COST=       0.000
S_16_ 4= 7464.3  OP=1.0  OV=0  REL=1.000  EL=1.000  DAB=0.0  COST=       0.000
S_16_ 5= 7292.4  OP=1.0  OV=0  REL=1.000  EL=1.000  DAB=0.0  COST=       0.000
S_16_ 6= 7047.1  OP=1.0  OV=0  REL=1.000  EL=1.000  DAB=0.0  COST=       0.000
S_16_ 7= 6923.7  OP=1.0  OV=0  REL=1.000  EL=1.000  DAB=0.0  COST=       0.000
S_16_ 8= 6923.2  OP=1.0  OV=0  REL=1.000  EL=1.000  DAB=0.0  COST=       0.000
```

```
S_16_ 9= 6866.9  OP=1.0  OV=0  REL=1.000  EL=1.000  DAB=0.0  COST=     0.000
S_16_10= 6931.1  OP=1.0  OV=0  REL=1.000  EL=1.000  DAB=0.0  COST=     0.000
S_16_11= 6282.6  OP=1.0  OV=0  REL=1.000  EL=1.000  DAB=0.0  COST=     0.000
S_16_12= 5572.7  OP=1.0  OV=0  REL=1.000  EL=1.000  DAB=0.0  COST=     0.000
S_17_ 1= 5559.6  OP=1.0  OV=0  REL=1.000  EL=1.000  DAB=0.0  COST=     0.000
S_17_ 2= 5716.1  OP=1.0  OV=0  REL=1.000  EL=1.000  DAB=0.0  COST=     0.000
S_17_ 3= 5545.8  OP=1.0  OV=0  REL=1.000  EL=1.000  DAB=0.0  COST=     0.000
S_17_ 4= 5213.6  OP=1.0  OV=0  REL=1.000  EL=1.000  DAB=0.0  COST=     0.000
S_17_ 5= 4880.6  OP=1.0  OV=0  REL=1.000  EL=1.000  DAB=0.0  COST=    45.000
S_17_ 6= 4522.9  OP=1.0  OV=0  REL=1.000  EL=1.000  DAB=0.0  COST=    75.000
S_17_ 7= 4297.3  OP=1.0  OV=0  REL=1.000  EL=1.000  DAB=0.0  COST=   105.000
S_17_ 8= 4083.2  OP=1.0  OV=0  REL=1.000  EL=0.120  DAB=0.0  COST=   368.987
S_17_ 9= 3962.6  OP=1.0  OV=0  REL=1.000  EL=1.000  DAB=0.0  COST=   150.000
S_17_10= 3795.0  OP=1.0  OV=0  REL=1.000  EL=0.034  DAB=0.0  COST=   231.865
S_17_11= 3792.1  OP=1.0  OV=0  REL=1.000  EL=0.328  DAB=0.0  COST=   803.263
S_17_12= 3914.3  OP=1.0  OV=0  REL=1.000  EL=1.000  DAB=0.0  COST=   165.000
S_18_ 1= 5129.8  OP=1.0  OV=0  REL=1.000  EL=1.000  DAB=0.0  COST=    90.000
S_18_ 2= 5815.3  OP=1.0  OV=0  REL=1.000  EL=1.000  DAB=0.0  COST=     0.000
S_18_ 3= 5776.4  OP=1.0  OV=0  REL=1.000  EL=1.000  DAB=0.0  COST=     0.000
S_18_ 4= 5495.0  OP=1.0  OV=0  REL=1.000  EL=1.000  DAB=0.0  COST=     0.000
S_18_ 5= 5202.1  OP=1.0  OV=0  REL=1.000  EL=1.000  DAB=0.0  COST=    15.000
S_18_ 6= 4856.2  OP=1.0  OV=0  REL=1.000  EL=1.000  DAB=0.0  COST=    45.000
S_18_ 7= 4642.6  OP=1.0  OV=0  REL=1.000  EL=1.000  DAB=0.0  COST=    75.000
S_18_ 8= 4591.1  OP=1.0  OV=0  REL=1.000  EL=0.103  DAB=0.0  COST=   290.929
S_18_ 9= 4655.4  OP=1.0  OV=0  REL=1.000  EL=1.000  DAB=0.0  COST=    90.000
S_18_10= 4691.7  OP=1.0  OV=0  REL=1.000  EL=1.000  DAB=0.0  COST=    75.000
S_18_11= 4798.1  OP=1.0  OV=0  REL=1.000  EL=1.000  DAB=0.0  COST=    75.000
S_18_12= 5518.6  OP=1.0  OV=0  REL=1.000  EL=1.000  DAB=0.0  COST=    30.000
S_19_ 1= 7500.0  OP=1.0  OV=0  REL=1.000  EL=1.000  DAB=0.0  COST=     0.000
S_19_ 2= 7500.0  OP=1.0  OV=0  REL=1.000  EL=1.000  DAB=0.0  COST=     0.000
S_19_ 3= 7500.0  OP=1.0  OV=0  REL=1.000  EL=1.000  DAB=0.0  COST=     0.000
S_19_ 4= 7381.1  OP=1.0  OV=0  REL=1.000  EL=1.000  DAB=0.0  COST=     0.000
S_19_ 5= 7164.7  OP=1.0  OV=0  REL=1.000  EL=1.000  DAB=0.0  COST=     0.000
S_19_ 6= 6892.4  OP=1.0  OV=0  REL=1.000  EL=1.000  DAB=0.0  COST=     0.000
S_19_ 7= 6754.1  OP=1.0  OV=0  REL=1.000  EL=1.000  DAB=0.0  COST=     0.000
S_19_ 8= 6708.8  OP=1.0  OV=0  REL=1.000  EL=1.000  DAB=0.0  COST=     0.000
S_19_ 9= 6908.6  OP=1.0  OV=0  REL=1.000  EL=1.000  DAB=0.0  COST=     0.000
S_19_10= 6957.2  OP=1.0  OV=0  REL=1.000  EL=1.000  DAB=0.0  COST=     0.000
S_19_11= 6303.5  OP=1.0  OV=0  REL=1.000  EL=1.000  DAB=0.0  COST=     0.000
S_19_12= 5725.2  OP=1.0  OV=0  REL=1.000  EL=1.000  DAB=0.0  COST=     0.000
S_20_ 1= 5739.2  OP=1.0  OV=0  REL=1.000  EL=1.000  DAB=0.0  COST=     0.000
S_20_ 2= 5704.0  OP=1.0  OV=0  REL=1.000  EL=1.000  DAB=0.0  COST=     0.000
S_20_ 3= 5503.4  OP=1.0  OV=0  REL=1.000  EL=1.000  DAB=0.0  COST=     0.000
S_20_ 4= 5167.7  OP=1.0  OV=0  REL=1.000  EL=1.000  DAB=0.0  COST=    15.000
S_20_ 5= 4838.1  OP=1.0  OV=0  REL=1.000  EL=1.000  DAB=0.0  COST=    45.000
S_20_ 6= 4476.0  OP=1.0  OV=0  REL=1.000  EL=1.000  DAB=0.0  COST=    75.000
S_20_ 7= 4256.9  OP=1.0  OV=0  REL=1.000  EL=1.000  DAB=0.0  COST=   105.000
S_20_ 8= 4045.4  OP=1.0  OV=0  REL=1.000  EL=0.120  DAB=0.0  COST=   368.987
S_20_ 9= 3927.9  OP=1.0  OV=0  REL=1.000  EL=0.329  DAB=0.0  COST=   789.702
S_20_10= 3991.4  OP=1.0  OV=0  REL=1.000  EL=0.337  DAB=0.0  COST=   804.506
S_20_11= 4175.8  OP=1.0  OV=0  REL=1.000  EL=1.000  DAB=0.0  COST=   135.000
S_20_12= 5725.8  OP=1.0  OV=0  REL=1.000  EL=1.000  DAB=0.0  COST=    45.000
S_21_ 1= 7500.0  OP=1.0  OV=0  REL=1.000  EL=1.000  DAB=0.0  COST=     0.000
S_21_ 2= 7500.0  OP=1.0  OV=0  REL=1.000  EL=1.000  DAB=0.0  COST=     0.000
S_21_ 3= 7500.0  OP=1.0  OV=0  REL=1.000  EL=1.000  DAB=0.0  COST=     0.000
S_21_ 4= 7372.8  OP=1.0  OV=0  REL=1.000  EL=1.000  DAB=0.0  COST=     0.000
S_21_ 5= 7190.6  OP=1.0  OV=0  REL=1.000  EL=1.000  DAB=0.0  COST=     0.000
S_21_ 6= 6940.8  OP=1.0  OV=0  REL=1.000  EL=1.000  DAB=0.0  COST=     0.000
S_21_ 7= 6818.1  OP=1.0  OV=0  REL=1.000  EL=1.000  DAB=0.0  COST=     0.000
S_21_ 8= 6680.1  OP=1.0  OV=0  REL=1.000  EL=1.000  DAB=0.0  COST=     0.000
S_21_ 9= 6810.7  OP=1.0  OV=0  REL=1.000  EL=1.000  DAB=0.0  COST=     0.000
S_21_10= 7020.5  OP=1.0  OV=0  REL=1.000  EL=1.000  DAB=0.0  COST=     0.000
S_21_11= 5805.3  OP=1.0  OV=0  REL=1.000  EL=1.000  DAB=0.0  COST=     0.000
S_21_12= 6067.7  OP=1.0  OV=0  REL=1.000  EL=1.000  DAB=0.0  COST=     0.000
S_22_ 1= 6406.3  OP=1.0  OV=0  REL=1.000  EL=1.000  DAB=0.0  COST=     0.000
S_22_ 2= 7061.0  OP=1.0  OV=0  REL=1.000  EL=1.000  DAB=0.0  COST=     0.000
S_22_ 3= 7084.8  OP=1.0  OV=0  REL=1.000  EL=1.000  DAB=0.0  COST=     0.000
S_22_ 4= 6812.6  OP=1.0  OV=0  REL=1.000  EL=1.000  DAB=0.0  COST=     0.000
S_22_ 5= 6491.8  OP=1.0  OV=0  REL=1.000  EL=1.000  DAB=0.0  COST=     0.000
S_22_ 6= 6129.5  OP=1.0  OV=0  REL=1.000  EL=1.000  DAB=0.0  COST=     0.000
S_22_ 7= 5949.0  OP=1.0  OV=0  REL=1.000  EL=1.000  DAB=0.0  COST=     0.000
S_22_ 8= 5790.7  OP=1.0  OV=0  REL=1.000  EL=1.000  DAB=0.0  COST=     0.000
S_22_ 9= 5735.9  OP=1.0  OV=0  REL=1.000  EL=1.000  DAB=0.0  COST=     0.000
S_22_10= 6069.6  OP=1.0  OV=0  REL=1.000  EL=1.000  DAB=0.0  COST=     0.000
```

```
S_22_11=  6507.0   OP=1.0   OV=0   REL=1.000   EL=1.000   DAB=0.0   COST=        0.000
S_22_12=  6909.7   OP=1.0   OV=0   REL=1.000   EL=1.000   DAB=0.0   COST=        0.000
S_23_ 1=  7500.0   OP=1.0   OV=0   REL=1.000   EL=1.000   DAB=0.0   COST=        0.000
S_23_ 2=  7500.0   OP=1.0   OV=0   REL=1.000   EL=1.000   DAB=0.0   COST=        0.000
S_23_ 3=  7500.0   OP=1.0   OV=0   REL=1.000   EL=1.000   DAB=0.0   COST=        0.000
S_23_ 4=  7331.3   OP=1.0   OV=0   REL=1.000   EL=1.000   DAB=0.0   COST=        0.000
S_23_ 5=  7086.9   OP=1.0   OV=0   REL=1.000   EL=1.000   DAB=0.0   COST=        0.000
S_23_ 6=  6805.0   OP=1.0   OV=0   REL=1.000   EL=1.000   DAB=0.0   COST=        0.000
S_23_ 7=  6655.5   OP=1.0   OV=0   REL=1.000   EL=1.000   DAB=0.0   COST=        0.000
S_23_ 8=  6542.0   OP=1.0   OV=0   REL=1.000   EL=1.000   DAB=0.0   COST=        0.000
S_23_ 9=  6506.2   OP=1.0   OV=0   REL=1.000   EL=1.000   DAB=0.0   COST=        0.000
S_23_10=  6522.0   OP=1.0   OV=0   REL=1.000   EL=1.000   DAB=0.0   COST=        0.000
S_23_11=  6156.1   OP=1.0   OV=0   REL=1.000   EL=1.000   DAB=0.0   COST=        0.000
S_23_12=  5880.6   OP=1.0   OV=0   REL=1.000   EL=1.000   DAB=0.0   COST=        0.000
S_24_ 1=  6188.1   OP=1.0   OV=0   REL=1.000   EL=1.000   DAB=0.0   COST=        0.000
S_24_ 2=  6139.1   OP=1.0   OV=0   REL=1.000   EL=1.000   DAB=0.0   COST=        0.000
S_24_ 3=  6010.7   OP=1.0   OV=0   REL=1.000   EL=1.000   DAB=0.0   COST=        0.000
S_24_ 4=  5672.9   OP=1.0   OV=0   REL=1.000   EL=1.000   DAB=0.0   COST=        0.000
S_24_ 5=  5344.8   OP=1.0   OV=0   REL=1.000   EL=1.000   DAB=0.0   COST=        0.000
S_24_ 6=  4988.4   OP=1.0   OV=0   REL=1.000   EL=1.000   DAB=0.0   COST=       30.000
S_24_ 7=  4770.2   OP=1.0   OV=0   REL=1.000   EL=1.000   DAB=0.0   COST=       60.000
S_24_ 8=  4828.7   OP=1.0   OV=0   REL=1.000   EL=0.095   DAB=0.0   COST=      244.233
S_24_ 9=  5117.1   OP=1.0   OV=0   REL=1.000   EL=1.000   DAB=0.0   COST=       45.000
S_24_10=  5337.3   OP=1.0   OV=0   REL=1.000   EL=1.000   DAB=0.0   COST=       30.000
S_24_11=  5605.3   OP=1.0   OV=0   REL=1.000   EL=1.000   DAB=0.0   COST=        0.000
S_24_12=  6053.6   OP=1.0   OV=0   REL=1.000   EL=1.000   DAB=0.0   COST=        0.000
S_25_ 1=  6221.1   OP=1.0   OV=0   REL=1.000   EL=1.000   DAB=0.0   COST=        0.000
S_25_ 2=  6103.1   OP=1.0   OV=0   REL=1.000   EL=1.000   DAB=0.0   COST=        0.000
S_25_ 3=  5909.1   OP=1.0   OV=0   REL=1.000   EL=1.000   DAB=0.0   COST=        0.000
S_25_ 4=  5586.3   OP=1.0   OV=0   REL=1.000   EL=1.000   DAB=0.0   COST=        0.000
S_25_ 5=  5252.7   OP=1.0   OV=0   REL=1.000   EL=1.000   DAB=0.0   COST=        0.000
S_25_ 6=  4909.3   OP=1.0   OV=0   REL=1.000   EL=1.000   DAB=0.0   COST=       30.000
S_25_ 7=  4698.3   OP=1.0   OV=0   REL=1.000   EL=1.000   DAB=0.0   COST=       60.000
S_25_ 8=  4487.2   OP=1.0   OV=0   REL=1.000   EL=0.095   DAB=0.0   COST=      274.233
S_25_ 9=  4985.9   OP=1.0   OV=0   REL=1.000   EL=1.000   DAB=0.0   COST=       75.000
S_25_10=  5135.8   OP=1.0   OV=0   REL=1.000   EL=0.004   DAB=0.0   COST=       52.254
S_25_11=  5829.6   OP=1.0   OV=0   REL=1.000   EL=1.000   DAB=0.0   COST=        0.000
S_25_12=  5875.6   OP=1.0   OV=0   REL=1.000   EL=1.000   DAB=0.0   COST=        0.000
S_26_ 1=  6225.8   OP=1.0   OV=0   REL=1.000   EL=1.000   DAB=0.0   COST=        0.000
S_26_ 2=  6276.6   OP=1.0   OV=0   REL=1.000   EL=1.000   DAB=0.0   COST=        0.000
S_26_ 3=  6232.6   OP=1.0   OV=0   REL=1.000   EL=1.000   DAB=0.0   COST=        0.000
S_26_ 4=  6029.5   OP=1.0   OV=0   REL=1.000   EL=1.000   DAB=0.0   COST=        0.000
S_26_ 5=  5810.7   OP=1.0   OV=0   REL=1.000   EL=1.000   DAB=0.0   COST=        0.000
S_26_ 6=  5573.1   OP=1.0   OV=0   REL=1.000   EL=1.000   DAB=0.0   COST=        0.000
S_26_ 7=  5432.8   OP=1.0   OV=0   REL=1.000   EL=1.000   DAB=0.0   COST=        0.000
S_26_ 8=  5259.7   OP=1.0   OV=0   REL=1.000   EL=1.000   DAB=0.0   COST=       15.000
S_26_ 9=  5229.3   OP=1.0   OV=0   REL=1.000   EL=1.000   DAB=0.0   COST=       15.000
S_26_10=  5417.9   OP=1.0   OV=0   REL=1.000   EL=1.000   DAB=0.0   COST=       15.000
S_26_11=  5945.6   OP=1.0   OV=0   REL=1.000   EL=1.000   DAB=0.0   COST=        0.000
S_26_12=  6730.9   OP=1.0   OV=0   REL=1.000   EL=1.000   DAB=0.0   COST=        0.000
S_27_ 1=  7500.0   OP=1.0   OV=0   REL=1.000   EL=1.000   DAB=0.0   COST=        0.000
S_27_ 2=  7500.0   OP=1.0   OV=0   REL=1.000   EL=1.000   DAB=0.0   COST=        0.000
S_27_ 3=  7497.8   OP=1.0   OV=0   REL=1.000   EL=1.000   DAB=0.0   COST=        0.000
S_27_ 4=  7278.6   OP=1.0   OV=0   REL=1.000   EL=1.000   DAB=0.0   COST=        0.000
S_27_ 5=  7003.1   OP=1.0   OV=0   REL=1.000   EL=1.000   DAB=0.0   COST=        0.000
S_27_ 6=  6693.9   OP=1.0   OV=0   REL=1.000   EL=1.000   DAB=0.0   COST=        0.000
S_27_ 7=  6507.0   OP=1.0   OV=0   REL=1.000   EL=1.000   DAB=0.0   COST=        0.000
S_27_ 8=  6367.4   OP=1.0   OV=0   REL=1.000   EL=1.000   DAB=0.0   COST=        0.000
S_27_ 9=  6371.2   OP=1.0   OV=0   REL=1.000   EL=1.000   DAB=0.0   COST=        0.000
S_27_10=  6498.9   OP=1.0   OV=0   REL=1.000   EL=1.000   DAB=0.0   COST=        0.000
S_27_11=  6316.8   OP=1.0   OV=0   REL=1.000   EL=1.000   DAB=0.0   COST=        0.000
S_27_12=  6449.5   OP=1.0   OV=0   REL=1.000   EL=1.000   DAB=0.0   COST=        0.000
S_28_ 1=  7332.8   OP=1.0   OV=0   REL=1.000   EL=1.000   DAB=0.0   COST=        0.000
S_28_ 2=  7500.0   OP=1.0   OV=0   REL=1.000   EL=1.000   DAB=0.0   COST=        0.000
S_28_ 3=  7467.8   OP=1.0   OV=0   REL=1.000   EL=1.000   DAB=0.0   COST=        0.000
S_28_ 4=  7211.2   OP=1.0   OV=0   REL=1.000   EL=1.000   DAB=0.0   COST=        0.000
S_28_ 5=  6918.3   OP=1.0   OV=0   REL=1.000   EL=1.000   DAB=0.0   COST=        0.000
S_28_ 6=  6596.5   OP=1.0   OV=0   REL=1.000   EL=1.000   DAB=0.0   COST=        0.000
S_28_ 7=  6456.3   OP=1.0   OV=0   REL=1.000   EL=1.000   DAB=0.0   COST=        0.000
S_28_ 8=  6321.7   OP=1.0   OV=0   REL=1.000   EL=1.000   DAB=0.0   COST=        0.000
S_28_ 9=  6222.3   OP=1.0   OV=0   REL=1.000   EL=1.000   DAB=0.0   COST=        0.000
S_28_10=  6258.6   OP=1.0   OV=0   REL=1.000   EL=1.000   DAB=0.0   COST=        0.000
S_28_11=  6228.1   OP=1.0   OV=0   REL=1.000   EL=1.000   DAB=0.0   COST=        0.000
S_28_12=  6315.7   OP=1.0   OV=0   REL=1.000   EL=1.000   DAB=0.0   COST=        0.000
```

```
S_29_ 1= 7223.5  OP=1.0  OV=0  REL=1.000  EL=1.000  DAB=0.0  COST=       0.000
S_29_ 2= 7500.0  OP=1.0  OV=0  REL=1.000  EL=1.000  DAB=0.0  COST=       0.000
S_29_ 3= 7451.4  OP=1.0  OV=0  REL=1.000  EL=1.000  DAB=0.0  COST=       0.000
S_29_ 4= 7163.3  OP=1.0  OV=0  REL=1.000  EL=1.000  DAB=0.0  COST=       0.000
S_29_ 5= 6852.6  OP=1.0  OV=0  REL=1.000  EL=1.000  DAB=0.0  COST=       0.000
S_29_ 6= 6505.8  OP=1.0  OV=0  REL=1.000  EL=1.000  DAB=0.0  COST=       0.000
S_29_ 7= 6289.8  OP=1.0  OV=0  REL=1.000  EL=1.000  DAB=0.0  COST=       0.000
S_29_ 8= 6343.3  OP=1.0  OV=0  REL=1.000  EL=1.000  DAB=0.0  COST=       0.000
S_29_ 9= 6419.7  OP=1.0  OV=0  REL=1.000  EL=1.000  DAB=0.0  COST=       0.000
S_29_10= 6486.5  OP=1.0  OV=0  REL=1.000  EL=1.000  DAB=0.0  COST=       0.000
S_29_11= 6175.9  OP=1.0  OV=0  REL=1.000  EL=1.000  DAB=0.0  COST=       0.000
S_29_12= 5697.0  OP=1.0  OV=0  REL=1.000  EL=1.000  DAB=0.0  COST=       0.000
S_30_ 1= 6324.1  OP=1.0  OV=0  REL=1.000  EL=1.000  DAB=0.0  COST=       0.000
S_30_ 2= 6609.9  OP=1.0  OV=0  REL=1.000  EL=1.000  DAB=0.0  COST=       0.000
S_30_ 3= 6598.5  OP=1.0  OV=0  REL=1.000  EL=1.000  DAB=0.0  COST=       0.000
S_30_ 4= 6307.1  OP=1.0  OV=0  REL=1.000  EL=1.000  DAB=0.0  COST=       0.000
S_30_ 5= 5996.4  OP=1.0  OV=0  REL=1.000  EL=1.000  DAB=0.0  COST=       0.000
S_30_ 6= 5663.8  OP=1.0  OV=0  REL=1.000  EL=1.000  DAB=0.0  COST=       0.000
S_30_ 7= 5454.9  OP=1.0  OV=0  REL=1.000  EL=1.000  DAB=0.0  COST=       0.000
S_30_ 8= 5255.3  OP=1.0  OV=0  REL=1.000  EL=1.000  DAB=0.0  COST=      15.000
S_30_ 9= 5271.3  OP=1.0  OV=0  REL=1.000  EL=1.000  DAB=0.0  COST=      15.000
S_30_10= 5262.7  OP=1.0  OV=0  REL=1.000  EL=1.000  DAB=0.0  COST=      15.000
S_30_11= 5206.6  OP=1.0  OV=0  REL=1.000  EL=1.000  DAB=0.0  COST=      30.000
S_30_12= 5136.8  OP=1.0  OV=0  REL=1.000  EL=1.000  DAB=0.0  COST=      30.000
S_31_ 1= 5216.7  OP=1.0  OV=0  REL=1.000  EL=1.000  DAB=0.0  COST=      30.000
S_31_ 2= 5186.5  OP=1.0  OV=0  REL=1.000  EL=1.000  DAB=0.0  COST=      30.000
S_31_ 3= 4971.4  OP=1.0  OV=0  REL=1.000  EL=1.000  DAB=0.0  COST=      45.000
S_31_ 4= 4615.7  OP=1.0  OV=0  REL=1.000  EL=1.000  DAB=0.0  COST=      60.000
S_31_ 5= 4262.7  OP=1.0  OV=0  REL=1.000  EL=1.000  DAB=0.0  COST=     105.000
S_31_ 6= 3895.3  OP=1.0  OV=0  REL=1.000  EL=1.000  DAB=0.0  COST=     135.000
S_31_ 7= 3657.8  OP=1.0  OV=0  REL=1.000  EL=1.000  DAB=0.0  COST=     165.000
S_31_ 8= 3663.2  OP=1.0  OV=0  REL=1.000  EL=0.158  DAB=0.0  COST=     487.283
S_31_ 9= 4164.7  OP=1.0  OV=0  REL=1.000  EL=1.000  DAB=0.0  COST=     150.000
S_31_10= 4425.0  OP=1.0  OV=0  REL=1.000  EL=1.000  DAB=0.0  COST=     120.000
S_31_11= 4933.4  OP=1.0  OV=0  REL=1.000  EL=1.000  DAB=0.0  COST=      75.000
S_31_12= 5208.7  OP=1.0  OV=0  REL=1.000  EL=0.004  DAB=0.0  COST=      52.254
S_32_ 1= 5931.7  OP=1.0  OV=0  REL=1.000  EL=1.000  DAB=0.0  COST=       0.000
S_32_ 2= 6119.5  OP=1.0  OV=0  REL=1.000  EL=1.000  DAB=0.0  COST=       0.000
S_32_ 3= 6006.4  OP=1.0  OV=0  REL=1.000  EL=1.000  DAB=0.0  COST=       0.000
S_32_ 4= 5708.5  OP=1.0  OV=0  REL=1.000  EL=1.000  DAB=0.0  COST=       0.000
S_32_ 5= 5379.7  OP=1.0  OV=0  REL=1.000  EL=1.000  DAB=0.0  COST=       0.000
S_32_ 6= 5021.8  OP=1.0  OV=0  REL=1.000  EL=1.000  DAB=0.0  COST=      30.000
S_32_ 7= 4797.9  OP=1.0  OV=0  REL=1.000  EL=1.000  DAB=0.0  COST=      60.000
S_32_ 8= 4679.8  OP=1.0  OV=0  REL=1.000  EL=0.095  DAB=0.0  COST=     259.233
S_32_ 9= 4767.7  OP=1.0  OV=0  REL=1.000  EL=1.000  DAB=0.0  COST=      75.000
S_32_10= 4744.4  OP=1.0  OV=0  REL=1.000  EL=1.000  DAB=0.0  COST=      75.000
S_32_11= 5027.1  OP=1.0  OV=0  REL=1.000  EL=1.000  DAB=0.0  COST=      60.000
S_32_12= 5351.8  OP=1.0  OV=0  REL=1.000  EL=1.000  DAB=0.0  COST=      30.000
S_33_ 1= 5706.5  OP=1.0  OV=0  REL=1.000  EL=1.000  DAB=0.0  COST=       0.000
S_33_ 2= 6730.3  OP=1.0  OV=0  REL=1.000  EL=1.000  DAB=0.0  COST=       0.000
S_33_ 3= 6798.9  OP=1.0  OV=0  REL=1.000  EL=1.000  DAB=0.0  COST=       0.000
S_33_ 4= 6512.1  OP=1.0  OV=0  REL=1.000  EL=1.000  DAB=0.0  COST=       0.000
S_33_ 5= 6196.7  OP=1.0  OV=0  REL=1.000  EL=1.000  DAB=0.0  COST=       0.000
S_33_ 6= 5856.5  OP=1.0  OV=0  REL=1.000  EL=1.000  DAB=0.0  COST=       0.000
S_33_ 7= 5631.7  OP=1.0  OV=0  REL=1.000  EL=1.000  DAB=0.0  COST=       0.000
S_33_ 8= 5500.1  OP=1.0  OV=0  REL=1.000  EL=1.000  DAB=0.0  COST=       0.000
S_33_ 9= 5681.7  OP=1.0  OV=0  REL=1.000  EL=1.000  DAB=0.0  COST=       0.000
S_33_10= 5689.8  OP=1.0  OV=0  REL=1.000  EL=1.000  DAB=0.0  COST=       0.000
S_33_11= 5694.1  OP=1.0  OV=0  REL=1.000  EL=1.000  DAB=0.0  COST=       0.000
S_33_12= 6665.8  OP=1.0  OV=0  REL=1.000  EL=1.000  DAB=0.0  COST=       0.000
S_34_ 1= 7425.6  OP=1.0  OV=0  REL=1.000  EL=1.000  DAB=0.0  COST=       0.000
S_34_ 2= 7500.0  OP=1.0  OV=0  REL=1.000  EL=1.000  DAB=0.0  COST=       0.000
S_34_ 3= 7357.1  OP=1.0  OV=0  REL=1.000  EL=1.000  DAB=0.0  COST=       0.000
S_34_ 4= 7031.6  OP=1.0  OV=0  REL=1.000  EL=1.000  DAB=0.0  COST=       0.000
S_34_ 5= 6697.6  OP=1.0  OV=0  REL=1.000  EL=1.000  DAB=0.0  COST=       0.000
S_34_ 6= 6328.8  OP=1.0  OV=0  REL=1.000  EL=1.000  DAB=0.0  COST=       0.000
S_34_ 7= 6103.4  OP=1.0  OV=0  REL=1.000  EL=1.000  DAB=0.0  COST=       0.000
S_34_ 8= 6363.9  OP=1.0  OV=0  REL=1.000  EL=1.000  DAB=0.0  COST=       0.000
S_34_ 9= 6379.1  OP=1.0  OV=0  REL=1.000  EL=1.000  DAB=0.0  COST=       0.000
S_34_10= 7084.1  OP=1.0  OV=0  REL=1.000  EL=1.000  DAB=0.0  COST=       0.000
S_34_11= 6476.6  OP=1.0  OV=0  REL=1.000  EL=1.000  DAB=0.0  COST=       0.000
S_34_12= 7500.0  OP=1.0  OV=0  REL=1.000  EL=1.000  DAB=0.0  COST= 300000.000
S_35_ 1= 7500.0  OP=1.0  OV=0  REL=1.000  EL=1.000  DAB=0.0  COST=       0.000
S_35_ 2= 7500.0  OP=1.0  OV=0  REL=1.000  EL=1.000  DAB=0.0  COST=       0.000
```

```
S_35_ 3= 7461.8  OP=1.0  OV=0  REL=1.000  EL=1.000  DAB=0.0  COST=       0.000
S_35_ 4= 7227.6  OP=1.0  OV=0  REL=1.000  EL=1.000  DAB=0.0  COST=       0.000
S_35_ 5= 6963.7  OP=1.0  OV=0  REL=1.000  EL=1.000  DAB=0.0  COST=       0.000
S_35_ 6= 6658.7  OP=1.0  OV=0  REL=1.000  EL=1.000  DAB=0.0  COST=       0.000
S_35_ 7= 6473.7  OP=1.0  OV=0  REL=1.000  EL=1.000  DAB=0.0  COST=       0.000
S_35_ 8= 6314.9  OP=1.0  OV=0  REL=1.000  EL=1.000  DAB=0.0  COST=       0.000
S_35_ 9= 6198.2  OP=1.0  OV=0  REL=1.000  EL=1.000  DAB=0.0  COST=       0.000
S_35_10= 6205.9  OP=1.0  OV=0  REL=1.000  EL=1.000  DAB=0.0  COST=       0.000
S_35_11= 6067.3  OP=1.0  OV=0  REL=1.000  EL=1.000  DAB=0.0  COST=       0.000
S_35_12= 6748.9  OP=1.0  OV=0  REL=1.000  EL=1.000  DAB=0.0  COST=       0.000
S_36_ 1= 7500.0  OP=1.0  OV=0  REL=1.000  EL=1.000  DAB=0.0  COST=       0.000
S_36_ 2= 7500.0  OP=1.0  OV=0  REL=1.000  EL=1.000  DAB=0.0  COST=       0.000
S_36_ 3= 7370.3  OP=1.0  OV=0  REL=1.000  EL=1.000  DAB=0.0  COST=       0.000
S_36_ 4= 7066.6  OP=1.0  OV=0  REL=1.000  EL=1.000  DAB=0.0  COST=       0.000
S_36_ 5= 6734.9  OP=1.0  OV=0  REL=1.000  EL=1.000  DAB=0.0  COST=       0.000
S_36_ 6= 6379.5  OP=1.0  OV=0  REL=1.000  EL=1.000  DAB=0.0  COST=       0.000
S_36_ 7= 6161.1  OP=1.0  OV=0  REL=1.000  EL=1.000  DAB=0.0  COST=       0.000
S_36_ 8= 6041.0  OP=1.0  OV=0  REL=1.000  EL=1.000  DAB=0.0  COST=       0.000
S_36_ 9= 6372.7  OP=1.0  OV=0  REL=1.000  EL=1.000  DAB=0.0  COST=       0.000
S_36_10= 6412.0  OP=1.0  OV=0  REL=1.000  EL=1.000  DAB=0.0  COST=       0.000
S_36_11= 6275.5  OP=1.0  OV=0  REL=1.000  EL=1.000  DAB=0.0  COST=       0.000
S_36_12= 6172.1  OP=1.0  OV=0  REL=1.000  EL=1.000  DAB=0.0  COST=       0.000
S_37_ 1= 6858.7  OP=1.0  OV=0  REL=1.000  EL=1.000  DAB=0.0  COST=       0.000
S_37_ 2= 6919.7  OP=1.0  OV=0  REL=1.000  EL=1.000  DAB=0.0  COST=       0.000
S_37_ 3= 6755.6  OP=1.0  OV=0  REL=1.000  EL=1.000  DAB=0.0  COST=       0.000
S_37_ 4= 6439.5  OP=1.0  OV=0  REL=1.000  EL=1.000  DAB=0.0  COST=       0.000
S_37_ 5= 6107.0  OP=1.0  OV=0  REL=1.000  EL=1.000  DAB=0.0  COST=       0.000
S_37_ 6= 5736.8  OP=1.0  OV=0  REL=1.000  EL=1.000  DAB=0.0  COST=       0.000
S_37_ 7= 5504.3  OP=1.0  OV=0  REL=1.000  EL=1.000  DAB=0.0  COST=       0.000
S_37_ 8= 5311.2  OP=1.0  OV=0  REL=1.000  EL=1.000  DAB=0.0  COST=       0.000
S_37_ 9= 5116.5  OP=1.0  OV=0  REL=1.000  EL=1.000  DAB=0.0  COST=      30.000
S_37_10= 5074.4  OP=1.0  OV=0  REL=1.000  EL=0.078  DAB=0.0  COST=     181.174
S_37_11= 4966.0  OP=1.0  OV=0  REL=1.000  EL=1.000  DAB=0.0  COST=      45.000
S_37_12= 5359.8  OP=1.0  OV=0  REL=1.000  EL=1.000  DAB=0.0  COST=      30.000
S_38_ 1= 5619.4  OP=1.0  OV=0  REL=1.000  EL=1.000  DAB=0.0  COST=       0.000
S_38_ 2= 5528.1  OP=1.0  OV=0  REL=1.000  EL=1.000  DAB=0.0  COST=       0.000
S_38_ 3= 5308.5  OP=1.0  OV=0  REL=1.000  EL=1.000  DAB=0.0  COST=       0.000
S_38_ 4= 4962.4  OP=1.0  OV=0  REL=1.000  EL=1.000  DAB=0.0  COST=      30.000
S_38_ 5= 4605.5  OP=1.0  OV=0  REL=1.000  EL=1.000  DAB=0.0  COST=      60.000
S_38_ 6= 4228.0  OP=1.0  OV=0  REL=1.000  EL=1.000  DAB=0.0  COST=     105.000
S_38_ 7= 4015.3  OP=1.0  OV=0  REL=1.000  EL=1.000  DAB=0.0  COST=     135.000
S_38_ 8= 3802.2  OP=1.0  OV=0  REL=1.000  EL=0.137  DAB=0.0  COST=     417.045
S_38_ 9= 4228.8  OP=1.0  OV=0  REL=1.000  EL=0.337  DAB=0.0  COST=     804.506
S_38_10= 4224.2  OP=1.0  OV=0  REL=1.000  EL=1.000  DAB=0.0  COST=     120.000
S_38_11= 4251.8  OP=1.0  OV=0  REL=1.000  EL=1.000  DAB=0.0  COST=     120.000
S_38_12= 5333.6  OP=1.0  OV=0  REL=1.000  EL=1.000  DAB=0.0  COST=      75.000
S_39_ 1= 6977.6  OP=1.0  OV=0  REL=1.000  EL=1.000  DAB=0.0  COST=       0.000
S_39_ 2= 7500.0  OP=1.0  OV=0  REL=1.000  EL=1.000  DAB=0.0  COST=       0.000
S_39_ 3= 7500.0  OP=1.0  OV=0  REL=1.000  EL=1.000  DAB=0.0  COST=       0.000
S_39_ 4= 7328.0  OP=1.0  OV=0  REL=1.000  EL=1.000  DAB=0.0  COST=       0.000
S_39_ 5= 7086.6  OP=1.0  OV=0  REL=1.000  EL=1.000  DAB=0.0  COST=       0.000
S_39_ 6= 6788.6  OP=1.0  OV=0  REL=1.000  EL=1.000  DAB=0.0  COST=       0.000
S_39_ 7= 6619.6  OP=1.0  OV=0  REL=1.000  EL=1.000  DAB=0.0  COST=       0.000
S_39_ 8= 6508.6  OP=1.0  OV=0  REL=1.000  EL=1.000  DAB=0.0  COST=       0.000
S_39_ 9= 6912.1  OP=1.0  OV=0  REL=1.000  EL=1.000  DAB=0.0  COST=       0.000
S_39_10= 7500.0  OP=1.0  OV=0  REL=1.000  EL=0.004  DAB=0.0  COST=       7.588
S_39_11= 6744.9  OP=1.0  OV=0  REL=1.000  EL=1.000  DAB=0.0  COST=  300000.000
S_39_12= 6974.7  OP=1.0  OV=0  REL=1.000  EL=1.000  DAB=0.0  COST=       0.000
S_40_ 1= 7500.0  OP=1.0  OV=0  REL=1.000  EL=1.000  DAB=0.0  COST=       0.000
S_40_ 2= 7500.0  OP=1.0  OV=0  REL=1.000  EL=1.000  DAB=0.0  COST=       0.000
S_40_ 3= 7500.0  OP=1.0  OV=0  REL=1.000  EL=1.000  DAB=0.0  COST=       0.000
S_40_ 4= 7304.6  OP=1.0  OV=0  REL=1.000  EL=1.000  DAB=0.0  COST=       0.000
S_40_ 5= 7061.5  OP=1.0  OV=0  REL=1.000  EL=1.000  DAB=0.0  COST=       0.000
S_40_ 6= 6769.5  OP=1.0  OV=0  REL=1.000  EL=1.000  DAB=0.0  COST=       0.000
S_40_ 7= 6599.9  OP=1.0  OV=0  REL=1.000  EL=1.000  DAB=0.0  COST=       0.000
S_40_ 8= 6584.4  OP=1.0  OV=0  REL=1.000  EL=1.000  DAB=0.0  COST=       0.000
S_40_ 9= 6809.1  OP=1.0  OV=0  REL=1.000  EL=1.000  DAB=0.0  COST=       0.000
S_40_10= 7223.4  OP=1.0  OV=0  REL=1.000  EL=0.004  DAB=0.0  COST=       7.588
S_40_11= 6288.0  OP=1.0  OV=0  REL=1.000  EL=1.000  DAB=0.0  COST=       0.000
S_40_12= 6241.6  OP=1.0  OV=0  REL=1.000  EL=1.000  DAB=0.0  COST=       0.000
S_41_ 1= 6645.7  OP=1.0  OV=0  REL=1.000  EL=1.000  DAB=0.0  COST=       0.000
S_41_ 2= 6715.8  OP=1.0  OV=0  REL=1.000  EL=1.000  DAB=0.0  COST=       0.000
S_41_ 3= 6570.3  OP=1.0  OV=0  REL=1.000  EL=1.000  DAB=0.0  COST=       0.000
S_41_ 4= 6254.4  OP=1.0  OV=0  REL=1.000  EL=1.000  DAB=0.0  COST=       0.000
```

```
S_41_ 5= 5922.8  OP=1.0  OV=0  REL=1.000  EL=1.000  DAB=0.0  COST=     0.000
S_41_ 6= 5564.2  OP=1.0  OV=0  REL=1.000  EL=1.000  DAB=0.0  COST=     0.000

S=reservoir  space
op=operation
```

IT Absorption & Diffusion Readiness Index (ITADRI): Conceptual Model, Factors and Measures

AMROLAH AMINI (Ph.D)

Associate Professor, Allameh Tabatabaei University (ATU), Tehran, Iran.

aminij@atu.ac.ir

ALIREZA EMAMI

Master of Science, Tehran University, Tehran, Iran

memami@alumni.ut.ac.ir

MOSTAFA EMAMI*

Master of Science, Michigan Technological University (MTU)

memami@mtu.edu

***Corresponding Address**

Applied Research and Technology Office, Michigan Technological University

1400 Townsend Dr, Houghton, MI 49931

Tel & Fax : +1-(816) 237-0018

E-mail: memami@mtu.edu

IT Absorption & Diffusion Readiness Index (ITADRI): Conceptual Model, Factors and Measures

Abstract

Denspite of widespread belief in the potential value of information technology (IT) on organizations and nations' developments, the literature shows a Paradox in the results (IT

Paradox). However, there is a significant digital divide between developed and developing countries in the use of IT and the availability of complementary assets such as telecommunications networks and skilled IT professionals. Accordingly, the main question now is not whether, but what factors affect and moderate the relation between IT and performance. This paper aims to achieve three following objectives; 1) reveiewing the related literature, 2) determining and classifying the most important influence factors that modify the relation between IT and performance, and 3) introducing a basical conceptual model of calculationg IT Absorption and Diffusion Readiness Index (ITADRI) as a strategic level moderator variable.

Key words: IT Absorption, IT Diffusion, Readiness Index, Conceptual Model

1. Introduction

Most of researchers and development specialist believe that information technology (IT) has a great impact on organizations performance and nations' developments and the amount of investments on IT has rapidly increased in recent years. (Adkinson, Lenard and Pickford 2004) Despite of positive viewpoints on the effects of IT on organizational and national performances, some researchers are concern. In other words, they question about the positive relationship between IT investments and the performance. Accordingly, their main question is "Does IT investment improves the organizational and national performance?"

There are a huge number of papers in literature in order to answer this question and explaining the relation between IT and performance. Moreover, some researchers studied the effects of IT investments on various areas of IT (e.g. on infrastructures, applications, hardware and software systems). The application of IT to development goals has not always succeeded to date and there are many cases of partial or complete failure. (Avgerou and Walsham 2000) In other words, the literature shows a Paradox in the results. (Brynjolfsson 1993; Brynjolfsson & Yang 1996; Lubbe, Parker & Hoard 1995; Brynjolfsson & Hitt 1996; Bakos 1998; Kennerley & Andy 1998; Bharadwaj Anandhi, Bharadwaj & Konsynski 1999; Smith, Bullers & Piland 2000; Kohli Rajiv & Sarv Devaraj 2003; Motohashi Kazuyuki 2003; Dowlatshahi Shad & Cao Qing 2006; Huang, Shi-Ming, Qu Chin-Shyh, Chen Chyi-Miaw, Lin Binshan 2006)

As mention above, although there is a widespread belief in the potential value of information technology (IT) on organizations and nations' developments, however there is paradox and a significant digital divide between developed and developing countries in the use of IT and the availability of complementary assets such as telecommunications networks and skilled IT professionals. We focuses on developing countries because they have the majority of the world's population; contain millions of people who lack access to resources such as clean water, adequate housing, education, and freedom to choices their own lives. (Sen 1999; Walsham, Robey, and Sahay 2007)

Respecting the Paradox, the main question of researchers has now become not whether, but what factors affecting IT absorption and disfusion. The literature suggests several influence factors especially at the country level and shows that there are various differences in these factors between developed and developing countries.

The purpose of this paper is to reveiew the related literature, determine and classify important influence factors that modify the relation between IT and performance, and introduce a basic conceptual model for considering IT Absorption and Diffusion Readiness Index (ITADRI) as a strategic level moderator variable. For this purpose, the remainder of the paper is structurized as follows. Section 2 explains a brief review of literature. Section 3 provides a framework to classify affecting factors and measures. Section 4 describes the conceptual model and the potenial research hypotheses that can be investigated in future researches. In this section, we will introduce the IT Absorption and Diffusion Readiness Index (ITADRI) as a strategic level moderator variable. Finally, the paper ends with conclusions and final remarks.

2. The Literature

Two main questions on IT usage are "what factors influence IT usage at organizational and the country level?" and "are there any significant differences in these factors between developed and developing countries?"

At organizational level, Mahmood Adam and Swanberg (2001) attempt to determine organizational factors affecting IT usage using a meta- analysis of empirical literature. They provide a combined model of IT usage and IT effectiveness. In this model, IT effectiveness is a function of IT usage and IT usage, in turn, consists of four main factors, organizational IT application, organization characteristics, individual characteristics, and perceived benefits. Results of their meta-analysis confirm a strong and significant positive relation between the perception of ease of use and the perceived usefulness of an IT system to the actual amount of usage. Although the factors of education level, training level, and professional level were found to have a substantial effect on IT usage, the magnitude of these effects were lower than those of the perceptions of the user and organizational support.

Meyer, Srinivas, Lal and Topolnytsky (2007) study the relations between the commitment components and behavioral support for a change using Herscovitch and Meyer's (2002) three-component model (affective, normative and continuance commitments) of commitment to an organizationa. They found a considerable support for the relations between commitment and support predicted by the model. However, they also found evidence for potential culture differences.

Mutula and Brakel (2006) propose an assessment tool for evaluating e-readiness at organizational level. Their proposed model includes five main components: enterprise readiness, ICT readiness, external environment readiness, human resource readiness, and information readiness. They define 29 measures for enterprise readiness, 19 measures for human resource readiness, 21 measure for information readiness, 22 measures for ICT readiness, and finally 21 measures for environment readiness component (totally 112 measures).

Although there is a widespread belief in potential value of IT and its supportive roles in human and nations' economic development, however there is significant differences between developed and developing countries in the use of IT. Several researches have been conducted to determine issues creating and affecting the differences in IT usage between developed and developing countries. The literature review shows a huge number of issues. For example, Dewan and Kraemer (2000) compare developed and developing countries and find a significant positive relationship between IT investment and productivity growth at the macroeconomic level in developed countries, but not in developing countries.

Moreover, Madon (2000) examine the use of the internet in sectors such as health and education, and in domains such as economic productivity and sustainable development.

Some researches and international documents confirms the effect of the availability of complementary assets such as telecommunications networks and skilled IT professionals and their drives for IT investments. (UNDP Report 2001; World Bank Group 2002; Shih, Kraemer & Dedrick 2008). Although the studies show that IT investment is correlated with the level of national wealth, other factors, resources for technology investments, structure of the economy, and openness to external influences, have been shown to be significant as well.

Bui, Sankaran and Sebastian (2003) propose a framework to evaluate the IT e-readiness of a nation based on eight factors: digital infrastructure, macro economy, ability to invest, knowledgeable citizens, competitiveness, access to skilled workforce, culture, and cost of living and pricing. They identify 52 measures to quantify these eight factors and provide a simple algorithm to calculate an overall e-readiness index for a country. Finally, they provide just a simple benchmarking e-readiness using a 5-point scale diagram. In their research, the measures are as follows:

- Six measures that quantify knowledge citizens' factors are: 1)adult tertiary rate, 2)secondary enrollment, 3)tertiary enrollment, 4) 8th grade achievement in science, 5)MGMT education locally available in first-class business schools, and 6)flexibility of people to adapt to new challenges.
- Twelve measures that quantify macro economy factor are: 1)trade as % of GDP, 2)adequate regulations and supervision of financial institutions, 3)protection of property rights, 4)tariff and non-tariff barriers, 5)soundness of banks, 6)local competition, 7)regulatory framework, 8)government effectiveness, 9)political stability, 10)press freedom, 11)rule of Law, and 12)control of corruption.
- Seven measures that quantify the competitiveness are: 1)technology assessment index, 2)tertiary science and engineering enrollment, 3)administration burden for start-Ups, 4)patent applications granted, 5)private sector spending on R&D, 6)total expenditure for R &D as % of GNI, and 7)high-technology exports.
- Four measures that quantify ability, willingness to invest are: 1)composite ICRG Risk Rating, 2)availability of venture capital, 3)entrepreneurship among managers, and 4)FDI as % of GDP.
- Six measures that quantify access to skilled workforce are: 1)public spending on education, 2)university education meets the needs of competitive economy, 3)well educated people do not emigrate abroad, 4)extent of staff training, 5)research collaboration companies/universities, and 6)technical papers per million population.
- Ten measures that quantify digital infrastructure are: 1)telephone per 1000 people, 2)mobile phones per 1000 people, 3)computers per 1000 people, 4)internet hosts per 10000 people, 5)international telecommunications, 6)cost of call to the USA, 7)investment in telecom, 8)computer processing power (% of total worldwide MIPS), 9)e-government (2001 WEF), 10)ICT expenditure as % of GDP, and 10)freedom on the internet.
- Three measures that quantify cost of living and pricing are: 1)international cost of living indices based on $100 US, 2)inflation rate-CPI in %, and 3)GDP per capita (PPP) in US$.

- Finally, four measures that quantify culture are: 1)national culture is open to foreign influence, 2)English language, 3)percentage of urban population, and 4)percent of population 65 years or older.

Caselli and Coleman (2001), Kraemer and Dedrick (1994) and Robinson and Crenshaw (2002) point out structure of the economy (such as size of country's services sector because of existing significant positive association between the size of a country's services sector and IT investment) as important affecting factor. They also believe that inadequate complementary assets such as telecommunications networks and/or infrastructures and skilled human resources (SHR) are also important in increasing differences in IT usage between developed and developing countries. They emphasis on SHR because it has less opposition to social changes associated with adoption of new technologies and empirical studies strongly support the association between education levels and IT use at the country level.

Dewan and Kraemer (2000) show that marginal impact of complementary assets is greater in developing countries, which are still in the process of creating adequate levels of such assets than developed countries and openness to external influences, foreign trade especially Foreign Direct Investment FDI, as an indicator, facilitates the diffusion of managerial and technical knowledge across borders. Moreover, Coe, Helpman and Hoffmaister (1997) and Shih, Kraemer and Dedrick (2008) find that FDI has a positive impact on technical progress in the host country.

Barrel and Pain (1997) and Kraemer and Dedrick (1994) determine factors influencing the level of IT investment. They find that IT investment is associated with diffusion of telecommunications, infrastructure, education levels, technical skills, and the percent of the economy in services industries. Moreover, Caselli and Coleman (2001) findings show association between computer hardware imports, an indicator of IT investment, with educational attainment, openness to imports and property rights protection.

Shih, Kraemer and Dedrick (2007) found a negative relationship between IT investment and interest rates, but significant positive relationships between investment, openness to trade, and tele-communications infrastructure. When they include interaction effects between national income levels and country variables, they find that the impacts of interest rates, size of the financial sector, teledensity, and intellectual property rights are strongest in shaping IT investment for developed countries. In contrast, they find that the impact of openness to trade is greater for developing countries, as is the size of government and education levels.

Hanafizadeh, Khodabakhshi and Hanafizadeh (2008) provide a set of recommendations for e-business development in developing countries. They test the recommendations by study of case of Iran. Based on benchmarking 19 countries and 4 regions, 339 recommendations for e-business development are finally using content analysis, they select 36 of 339 recommendations and categorize them into four groups of human resource, security, e-infrastructure, and policies and plans. They also provide a national survey to test the recommendations that fit with Iran internal situations. Finally, they rank the recommendations based on pundits' opinions.

Shih, Kraemer and Dedrick (2008) consider poverty, lack of infrastructure, inadequate education, policy making based on incorrect assumptions about IT usage, low level of IT investment to achieve measurable productivity gains, technology accumulation (evolutionary process of continuous innovation and imitation), and lack of resources for technology investments (because of credit, loan and capital gathering problems and operating in more ill-developed and not matured monetary and stock markets) as important issues that make differences between developed and developing countries.

In addition to earlier mentioned economic, social and infrastructural issues, there is also a long history for the cultural issues and their effects on the differences between developed and developing countries. Although there is a general agreement on the cultural issues and their effects on the differences in IT usage and governance between developed and developing countries, but each research in literature has its own angle of view. It should be mind that there are two major areas for cultural studies: organizational culture and national culture. (Trice and Beyer 1993)

Hofstede, Neuijen, Ohayv and Sanders (1990) study the relationships between organizational culture and organizational characteristics. They gathered data on organizational cultures in twenty units from ten different organizations in Denmark and the Netherlands. Based on the gathered data, they study the relationships between organizational culture and organizational characteristics.

According to Rossouw (1994), business ethics, as an integral part of business culture, has a much larger extent become part of the business culture in developed countries than in developing countries. Rossouw provides an explanation for the fact that business ethics is fighting an uphill battle in becoming part of the business culture in developing countries. Although cultural factors in developing countries set limits to organizational effectiveness, variations in effectiveness nevertheless do exist within countries.

Ryan, Chang, Ployhart and Slade (1999) study the cross-cultural equivalence of a multinational employee opinion using multiple-groups covariance structure analysis in four countries (U.S. and Australia, Mexico and Spain). Conceptual equivalence occurs when a construct can be meaningfully discussed in each culture and has a similar meaning across cultures. (Brett, Tinsley, Janssens, Barsness & Lytle 1997) Cultural and linguistic influences considered by assessing equivalence across two pairs of countries having the same language but different cultures (U.S. and Australia, Mexico and Spain) and across countries differing in culture and language (U.S. and Mexico). The measure was equivalent across U.S. and Australian samples only. One cause source of lack of invariance was translation problems.

Brewster (1999) and Dowling, Welch and Schuler (1999) identify national culture as one of five variables that moderate (i.e. either diminish or accentuate) differences between domestic and international human resource management. These include differences in the centrality of markets, institutions, regulations, collective bargaining, and labor-force characteristics.

Namazi (1999) determines the behavior considerations that should be taken into account in implementing Activity Based Costing (ABC) system in Iran. His study emphasis on the importance of considering international, national, organizational and management cultures in successful design and implementation of ABC in Iranian firms.

Hofstede (2001) studies cultural consequences comparing values, behaviors, institutions, and organizations across nations. It is well known that countries are different in terms of cultures, values and mental programs developed in the family and in schools and organizations. What do we mean of culture, value and mental program?

Culture is the collective programming of the mind that distinguishes the members of one group or category of people from another. Cultures, especially national cultures, are extremely stable over the time and changes in cultures come from the outside. To structurize the culture concept, five following main dimensions (indices) on which country cultures differs proposed in literature. Power Distance Index (PDI) measures the extent to which the power is distributed unequally. PDI shows inequality in society (such as inequality in physical and mental characteristics, social status and prestige, wealth, in power, and in law, rights and rule) and in organization. Uncertainty Avoidance Index (UAI) shows the extent to which a culture programs its members to feel either uncomfortable or comfortable in unstructured situations. Individualism versus Collectivism Index (IDV) measures the degree to which individuals are suspects to look after themselves or remain integrated into groups. Masculinity versus Femininity Index (MAS) refers to the distribution of emotional roles between genders. Finally, Long-term versus Short-term Orientation Index (LTO) measures the extent to which a culture programs its member to accept delayed gratification of their material, social and emotional needs.

A value is a broad tendency to perform certain states of affairs over others. (Kluckhohn 1967) In fact, values determine our subjective definition of rationality. Each value has a plus and minus pole such as evil versus good, dirty vesus clean, dangerous versus safe, and so on. (Bem, 1970, p 16)

Three levels of human mental programming are individual programs that are truly partly unique and partly shared, collective programs that are shared with some but not all other humans, and universal programs, that are shared by all or almost all human kinds. Four different strategies or methods for operationalizing constructs about human mental programming are interview (questionnaire and projective tests), content analysis of speeches (discussions and documents), laboratory experiments and field experiments and direct observation (use of available descriptive statistics). Interview and laboratory experiments and field experiments are provoked-word base and content analysis of speeches and direct observation are natural-deed base strategies. (Hofstede 2001, p 4) Two available research strategies for comparing multi-society studies are focus on similarities between societies and focus on differences between societies. For example, countries can be compared by the language difference or homogeneities (single language countries or multilanguage countries), some economic, geographic, and demographic indicators (such as wealth (GNP), economic growth in the past periods (EGP), economic growth in the following periods (EGF), latitude (LAT), population size (POP), population growth (PGR), population density (PDN), organizational size (ORS), relatives organizational size (ROS)), and /or occupation, gender, and even age. Considering two situations (low and high) for each of cultural indices (PDI, UAI, IDV, MAS and LTO), countries can easilty be positioned and compared based on their situations in terms of each cultural index, pair of indices (totally $n(n-1)$, where n denotes the number of cultural indices), or all indices. According to nationality constraints rationality and cultures and organizational theories, some scientists, as Mintzberg, try to classifiy organizational structures and what country configurations. (Hofstede 2001, p 376) Some management scientists relate countries' 5 cultural characteristics to their organizational functions and characteristics such as to planning and control, corporate governance, motivations and compensation, leadership and empowerment, management and organizational developments, and performance appraisal and management by objectives. Some kinds of dimensions of organizational culture are process oriented versus result oriented, employee oriented versus job oriented, parochial versus professional, open system versus closed system, loose control versus tight control and normative versus pragmatic. As a generl, globalization forced organizations to pay more attention to intercultural interactions (language and discourses, training in intercultural competence, and intercultural negotiations). They also need to monitor political issues such as minorities, migrants and refuges, international politics and international organizations issues. In other words, suceesful multinational businesses try to develop intercultural communications and cooperations, take advantages of different cultural profiles in international competitions, and consider cultural differences in their international acquisitions, mergers and joint ventures, international marketing, adverstisement and consumer behavior analysis. (Hofstede 2001)

Awasthi, Chow, and Wu (2001) examine the effects of national cultural differences on the behavioral consequences of imposing performance evaluation and reward systems (PERS). They conclude that two cultural dimensions (individualism versus collectivism and power distance) can modify employees' decisions and satisfaction under imposed performance evaluation and rewards aimed at modifying their work-related behavior. US nationals had significantly lower satisfaction under imposed rather than self-selected performance evaluation and reward structures, while Chinese counterparts did not have a similar adverse reaction. Their results were consistent with prior Anglo-American-based research that the significantly affects employee behavior. They suggest that thier finding may not be directly generalizable to employees whose national cultures differ from those of Anglo-Americans.

Salter and Sharp (2001) investigate the effects of national culture on management control systems. Results of their study show that even apparently small cultural differences, such as between the USA and Canada, can be particularly troublesome. In fact, their study explores the effect of an apparently small difference in national culture on the ability of agency theory to explain escalation of commitment to failing projects in two countries with significant cross-border investment, i.e., USA and Canada. They found that the effect of adverse selection conditions was significantly stronger among managers from the more individualist USA and that more experienced managers were less likely to escalate commitment.

Pothukuchi, Damanpour, Choi, Chen and Park (2002) examine the effects of national and organizational cultural differences on international Joint Venture (JV) performance. They found that negative effects from cultural distance stems from organizational culture than from national culture. In other words, their study shows the importance of organizational culture similarity for JV success. They argue that distance in the open (with a better communication climate) versus closed system dimension negatively affects all measures of International JV performance. Some organizations are traditionally more closed whereas others have a tradition of openness. A major characteristic of the open versus closed dimension is information sharing. If one partner engages in high information sharing activity (open system] and the other does not (closed system), partners cannot capitalize on the synergy effect of JV, and the open system partner may come to suspect the closed system partner's commitment and loyalty toward the venture. In order to be successful, JV partners should have a similar level of information sharing tendency and foster an open communication climate. The results suggest that while JVs have little control over each other's national culture, they could nevertheless engage in shaping similar organizational practices.

Silva and Figueroa (2002) discuss how to promote the use of IT in the context of Chile. They discuss that Strategic Information Systems (SIS) can fail to become institutionalized in a developing country despite adequate planning, strong leadership, and knowledgeable IS professionals. They state some factors including core values and beliefs, political time, the distribution of power, formal organizational structure, and control systems prevent achieving to the developmental goals.

Bada (2002) explain a longitudinal case study of radical organizational change related to the computerization and networking of branches in the Nigerian banking sector. He implies that cultural homogeneity is not becoming the norm. It is needed to understand and value local practices.

Walsham (2002) dealt with cross-cultural issues in software production and use, drawing on secondary data from two case studies, including that of a joint Jamaican/Indian software team.

Considering Gray's (1988) and Hofsted's (2001) studies, Noravesh (2002) conclude that Iranian special national culture, economic and political characteristics should affects on Iranian accounting profession differently from the other countries. Consequently, he hypothesis and examines the relationships between national cultural characteristics and the accounting systems and values. For this purpose, according Gary's model, he creates a matrix to relate each cultural values (power distance, uncertainty avoidance, individualism versus collectivism, masculinity versus femininity, and long-term versus short-term orientation) to accounting values (professionalism versus statutory control, uniformity versus flexibility, secrecy vesus transparency).

Spony (2003) examine an analytical model, which enables the operationalization of cultural concepts related to the work context at both the individual and cultural levels of analysis. The model was empirically tested using a population of French and British managers from two different sectors, bank/insurance and pharmaceutical/ healthcare organizations. They try to control the impact of organizational culture differences. The final four work-value scales (self-enhancement, individual dynamics, consideradon for others and group dynamics) elicited through five-step analysis successfully achieved the purpose of the model's development.

Fang and Rau (2003) examine the effects of cultural differences between the Chinese and the US people in terms of the perceived usability and search performance of World Wide Web portal sites. They found significant differences of satisfaction and steps in performing some tasks between Chinese and American. The results also provide more detailed insights into the cultural differences among countries' users and indicate that the cultural differences have significant impact on users' perception and usage of the same portal Website. Their study provides important insights in designing portal sites for different users with different cultures.

Aman and Nicholson (2003) study the case of Malaysia. Their study emphasizes on the specific difficulty in remote communication when working across cultures.

Noravesh and Dianati Deylami (2003) provide an empirical evidence for the effects of culture on accounting values in Iran. They implemented the Gary's model (1988) in Iran. They found the same results that were obtained by Suderwan and Fogarty (1996) in Indonesia. It means that among 20 hypotheses that were tested by Gary, just two hypotheses were confirmed in both countries of Iran and Indonesia. In other words, the results clearly confirm that Gary's model do not performs well in Iran as well as in Indonesia.

Avgerou (2003) shows the complex dynamics of the link between IT and development. She discusses that an effective action requires involvement and collaboration between industry, government, and international organizations.

Adam and Myers (2003) using case study of the Maldives customs service addressed the challenge of culturally inappropriate impositions of IT.

Shoib and Nandhakumar (2003) used two case studies to argue that multiple forms of rationality exist in any context and that national culture is only one aspect of actors' sense-making activities. They suggest need to the notion of culture rather than seeing it as a fixed entity.

Liu and Westrup (2003) examine a case study of coordination and control between the United Kingdom and China in a multinational corporation. They discuss that IT-enabled coordination is only effective when linked with other approaches such as the use of expatriates and face-to-face contacts. These studies emphasize the crucial importance of IT in cross-cultural working in the contemporary world.

Dunkel and Meierewert (2004) investigate the impact of different cultural standards on the processes and performances of Austrian, Spanish, German and Hungarian task groups using 201 qualitative interviews. They conclude that culturally heterogeneous teams have more potential for conflicts, thus, resulting in more challenges for the team members.

Anvary Rostamy and Lari Semnani (2004) determine the factors make stock markets more attractive for foreign investors. They classify the factors in two groups, country related factors and stock market related factors. Among the country factors, they find factors such as cultural homogeneity, language commonality and legal similarity.

Saad and Zawdie (2005) reveal the need for both technology transfer and the development of the triple helix culture in developing countries. They believe that the business incubation system as an aspect of the triple helix model of innovation in which universities, industry, government and non-government organizations feature as principal actors in the national innovation system. The culture of bureaucracy and institutional fragmentation has been major factors militating against initiatives for technological capability development; and the conventional technology transfer practice has reinforced this culture. They beleive that a major policy initiative is needed in developing countries to put the national system of innovation in place, and remove the constraints on the development of the triple helix culture.

Adler's book International Dimensions of Organizational Behavior (2002) focuses heavily on the importance and consequences of national culture differences. Gerhart and Fang (2005) studied the national culture and human resource management. Their study implies that although countries can be differ in many ways (e.g. institutional and regulatory environment, labor-force characteristics such as education), a dominant focuses of the international management literature is on national differences in culture, especially culture values. They conclude that while national culture difference can be important, their role needs to be put in the context of other important contextual factors, including organizational culture.

Dastgir and Arab Yarmohammadi (2005) attempt to determine issues affecting implementation of target costing systems in Iranian firms operate in Tehran Stock Exchange (TSE). Their research confirms existing two main cultural issues in Iranian firms, lacking attention to customer needs and satisfaction and lack of team working.

Noravesh and Sepasi (2005) examine the relationship between cultural values and profit smoothing/management in Iran. Using 64 of 90 Iranian firms' data, they confirm that there is a significant relationship between cultural values and profit smoothing/management in Iran.

Some researchers consider local adaptation and new technologies as important factor. For example, Sayed and Westrup (2003) study the case of Egypt and explains the role of a specific IT, Enterprise Resource Planning (ERP) systems networks in country development. Macome (2003) shows that the local context was crucial in the implementation process and that it was essential to involve local stakeholders in the entire process. D'Mello (2003) concerned with local adaptation related to new ICTs. She addresses the adaptation of people in the context of global software outsourcing and argues that adaptation has produced a new breed of knowledge workers in the software industry in countries such as India from where she drew her field data.

As Walsham, Robey, and Sahay 2007 state, IT disffusion consequences emerge from a complex set of processes over a significant period. It needs involving a wide range of actors and institutions. IT has no deterministic effects on development because it being applied to complex social issues. In other words, social influences are crucially important to the trajectory of any technology-based project. (Walsham, Robey, and Sahay 2007) Accordingly, the studies on the developing countries and the potential role of IT to support their development emphasize on a complex set of factors such as social, political, and cultural contexts. According to Walsham, Robey, and Sahay (2007), we need to conduct more researchers to consider geographical spread, Non Govrnmental Organizations (NGOs) roles as important intermediaries in IT related development, and different level of analysis such as individuals, groups, organizations, industry sectors, societies, and international organizations. (Walsham 2001) Work at the community level also promises to contribute to an understanding of IT in marginalized groups in developed countries (e.g., Kvasny 2006). Research is also needed on society-wide critical issues (such as HIV/AIDS or gender) in developing countries. Gender studies received more attentions in IT research (Adam, Howcroft and Richardson 2005), but there is little work as yet which addresses the role of women in connection with IT in developing countries. (Walsham, Robey, and Sahay 2007)

Brief review of the literature implies that there are a numerous factors affecting IT usage. In addition, there are various differences in these factors between developed and developing countries. In order to direct the future researches, we need to sammurize and classify these factors in a scientific way. For this purpose, next setion of the paper sammurizes and classifies the most important factors and measures that affecting the relation between IT and performance and make difference between developed and developing countries in use of IT.

3. Economic, cultural, social, and infrastructural factors and measures

Tables 1, 2, and 3 show the important factors, the most widely used independent, depended, and moderator variables, and measures that are supported by the literature and the international data based (such as the World Bank, International Monetary Funds (IMF), United Nations (UN) data base, International Telecommunication Union (ITU) data bases), respectively.

Table 1: Factors affecting IT diffusion

Factors	Factors

- *Educational level* (Kraemer & Dedrick 1994; Barrel & Pain 1997; Sen 1999; Caselli and Coleman 2001; Mahmood Adam & Swanberg 2001; Walsham, Robey, Sahay 2007)
- *Professional and Training level* (Kraemer & Dedrick 1994; Barrel & Pain 1997; Mahmood Adam & Swanberg 2001)
- *Perception of user toward IT* (Mahmood Adam & Swanberg 2001)
- *Commitement level* (Meyer, Srinivas, Lai & Topolnystky 2007)
- *Enterprice readiness* (Multula & Brakel 2006)
- *ICT readiness* (Multula & Brakel 2006)
- *External Environmen readiness* (Multula & Brakel 2006)
- *Human readiness* (Multula & Brakel 2006)
- *Information readiness* (Multula & Brakel 2006)
- *Completeness assets* (Kraemer & Dedrick 1994; Dewan and Kraemer 2000); Caselli & Coleman 2001; UN Development Report 2001; Robinson & Crenshaw 2002; World Bank Group 2002; Shih, Kraemer & Dedrick 2008)
- *Telecomunications networks* (Kraemer & Dedrick 1994; Caselli & Coleman 2001; UN Development Report 2001; Robinson & Crenshaw 2002, World Bank Group 2002; Shih, Kraemer & Dedrick 2008)
- *Skilled IT professionals* (UN Development Report 2001; World Bbank Group 2002; Shih, Kraemer & Dedrick 2008)
- *Lack of resourece for technology investments* (Sen 1999; UN development report 2001; World Bank Group 2002; Walsham, Robey, and Sahay 2007; Shih, Kraemer & Dedrick 2008)
- *Structure of economy* (Kraemer & Dedrick 1994; Barrel & Pain 1997; Caselli & Coleman 2001; UN development report 2001; Robinson & Crenshaw 2002; World bank group 2002; Shih, Kraemer and Dedrick 2007; Shih, Kraemer & Dedrick 2008)
- *Openness to external influence* (Dewan & Kraemer 2000; Caselli & Coleman 2001; UN Development Report 2001; World Bank Group 2002; Shih, Kraemer & Dedrick 2008)
- *Digital infrastructure* (Kraemer & Dedrick 1994; Barrel & Pain 1997; Bui, Sankaran & Sebastian 2003)
- *Macro econy situation* (Bui, Sankaran & Sebastian 2003)
- *Ability to invest* (Bui, Sankaran & Sebastian 2003)
- *Knowledge citizens* (Bui, Sankaran & Sebastian 2003)
- *Competitiveness* (Bui, Sankaran & Sebastian 2003)
- *Access to skilled workforce* (Bui, Sankaran & Sebastian 2003)
- *Cost of living and pricing* (Bui, Sankaran & Sebastian 2003)
- *Poverty* (Shih, Kraemer & Dedrick 2008)
- *Lack of infrastructure* (Shih, Kraemer & Dedrick 2008)
- *Inadequate educaton* (Shih, Kraemer &d Dedrick 2008)

- *Incorrect assumptions and policy makings* (Shih, Kraemer & Dedrick 2008)
- *Technology accumulation* (Shih, Kraemer & Dedrick 2008)
- *Lack of resources fortechnology investment (*Shih, Kraemer & Dedrick 2008)
- *Infrastructures (*Kraemer & Dedrick 1994; Caselli & Coleman 2001; Robinson & Crenshaw 2002; Shih, Kraemer & Dedrick 2008)
- *Skilled human resource (*Kraemer & Dedrick 1994; Caselli & Coleman 2001; Robinson & Crenshaw 2002; Shih, Kraemer & Dedrick 2008)
- *Proterty rights protection* (Caselli & Coleman 2001; Shih, Kraemer & Dedrick 2007)
- *Lack of clean water, inadequate housing and freedom* (Sen 1999; Walsham, Robey, & Sahay 2007),
- *National culture and cross cultural differences* (Gray 1988; Rossouw 1994; Suderwan & Fogarty 1996; Ryan, Chang, Ployhart & Slade 1999; Brett, Tinsley, Janssens, Barsness & Lytle 1997; Brewster 1999; Dowling et al 1999; Awasthi, Chow & Wu 2001; Salter & Sharp 2001; Hofsted 2001; Pothukuchi, Damanpour, Choi, Chen & Park 2002; Walsham 2002; Noravesh 2002; Silva & Figueroa 2002; Spony 2003; Bui, Sankaran & Sebastian 2003; Fang & Rau 2003; Aman & Nicholson 2003; Noravesh & Dianati Deylami 2003; Avgerou 2003; Adam & Myers 2003; Shoib & Nandhakumar 2003; Liu & Westrup 2003; Noravesh & Sepasi 2005)
- *Organizational culture* (Hofstede, Neuijen, Ohayv & Sanders 1990; Gerhart and Fang 2005)
- *Business Ethics* (Rossouw 1994)
- *Language and translation problems* (Brett, Tinsley, Janssens, Barsness & Lytle 1997; Anvary Rostamy & Lari Semnani 2004)
- *International, national, organizational and management cultures* (Namazi 1999)
- *Culturally heterogeneous teams* (Dunkel & Meierewert 2004; Anvary Rostamy & Lari Semnani 2004; Bada 2002)
- *Culture of bureaucracy and institutional fragmentation* (Saad and Zawdie 2005)
- *Lacking attention to customer needs and satisfaction* (Dastgir & Arab Yarmohammadi 2005)
- *Lack of team working* (Dastgir & Arab Yarmohammadi 2005)
- *Cultural homogeneity* (Anvary Rostamy & Lari Semnani 2004)
- *Language commonality* (Anvary Rostamy & Lari Semnani 2004)
- *Legal similarity* (Anvary Rostamy & Lari Semnani 2004)

Table 2: Most widely used independent, depended and moderator variables

Type of Variables	Factors	Measures
Independent Variable	**ITechnology Investments**	• *IT investment* (Kraemer & and Dedrick 1994; Barrel & Pain 1997; Dewan & Kraemer 2000; UN Development Report 2001; World Bank Group 2002; Shih, Kraemer & Dedrick 2007; Shih, Kraemer & Dedrick 2008) • *IT use at country level* (Kraemer and Dedrick 1994; Caselli & Coleman 2001; Robinson & Crenshaw 2002; Fang & Rau 2003; Shih, Kraemer & Dedrick 2008) • *IT spending on hardware and software as percent of GDP* (Shih, Kraemer & Dedrick 2007) • *Computer hardware imports and production* (Caselli & Coleman 2001)
Dependent Variable	**Productivity Level**	• *Productivity growth at the macroeconomic level* (Dewan & Kraemer 2000; Madon 2000; Caselli & Coleman 2001;) • *Level of national wealth* (UN Development Report 2001; World Bank Group 2002; Shih, Kraemer & Dedrick 2008) • *Technical progress* (Coe, Helpman and Hoffmaister 1997; Shih, Kraemer & Dedrick 2008)
Common Used General Moderator Variables	**Most widely-used, official-source development data from the World Bank and other international agencies**	• *Total external debt to gross national income* (Economic Indicator) • *GDP (current US$) (billions)* (Economic Indicator) • *GNI per capita, Atlas method (current US$)* (Economic Indicator) • *Life expectancy at birth, total (years)* (Social Indicator) • *Population, total (millions)* (Social Indicator) • *Population growth (annual %)* (Social Indicator) • *Surface area (sq. km) (thousands)* (Infrastructural & Natural Indicator)

Moderator Variables	Factors	Measures/Indicators		
Infrastructural and Natural Moderator Variable	Geographical Environmental General Infrastructural ICT Infrastructural	• Roads, total network (thousands km) • Vehicles (per 1,000 people) • Airports, Heliports • Merchant marine (ships) • Pipelines (km) • Railways (km) • Roadways (km) • Computers per 1,000 People • Television broadcast stations • Internet Hosts per 10,000 People • Internet users per 10,000 People • Households with television (%) • Waterways(km) Oil and Gas proved reserves • Passenger cars (per 1,000 people) • Price basket for internet • Fixed line and mobile phone subscribers (per 1,000 people) • International Telecommunications • Total Investments in Telecommunications Telecommunication equipment (Export) (US$) • Telecommunication equipment (Import) (US$) • % of households with a telephone • Public payphones • Main (fixed) telephone lines in operation • Main (fixed) telephone lines in largest city • Total telephone subscribers (fixed + mobile) • % automatic main lines • % digital main lines • % residential main lines • % of main lines in urban areas • Total capacity of local public switching exchanges • International telephone circuits • Waiting list for main (fixed) lines • Number of local (fixed) telephone (calls) • Number of local (fixed) telephone (minutes) • Number of national (fixed) long distance telephone (calls) • Number of national (fixed) long distance telephone (minutes) • Total national (fixed) telephone traffic (calls) • Total national (fixed) telephone traffic (minutes) • International outgoing fixed telephone traffic (calls) • International incoming fixed telephone traffic (calls) • International incoming fixed telephone traffic (minutes) • International outgoing fixed telephone traffic (minutes) • %of telephone faults cleared by next working day • Faults per 100 main (fixed) lines per year • Residential telephone connection charge • Residential telephone connection charge (US$) • Business telephone connection charge • Business telephone connection charge (US$) • Mobile cellular connection charge • Mobile cellular connection charge (US$) • Residential monthly telephone subscription	• Residential monthly telephone subscription (US$) • Business telephone monthly subscription Business telephone monthly subscription (US$) • Mobile cellular monthly subscription • Mobile cellular monthly subscription (US$) • Price of a 3-minute fixed telephone local call (peak rate) • Price of a 3-minute fixed telephone local call (peak rate - US$) • Mobile cellular - price of 3-minute local call (peak) • Mobile cellular - price of 3-minute local call (peak - US$) • Mobile cellular - price of 3-minute local call (off-peak) • Mobile cellular - price of 3-minute local call (off-peak - US$) • Price of a 3-minute fixed telephone local call (off-peak rate) • Price of a 3-minute fixed telephone local call (off-peak rate - US$) • Households Mobile cellular telephone subscribers - (Post-paid + Pre-paid) • Mobile cellular telephone subscribers (Digital) • Mobile cellular telephone subscribers -prepaid subscribers • POP Coverage of mobile cellular network (population, in %) • Staff (Total full-time telecommunications staff) • Staff (Female telecommunication staff) • Mobile communications staff • Revenue from fixed telephone service • Revenue from fixed telephone service (US$) • Revenue from mobile communication • Revenue from mobile communication (US$) • Total revenue from all telecommunication services • Total revenue from all telecommunication services (US$) • Total annual investment in telecom • Total annual investment in telecom (US$) • Fixed telephone service investment • Fixed telephone service investment (US$) • Mobile communication investment • Mobile communication investment (US$) • Main (fixed) telephone lines per 100 inhabitants • Mobile cellular telephone subscribers per 100 inhabitants • Total telephone subscribers (fixed + mobile) per 100 inhabitants • Public payphones per 1000 inhabitants • Radio sets • Radio equipped households • % of households with a radio • Television receivers • Television receivers per 100 inhabitants • Cable television subscribers • Television equipped households • % of households with a television • Home satellite antennas • ISDN subscribers • SDN Channels • Estimated Internet users • Total (fixed) Internet subscribers • Cable modem Internet subscribers • Dial-up Internet subscribers • DSL Internet subscribers	• % of homes with Internet • Total fixed broadband Internet subscribers • International Internet Bandwidth (Mbps) • Personal computers • % of homes with a Personal Computer • Personal computers per 100 inhabitants • Internet users per 100 inhabitants • Total fixed broadband Internet subscribers per 100 inhabitants • Total (fixed) Internet subscribers per 100 inhabitants • International Internet Bandwidth per inhabitant (bit/s) • Schools connected to internet (%) • Broadband subscribers (per 1000 people) • International voice traffic (minutes per person) • Daily newspapers (per 1,000 people) • Telephone mainlines (per 1,000 people) • Technology Assessment Index • Patent Applications Granted • Computer Processing Power (% of total worldwide MIPS) • E-Government Index • Freedom on the Internet • ICT Expenditure as % of GDP • International internet bandwidth bits (per capita) • Internet servers per million people • Permanent cropland (% of land area) • Arable land (% of land area) • Land use - arable land(%) • Land use - permanent crops(%) • Electricity - consumption(kWh) • Electricity - exports (kWh) • Electricity - imports (kWh) • Electricity - production(kWh) • Natural gas and oil consumption, production, exports, import Electric power consumption (kWh per capita) Coastline • Elevation extremes - highest point • Elevation extremes - lowest point • Irrigated land • Land boundaries - km • Surface area (sq. km) • Forest area (sq. km) • Agricultural land (% of land area) • Land and water area sq km • Total Area - sq km • CO2 emissions (kt) (thousands) • CO2 emissions (metric tons per capita) • Improved water source, rural (% of rural population with access) • Improved water source, urban (% of urban population with access) • Improved water source (% of population with access) • Improved sanitation facilities, urban (% of urban population with access) • Land area (sq. km) (thousands) • Organic water pollutant (BOD) emissions (kg per day) • Energy use (kg of oil equivalent per capita) Energy imports, net (% of energy use)

Table 3: Moderator variables factors and measures classification (continued)

Moderator Variables	Factors	Measures/Indicators	
Cultural & Educational Moderator Variable	Cultural (Education /Literacy)	<ul><li>Expenditure per student, primary (% of GDP per capita)</li><li>Public Spending on Education</li><li>Literacy rate, adult total (% of people ages 15 and above)</li><li>Literacy rate, adult female (% of females ages 15 and above)</li><li>Literacy rate, adult male (% of males ages 15 and above)</li><li>Persistence to grade 5, total (% of cohort)</li><li>Pupil-teacher ratio, primary</li><li>School enrollment, primary (% gross)</li><li>School enrollment, primary, female (% gross)</li><li>School enrollment, primary, male (% gross)</li><li>Primary completion rate, total (% of relevant age group)</li><li>School enrollment, tertiary (% gross)</li><li>School enrollment, tertiary, female (% gross)</li><li>School enrollment, secondary (% gross)</li><li>Adult Literacy Rate</li></ul>	<ul><li>Tertiary Enrollment</li><li>8th Grade Achievement in Science</li><li>MGMT Education Locally Available in first-class Business Schools</li><li>Flexibility of People to Adapt to New Challenges</li><li>Tertiary Science & Engineering Enrollment</li><li>University Education Meets the Needs of Competitive Economy</li><li>Well Educated People Do not Emigrate Abroad</li><li>Extent of Staff Trainings</li><li>Research Collaboration Companies/Universities</li><li>Technical Papers per Million Population</li><li>Labor force with tertiary education (% of total)</li><li>Business ethics as an integral part of business culture</li><li>Educational level measured by tertiary school enrollment as percent of relevant age group</li><li>skilled human resources</li></ul>
Social & Demographical Moderator Variable	Social Development Gender and Population Health Rural and Urban Development	<ul><li>Proportion of seats held by women in national parliament (%)</li><li>Ratio of girls to boys in primary and secondary education (%)</li><li>Mortality rate, under-5 (per 1,000)</li><li>Mortality rate, infant (per 1,000 live births)</li><li>Health expenditure per capita (current US$)</li><li>Health expenditure, total (% of GDP)</li><li>Hospital beds (per 1,000 people)</li><li>Immunization, DPT (% of children ages 12-23 months)</li><li>Immunization, measles (% of children ages 12-23 months)</li><li>Malnutrition prevalence, weight for age (% of children under 5)</li><li>Mortality rate, under-5 (per 1,000)</li><li>Physicians (per 1,000 people)</li><li>Prevalence of HIV, total (% of population ages 15-49)</li><li>Death rate (birth/1000 population)</li><li>Gender, and even age</li><li>Fertilizer consumption (metric tons) (thousands)</li><li>Land under cereal production (hectares)</li><li>Agricultural machinery, tractors per 100 sq. km of arable land</li><li>Rural population density (rural population per sq. km of arable land)</li><li>Population in the largest city (% of urban population)</li><li>Population in urban agglomerations > 1 million (% of total population)</li></ul>	<ul><li>Poverty headcount ratio at urban poverty line (% of urban population)</li><li>Urban population</li><li>Urban population (% of total)</li><li>Latitude (LAT)</li><li>Organizational size (ORS)</li><li>Relatives organizational size (ROS)</li><li>Population size (POP)</li><li>Population growth (PGR)</li><li>Population density (PDN)</li><li>Population, total (millions)</li><li>Population, female</li><li>Population, female (% of total)</li><li>Population growth (annual %)</li><li>Population density (people per sq. km)</li><li>Births attended by skilled health staff (% of total)</li><li>Age dependency ratio (dependents to working-age population)</li><li>Fertility rate, total (births per woman)</li><li>Age structure in terms of ages (0-14, 15-64, 65 and over) and the gender (male and female) (%)</li><li>Life expectancy at birth, female (years)</li><li>Life expectancy at birth, male (years)</li><li>Life expectancy at birth, total (years)</li><li>Occupation</li></ul>

*(in Agriculture & Food, Information & Communications, Mining, Public Sector, Social Protection, Tourism, Transport, Urban Development, Water Services , Construction, Energy, Environment, Finance, Health & Population, Industry). http://www.dgmarket.com

** in Energy sector (include those related to the exploration, extraction, and refinement of hydrocarbons, oil, and natural gas), Financial Sector (those related to banks, insurance, real estate, and other financial services), Manufacturing and Services (those in agribusiness, cement, chemicals, construction, steel, hotels, tourism, airlines, maritime services, and other sub-sectors that are not infrastructure or finance related), Infrastructure (those in transportation, water and sewerage, telecommunications, natural gas transmission and distribution, and electricity generation, transmission, and distribution), Primary (include those related to the extraction, refinement, and sale of primary minerals and metals, such as coal and iron ore). http://rru.worldbank.org/Privatization

*** in terms of Starting a Business, Dealing with Licenses, Employing Workers, Registering Property, Getting Credit, Protecting Investors, Paying Taxes, Trading Across Borders, Enforcing Contracts, Closing a Business. http://www.doingbusiness.org

****http://www.unctad.org/wir

*****http://aida.developmentgateway.org/aida/AidaAbout.do
http://www.imf.org/external/data.htm#data

4. The conceptual model, potential research hypotheses, and ITADRI

4.1 Conceptual model

Figure 1 and 2 show the general and the extended version of the proposed conceptual model. Although this research focuses on the developed and developing countries, but in fact, the proposed model can be used for four different levels of analysis. For example, it can be used for country level analysis, for analyzing a group of countries (such as developed, developing, advanced economies, Euro area, major advanced economies, European Union, newly industrialized Asian economies, advanced economies excluding G7 and euro area, and emerging market countries) for regional analysis and/or even for a global level of analysis.

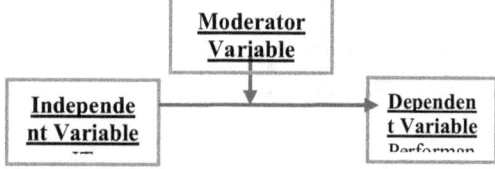

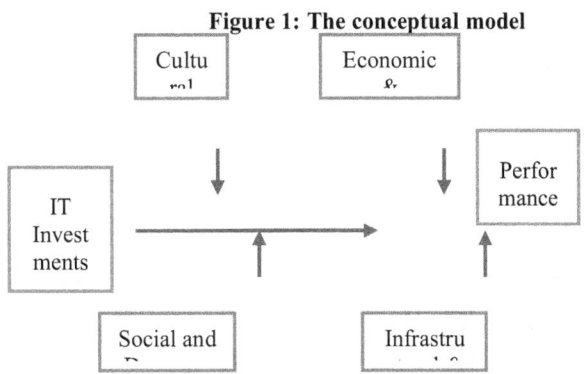

Figure 1: The conceptual model

Figure 2: Extended vesion of the conceptual model

4.2. Potential research hypotheses for future researches

According Figure 2, the potential research hypotheses can be defined as follows:

H1: *IT investments* is significantly associated with the *performance*.

H2: *The effects of IT investments on the performance* are significantly different between developed and developing countries.

H3: *IT absorption and diffusion readiness* (including economic & business, cultural, social & demographical, and infrastructural & natural readiness) moderates the relation between *IT investments* and *performance*.

H4: The effects of *IT absorption and diffusion readiness on the relation between IT investments and performance* are significantly different between developed and developing countries.

    H41: *economic & business readiness* moderates the relation between IT investments and country performance.

    H42: *cultural readiness* moderates the relation between IT investments and country performance.

    H43: *social and demographical readiness* moderates the relation between IT investments and country performance.

    H44: *infrastructural & natural readiness* modifies the relation between investments on IT and country performance.

H5: The effects of *economic & business*, *cultural*, *social and demographical* and *infrastructural & natural readiness* are significantly different between developed and developing countries.

In this research, ITDRI regards as a strategic level moderator variable that modifies the relation between IT investments and performance. According to Baron and Kenny (1986), a moderator variable is a qualitative or quantitative variable that affects the direction and/or strength of the relation between an independent or predictor variable and a dependent or criterion variable. A moderator effect within a correlational framework may also be said to occur where the direction of the correlation changes. That is, moderator variables always function as independent variables, whereas mediating events shift roles from effects to causes, depending on the focus of the analysis. Moderator variables apply when there is an unexpectedly weak or inconsistent relation between a predictor and a criterion variable (e.g., a relation holds in one setting but not in another, or for one subpopulation but not for another). Accordingly, ITDRI is a moderator variable that modifies the relation between IT investments and performance.

5. Conclusion and final remarks

There is a widespread belief in the positive relation between information technology (IT) and organizations and nations' performance improvement. The application of IT to development goals has not always succeeded to date and there are many cases of partial or complete failure. Results of the literature review show a Paradox in the results (IT Paradox). Moreover, there are significant differences between developed and developing countries in the use of IT. Accordingly, the main question of the researchers is not whether, but what factors affect and moderate the relation between IT and performance.

This paper is an attempt to determine and classifying the most important influence factors that modify the relation between IT and performance. In addition, it provides a general basic conceptual model and introduces some potential research hypotheses that can be directive for the future studies. Finally, based on the literature, it introduces ITADRI as a strategic level moderator variable (including economic and business, cultural, social, and infrastructural and demographical readiness components) that facilitate the systematic thinking in future studies.

References

Adam, M., and Myers, M. (2003) Have You Got Anything to Declare? Neo-colonialism, Information Systems, and the Imposition of Customs and Duties in a Third World Country, in Organizational Information Systems in the Context of Globalization, M. Korpela, R. Montealegre, and A. Poulymenakou (eds.), Kluwer Academic Publishers, Boston, 2003, pp. 101-116.

Adam, A., Howcroft, D., and Richardson, H. (2005) A Decade of Neglect: Reflecting on the Gender and IS Field," New Technology, Work and Employment (19:3), pp. 222-240.

Adkinson, W. F., Lenard, T. M., and Pickford, M. J. (2004) *The Digital Economy Fact Book*. 6th Ed., Washington D.C., The Progress and Freedom Foundation.

Adler, N. J. (2002) *International Dimensions of Organizational Behavior*. 4th edn, Cincinnati, OH: South-Western.

Aman, A., and Nicholson, B. (2003) The Process of Offshore Development: Preliminary Studies of UK Companies in Malaysia," in Organizational Information Systems in the Context of Globalization, M. Korpela, R. Montealegre, and A. Poulymenakou (eds.), Kluwer Academic Publishers, Boston, 2003, pp. 201-216.

Anvary Rostamy, A. A. and Lari Semnani, B. (2004) What Factors Make Stock Markets more Attractive? Case of Tehran Stock Exchange. *Journal of Iranian Accounting and Auditing Review*, 35: 101.

Avgerou, C., and Walsham, G. (2000) Information Technology inContext: Studies from the Perspective of Developing Countries, Ashgate Publishing, Aldershot, UK.

Avgerou, C. (2003) The Link Between ICT and Economic Growth in the Discourse of Development," in Organizational InformationSystems in the Context of Globalization, M. Korpela, R. Montealegre, and A. Poulymenakou (eds.), Kluwer Academic Publishers, Boston, pp. 373-386.

Awasthi, V. N. Chow, C. W. and Wu, A. (2001) Cross-cultural Differences in the Behavioral Consequences of Imposing Performance Evaluation and Reward Systems: An Experimental Investigation. *International Journal of Accounting*, 36(3): 291-309.

Bada, A. O. (2002) Local Adaptation to Global Trends: A Study of an IT-Based Organizational Change Program in a Nigerian Bank," The Information Society (18:2), pp. 77-86.

Bakos Y. (1998) The Productivity Payoff of Computers, A Review of Computer Revolution: An Economic Perspective, *Daniel E. Sichel Science*, 52(3).

Baron, R. M. and Kenny, D. A. (1986) The Moderator-Mediator Variable Distinction in Social Psychological Research: Conceptual, Strategic, and Statistical Considerations. Journal of Personality and Social Psychology, 51, No. 6, 1173-1182.

Bem, D. J. (1970) *Belifes, Attitudes, and Human Affairs*. Belmont, CA: Brook/Cole.

Barrell, R. and Pain, N. (1997) Foreign Direct Investment, Technological Change, and Economic Growth within Europe. *Economic Journal,* 107, 445: 1770–1786.

Bharadwaj Anandhi S., Sundar G. Bharadwaj, Benn R. Konsynski (1999) Information Technology Effects on Firm Performance as Measured by Tobin's Q. *Management Science*, 45(6).

Brett, J. M. Tinsiey, C. H. Janssens, M. Barsness Z. I. and Lytle A. L. (1997) New Approaches to the Study of Culture in Industrial/Organizational Psychology. In Eariey P.C., Erez M (Eds.), New Perspectives on Intemationai Industrial/Organizational Ssychology. San Francisco: New Lexington Press.

Brewster, C. (1999) Different Paradigms in Strategic HRM: Questions Raised by Comparative Research. In Wright, P. Dyer, L. Boudreau, J. and Milkovich, G. (eds) Research in Personnel and HRM. Supplement 4, Greenwich, CT: JAI Press.

Brynjolfsson, E. (1993) The Productivity Paradox of Information Technology, *Comm. ACM*, 36(12).

Brynjolfsson E. and Hitt, L. M. (1996) Paradox Lost? Firm Level Evidence on the Returns to Information Technology Spending. *Management Science*, 42(4).

Brynjolfsson E. and Yang, S. (1996) Information Technology and Productivity: A Review of the Literature. *Advances in Computers*, Academic Press, 43.

Bui, T. X. Sankaran, S. and Sebastian I. M. (2003) A Framework for Measuring National Readiness. *International Journal of Electronic Business*, 1(1): 3-22.

Coe, D.T. Helpman, E. and Hoffmaister, A. W. (1997) North-south R&D Spillovers. *The Economic Journal,* 107, 440: 134–149.

Caselli, F. and Coleman II, W. J. (2001) Cross-country Technology Diffusion: The Case of Computers. *The American Economic Review*, 91, 2.

Dastgir, M. and Arab Yarmohammadi, J. (2005) Issues Affecting Implementation of Target Costing Systems in Iranian Firms Operate in Tehran Stock Exchange (TSE). *Journal of Iranian Accounting and Auditing Review*, 12(39): 63-75.

D'Mello, M. (2003) Thinking Local, Acting Global: An Analysis of Identity Related Issues in a GSO in India," Research in Progress paper presented at the IFIP 9.4/8.2 Joint Conference on Organizational Information Systems in the Context of Globalization, 2003 (available on CD).

Dowlatshahi Shad and Cao Qing (2006) The Relationships among Virtual Enterprise, Information Technology and Business Performance in Sgile Manufacturing: An Industry Perspective. *European Journal of Operational Research*, 174 (2).

Dewan, S., and Kraemer, K.L. Information technology and productivity: Evidence from country-level data. Management Science 46, 4, (2000), 548–562.

Dowling, P. J. Welch, D. E. and Schuler, R. S. (1999) International Human Resource Management. Cincinnati, OH: South-Western.

Dunkel, A. and Meierewert, S. (2004) Culture Standards and Their Impact on Teamwork–An Empirical Analysis of Austrian, German, Hungarian and Spanish Culture Differences. *Journal for East European Management Studies*, 2, 147-174.

Fang, X. and Rau, P-L. P. (2003) Culture Differences in Design of Portal Sites. *Ergonomics*, 46(1-3): 242-254.

Gerhart, B. and Fang, M. (2005) National Culture and Human Resource management: Assumptions and Evidence. *International Journal of Human Management*, 16(6): 971-986.

Gray, S. J. (1988) Toward a Theory of Cultural Influence on the Development of Accounting Systems Internationally, *Abacus*, p. 8.

Hanafizadeh, P. Khodabakhshi, M. and Hanafizadeh, M. R. (2008) Recommendations for E-business Development in Developing Countries: A Case Study of Iran. European and Mediterranean Conference on Information Systems 2008 (EMCIS 2008), May 25-26 2008, Dubai, UEA.

Huang, Shi-Ming, Qu Chin-Shyh, Chen Chyi-Miaw, Lin Binshan (2006) An Empirical Study of Relationship between IT Investment and Firms Performance: A Resource–Based Perspective. *European Journal of Operational Research*, 173(3).

Herscovitch, L. and Meyer, J. P. (2002) Commitment to Organizational Change: Extension of a Three Component, Model. *Journal of Applied Psychology*, 87: 474–487.

Hofstede, G. Neuijen, B. Ohayv, D. D. and Sanders, G. (1990) Measuring Organizational Cultures: A Qualitative and Quantitative Study across Twenty Cases. *Administrative Science Quarterly*, 35(2): 286-316.

Hofstede, G. (2001) *Cultural Consequences: Comparing Values, Behaviors, Institutions, and Organizations across Nations*. Second Edition, Sage Publication Inc., Thousand Oaks, California, USA.

Kennerley, M. and Andy, N. (1998) Evaluating the Impact of Information Technology on Business Performance, Presented at the Fifth International Conference of the European Operations Management Association, Trinity College, Dublin, Ireland..

Kluckhohn, C. (1967) Values and Value-orientation in Theory of Action: An exploration in definition and classification. In T. Parsons & E. A. Shils (Eds.), *Toward a general theory of action*, Cambridge, MA, Harvard University Press.

Kohli Rajiv and Sarv Devaraj (2003) Measuring Information Technology Payoff: A Meta-Analysis of Structural Variables in Firm-Level Empirical Research. *Information Systems Research*, 14(2).

Kraemer, K. L. and Dedrick, J. (1994) Payoffs from Investment in Information Technology: Lessons from Asia-Pacific Region. *World Development*, 22: 1921–1931.

Kvasny, L. (2006) Cultural (Re) Production of Digital Inequality in a US Community Technology Initiative," Information, Communication & Society (9:2), pp. 160-181.

Liu, W., and Westrup, C. (2003) ICTs and Organizational Control Across Cultures: The Case of a UK Multinational Operating in China, in Organizational Information Systems in the Context of Globalization, M. Korpela, R. Montealegre, and A. Poulymenakou (eds.), Kluwer Academic Publishers, Boston, 2003, pp. 155-168.

Lubbe, S. Parker, G. and Hoard, A. (1995) The Profit Impact of IT Investment. *Journal of Information Technology*, 10: 44-51.

Macome, E. (2003) On the Implementation of an Information System in the Mozambican Context: The EDM Case," in Organizational Information Systems in the Context of Globalization, M. Korpela, R. Montealegre, and A. Poulymenakou (eds.), Kluwer Academic Publishers, Boston, pp. 169-184.

Madon, S. (2000) The Internet and Socio-Economic Development: Exploring the Interaction, Information Technology and People (13:2), pp. 85-101.

Mahmood Adam, M. A. and Swanberg, D. L. (2001) Factors Effecting Information Technology Usage: A Meta-Analysis of the Empirical Literature. *Journal of Organizational Computing and Electronic Commerce*, 11(2): 107-130.

Meyer, J. P. Srinivas, E. S. Lal, J. B. and Topolnytsky, L. (2007) Employee Commitment and Support for an Organizational Change: Test of the Three-component Model inTwo Cultures. *Journal of Occupational and Organizational Psychology*, 80, 185–211.

Milne, R. S. (1970) Mechanistic and Organic Models of, Public Administration in Developing Countries, pp. 57-67.

Motohashi Kazuyuki (2003) Firm Level Analysis of Information Network Use and Productivity in Japan. Comparative Analysis of Enterprise Data (CAED) Conference, London.

Mutula, S. M. and Brakel P. V. (2006) An evaluation of E-readiness Assessment Tools with Respect to Information Access: Towards an Integrated Information Rich Tool. *International Journal of Information Management*, 26(3): 212–223.

Namazi, M. (1999) Behavior Consideration in Implementing Activity Based Costing (ABC) System. *Journal of Iranian Accounting and Auditing Review*, 7(26-27): 71-106.

Noravesh, I. (2002) Cultural Values in Iran and Feasibility of Achieving to an Optimal International Accounting Standards. *Journal of Iranian Accounting and Auditing Review*, 9(30): 59-79.

Noravesh, I. and Dianati Deylami Z. (2003) Assessing the Effects of Culture on Accounting Values: An Empirical Evidence. *Journal of Iranian Accounting and Auditing Review*, 10(33): 3-40.

Noravesh, I. and Sepasi, S. (2005) Examining the Relationship between Cultural Values and Profit Smoothing/Management. *Journal of Iranian Accounting and Auditing Review*, 12(40): 81-96.

Pothukuchi, V. Damanpour, F. Choi, J. Chen, C. C. and Park, S. H. (2002) National and Organizational Culture Differences and International Joint Venture Performance. *Journal of International Business Studies*, 32(2): 243-265.

Robison, K. K. and Crenshaw, E. M. (2002) Post-industrial Transformations and Cyber-space: A Cross-national Analysis of Internet Development. *Social Science Research*, 31: 334–363.

Rossouw, G. J. (1994) Business Ethics In Developing Countries. *Business Ethics Quarterely*, 4(1): 0043-051.

Ryan, A. M. Chang, D. Ployhart, R. E. and Slade, L. A. (1999) Employee Attitude Surveys in a Multinational Organization: Considering Language and Culture in Assessing Measurement Equivalence. *Personnel Psychology*, 52: 37-58.

Saad, M. and Zawdie, G. (2005) From Technology Transfer to the Emergence of a Triple Helix Culture: The Experience of Algeria in Innovation and Technological Capability Development. *Technology Analysis & Strategic Management*, 17(1): 89–103.

Salter, S. B. and Sharp, D. J. (2001) Agency Effects and Escalation of Commitment Do Small National Culture Differences Matter?. *International Journal of Accounting*, 36(1): 33-45.

Sayed, E. H., and Westrup, C. (2003) Egypt and ICTs Bring National Initiatives, Global Actors and Local Companies Together," Information Technology and People (16:1), 2003, pp. 93-110.

Sen, A. (1999) Development as Freedom, Oxford University Press, Oxford, UK.

Shih, E. Kraemer, K. L. and Dedrick, J. (2008) IT Diffusion in Developing Countries. 51(2): 42-48.

Shih, E. Kraemer, K. L. and Dedrick, J. (2007) Research Note: Determinants of Country-level Investment in Information Technology. *Management Science,* 53(3): 521–528.

Shoib, G. M., and Nandhakumar, J. (2003) Cross-Cultural IS Adoption in Multinational Corporations: A Study of Rationality," in Organizational Information Systems in the Context of Globalization, M. Korpela, R. Montealegre, and A. Poulymenakou (eds.), Kluwer Academic Publishers, Boston, pp. 435-454.

Silva, L., and Figueroa, E. B. (2002) Institutional Intervention and the Expansion of ICTs in Latin America: The Case of Chile," Information Technology and People (15:1), pp. 8-25.

Smith Howard, L. Bullers, W. I. and Piland, N. F. (2000) Does Information Technology Make Difference in Healthcare Organization Performance?. *Hospital Topics: Research and Perspectives on Healthcare*, 78(2).

Spony, G. (2003) The Development of a Work-value Model Assessing the Cumulative Impact of Individual and Cultural Differences on Managers' Work-value Systems: Empirical Evidence from French and British Managers. *International Journal of Human Resource Management.* 14(4): 658-679.

Suderwan, M. and Fogarty, T. J. (1996) Culture and Accounting in Indonesia: An Empirical Examination. *The International Journal of Accounting*, 31(4): 463-481.

Trice, H. M. and J. M. Beyer (1993) *The Cultures of Work Organizations*, Englewood Cliffs, NJ: Prentice Hall.

United Nations Development Program (UNDP) Human Development Report 2001: Making New Technologies Work for Human Development, Oxford University Press, New York.

Walsham, G. (2001) Making a World of Difference: IT in a Global Context, Wiley, Chichester, UK.

Walsham, G. (2002) Cross-Cultural Software Production and Use: A Structurational Analysis," MIS Quarterly (26:4), pp. 359-380.

Walsham, G. Robey, D. Sahay, S. (2007) Forwadr: Special issue on Information Systems in Developing Countries, MIS Quarterly, 31(2): 317-326.

World Bank Group (2002) Information and Communication Technologies: A World Bank Group Strategy. Washington D.C..

http://web.worldbank.org

http://www.dgmarket.com

http://rru.worldbank.org

http://www.doingbusiness.org

http://www.unctad.org/wir
http://aida.developmentgateway.org/aida/AidaAbout.do
http://www.imf.org/external/data.htm#data
http://www.itu.int/ITU-D/icteye/Indicators/Indicators.aspx
http://www.photius.com/rankings/transportation/roadways_2007_0.html

IT Diffusion in Developing and Developed Countries: A Conceptual Analytical Model

AMROLAH AMINI (Ph.D)

Associate Professor, Allameh Tabatabaei University (ATU), Tehran, Iran.

aminij@atu.ac.ir

ALIREZA EMAMI

Master of Science, Tehran University, Tehran, Iran

memami@alumni.ut.ac.ir

MOSTAFA EMAMI*

Master of Science, Michigan Technological University (MTU)

memami@mtu.edu

*Corresponding Address

Applied Research and Technology Office, Michigan Technological University

1400 Townsend Dr, Houghton, MI 49931

Tel & Fax : +1-(816) 237-0018

E-mail: memami@mtu.edu

IT Diffusion in Developing and Developed Countries: A Conceptual Analytical Model

Abstract

According to the literature, there is a paradox in IT results and significant difference between developed and developing countries in the IT diffusion. Consequently, one of the most important questions of development researchers is now what factors affecting the relation between IT and national development in developed and developing countries. This paper determines and classifies factors affecting the relation between IT diffusion and nations' performance in developed and developing countries. Moreover, in order to facilitate future empirical studies on developed and developing countries, a general conceptual model, some key potential research hypotheses, and a new calculation methodology are provided.

Key words: IT diffusion, Conceptual model, Developing countries, Developed countries

1. Introduction

Most of researchers and development specialist believe that information technology (IT) has a great impact on organizations performance and nations' developments. On the other hand, the amount of investments on IT has rapidly increased in recent years. [3] In spite of positive viewpoints about the effects of IT on organizational and national performances, some researchers are concern. In other words, they question about the positive relationship between IT investments and the performance. Accordingly, their main question about IT is "does IT investments improve the performance?" There is huge number of papers in literature to answer this question and explain the relation between IT and national performance and development. However, the results show a Paradox in the results. [8][12][15][16][17][22][29][33][35][39][45][59] General speaking, the application of IT to development goals has not always succeeded to date and there are many cases of partial or complete failure. [4]

Respecting the paradox in the results of IT, the researchers find it more useful to answer a new question of "what factors influence IT usage?" In other words, the main question has now become not whether, but how IT can be benefial for development and what factors affect its disfusion. Although the literature introduces a numerous number of factors that affecting IT usage and shows various differences in these factors between developed and developing countries, however, there are few general conceptual models to identify, classify and quantify the factors in a systematic way.

This research aims to achieve three following objectives; 1)review the literature and determine factors affecting IT usage, 2)introduce some main measures and ndicators that quantify the factors, and 3)provide a generic conceptual model that facilitate future studies on IT diffusion in developed and developing countries. It focuses on the differences between developed and developing countries in IT usage and emphasis on developing countries because they have the majority of the world's population, contain millions of people who lack access to resources such as clean water, adequate housing, education, and freedom to choices their own lives. [54][65] For this purpose, the remainder of the paper is structurized as follows. Tthe following section explains a brief review of literature. Section 3 provides a framework to classify affecting factors and measures. Section 4 describes the conceptual model, the research potential hypotheses, and the computational methodology for future empirical analysis. Finally, the paper ends with conclusions and final remarks.

2. Review of the Literature

Two main questions on IT usage are "what factors influence IT usage?" and "are there any significant differences in these factors between developed and developing countries?" To answer these questions several researches have been conducted. For example, Mahmood Adam and Swanberg attempt to determine organizational factors affecting IT usage using a meta-analysis of empirical literature. They provide a combined model of IT usage and IT effectiveness. In this model, IT effectiveness is a function of IT usage and IT usage, in turn, consists of four main factors, organizational IT application, organization characteristics, individual characteristics, and perceived benefits. Results of their meta-analysis confirm a strong and significant positive relation between the perception of ease of use and the perceived usefulness of an IT system to the actual amount of usage. [42]

Mutula and Brakel propose an assessment tool for evaluating e-readiness at organizational level. Their proposed model includes five main components of enterprise readiness, ICT readiness, external environment readiness, human resource readiness, and information readiness. They define 29 measures for enterprise readiness, 19 measures for human resource readiness, 21 measure for information readiness, 22 measures for ICT readiness, and finally 21 measures for environment readiness component (totally 112 measures). [46]

Meyer, Srinivas, Lal and Topolnytsky study the relations between the commitment components and behavioral support for a change using Herscovitch and Meyer's three-component model (affective, normative and continuance commitments) of commitment to an organizationa. They found a considerable support for the relations between commitment and support predicted by the model. However, they also found evidence for potential culture differences. [30][43]

Although there is a widespread belief in potential value of IT and its supportive roles in human and nations' economic development, however there is significant differences between developed and developing countries in the use of IT. Several researches have been conducted to determine factors affecting the differences in IT usage between developed and developing countries. For example, Barrel and Pain, and Kraemer and Dedrick determine factors influencing the level of IT investment. They find that IT investment is associated with diffusion of telecommunications, infrastructure, education levels, technical skills, and the percent of the economy in services industries. [10][11][36]

Dewan and Kraemer compare developed and developing countries and find a significant positive relationship between IT investment and productivity growth at the macroeconomic level in developed countries, but not in developing countries. [23] Moreover, Madon examined the use of the Internet in sectors such as health and education, and in domains such as economic productivity and sustainable development. [41]

Caselli and Coleman findings show association between computer hardware imports, an indicator of IT investment, with educational attainment, openness to imports and property rights protection. [20]

Some researches and international documents confirm the effect of the availability of complementary assets such as telecommunications networks and skilled IT professionals and their drives for IT investments. [55][62][66] Although the studies show that IT investment is correlated with the level of national wealth, other factors such as resources for technology investments, structure of the economy, and openness to external influences have been shown to be significant as well.

Bui, Sankaran and Sebastian propose a framework to evaluate the IT e-readiness of a nation based on eight factors of digital infrastructure, macro economy, ability to invest, knowledgeable citizens, competitiveness, access to skilled workforce, culture, and cost of living and pricing. They identify 52 measures to quantify these eight factors and provide a simple algorithm to calculate an overall e-readiness index for a country. Finally, they provide benchmarking e-readiness using a 5-point scale diagram. [18]

Caselli and Coleman, Kraemer and Dedrick, and Robinson and Crenshaw point out structure of the economy (such as size of country's services sector because of existing significant positive association between the size of a country's services sector and IT investment) as important affecting factor. [20][36][48] They also believe that inadequate complementary assets such as telecommunications networks and/or infrastructures and skilled human resources (SHR) are also important in increasing differences in IT usage between developed and developing countries. They emphasis on SHR because it has less opposition to social changes associated with adoption of new technologies and empirical studies strongly support the association between education levels and IT use at the country level.

Dewan and Kraemer show that marginal impact of complementary assets is greater in developing countries, which are still in the process of creating adequate levels of such assets than developed countries and openness to external influences, foreign trade especially Foreign Direct Investment FDI, as an indicator, facilitates the diffusion of managerial and technical knowledge across borders. [23] In addition, Coe, Helpman and Hoffmaister, and Shih, Kraemer and Dedrick find that FDI has a positive impact on technical progress in the host country. [19][55]

Shih, Kraemer and Dedrick found a negative relationship between IT investment and interest rates, but significant positive relationships between investment, openness to trade, and tele-communications infrastructure. When they include interaction effects between national income levels and country variables, they find that the impacts of interest rates, size of the financial sector, teledensity, and intellectual property rights are strongest in shaping IT investment for developed countries. In contrast, they find that the impact of openness to trade is greater for developing countries, as is the size of government and education levels. [56]

Hanafizadeh, Khodabakhshi and Hanafizadeh provide a set of recommendations for e-business development in developing countries. They test the recommendations by study of case of Iran. Based on benchmarking 19 countries and 4 regions, 339 recommendations for e-business development are determined and finally using content analysis, 36 of 339 recommendations were selected and categorized into four groups of human resource, security, e-infrastructure, and policies and plans. They also provide a national survey to test the recommendations that fit with Iran internal situations. Finally, they ranked the recommendations based on pundits' opinions. [28]

Shih, Kraemer and Dedrick consider poverty, lack of infrastructure, inadequate education, policy making based on incorrect assumptions about IT usage, low level of IT investment to achieve measurable productivity gains, technology accumulation (evolutionary process of continuous innovation and imitation), and lack of resources for technology investments (because of credit, loan and capital gathering problems and operating in more ill-developed and not matured monetary and stock markets) as important issues make differences between developed and developing countries. [55]

In addition to earlier mentioned economic and business, social and infrastructural issues, there is also a long history for the cultural issues and their effects on the differences between developed and developing countries. Although there is a general agreement on the effects on culture on the differences in IT usage and governance between developed and developing countries, however each research in literature has its own angle of view. It should be mind that there are two major areas for cultural studies: organizational culture and national culture. [61] The following researches are some evidence of cultural effects.

Hofstede, Neuijen, Ohayv and Sanders study the relationships between organizational culture and organizational characteristics. They gathered data on organizational cultures in twenty units from ten different organizations in Denmark and the Netherlands. Based on gathered data on organizational cultures in twenty units from ten different organizations in Denmark and the Netherlands, they study the relationships between organizational culture and organizational characteristics. [31]

According to Rossouw, business ethics, as an integral part of business culture, has a much larger extent become part of the business culture in developed countries than in developing countries. Rossouw provides an explanation for the fact that business ethics is fighting an uphill battle in becoming part of the business culture in developing countries. Although cultural factors in developing countries set limits to organizational effectiveness, variations in effectiveness nevertheless do exist within countries. [49]

Ryan, Chang, Ployhart and Slade study the cross-cultural equivalence of a multinational employee opinion using multiple-groups covariance structure analysis in four countries (U.S. and Australia, Mexico and Spain). [50] Conceptual equivalence occurs when a construct can be meaningfully discussed in each culture and has a similar meaning across cultures. [13] Cultural and linguistic influences were considered by assessing equivalence across two pairs of countries having the same language but different cultures (U.S. and Australia, Mexico and Spain) and across countries differing in culture and language (U.S. and Mexico). The measure was equivalent across U.S. and Australian samples only. One cause source of lack of invariance was translation problems.

Brewster and Dowling, Welch and Schuler identify national culture as one of five variables that 'moderate (i.e. either diminish or accentuate) differences between domestic and international human resource management. [14][24] These include differences in the centrality of markets, institutions, regulations, collective bargaining, and labor-force characteristics. Hofstede study cultural consequences comparing values, behaviors, institutions, and organizations across nations. [32]

Awasthi, Chow, and Wu examine the effects of national cultural differences on the behavioral consequences of imposing performance evaluation and reward systems (PERS). They conclude that two cultural dimensions (individualism versus collectivism and power distance) can modify employees' decisions and satisfaction under imposed performance evaluation and rewards aimed at modifying their work-related behavior. US nationals had significantly lower satisfaction under imposed rather than self-selected performance evaluation and reward structures, while Chinese counterparts did not have a similar adverse reaction. Their results were consistent with prior Anglo-American-based research that the significantly affects employee behavior. They suggest that thier finding may not be directly generalizable to employees whose national cultures differ from those of Anglo-Americans. [6][34]

Salter and Sharp investigate the effects of national culture on management control systems and performance. Results of their study show that even apparently small cultural differences, such as that between the USA and Canada, can be particularly troublesome. In fact, their study explores the effect of an apparently small difference in national culture on the ability of agency theory to explain escalation of commitment to failing projects in two countries with significant cross-border investment, i.e., USA and Canada. They found that the effect of adverse selection conditions was significantly stronger among managers from the more individualist USA and that more experienced managers were less likely to escalate commitment. [52]

Pothukuchi, Damanpour, Choi, Chen and Park examined the effects of national and organizational cultural differences on international joint venture performance. They found that negative effects from cultural distance stems from organizational culture than from national culture. In other words, their study shows the importance of organizational culture similarity for joint venture (JV) success. They found that distance in the open (with a better communication climate) versus closed system dimension negatively affects all measures of International JV performance. The results suggest that while JVs have little control over each other's national culture, they could nevertheless engage in shaping similar organizational practices. [44][47]

Silva and Figueroa discuss how to promote the use of IT in the context of Chile. They discuss that SIS can fail to become institutionalized in a developing country despite adequate planning, strong leadership, and knowledgeable IS professionals. They state some factors including core values and beliefs, political time, the distribution of power, formal organizational structure, and control systems prevent achieving to the developmental goals. [58]

Bada explained a longitudinal case study of radical organizational change related to the computerization and networking of branches in the Nigerian banking sector. He implies that cultural homogeneity is not becoming the norm; it is needed to understand and value local practices. [7]

Walsham dealt with cross-cultural issues in software production and use, drawing on secondary data from two case studies, including that of a joint Jamaican/Indian software team. [64]

Spony examined an analytical model, which enables the operationalization of cultural concepts related to the work context at both the individual and cultural levels of analyses. The model was empirically tested using with a population of French and British managers from two different sectors, bank/insurance and pharmaceutical/ healthcare organizations. They have tyried to control the impact of organizational culture differences. The final four work-value scales (self-enhancement, individual dynamics, consideradon for others and group dynamics) elicited through five-step analysis successfully achieved the purpose of the model's development. [60]

Fang and Rau examined the effects of cultural differences between the Chinese and the US people in terms of the perceived usability and search performance of World Wide Web portal sites. They found significant differences of satisfaction and steps in performing some tasks between Chinese and American. The results also provided more detailed insights into the cultural differences among countries' users. Results of their study indicate that the cultural differences have significant impact on users' perception and usage of the same portal Website.

Their studies provided important insights in designing portal sites for different users with different cultures. [26]

Avgerou show the complex dynamics of the link between IT and development. She discuss that an effective action requires involvement and collaboration between industry, government, and international organizations. [5]

Adam and Myers using case study of the Maldives customs service addressed the challenge of culturally inappropriate impositions of IT. [1]

Shoib and Nandhakumar used two case studies to argue that multiple forms of rationality exist in any context and that national culture is only one aspect of actors' sense-making activities. They suggest need to the notion of culture rather than seeing it as a fixed entity. [57]

Liu and Westrup examined a case study of coordination and control between the United Kingdom and China in a multinational corporation. They discuss that IT-enabled coordination is only effective when linked with other approaches such as the use of expatriates and face-to-face contacts. These studies emphasize the crucial importance of IT in cross-cultural working in the contemporaryworld. [38]

Dunkel and Meierewert examined the impact of different cultural standards on the processes and performances of Austrian, Spanish, German and Hungarian task groups using 201 qualitative interviews. They concluded that culturally heterogeneous teams have more potential for conflicts, thus, resulting in more challenges for the team members. [25]

Saad and Zawdie reveal the need for both technology transfer and the development of the triple helix culture in developing countries. They believe that the business incubation system as an aspect of the triple helix model of innovation in which universities, industry, government and non-government organizations feature as principal actors in the national innovation system. The culture of bureaucracy and institutional fragmentation has been major factors militating against initiatives for technological capability development; and the conventional technology transfer practice has reinforced this culture. They beleive that a major policy initiative is needed in developing countries to put the national system of innovation in place and remove the constraints on the development of the triple helix culture. [51]

Gerhart and Fang studied the national culture and human resource management. Their study implies that although countries can be differ in many ways (e.g. institutional and regulatory environment, labor-force characteristics such as education), a dominant focuses of the international management literature is on national differences in culture, especially culture values. They conclude that while national culture difference can be important, their role needs to be put in the context of other important contextual factors, including organizational culture. [27]

Some researchers consider local adaptation and new technologies as important factor as well as cultural factors. For example, Sayed and Westrup study the case of Egypt and explains the role of a specific IT, Enterprise Resource Planning (ERP) systems networks in country development. [53] Some researchers study the local adaptation and cultivation of IT. Macome shows that the local context was crucial in the implementation process and that it was essential to involve local stakeholders in the entire process. [40] D'Mello was also concerned with local adaptation related to new ICTs she addressed the adaptation of people in the context of global software outsourcing and argued that adaptation has produced a new breed of knowledge workers in the software industry in countries such as India from where she drew her field data. [21]

As Walsham, Robey, and Sahay state, IT disffusion consequences emerge from a complex set of processes over a significant period. It needs involving a wide range of actors and institutions. IT has no deterministic effects on development because it has being applied to complex social issues. In other words, social influences are crucially important to the trajectory of any technology-based project. [65] Accordingly, the studies on the developing countries and the potential role of IT to support their development emphasis on a complex set of factors such as social, political, and cultural contexts. According to Walsham, Robey and Sahay, we need to conduct more researchers to consider geographical spread, NGOs roles as important intermediaries in IT related development, and different level of analysis such as individuals, groups, organizations, industry sectors, societies, and international organizations. [63] Work at the community level also promises to contribute to an understanding of IT in marginalized groups in developed countries. [37] Research is also needed on society-wide critical issues (such as HIV/AIDS or gender) in developing countries. Gender studies received more attentions in IT research, but there is little work as yet which addresses the role of women in connection with IT in developing countries. [2][65]

3. Factors Affecting IT Diffusion

Brief review of the literature shows that there are a numerous number of factors affecting IT usage and there are various differences in these factors between developed and developing countries. Tables 1, 2 and 3 will sammurize and classfify the most important factors that affecting the relation between IT and performance and make difference between developed and developing countries. These Tables facilitate answering to the main question of "what factors affecting IT diffusion and create differences between developed and developing countries?"

Table 1: Most widely used variables in literature

Type of Variables	Factors	Measures
Independent Variable	ITechnology Diffusion (Investments)	• IT investment [11][23][36][55][56][62][66] • IT use at country level [20][26][36][48][55] • IT spending on hardware and software as percent of GDP [56] • Computer hardware imports and production [20]
Dependent Variable	National Productivity Level	• Productivity growth at the macroeconomic level [20][23][36][41] • Level of national wealth [55][62][66] • Technical progress [19][55]
Common Used General Moderator Variables	Most widely-used, official-source development data from the World Bank and other international agencies	• Total external debt to gross national income (Economic Indicator) • GDP (current US$) (billions) (Economic Indicator) • GNI per capita, Atlas method (current US$) (Economic Indicator) • Life expectancy at birth, total (years) (Social Indicator) • Population, total (millions) (Social Indicator) • Population growth (annual %)(Social Indicator) • Surface area (sq. km) (thousands) (Infrastructural &Natural Indicator)

Table 2: Factors affecting IT diffusion

Factors	Factors
• Educational level [11][20][36][42][54][65]	• Cost of living and pricing [18]
• Professional and Training level [11][36][42]	• Techmology accumulation [55]
• Perception of user toward IT [42]	• Lack of resources fortechnology investment [55]
• Commitement level [43]	• Infrastructures [20][36][48][55]
• Enterprice readiness [46]	• Skilled human resource [20][36][48][55]
• ICT readiness [46]	• Proterty rights protection [20][56]
• External Environmen readiness [[46]	• Lack of clean water, inadequate housing and freedom [54][65]
• Human readiness [46]	• National culture and cross cultural differences [1][5][6][13][14][18][24][26][32][38][47][49][50][52][57][58][60][64]
• Information readiness [46]	
• Completeness assets [20][23][36][48][55][62][66]	
• Telecomunications networks [20][36][48][62][66][55]	• Organizational culture [27][31]
• Skilled IT professionals [55][62][66]	• Business Ethics [49]
• Lack of resourece for technology investments [54][55][62][65][66]	• Language and translation problems [13]
	• Culturally heterogeneous teams [7][25]
• Structure of economy [11][20][36][48][55][56][62][66]	• Culture of bureaucracy and institutional fragmentation [51]
• Openness to external influence [20][23][55][62][66]	
• Digital infrastructure [11][18][36]	• Poverty [55]
• Macro econy situation [18]	• Lack of infrastructure [55]
• Ability to invest [18]	• Inadequate educaton [55]
• Knowledge citizens [18]	• Incorrect assumptions and policy makings [55]
• Competitiveness [18]	• Legal similarity [58]
• Access to skilled workforce [18]	• Political context [58][65]

Table 3: Moderator variables/factors and their measures classfification

Moderator Variables	Factors	Measures/Indicators		
Economic & Business Moderator Variable	Globalization and International Trade	• Merchandise exports (current US$) (millions) • Merchandise imports (current US$) (millions) • Merchandise trade (% of GDP) • Trade Balance (• Trade (% of GDP) • Tariff & Non-tariff Barriers • Net financial flows	• Merchandise trade (% of GDP) • Net barter terms of trade (2000 = 100) • Commercial service exports (current US$) (millions) • Commercial service imports (current US$) (millions) • Manufactures exports (% of merchandise exports) • Manufactures imports (% of merchandise imports) • Foreign direct investment, net inflows (BoP, current US$) (millions)	• International tourism, receipts (current US$) • International tourism, number of departures • International tourism, number of arrivals • Bank and trade-related lending (PPG + PNG) (NFL, current US$) (millions) • Private capital flows, total (BoP, current US$) • Foreign direct investment, net inflows (% of GDP)
	Macroeconomics Situation	• GDP (current US$) (millions) • GDP growth (annual %) • GDP per capita, Shih, Kraemer and Dedrick (2007) • GDP - real growth rate(%) • GNI, Atlas method (current US$) (millions) • GNI per capita, Atlas method (current US$) • Budget expenditures • Budget-capital (%) • Budget deficit • Current account balance • Industrial production growth rate (%) • Investment (gross fixed)(% of GPD) • Industry, value added (current US$) (millions) • Adequate Regulations & Supervision of Financial Institutions	• Soundness of Banks • Local Competition • Regulatory Framework • Government Effectiveness • Political Stability • Rule of Law and Control of Corruption • Industry, value added (% of GDP) • Cereal yield (kg per hectare) • Economic growth in the following periods (EGF) • Size of the financial sector • Interest rates • Wealth (GNP), economic growth in the past periods (EGP) • Structure of the economy such as size of country's services sector • Protection of Property Rights	• Agriculture, value added (% of GDP) • Total debt service (% of GNI) • Total debt service (% of exports of goods, services and income) • Current account balance (% of GDP) • Exports of goods and services (% of GDP) • GNI per capita, PPP (current international $) • Inflation, GDP deflator (annual %) • Gross capital formation (current US$) (millions) • Gross capital formation (% of GDP) • Services, etc., value added (% of GDP) • Imports of goods and services (% of GDP) • Industry, value added (annual % growth) • The size of government • Cash surplus/deficit (% of GDP)
	Labor and Employment	• Labor force, female (% of total labor force) • Labor force, total (millions) • Labor force with primary education (% of total) • Worker remittances and compensation of employees, received (US$)	• Employment in industry (% of total employment) • Employment in services (% of total employment) • Labor force - by occupation - in agriculture, • Employees, agriculture, male (% of male employment)	• Population ages 15-64, total (millions) • Unemployment, total (% of total labor force) • Employees, agriculture, female (% of female employment)
	Private and Public Sectors	• Domestic credit to private sector (% of GDP) • GFCF, private sector (% of GDP) • Private Sector Spending on R&D • Credits made to the private sector as percent of GDP	• Global Fund for Community Foundations GFCF, public sector (current LCU) • Public sector long-term debt of public sector LDOD (current US$) • Privatization transactions values by country, region or sector**	• Claims on private sector (annual growth as % of M2) • PNG, total private nonguaranteed L-T debt service (TDS, current US$) • Expense (% of GDP) • Revenue, excluding grants (% of GDP)
	States, Markets & Competitiveness	• Total Expenditure for R&D as % of GNI • Stocks traded, total value (% of GDP) • Market capitalization of listed companies (% of GDP) • Market capitalization (% of GDP) • Inward foreign direct investment as percent of GDP • Intellectual property rights • Property rights protection	• Composite ICRG Risk Rating • Availability of Venture Capital • Openness to external influences, foreign trade specially Foreign Direct Investment FDI as % of GDP • openness to imports/trades trade as percent of GDP • Values of AiDA or official development aid activities by Country*****	• Time required to start a business (days) • Easiness of Doing Business (rank) *** • Admin. Burden for Start-Ups a business (rank) • Military expenditure (% of GDP) • Entrepreneurship among Managers • High-technology exports (% of manufactured exports) • Tenders and procurement opportunities worldwide or Tenders and consulting opportunities worldwide*
	Poverty, Debts & Aids	• Cost of Living and Pricing • International Cost of Living Indices • Income share held by lowest 10% and 20% • Poverty gap at $1 and $2 a day (PPP) (%) • Poverty headcount ratio at $1 and $2 a day (PPP) (% of population) • Malnutrition prevalence, weight for age (% of children under 5) • PPP conversion factor to official exchange rate ratio • Purchasing power parity conversion factor (LCU per international $) • Inflation Rate-CPI in % • GDP per capita (PPP) • Poverty index	• Food production index (1999-2001 = 100) • Homeownership Rates • Population below poverty line(%) • Reserves of foreign exchange and gold • GDP - composition by sector - agriculture, industry and services • Inflation rate(consumer prices) (%) • Household income or consumption by percentage share - highest 10% • Present value of debt (% of GNI) • Total debt service (TDS, current US$) (millions) • Total debt service, total long-term (TDS, current US$) (millions) • Long-term debt (DOD, current US$) (millions) • Present value of debt (current US$) (millions)	• External debt (% of exports of goods and services) • External debt (% of GNI) • External debt, total (DOD, current US$) (millions) • Economic aid - donor • Economic aid - recipient • Official development assistance and official aid (current US$) (millions) • Aid per capita (current US$) • Aid (% of GNI)**** • Aid (% of gross capital formation) • Aid (% of imports of goods and services) • Short-term debt (% of total external debt) • Lending interest rate (%)

Table 3: Moderator variables factors and measures classfification (continued

Moderator Variables	Factors	Measures/Indicators		
Infrastructural and Natural Moderator Variable	Geographical Environmental General Infrastructural ICT Infrastructural	• Roads, total network (thousands km) • Vehicles (per 1,000 people) • Airports, Heliports • Merchant marine (ships) • Pipelines (km) • Railways (km) • Roadways (km) • Computers per 1,000 People • Television broadcast stations • Internet Hosts per 10,000 People • Internet users per 10,000 People • Households with television (%) • Waterways(km) Oil and Gas proved reserves • Passenger cars (per 1,000 people) • Price basket for internet • Fixed line and mobile phone subscribers (per 1,000 people) • International Telecommunications • Total Investments in Telecommunications Telecommunication equipment (Export) (US$) • Telecommunication equipment (Import) (US$) • % of households with a telephone • Public payphones • Main (fixed) telephone lines in operation • Main (fixed) telephone lines in largest city • Total telephone subscribers (fixed + mobile) • % automatic main lines • % digital main lines • % residential main lines • % of main lines in urban areas • Total capacity of local public switching exchanges • International telephone circuits • Waiting list for main (fixed) lines • Number of local (fixed) telephone (calls) • Number of local (fixed) telephone (minutes) • Number of national (fixed) long distance telephone (calls) • Number of national (fixed) long distance telephone (minutes) • Total national (fixed) telephone traffic (calls) • Total national (fixed) telephone traffic (minutes) • International outgoing fixed telephone traffic (calls) • International incoming fixed telephone traffic (calls) • International incoming fixed telephone traffic (minutes) • International outgoing fixed telephone traffic (minutes) • %of telephone faults cleared by next working day • Faults per 100 main (fixed) lines per year • Residential telephone connection charge • Residential telephone connection charge (US$) • Business telephone connection charge • Business telephone connection charge (US$) • Mobile cellular connection charge • Mobile cellular connection charge (US$) • Residential monthly telephone subscription	• Residential monthly telephone subscription (US$) • Business telephone monthly subscription Business telephone monthly subscription (US$) • Mobile cellular monthly subscription • Mobile cellular monthly subscription (US$) • Price of a 3-minute fixed telephone local call (peak rate) • Price of a 3-minute fixed telephone local call (peak rate - US$) • Mobile cellular - price of 3-minute local call (peak) • Mobile cellular - price of 3-minute local call (peak - US$) • Mobile cellular - price of 3-minute local call (off-peak) • Mobile cellular - price of 3-minute local call (off-peak - US$) • Price of a 3-minute fixed telephone local call (off-peak rate) • Price of a 3-minute fixed telephone local call (off-peak rate - US$) • Households Mobile cellular telephone subscribers - (Post-paid + Pre-paid) • Mobile cellular telephone subscribers (Digital) • Mobile cellular telephone subscribers - prepaid subscribers • POP Coverage of mobile cellular network (population, in %) • Staff (Total full-time telecommunications staff) • Staff (Female telecommunication staff) • Mobile communications staff • Revenue from fixed telephone service • Revenue from fixed telephone service (US$) • Revenue from mobile communication • Revenue from mobile communication (US$) • Total revenue from all telecommunication services • Total revenue from all telecommunication services (US$) • Total annual investment in telecom • Total annual investment in telecom (US$) • Fixed telephone service investment • Fixed telephone service investment (US$) • Mobile communication investment • Mobile communication investment (US$) • Main (fixed) telephone lines per 100 inhabitants • Mobile cellular telephone subscribers per 100 inhabitants • Total telephone subscribers (fixed + mobile) per 100 inhabitants • Public payphones per 1000 inhabitants • Radio sets • Radio equipped households • % of households with a radio • Television receivers • Television receivers per 100 inhabitants • Cable television subscribers • Television equipped households • % of households with a television • Home satellite antennas • ISDN subscribers • SDN Channels • Estimated Internet users • Total (fixed) Internet subscribers • Cable modem Internet subscribers • Dial-up Internet subscribers • DSL Internet subscribers	• % of homes with Internet • Total fixed broadband Internet subscribers • International Internet Bandwidth (Mbps) • Personal computers • % of homes with a Personal Computer • Personal computers per 100 inhabitants • Internet users per 100 inhabitants • Total fixed broadband Internet subscribers per 100 inhabitants • Total (fixed) Internet subscribers per 100 inhabitants • International Internet Bandwidth per inhabitant (bit/s) • Schools connected to internet (%) • Broadband subscribers (per 1000 people) • International voice traffic (minutes per person) • Daily newspapers (per 1,000 people) • Telephone mainlines (per 1,000 people) • Technology Assessment Index • Patent Applications Granted • Computer Processing Power (% of total worldwide MIPS) • E-Government Index • Freedom on the Internet • ICT Expenditure as % of GDP • International internet bandwidth bits (per capita) • Internet servers per million people • Permanent cropland (% of land area) • Arable land (% of land area) • Land use - arable land(%) • Land use - permanent crops(%) • Electricity - consumption(kWh) • Electricity - exports (kWh) • Electricity - imports (kWh) • Electricity - production(kWh) • Natural gas and oil consumption, production, exports, import Electric power consumption (kWh per capita) Coastline • Elevation extremes - highest point • Elevation extremes - lowest point • Irrigated land • Land boundaries - km • Surface area (sq. km) • Forest area (sq. km) • Agricultural land (% of land area) • Land and water area sq km • Total Area - sq km • CO_2 emissions (kt) (thousands) • CO_2 emissions (metric tons per capita) • Improved water source, rural (% of rural population with access) • Improved water source, urban (% of urban population with access) • Improved water source (% of population with access) • Improved sanitation facilities, urban (% of urban population with access) • Land area (sq. km) (thousands) • Organic water pollutant (BOD) emissions (kg per day) • Energy use (kg of oil equivalent per capita) Energy imports, net (% of energy use)	

Table 3: Moderator variables factors and classfification (continued)

Moderator Variables	Factors	Measures	
Cultural & Educational Moderator Variable	Cultural (Education /Literacy)	• Expenditure per student, primary (% of GDP per capita) • Public Spending on Education • Literacy rate, adult total (% of people ages 15 and above) • Literacy rate, adult female (% of females ages 15 and above) • Literacy rate, adult male (% of males ages 15 and above) • Persistence to grade 5, total (% of cohort) • Pupil-teacher ratio, primary • School enrollment, primary (% gross) • School enrollment, primary, female (% gross) • School enrollment, primary, male (% gross) • Primary completion rate, total (% of relevant age group) • School enrollment, tertiary (% gross) • School enrollment, tertiary, female (% gross)	• School enrollment, secondary (% gross) • Adult Literacy Rate • Tertiary Enrollment • 8th Grade Achievement in Science • MGMT Education Locally Available in first-class Business Schools • Flexibility of People to Adapt to New Challenges • Tertiary Science & Engineering Enrollment • University Education Meets the Needs of Competitive Economy • Well Educated People Do not Emigrate Abroad • Extent of Staff Trainings • Research Collaboration Companies/Universities • Technical Papers per Million Population • Labor force with tertiary education (% of total) • Business ethics as an integral part of business culture • Educational level measured by tertiary school enrollment as percent of relevant age group • skilled human resources
Social & Demographical Moderator Variable	Social Development Gender and Population Health Rural and Urban Development	• Proportion of seats held by women in national parliament (%) • Ratio of girls to boys in primary and secondary education (%) • Mortality rate, under-5 (per 1,000) • Mortality rate, infant (per 1,000 live births) • Health expenditure per capita (current US$) • Health expenditure, total (% of GDP) • Hospital beds (per 1,000 people) • Immunization, DPT (% of children ages 12-23 months) • Immunization, measles (% of children ages 12-23 months) • Malnutrition prevalence, weight for age (% of children under 5) • Mortality rate, under-5 (per 1,000) • Physicians (per 1,000 people) • Prevalence of HIV, total (% of population ages 15-49) • Death rate (birth/1000 population) • Gender, and even age • Fertilizer consumption (metric tons) (thousands) • Land under cereal production (hectares) • Agricultural machinery, tractors per 100 sq. km of arable land • Rural population density (rural population per sq. km of arable land) • Population in the largest city (% of urban population)	• Population in urban agglomerations > 1 million (% of total population) • Poverty headcount ratio at urban poverty line (% of urban population) • Urban population • Urban population (% of total) • Latitude (LAT) • Organizational size (ORS) • Relatives organizational size (ROS) • Population size (POP) • Population growth (PGR) • Population density (PDN) • Population, total (millions) • Population, female • Population, female (% of total) • Population growth (annual %) • Population density (people per sq. km) • Births attended by skilled health staff (% of total) • Age dependency ratio (dependents to working-age population) • Fertility rate, total (births per woman) • Age structure in terms of ages (0-14, 15-64, 65 and over) and the gender (male and female) (%) • Life expectancy at birth, female (years) • Life expectancy at birth, male (years) • Life expectancy at birth, total (years) • Occupation

http://web.worldbank.org
http://www.dgmarket.com
http://rru.worldbank.org
http://www.doingbusiness.org
http://www.unctad.org/wir
http://aida.developmentgateway.org/aida/AidaAbout.do
http://www.imf.org/external/data.htm#data
http://www.itu.int/ITU-D/icteye/Indicators/Indicators.aspx

4. Cnoceptual Model, Hypotheses and Computational Methodology

4.1 The Conceptual Model

Figure 1 and 2 show the general and the extended version of the proposed conceptual model. Although this research focuses on the developed and developing countrirs, but in fact, the proposed model can be used for four diffeenrt levels of analysis. For example, it can be used for country level analysis, for analyzing a group of countries (such as developed, developing, advanced economies, Euro area, major advanced economies, European Union, newly industrialized Asian economies, advanced economies excluding G7 and euro area, and emerging market countries), for regional analysis and even for a global level of analysis.

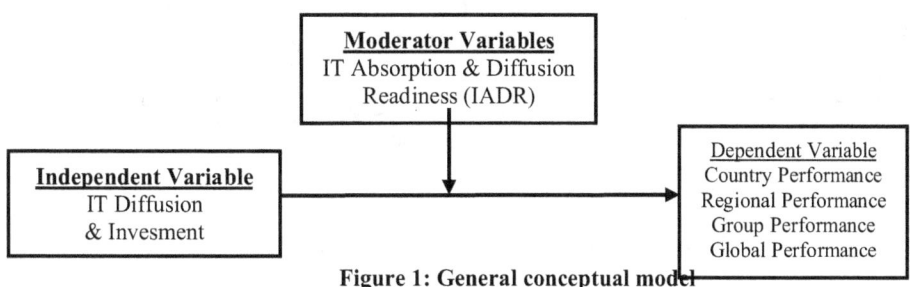

Figure 1: General conceptual model

As shown in figure 1, a given country's performance, performance of countries in a given region (such as Asian, European, American, Ocenia and/or African countries), the performance of a given group of countries (such as developing and/or developed coutries) or even global performance is a function of IT investment and diffusion. In other words, we can investigate the relation between independent variable (IT investment and diffusion) and performance at four different levels. What that moderate these relations are called "IT Absorption and Diffusion Readiness (ITADR)". ITADR, in turns, is constituted by four components of cultural, economic and business, social and demographical, and infrastructural and natural readiness. Accordingly, an extended version of the conceptual model can be shown as figure 2.

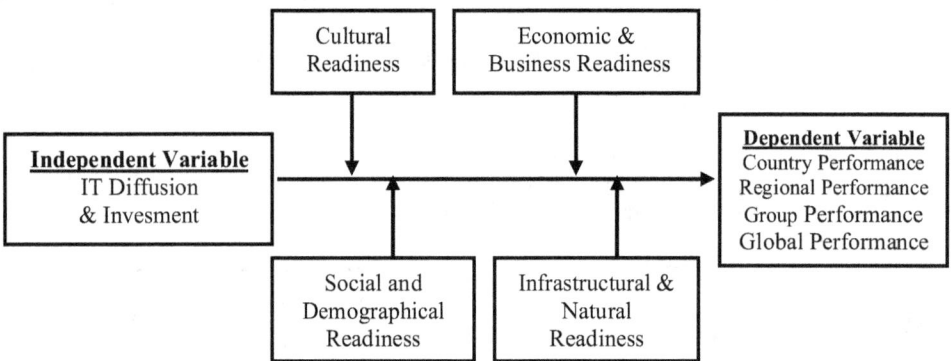

Figure 2: Extended vesion of the conceptual model

4.2. Potential Research Hypotheses

Considering Figure 2, the following potential research hypotheses can be defined:

H1: The effects of IT investments on the performance are significantly different between developed and developing countries.

H2: IT diffusion readiness (consistes of economic & business, cultural, social & demographical, and infrastructural & natural readiness) moderates the relation between countrirs' IT investments and the performances in both developed and developing countries.

H3: Economic & business readiness moderates the relation between IT investments and country performance in both developed and developing countries.

H4: Cultural readiness moderates the relation between IT investments and country performance in both developed and developing countries.

H5: Social and demographical readiness moderates the relation between IT investments and country performance in both developed and developing countries.

H6: Infrastructural & natural readiness modifies the relation between investments on IT and country performance in both developed and developing countries.

H7: The effects of each of readiness elements (economic & business readiness, cultural readiness, social and demographical readiness and infrastructural & natural readiness) are significantly different in each of developed and developing countries.

H8: The effects of economic & business readiness, cultural readiness, social and demographical readiness and infrastructural & natural readiness are significantly different between developed and developing countries.

According to Baron and Kenny, a moderator variable is a qualitative or quantitative variable that affects the direction and/or strength of the relation between an independent or predictor variable and a dependent or criterion variable. [9] A moderator effect within a correlational framework may also be said to occur where the direction of the correlation changes. That is, moderator variables always function as independent variables, whereas mediating events shift roles from effects to causes, depending on the focus of the analysis. Moderator variables apply when there is an unexpectedly weak or inconsistent relation between a predictor and a criterion variable (e.g., a relation holds in one setting but not in another, or for one subpopulation but not for another). In this research, IT Diffusion Readiness Index (ITDRI) is a moderator variable that affects the relation between IT investments and performances at different levels.

4.3 Computational methodology

In order to test the conceptual model and its related hypotheses, we need to an operational model. Generally, we can classify different kinds of conceptual models into seven following groups:

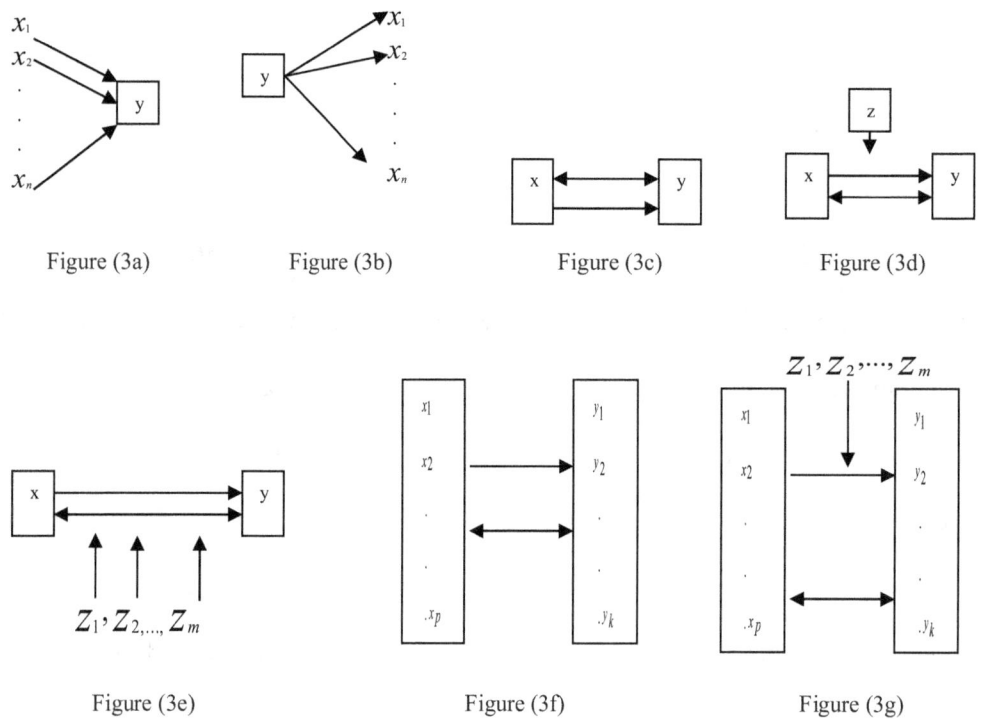

Figure 3: Seven popular for of conceptual models without moderator variables

Figure (3a) shows the effects of different drivers or independent variables on single dependent variable. Figure (3b) shows the effects of a given variable (independent variable) on several later dependent variables. Figure (3c) shows simple relations between single independent and dependent variables. In this case, there are no moderator and/or mediator variables. Figure (3d) explains how the relationships between an independent and dependent variables may be affected by a moderator variable. Figure (3e) explains how a relationship may be affected by several moderator variables. Figure (3f) describes the relationships among several independent and dependent variabls. Finally, Figure (3g) explains how the relationships among several independent and dependent variables may be affected by some moderator variables.

For the real cases when we have huge number of factors and measures to quantify independent, dependent, and moderator variables, we face to case of Figure (3g). In this case, it is difficult to solve the problem by well-known classical statistical methods. For this case, we suggest first to reduce the complexity and multidimensionality (change the complex problem to a simple one as shown in Figure 3d) and then apply statistical methods for each group.

In reality and as shown in Tables 1, 2, 3, a variety of measures can be applied to quantify the research variables. In other worlds, we have a problem with a huge number of measures for each of independent, dependent and moderator variables. Suppose a problem in which for each country (or groups of countries named developing or developed countries) i, we can define Ni, Yi, and Mi as the number of measures for independent, dependent and moderator variables, respectively. In this case, the problem is naturally a Multi Attribute Decision Making (MADM) problem. For this real situation, using a MADM model (such as TOPSIS) helps analysts to reduce the dimeniond and the complexity of real problem and consider maximum possible measures. Let us consider general version of the problem as following:

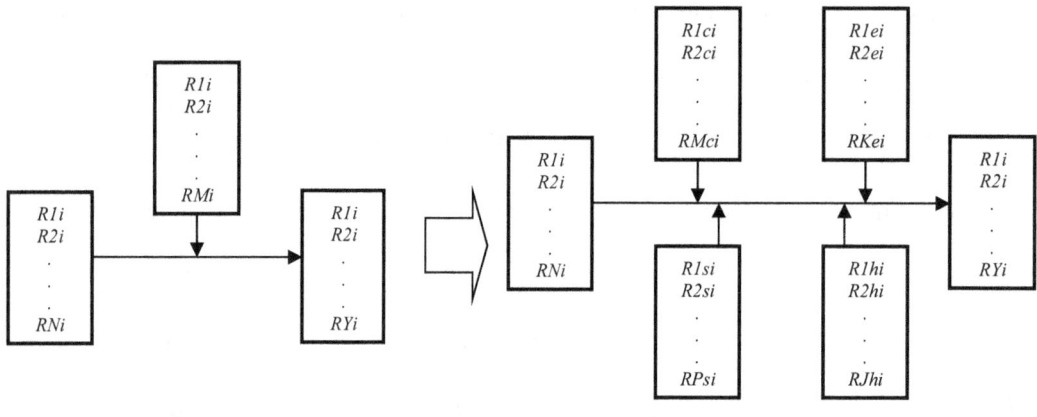

Figure 4a   **Figure 4a**

In Figure 4a, *RNi, RYi, and RMi* denote number of independent, dependent and moderator variables measures for country (or a given group of countries) *i*, respectively. Accordingly, the real problem can be redefined as Figure 4b where:

Rni: value (rank) of *nth* measure of independent variable for country (group of country) *i*

Ryi: value (rank) of *yth* measure of dependent variable for country (group of country) *i*

Rmci: value (rank) of *mth* cultural measure of moderator variable for country (group of country) *i*

Rkei: value (rank) of *kth* economic & business measure of moderator variable for country (group of country) *i*

Rpsi: value (rank) of *pth* social and demographical measure moderator variable for country (group of country) *i*

Rjhi: value (rank) of *jth* infrastructural & natural measure of moderator variable for country (group of country) *i*

We propose using TOPSIS technique because it reduces the dimensions and the complexity of a real problem and let's to evaluate each alternative with the best virtual benchmark and select the best alternative. Best alternative is an alternative with maximum relative closeness index to the best virtual benchmark among m alternatives in terms of n decision criteria. TOPSIS solution steps are as follows:

Step 1: Prepare dimensionless matrix N_D using norm method ($n_{ij} = r_{ij} / \sqrt{\sum_{i=1}^{m} r_{ij}^2}$)

Step 2: Calculate $V = N_D.W_{n.n}$ matrix where $W_{n.n}$ is the weight vector that can be calculated by some well-known mwthods (e.g. Shannon Entropy Method).

Step 3: Calculate V_j^+ denote V_j^- and V_j^+ vectors where V_j^- and virtual ideal point/vector with the highest positive and negative values in terms of all criteria.

Step 4: Calculate total positive and negative distance values for each alternative i by

$$d_i^- = \sqrt{\sum_{j=1}^{n}(V_{ij} - V_j^-)^2} \quad i=1,2,\ldots,m. \quad \text{and} \quad d_i^+ = \sqrt{\sum_{j=1}^{n}(V_{ij} - V_j^+)^2} \quad i=1,2,\ldots,m.$$

Step 5: Calculate $cl_i^* = \dfrac{d_i^-}{d_i^- + d_i^*}$ as relative closeness index to the best virtual benchmark.

In our problem, the global IT Absorbtion & Diffusion Readiness Index (ITADRI) for a given country (or a given group of countries such as developed or developing countries) can be easily calculated by using its four component partial readiness vectors (cultural readiness vector, economic & business readiness vector, social & demographical readiness vector, and infrastructural & natural readiness vector). Finally, having independent, dependent and moderator/readiness vectors, we can easily apply well-known statistical methods to analyze and compare empiricaly the effects of moderator variable(s) on the relation between IT diffusion and country performance and developed with developing countries.

The most advantages of the proposed methodology are as follows:

- Let analysts to consider maximum number of independent, dependent and moderator variables' factors and measures.
- Reduces the dimensions and the complexity of a large-scale problem, which includes a huge number of measures and data.
- Let analysts to use an optimization and benchmarking method.
- Applies operational research (OR) technique (TOPSIS) to facilitate using well known classical statistical methods.
- Let analysts to calculate global IT Absorbtion & Diffusion Readiness Index (ITADRI) as well as partial readiness indices for each of moderator variables, separately.
- Let analysts do sensitivity analysis and simulate the behavior of system and its trend.
- Finally, let analysts to develop an intelligent system to helps them in better planning and controlling and monitoring the relations between independent, dependent and moderator variables using efficient and effective related factors and measures.

5. Summary and Conclusions

This paper, based on the literature and the international organizations' database, determined and classifyied most important factors affecting the relation between IT and performance in developed and developing countries. Moreover, it provided a new general conceptual model to facilitates the investigation of the IT absorption and diffusion readiness as a strategic level moderator variable. To operationalize the proposed general conceptual model, eight potential research hypotheses were introduced. Finally, for the future empirical researches, a new calculation methodology was sugested. The proposed model, potential research hypotheses, and the suggested calculation methodology facilitate future studies on the effects of various influence factors on the relations between IT and national performance in developed and developing countries.

References

67. Adam, M., and Myers, M. Have You Got Anything to Declare? Neo-colonialism, Information Systems, and the Imposition of Customs and Duties in a Third World Country, 2003, In Organizational Information Systems in the Context of Globalization, M. Korpela, R. Montealegre, and A. Poulymenakou (eds.), Kluwer Academic Publishers, Boston, 2003: 101-116.

68. Adam, A., Howcroft, D., and Richardson, H. A Decade of Neglect: Reflecting on the Gender and IS Field," New Technology, Work and Employment, 19(3), 2005: 222-240.

69. Adkinson, W. F., Lenard, T. M., and Pickford, M. J. The Digital Economy Fact Book, 6th Ed., Washington D.C., The Progress and Freedom Foundation, 2004.

70. Avgerou, C., and Walsham, G. Information Technology in Context: Studies from the Perspective of Developing Countries, Ashgate Publishing, Aldershot, UK, 2000.

71. Avgerou, C. The Link Between ICT and Economic Growth in the Discourse of Development, in Organizational InformationSystems in the Context of Globalization, M. Korpela, R. Montealegre, and A. Poulymenakou (eds.), Kluwer Academic Publishers, Boston, 2003: 373-386.

72. Awasthi, V. N. Chow, C. W. and Wu, A. Cross-cultural Differences in the Behavioral Consequences of Imposing Performance Evaluation and Reward Systems: An Experimental Investigation, International Journal of Accounting, 36(3), 2001: 291-309.

73. Bada, A. O. Local Adaptation to Global Trends: A Study of an IT-Based Organizational Change Program in a Nigerian Bank," The Information Society, 18(2), 2002: 77-86.

74. Bakos Y. The Productivity Payoff of Computers, a Review of Computer Revolution: An Economic Perspective, Daniel E. Sichel Science, 52(3), 1998.

75. Baron, R. M. and Kenny, D. A. The Moderator-Mediator Variable Distinction in Social Psychological Research: Conceptual, Strategic, and Statistical Considerations, Journal of Personality and Social Psychology, 51(6), 1986: 1173-1182.

76. Bem, D. J. Belifes, Attitudes, and Human Affairs, Belmont, CA: Brook/Cole, 1970.

77. Barrell, R. and Pain, N. Foreign Direct Investment, Technological Change and Economic Growth within Europe, Economic Journal, 107(445), 1997: 1770–1786.

78. Bharadwaj Anandhi S., Sundar G. Bharadwaj, Benn R. Konsynski Information Technology Effects on Firm Performance as Measured by Tobin's Q. Management Science, 45(6), 1999.

79. Brett, J. M. Tinsiey, C. H. Janssens, M. Barsness Z. I. and Lytle A. L. New Approaches to the Study of Culture in Industrial/Organizational Psychology, In Eariey P.C., Erez M (Eds.), New Perspectives on Intemationai Industrial/Organizational Ssychology, San Francisco: New Lexington Press, 1997.

80. Brewster, C. Different Paradigms in Strategic HRM: Questions Raised by Comparative Research, in Wright, P. Dyer, L. Boudreau, J. and Milkovich, G. (eds) Research in Personnel and HRM. Supplement 4, Greenwich, CT: JAI Press, 1999.

81. Brynjolfsson, E. The Productivity Paradox of Information Technology, Communications of ACM, 36(12), 1993.

82. Brynjolfsson E. and Hitt, L. M. Paradox Lost? Firm Level Evidence on the Returns to Information Technology Spending, Management Science, 42(4), 1996.

83. Brynjolfsson E. and Yang, S. Information Technology and Productivity: A Review of the Literature, Advances in Computers, Academic Press, 43, 1996.

84. Bui, T. X. Sankaran, S. and Sebastian I. M. A Framework for Measuring National Readiness, International Journal of Electronic Business, 1(1), 2003: 3-22.

85. Coe, D.T. Helpman, E. and Hoffmaister, A. W. North-south R & D Spillovers, The Economic Journal, 107(440), 1997: 134–149.

86. Caselli, F. and Coleman II, W. J. Cross-country Technology Diffusion: The Case of Computers, The American Economic Review, 91(2), 2001.

87. D'Mello, M. Thinking Local, Acting Global: An Analysis of Identity Related Issues in a GSO in India, Research in Progress paper presented at the IFIP 9.4/8.2 Joint Conference on Organizational Information Systems in the Context of Globalization, 2003.

88. Dowlatshahi Shad and Cao Qing The Relationships among Virtual Enterprise, Information Technology and Business Performance in Sgile Manufacturing: An Industry Perspective, European Journal of Operational Research, 174 (2), 2006.

89. Dewan, S., and Kraemer, K.L. Information Technology and Productivity: Evidence from Country-level Data, Management Science 46, 4, 2000: 548–562.

90. Dowling, P. J. Welch, D. E. and Schuler, R. S. International Human Resource Management. Cincinnati, OH: South-Westem, 1999.

91. Dunkel, A. and Meierewert, S. Culture Standards and Their Impact on Teamwork–An Empirical Analysis of Austrian, German, Hungarian and Spanish Culture Differences, Journal for East European Management Studies, 2, 2004: 147-174.

92. Fang, X. and Rau, P-L. P. Culture Differences in Design of Portal Sites, Ergonomics, 46(1-3), 2003: 242-254.

93. Gerhart, B. and Fang, M. National Culture and Human Resource Management: Assumptions and Evidence, International Journal of Human Management, 16(6), 2005: 971-986.

94. Hanafizadeh, P. Khodabakhshi, M. and Hanafizadeh, M. R. Recommendations for E-business Development in Developing Countries: A Case Study of Iran, European and Mediterranean Conference on Information Systems 2008 (EMCIS 2008), May 25-26 2008, Dubai, UEA.

95. Huang, Shi-Ming, Qu Chin-Shyh, Chen Chyi-Miaw, Lin Binshan An Empirical Study of Relationship between IT Investment and Firms Performance: A Resource–based Perspective, European Journal of Operational Research, 173(3), 2006.

96. Herscovitch, L. and Meyer, J. P. Commitment to Organizational Change: Extension of a Three Component Model, Journal of Applied Psychology, 87, 2002: 474–487.

97. Hofstede, G. Neuijen, B. Ohayv, D. D. and Sanders, G. Measuring Organizational Cultures: A Qualitative and Quantitative Study across Twenty Cases, Administrative Science Quarterly, 35(2), 1990: 286-316.

98. Hofstede, G. Cultural Consequences: Comparing Values, Behaviors, Institutions, and Organizations across Nations, Second Edition, Sage Publication Inc., Thousand Oaks, California, USA, 2001.

99. Kennerley, M. and Andy, N. Evaluating the Impact of Information Technology on Business Performance, Presented at the Fifth International Conference of the European Operations Management Association, Trinity College, Dublin, Ireland, 1998.

100. Kluckhohn, C. Values and Value-orientation in Theory of Action: An Exploration in Definition and Classification, in T. Parsons & E. A. Shils (Eds.), Toward a General Theory of Action, Cambridge, MA, Harvard University Press, 1967.

101. Kohli Rajiv and Sarv Devaraj Measuring Information Technology Payoff: A Meta-Analysis of Structural Variables in Firm-Level Empirical Research, Information Systems Research, 14(2), 2003.

102. Kraemer, K. L. and Dedrick, J. Payoffs from Investment in Information Technology: Lessons from Asia-Pacific Region, World Development, 22, 1994: 1921–1931.

103. Kvasny, L. Cultural (Re) Production of Digital Inequality in a US Community Technology Initiative, Information, Communication & Society, 9(2), 2006: 160-181.

104. Liu, W., and Westrup, C. ICTs and Organizational Control across Cultures: The Case of a UK Multinational Operating in China, in Organizational Information Systems in the Context of Globalization, M. Korpela, R. Montealegre, and A. Poulymenakou (eds.), Kluwer Academic Publishers, Boston, 2003: 155-168.

105. Lubbe, S. Parker, G. and Hoard, A. The Profit Impact of IT Investment, Journal of Information Technology, 10, 1995: 44-51.

106. Macome, E. On the Implementation of an Information System in the Mozambican Context: The EDM Case, in Organizational Information Systems in the Context of Globalization, M. Korpela, R. Montealegre, and A. Poulymenakou (eds.), Kluwer Academic Publishers, Boston, 2003: 169-184.

107. Madon, S. The Internet and Socio-Economic Development: Exploring the Interaction, Information Technology and People, 13(2), 2000: 85-101.

108. Mahmood Adam, M. A. and Swanberg, D. L. Factors Effecting Information Technology Usage: A Meta-Analysis of the Empirical Literature, Journal of Organizational Computing and Electronic Commerce, 11(2), 2001: 107-130.

109. Meyer, J. P. Srinivas, E. S. Lal, J. B. and Topolnytsky, L. Employee Commitment and Support for an Organizational Change: Test of the Three-component Model inTwo Cultures, Journal of Occupational and Organizational Psychology, 80, 2007: 185–211.

110. Milne, R. S. Mechanistic and Organic Models of Public Administration in Developing Countries, Administrative Science Quarterely, 1970: 57-67.

111. Motohashi K. Firm Level Analysis of Information Network Use and Productivity in Japan, Comparative Analysis of Enterprise Data (CAED) Conference, London, 2003.

112. Mutula, S. M. and Brakel P. V. An evaluation of E-readiness Assessment Tools with Respect to Information Access: Towards an Integrated Information Rich Tool, International Journal of Information Management, 26(3), 2006: 212–223.

113. Pothukuchi, V. Damanpour, F. Choi, J. Chen, C. C. and Park, S. H. National and Organizational Culture Differences and International Joint Venture Performance, Journal of International Business Studies, 32(2), 2002: 243-265.

114. Robison, K. K. and Crenshaw, E. M. Post-industrial Transformations and Cyber-space: A Cross-national Analysis of Internet Development, Social Science Research, 31, 2002: 334–363.

115. Rossouw, G. J. Business Ethics in Developing Countries, Business Ethics Quarterely, 4(1), 1994: 43-51.

116. Ryan, A. M. Chang, D. Ployhart, R. E. and Slade, L. A. Employee Attitude Surveys in a Multinational Organization: Considering Language and Culture in Assessing Measurement Equivalence, Personnel Psychology, 52, 1999: 37-58.

117. Saad, M. and Zawdie, G. From Technology Transfer to the Emergence of a Triple Helix Culture: The Experience of Algeria in Innovation and Technological Capability Development, Technology Analysis and Strategic Management, 17(1), 2005: 89–103.

118. Salter, S. B. and Sharp, D. J. Agency Effects and Escalation of Commitment Do Small National Culture Differences Matter? International Journal of Accounting, 36(1), 2001: 33-45.

119. Sayed, E. H., and Westrup, C. Egypt and ICTs Bring National Initiatives, Global Actors and Local Companies Together, Information Technology and People (16:1), 2003: 93-110.

120. Sen, A. Development as Freedom, Oxford University Press, Oxford, UK, 1999.

121. Shih, E. Kraemer, K. L. and Dedrick, J. IT Diffusion in Developing Countries, Communications of the ACM, 51(2), February 2008: 43-48.

122. Shih, E. Kraemer, K. L. and Dedrick, J. Research Note: Determinants of Country-level Investment in Information Technology, Management Science, 53(3), 2007: 521–528.

123. Shoib, G. M., and Nandhakumar, J. Cross-Cultural IS Adoption in Multinational Corporations: A Study of Rationality, in Organizational Information Systems in the Context of Globalization, M. Korpela, R. Montealegre, and A. Poulymenakou (eds.), Kluwer Academic Publishers, Boston, 2003:435-454.

124. Silva, L., and Figueroa, E. B. Institutional Intervention and the Expansion of ICTs in Latin America: The Case of Chile, Information Technology and People, 15(1), 2002: pp. 8-25.

125. Smith Howard, L. Bullers, W. I. and Piland, N. F. Does Information Technology Make Difference in Healthcare Organization Performance? Hospital Topics: Research and Perspectives on Healthcare, 78(2), 2000.

126. Spony, G. The Development of a Work-value Model Assessing the Cumulative Impact of Individual and Cultural Differences on Managers' Work-value Systems: Empirical Evidence from French and British Managers, International Journal of Human Resource Management, 14(4), 2003: 658-679.

127. Trice, H. M. and J. M. Beyer The Cultures of Work Organizations, Englewood Cliffs, NJ: Prentice Hall, 1993.

128. United Nations Development Program (UNDP) Human Development Report 2001: Making New Technologies Work for Human Development, Oxford University Press, New York, 2001.

129. Walsham, G. Making a World of Difference: IT in a Global Context, Wiley, Chichester, UK, 2001.

130. Walsham, G. Cross-Cultural Software Production and Use: A Structurational Analysis, MIS Quarterly, (26:4), 2002: pp. 359-380.

131. Walsham, G. Robey, D. Sahay, S. Forwadr: Special issue on Information Systems in Developing Countries, MIS Quarterly, 31(2), 2007: 317-326.

132. World Bank Group, Information and Communication Technologies: A World Bank Group Strategy, Washington D.C., 2002.

Title Page

Stock Markets Efficiency, Attactiveness and the Nature of Information Investors Use to Trade: An Evidence from the Tehran Stock Exchange(TSE)

AMROLAH AMINI (Ph.D)

Associate Professor, Allameh Tabatabaei University (ATU), Tehran, Iran.

aminij@atu.ac.ir

ALIREZA EMAMI

Master of Science, Tehran University, Tehran, Iran

memami@alumni.ut.ac.ir

MOSTAFA EMAMI*

Master of Science, Michigan Technological University (MTU)

memami@mtu.edu

*Corresponding Address

Applied Research and Technology Office, Michigan Technological University

1400 Townsend Dr, Houghton, MI 49931

Tel & Fax : +1-(816) 237-0018

E-mail: memami@mtu.edu

Stock Markets Efficiency and Attactiveness and the Nature of Information Investors Use to Trade: An Evidence from the Tehran Stock Exchange(TSE)

Abstract
This paper is aimed to explain the relationships among efficiency of stock markets, stock markets attactiveness to foreign investors, and the nature of information that most of investors use in their trading decisions. To study the relationships, after reveiving the literature, a conceptual model is provided. The proposed model claims that there are clear relationships amonge the maturity of a stock market (third world, transitional or advanced markets), its efficiency degree (weak, semi or full efficient form) and the nature of information investors use in their trading decision making process. To test the proposed conceptual model, some research hypothesis have been defined and tested in the Tehran Stock Exchange (TSE). The results confirms the validity of the proposed model in TSE and clearly show that 1) TSE is in a weak form of efficiency, 2) TSE is not so attractive to foreign investors, and 3) in TSE, investors mostly use of the quantitative information rather qualitative, and 4) in TSE accounting performance indicators are more correlated to companies shares' market prices. In other words, accounting performance indicators outperforms economic indicators (EVA).
Key words: Tehran Stock Exchange (TSE), Attractiveness, Efficiency, Information

1. Introduction Attractiveness

capital markets strongly affect on all economic actvities. One of the critical questions about the stock markets is what makes a stock market atractive?

Results of the investigations show that the growth rate of investment and the gross fixed capital added in machinary and mines sections in Iran are not in a stisfactory. Increasing the attractiveness of the TSE for foreign investors can meaningfully rapid the economic growth in Iran [see Major Economic Indices, centra bank of The Islamic Republic of Iran, (Winter 2002]. On the other hand, according to The Economist Journal, Iran is ranked 55 among 60 countries in terms of investment risk. In June 2002, Iran ranked C (from A to D) in terms of political and economic risk. Also according to report of Heritage Foundation (a non governmental institute), Iran ranked 151 among 155 countries.

Respect to undesirable ranking of Iran in terms of political, economic and financial risks and because of the importance of new capitals and investments in development process of Iran, this research is planned. This research is aimed to help financial policy makers to increase their knowledge about the factors affecting on the attractiveness of a stock market. The evaluation of the TSE in terms of determined attractive factors not only declears the relative weaknesses of the TSE, but it can be regarded as a starting point in designing some improvement action plans.

This paper is divided into 4 sections. The next section reviews the literature. Section 3 explains questions, data, methodology and the results. The paper ends with a some concluding remarks.

EVA INTRODUCTION

According to financial theory, maximization of shareholers' wealth regards as the most important stockholder-oriented financial objective and one of the best of wealth indicator is share market price. Wealth maximization is in turn strongly depended on the qulity of companies' performances. In literature, several economicd, financial and accounting criteria have been developed to measure and evaluate companies' performances. One of the most famous and impotrant performance measures is Economic Value Added (EVA).

Although the EVA is not a new concept and a measure of performance, but It is first widely appled by Stern Stewart & Company.[9] According Stern Stewart, EVA no only shows a strong positive correlation with shareholers' wealth indicator (companies' share prices), but It also operates better in companies' performance evaluation process than some prevailent accounting performance measures (such as profit, earinig per share or EPS).

It is well known that a firm value is a function of two important factors; 1)return and 2)cost of capital. Considering these two factors, EVA is the best performance measure because It precisely considers both the return and the cost of capital in Its performance evaluation process. According these considerations, some researchers believe that the economic measure of EVA should be more positively correlated to companies' share prices than prevalent accounting performance measures.

This research is aimed to provide the results of an empirical test that is implemented in the Tehran Stock Exchange (TSE). It measures and compares the correlations of the EVA (as a well known economic performance measure), CFO and EBIT (as the well known accounting measures) with companies' wealth indicator (companies' shares market prices) in the TSE. It is to tetify the following hypothesis at $\alpha = \%5$ significant level (or $1-\alpha = 95\%$ confidence level):

- In the TSE, comparing to Cash from Operation (CFO) measure, the EVA is more positively correlated to share market values.
- In the TSE, comparing to Earning Before Interest and Taxe (EBIT) measure, the EVA is more positively correlated to share market values.

Next section of the paper explaines some performance evaluation approaches. Section 3 reviews literature and section 4 introduces research methodology was applied in this research. Results of the research hypothesis tests are provided in section 5. Finally, the paper ends with coclusions and final remarks.

PERFORMANCE EVALUATION APPROACHES

In literature, several approaches have been developed to evaluate companies' performance. Some of important apprraches are as follows:[11]

- **Accounting Approach:** This approach uses some financial statement indicators such as sales, profits, return on asset (ROA), return on equity (ROE), ... for comparative performance evaluation.
- **Combined Approach:** This approach uses some combined indicators from financial statements and markets such as price to earning (P/E), ratio of assets market value to book value, ...for comparative performance evaluation.
- **Financial Management Approach:** This approach uses some financial management models such as capital asset pricing model(CAPM),...for comparative performance evaluation.

- **Economic Approach:** This approach uses some economic indicators such as EVA and REVA for comparative performance evaluation.

In literature, EVA is regarded as one of the most useful measure for companies' performance evaluation and companies' future share price estimation.[12] EVA is a powerful economic measure of companies' performance, because It not only considers companies' profits, but It also take into account companies' cost of capital for comparative performance evaluation and analysis.. EVA is confirmed with some important financial concepts such as Net Present Value (NPV), Cash Value Added (CVA), Shareholders Value Added (SVA), and Cash Flow Return on Investmant (CFROI). Managers prefer EVA because they will be responsible for internal controlable criteria (suach as return and cost of capital) not for noncontrolable criteria (such as share market value). EVA implies that a firm value is depended on its managers' decisions.[9] EVA values are strongly corelated with share market values, because in reality, MV is a function of estimated EVA in the future. A positive EVA value means increasing companies value. EVA is a proper measure in determining performance measurement goals, strategy evaluation, capital allocations, designing incentive plans, capital increasing and also pricing. Also, EVA is more confidental than accounting performance measures.[3,8] EVA can be calculated by the following equations:[12]

$$EVA = (\gamma - C) * Cap$$

$$EVA = NOPAT_t - (WACC * Cap_{t-1})$$

where γ, C, NOPAT, WACC, Cap denote companies' rate of return and cost of capital, net profit after tax, weighted cost of capital and capital, respectively. Generally, maximization of EVA can be translates as real wealth maximization.

EVA considers economic concept of the capital not its accounting concept. Then, in order to calculate EVA, some adjustments in accounting profit are required. Some resaerchers as Zemermann believes that cost of adjustments is usually higher than its improvements.[8] Stwart and Yang explain some impotant accounting adjustments in references 12 and 16. [12,16]

After introducing EVA, some economists proposed an adjusted concept of EVA, as Retained Economic Value Added (REVA). In calculation of REVA, market values should be used in place of adjusted asstets' book values. REVA can be calculated by following equation:[9]

REVA= NOPAT$_t$ - [WACC (Maket Value of Debts+Market Value of Equity)]*

An other economic performance measure is Market Value Aded (MVA). MVA is the difference between firm market value and the value of capital applied. Theoritically, market value added is equal to the present value of all future EVAs or the future expected residual profits.

2. Exchange Attractiveness Literature

What makes stock exchange more attractive to investors? The attactiveness is likely to depend on the characteristics of the exchange and on the institutional features of the country where the exchange is located.

1-2- Country Characteristics

- **Accounting Standards:** Countries have on average lower but better accounting standards are more attractive from view point of investors because of their greater transparency, reducing the monitoring costs of shareholders and the required rate of return. This benefit does not come for free because switching to a different accounting system can have substantial costs [Biddle et al., 1989; Saudagaran and Biddle, 1992].
- **Legal Variables:** Investors are likely to prefer a country where contracts are easily enforce and the bureaucracy is efficient [Pagano et al., 2001].
- **Cultural Homogeneity:** Investors prefer to invest in countries that are culturally similar to their home country in terms of language and institutions, because this reduces costs of communication with foreign investors and legal/accounting costs [Pagano et al., 2001].
- **Degree of Openness of Stock Exchange:** The attractiveness may also be related to characteristics of the international openness of stock exchanges and their competitiveness that can be measured by two variables; 1) the ratio of foreign listings to the total listings for each market captures its ability to attract companies from abroa and 2) the fraction of domestic companies cross-listed abroad indicates instead the exchange's inability to fulfill all the needs of domestic companies [Pagano et al., 2001].
- **The tendency of domestic companies to seek a foreign trading forum**: This charactristic is measured by the proportion of the domestic public companies that have listed abroad. These numbers do not tell the whole story, however. The companies that cross-listed abroad and in the country may be qualitatively different. As shown by Pagano, those that cross-list in the U.S. are relatively high-growth, high-tech, R&D-intensive and strongly export oriented [Pagano et al., 2000].
- **Integration of Capital Markets:** Despite the increasing integration of capital markets, geography has not yet become irrelevant to finance. In the last two decades, technological

progress and liberalization of capital flows have lowered the barriers that isolated domestic stock markets from each other [Pagano et al.,2000]. As capital markets become more integrated, companies should be able to tap participate in initial public offerings abroad and trade shares cross-border, and brokers to operate directly in foreign stock markets via remote membership.

2-2-Exchange Charactristics

- **Liguidity:** The liquidity services is often regarded as the key function of a stock exchange. Greater liquidity can translate into a lower cost of capital for the investors concerned, insofar as it is valued by investors and factored into market prices. Investors prefer to invest in more liquid exchanges and the difference between the trading costs of the destination and home exchanges is a critical measurement. [Amihud and Mendelson, 1986; Brenna, 1996].
- **Stock Market Size:** Investors prefer larger stock markets because they provide access to a larger pool of potential investors and may confer greater visibility and reputation upon investors. Visibility and prestige can be measured by the difference in stock markets capitalization compare to the average exchange capitalization [Bancel and Mitto, 2001].
- **Analysts' Coverage:** One possible benefit of going abroad is exposing the investor to the attention of additional financial analysts, and thereby to a wider investor base [Pagano et al., 2001].
- **Be with your Peers:** If a company's managers observe many companies go to abroad on a particular stock exchange, they may infer that there is much to be gained from imitating them. The proporiton of firms are active in abroad to the total number of firms belonging to the same industry is a good measurement in this regards [see Pagano et al., 2001].
- **Market Opening Rules and Procedures:** Financial marekets around the world utilise different rules and procedures to open the market. Opening rules impact on stock market efficiency. Essentially, there are two mechanisms: call and continuous openings. In a call market, orders are entered prior to the opening but remain unexecuted until there is a simultaneous execution of matching orders. In contrast, continuous trading executes orders as they come to the market, assuming they match with an existing order. Use of a call enhances market efficiency by increasing liquidity and lowering volatility at the open [Comerton Forde, 1999]. A growing volume of empirical literature has analysed the opening mechanisms, in a number of markets, to determine how they affect price discovery, volatility and liquidity at the open. For example, Amihud et al. found that the volatility at the opening call on the NYSE was greater than the volatility at the close [Amihud and Mendelson, 1986; Stoll et al., 1983]. Despite the indications from the literature that a call market can enhance price discovery and liquidity and reduce volatility, particularly in an automated market, a number of exchanges choose not to open their markets with a call. This means that there is still a degree of uncertainty about the most appropriate way to open a market.
- **The Behaviors of the Returns:** Study the behavior of the returns and the volatility for stocks on a stock exchange are very important. For example, the results of a research show that opening transactions exhibit more volatility than closing transactions, daytime returns are more volatile than overnight returns, open-to-open and close-to-close returns exhibit positive serial correlation, and the correlations betwean daytime returas are negarive. Prices

adjust partiailly from transaction to transacuon, overnight returns tend to be reversed by the following day return, and price continuations exist from closing to next day's opening [Shastri et al., 1995].

Degree of Automation of Trading System: As equity markets continue to expand their international linkages and the technology of securities trading develops further, computerized trading is becoming more prominent among the world's stock exchanges. Adoption of a fully automated trading system affects on the nature and behavior of security returns. Automation will increased the transparency of the market and transparency, in turn, will addresses the dissemination of quotations as well as trading activity. Enhancing transparency increases market efficiency, improves investors protection and develops market's integrity and investor participation. Then, adoption of an automated trading system for equity trading will affect the attractiveness of a stock exchange because of increase the transparency of the markets and consequently enhancing the level of investor participation and confidence in it [Huang and Stoll, 1992; Ferris et al., 1997]. Shifting from a floor-based system to an electronic screen-based system make a market more atractive. Schmidt and Iversen show that different automated trading systems can produce different bid-ask spreads for the same stocks [Schmidt and Iversen, 1993].

Barriers to Transact and Regulatory Costs: Barriers to transact within a country may encaurage investors to seek foreign investment. Reducing regulatory costs and facilitate foreign listings strongly affects on stock markets attractiveness. Decker reports that in the early 1990s the Security Exchange Commission (SEC) became far more cooperative towards non-U.S. companies trying to register in the U.S. [Decker, 1994]. This change in attitude was at least partly prompted by stock exchange officials who regarded the listing of foreign investors as an attractive business opportunity [Cochrane, 1994].

• **Transaction Costs:** Transaction costs and minimum price changes, or tick sizes affecting on the attractiveness of a stock market. Some researchers show that indirect execution costs, of which the bid-ask spread is a major component, account for 35% of transactions costs [Stoll et al., 1983]. Some researchers show that in a competitive market, the spread is determined by activity, risk, information, and competition. Melnish and Wood, 1992] Tick sizes are set by exchanges and the minimum tick size determines the minimum market spread. The reduction of tick size will decrease the bid-ask spreads significantly and thereby reduces transactions costs [13]. The market bid-ask spread is the difference between the best offer to buy (a bid) and the best offer to sell (an ask). If the minimum tick size is larger than the spread warranted by these determinants, the market spread, and consequently trading costs, are artificially will increase. Harris concludes that smaller iminimum price variations would significantly reduce bid ask spreads. [Harris, 1994] The reduction in the minimum tick size resulted: 1)a reduction in bid-ask spreads and an economically significant decrease in transactions costs, 2)a large reduction in spreads for stocks that were more constrained by the prereduction minimum tick size, 3)a decrease in the sizes quoted at the best bid and ask, reflecting a typical response to higher purchase prices and lower sales prices, and 4)a decrease in the aggregate quoted size over all of the bids and asks entered into the system.

- **Leadership Role of the Stock Market:** Empirical studies showing that some stock exchanges leads other exchanges because of their market structure factors rather than "country effects" [Parisi et al., 2002]. Some of the factors that lead to a leadership role are deeper liquidity, more effective monitoring, and a greater concentration of speculators. Markets possessing these factors will be the first to attract investors and will lead other exchanges. Although, the leadership role of a given stock market creates a predictable flow of information between markets, the ability to create arbitrage opportunities is mitigated by transaction costs and the current order-processing mechanism. However, market's leadership could result in arbitrage opportunities in countries with lower transaction costs or different order-processing mechanisms. The current state of the literature on exchange leadership is mixed. While much of the existing research indicates a leadership role in the transmission of returns and variances, other research attributes this result to noise trading. Of the papers, which detect a leadership role are the market with greater liquidity, more effective monitoring, and a concentration of speculators exhibit the leadership role [Parisi et al., 2002]. This revelation is also of great import to developing countries attempting to reduce capital market frictions with single or multiplc stock exchanes.

General speaking, the following factors affecting on the attractiveness of a stock market:
- trading/transaction costs
- capitalization
- analysts' coverage
- degree of openness of stock exchange
- barriers to transact and regulatory costs
- jurisdiction
- degree of investors protection
- degree of enforceability of contracts
- bureaucratic delays efficiency of the bureaucracy
- efficiency and the quality of the accounting standards
- commonality and the sufficiency of the business laws
- commonality of language and legal system
- cultural homogeneity
- size of the stock market
- existing huge peers
- market liquidity
- degree of automation of trading system
- market opening rules and procedures
- return forecasting and estimation power
- facility of access to financial and related non finacial information
- market maturity or the power of using reported and published financial data
- the time interval between request and acceptance in stock market
- volitality or the behavior of returns and prices
- leadership role of the stock market
- integration of capital markets

- economic, political and financial risk of the investment

3. EVA LITERATURE

According to economic theory, a firm value increases when its return be greater than its cost of capital. To explain this simple economic theory, several concepts (abnormal profits, surplus profit or income, net profits and residual profits or incomes) have been developed in accounting and financial area.

In 1950, GMC applied residual profit to evaluate performance of its deccentralized units. [2] At the end of 1980 decade, Ston Stwart company applied EVA as both internal and external performance evaluation indicator for more than 300 big size international companies. In 1994, Stwart using the results of a research tried to prove and show that EVA is the best indicator of wealth generation. In 1995 it was also claimed that in future companies' performance reports to financial markets, EPS will be replaced by EVA. [1] In 1997, Melborne studied the correlation between EVA and REVA and concluded that REVA outperforms EVA in terms future wealth creation estimation. Using 6554 year-company data for interval 1985-1992, O'byrne concluded that there are positive correlations among companies' EVA, NOPAT and their share prices. [10] Using 100 companies data between interval 1986-1995, Uyemura studied the correlations among Earning Per Share (EPS), Net Profit (NP), Return on Equity (ROE), Return on Asset (ROA), EVA with companies market values. The correlation coefficients were 0.06 for EPS, 0.08 for NP, 0.1 for ROE, 0.13 for ROA and finally 0.14 for EVA. This research provided a higher correlation of EVA.[15] Piksoto studies, that were based on 156 year-company data between interval 1995-1998 related to 39 companies were listed in Lisbon stock exchange, show the correlation coefficients 0.7087, 0.7084 and 0.721 for the companies' Operational Profits (OP), NP and EVA with their share prices. Fernandez (2002) studied the correlation between companies' EVA and CSV. Based on 296 sample companies' data, he concluded that EVA is not a good predictor for determining companies' CVS. [4]

There is a lot of researches on EVA in Iran. Nazariyeh's research in 1998 show that in the TSE, there is no meaningful correlation between nonmetal product industry companies' EVA and their EPS. She also concluded that EVA is more effective than EPS for the performance evaluation of the nonmetal product companies.[13] Rezai's reasearch in 1999 show existing a meaningful correlation between motor vehicles industry companies' EVA and their ROE in TSE. [14] Ghanbari's research in 2000 show meaningful correlations among companies financial ratios and their EVA.[5] Kawoosi's research in 2001 show a meaningful relationship between EVA and Q-Twobin ratio. He concluded that EVA can be regarded as a good replacement for Q-Tobin Ratio in Iran capital markets.[7] Izadniya's research in 2003 just proves that in Iran capital markets, there are meaningful relationships among companies' EVA, Free Cash Flow FCF values with their share market prices.[6]

This research is to measure and compare the correlations of the EVA, CFO and EBIT with companies' shares market prices in the TSE. Next section is devoted to resaerch methdology we used.

Conceptual Model

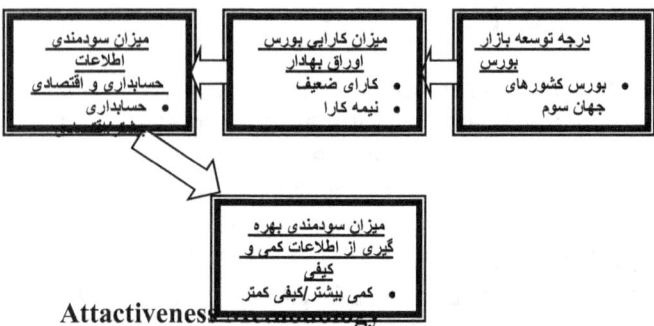

Attactiveness

Three critical resaerch questions were as follows:

1) what factors make a stock market more attractive from the stand point of investors?
2) how can we evaluate the existing attractiveness condition of a given stock market? and
3) how can improve a stock market atractiveness level?

We have answered to the first question by reviewing the literature. To answer the second question, a descriptive resaerch methodology was used. In this stage, the data measurement tool was a questionare. As a first step and in order to determine the factors affecting on the stock market attractiveness, we have reviewed the literature and determined 36 affecting factors (variables). Based on these variables, a questionair was developed. The questionare included 43 closed questions (questions No.1~33 and No. 35~44), designed according to Likert scale, and 5 semi-open questions (questions No. 34,45,46,47,48). After testing the validity and the reliablity of the developed questionair using a sample pretest, the questionares were distributed among financial experts and analysts of the TSE. The data was collected and statistically analyzed. The resraech main hypothesis was tested. It means, after calculation of statistics, considering $\alpha = \%1$ (or at the confidence levele of %99), statistical inference method (student's T-test) was applied and the research hypothesis tested.

The main hypothesis of this research was "from the view points of the experts, the TSE is not yet attractive for foreign investors/companies". In order to test this main hypothesis, we have defined and tested 12 sub-hypothesis as follows:

1) the TSE is in a weak condition in terms of financial analysts coverage,

2) the TSE is in a weak condition in terms of investors protection,

3) the TSE is in a weak condition in terms of efficiency of the beurucracy,

4) the TSE is in a weak condition in terms of accounting standards,

5) the TSE is in a weak condition in terms of proficiency in foreign languages and/or commonality of the language,

6) the TSE is in a weak condition in terms of returns and profit margins,

7) the TSE is in a weakcondition in terms of transaction costs,

8) the TSE is in a weakcondition in terms of ordering accepting procedures,

9) the TSE is in a weakcondition in terms of automation of trading and transactions,

10) the TSE is in a weakcondition in terms of number of dealers and investors,

11) the TSE is in a weakcondition in terms of leadership role relative to other stock exchanges, and

12) the TSE is in a weakcondition in terms of price and return sensitivity.

RESEARCH METHODOLOGY EVA

In this section, we will explain our research questions, research objectives, research hypothesis, data gathering methods, research hypothesis testing methods, and finally resaerch variables.

The main research question is that which of companies performance evaluation measurements (EVA, CFO or EBIT) are more correlated to share market prices? In other words, the main objective is to calculate the correlations among Iranian companies' EVA, CFO and EBIT with their share prices.

Two research hypothesis were defined as follows:

H1: *Iranian companies' EVA values are more correlated with their share prices than their CFO values*

H2: *Iranian companies' EVA values are more correlated with their share prices than their EBIT values.*

The data gathered from the TSE' companies for interval 1999-2002. Using random sampling method, among 320 company-year data from 64 sample companies, 221 company-year data with a meaningful β value were selected. Table 1 show the company-year data.

Table 1: Company-year data

	Years					Companies Names			Years					Companies Names	
	1381	1380	1379	1378	1377				1381	1380	1379	1378	1377		
				*		Margarin	33		*		*	*		Absal	1
		*	*	*	*	Mess Bahonar	34		*		*	*	*	Aluminum Iran	2
		*		*	*	Motozhen	35					*	*	Alyaf	3
			*	*	*	Roghan Nabati Nab	36						*	Ama Industrial	4
	*	*		*	*	Naft Behran	37					*	*	Azarit	5
		*	*	*	*	Navard Aluminum	38				*	*	*	Bastebandi Iran	6
			*	*	*	Navard Ghataat Foolad	39				*		*	Bastebandi Mashad	7
	*		*	*	*	Pars Darou	40		*		*	*	*	Behpak	8
	*	*		*	*	Pars Electric	41		*		*	*	*	Biscuit Gorji	9
		*	*	*	*	Pars Metal	42		*		*	*		Darouee Farabi	10
	*	*	*	*	*	Pars Minoo	43		*		*	*	*	Jaberebn Hayyan	11
		*	*	*	*	Pars Pamchal	44		*	*	*	*		Darousazi Kossar	12
		*	*	*	*	Pars Seram	45		*	*	*		*	Darouee Loghman	13
	*	*		*		Labaniat Pak	46				*		*	Darousazi Ossveh	14
	*		*	*		Plasiran	47		*	*	*	*	*	Darou Pakhsh	15
		*	*	*	*	Petroshimi Abadan	48		*	*	*	*		Dasht Morghab	16
			*	*		Petroshimi Farabi	49			*	*	*	*	Fibr Iran	17
	*	*	*	*	*	Pumpsazi Iran	50			*		*	*	Gand Neishaboor	18
	*	*	*	*		Darouee Razak	51					*	*	Ghovveh Pars	19
	*	*	*	*	*	Roghan Nabati Pars	52		*	*	*	*	*	Bahman Group	20
	*	*	*	*	*	Sassan	53		*			*	*	Iran Khodro	21
		*	*	*	*	Shahd Iran	54			*	*	*	*	Iran Merinoos	22
	*	*	*	*		Shisheh va Gaz	55					*	*	Iran Pooya	23
		*	*	*		Shisheh Hamadan	56			*			*	Iran Teransfo	24
		*	*	*		Shocopars	57				*	*	*	Iran Tayer	25
		*	*	*	*	Siman Fars Va khouzestan	58		*	*	*	*	*	Jam Darou	26
	*	*	*	*	*	Siman Kerman	59				*	*	*	Cabl Alborz	27
			*	*	*	Siman Mazandaran	60							Carbon Iran	28
		*	*	*	*	Siman Shomal	61		*		*	*	*	Carton Mashad	29
			*	*	*	Siman Soofian	62		*	*	*		*	Kashi Esfehan	30
		*	*		*	Siman Tehran	63			*	*			Kimi Darou	31
			*	*	*	Lavazem Khanegi Pars	64			*	*	*	*	Pars Shahab Lamp	32
28	36	50	57	50										Total	

* Implies the company-year data used for correlations calculation.

As shown in Table 1, the selected samples cover almost all important industries of the TSE. Industries and companies included in sample population with their related codes (in Table 1) are as follows:
- **Food Industry:** numbers 33,52,36,54,53,57,43,18,9,46,8,16
- **Textiles Industry**: number 22
- **Paper & Wood Industry**: numbers 17,29
- **Petroleum Industry:** numbers 37,48,49
- **Chemical and Pharmacy Industry**: numbers 3, 10, 28, 11, 12, 13, 14, 15, 31, 40, 44, 51
- **Rubber & Plastic Industry**: number 47
- **Non Metal Product Industry:** numbers 5, 30, 45, 55, 56, 58, 59, 60, 61, 62, 63
- **Basic Metal Industry:** numbers 2, 34, 38, 42, 39
- **Metal Product Industry:** numbers 4, 6, 7, 26
- **Machinery & Equipment Industry**: numbers 1, 50, 23, 64
- **Electrical Machinery & Apparatus Industry**: numbers 19, 24, 27, 32, 35
- **Radio & TV & Communication Industry**: number 41
- **Motor Vehicles Industry**: number 25
- **Transport Equipment Industry:** numbers 20,21

To test the resrearch hypothesis, satatistical correlation test was applied. In this research, three independent and one dependent variables were EVA, CFO, EBIT and Share Price (SP), respectively.

5. The RESULTS

Tables 1 and 2 show the results. The results show that despite of several recent improvement actions, plans and programs, the TSE is not yet attractive for foreign investors. Although the TSE attractiveness is generally near to the average level, but it is not satisfactory and desirable.

Table 1: Statistical Calculations for Hypothesis ($\alpha = 1\%$)

The Result	Critical Value $t:(\alpha, df)$	$t = \dfrac{\bar{X} - \sum_o}{S_{\bar{x}}}$	$S_{\bar{x}}$	Mean Scores	Numbers of Related Questions	Hypothesis No.
H₀ Accepted	2/998	-5/350	0/134	2/283	42,43 6~1	1
H₀ Accepted	3/747	-4/801	0/141	2/323	7~11	2
H₀ Accepted	2/896	-1/693	0/173	2/707	~18 41, 12	3
H₀ Accepted	6/965	-3/677	0/127	2/533	19~21	4
H₀ Accepted	–	–	–	1/818	22	5
H₀ Accepted	4/541	0/809	0/110	3/089	23~25	6
H₀ Accepted	31/821	0/017	0/340	3/006	26,28	7

Results of the Statistical Test	Critical Value		Mean Scores	Question No.
H₀ Accepted	31/821	-2/003	0/333	2/333	29,30	8
H₀ Accepted	6/965	-3/832	0/185	2/291	31~33	9
H₀ Accepted	–	–	–	2/714	35	10
H₀ Accepted	6/965	-15/052	0/096	1/555	36~39	11
H₀ Accepted	31/821	-0/860	0/608	2/477	40	12

Table 2: Statistical Calculations of the Questions ($\alpha = 1\%$)

Results of the Statistical Test	Critical Value $t = (\alpha, df)$	$t = \dfrac{\overline{X} - \sum_o}{S_{\overline{x}}}$	$S_{\overline{x}}$	Mean Scores	Question No.
H₀ Accepted	2/508	-1/5426	0/2541	2/608	1
H₀ Accepted	2/508	-0/2100	0/2095	2/956	2
H₀ Accepted	2/508	-5/1101	0/2043	1/956	3
H₀ Accepted	2/508	-3/2918	0/1850	2/391	4
H₀ Accepted	2/508	-2/8653	0/2429	2/304	5
H₀ Accepted	2/508	-5/3022	0/1886	2	6
H₀ Accepted	2/508	-8/6138	0/1414	1/782	7
H₀ Accepted	2/552	-2/5470	0/1861	2/526	8
H₀ Accepted	2/552	-2/9909	0/1762	2/473	9
H₀ Accepted	2/624	-1/2882	0/3625	2/533	10
H₀ Accepted	2/508	-2/9243	0/2380	2/304	11
H₀ Accepted	2/518	-1/5599	0/2045	2/681	12
H₀ Accepted	2/508	-1/4561	0/2692	2/608	13
H₀ Accepted	2/508	-2/4188	0/2340	2/434	14
H₀ Accepted	2/508	0	0/2393	3	15
H₀ Rejected	2/518	13/8823	0/0425	3/590	16
H₀ Accepted	2/508	0/9192	0/1882	3/173	17
H₀ Accepted	2/518	-2/5879	0/1932	2/5	18
H₀ Accepted	2/518	-2/9531	0/2157	2/363	19
H₀ Accepted	2/518	-2/1632	0/2524	2/454	20
H₀ Accepted	2/508	-1/2178	0/1790	2/782	21
H₀ Accepted	2/518	-6/8009	0/1738	1/818	22
H₀ Accepted	2/518	-0/6640	0/2063	2/863	23
H₀ Accepted	2/528	1/8962	0/1503	3/285	24
H₀ Accepted	2/528	1/8962	0/1503	3/285	25
H₀ Accepted	2/528	-0/2610	0/1839	2/952	26
H₀ Accepted	2/508	-15/9435	0/1664	3/347	27
H₀ Accepted	2/528	-1/7765	0/1880	2/666	28
H₀ Accepted	2/539	-3/9793	0/2513	2	29
H₀ Accepted	2/624	-1/1509	0/2902	2/666	30
H₀ Accepted	2/528	-3/6882	0/2066	2/238	31
H₀ Accepted	2/518	-3/8008	0/2631	2	32
H₀ Accepted	2/518	-1/9475	0/1869	2/636	33
H₀ Accepted	2/528	-1/0541	0/2713	2/714	34
H₀ Accepted	2/508	-7/5138	0/1621	1/782	35
H₀ Accepted	2/508	-5/2924	0/2137	1/869	36
H₀ Accepted	2/508	-10/8193	0/1367	1/521	37
H₀ Accepted	2/518	-11/5852	0/1413	1/363	38
H₀ Accepted	2/508	-0/3404	0/2526	3/086	39
H₀ Accepted	2/518	-7/4838	0/1701	1/727	40
H₀ Accepted	2/508	-7/6796	0/1586	1/782	41
H₀ Accepted	2/518	-3/7739	0/1929	2/272	42
H₀ Accepted	2/508	-1/5303	0/2274	2/652	43

In this research we tested two following hypothesis:

H1: *Iranian companies' EVA values are more correlated with their share prices than their CFO values*

H2: *Iranian companies' EVA values are more correlated with their share prices than their EBIT values.*

To test H1, two following equations were used, the linear relationships (between EVA with SP and EVA with CFO) were defined and finally their R^2 values were compared:

$$\frac{MV_t}{Capital_{t-1}} = \alpha + \beta \frac{\frac{EVA_t}{WACC}}{Capital_{t-1}} + e_t$$

$$\frac{MV_t}{Capital_{t-1}} = \alpha + \beta \frac{CFO_t}{Capital_{t-1}} + e_t$$

Statistical results, in Table 2, show that at 5% significant level, there is a meaningful positive linear relation between TSE companies' EVA values and their SP values.

Table 2: Regression Between EVA and MV

Multipl R	%754545
R Square	%569338
Adjusted R square	%567353
Standard Error	3/83E +11
Observations	221

ANOVA	d.f	SS	MS	F	Significanc F
Regression	1	4/21E + 25	E + 10 4/20912	28/87 6	0
Residual	219	3/18E + 25	E + 23		
Total	220	7/39E + 25	1/46723		

Also, statistical results, in Table 3, imply that at 5% significant level, there is a meaningful positive linear relation between TSE companies' CFO values and their SP values.

Table 3: Regression Between CFO and MV

Multipl R	0/649674
R Square	0/422076
Adjusted R Ssquare	0/419412
Standard Error	4/44E + 11
Observations	221

ANOVA	d.f	SS	MS	F	Significance F
Regression	1	4/21E + 25	4/20912E + 10	28/87 6	0
Residual	219	3/18E + 25	E + 23		
Total	220	7/39E + 25	1/46723		

Comparing the correlation coefficients for EVA with SP and CFO with SP, 0.567 and 0.419, and considering their standard errors, It can be concluded that in TSE, at 5% significant level, EVA values are more correlated with SP values than CFO. Then, hypothesis 1 is confirmed.

To test H2, two following equations were used, the linear relationships (between EVA with SP and EBIT with SP) were defined and finally their R^2 values were compared:

$$\frac{MV_t}{Capital_{t-1}} = \alpha + \beta \frac{\frac{EVA_t}{WACC}}{Capital_{t-1}} + e_t$$

$$\frac{MV_t}{Capital_{t-1}} = \alpha + \beta \frac{EBIT_t}{Capital_{t-1}} + e_t$$

Statistical results, in Table 4, show that at 5% significant level, there is a meaningful positive linear relation between companies' EBIT and their SP values.

Table 4: Regression Results Between EBIT and MV

Multipl R	0/774757671
R Square	0/60024945
Adjusted R square	0/598407281
Standard Error	3/69042E + 11
Observations	221

ANOVA	d.f	SS	MS	F	Significance F
Regression	1	E + 25 4/43765	E + 25 4/43765	32/83855	0
Residual	219	E + 25 2/95536	E + 23 1/36192		
Total	220	E + 25 7/39301			

Comparing the correlation coefficients, for EVA with SP and EBIT with SP, 0.567 and 0.6, and considering their standard errors, It can be concluded that in TSE, at 5% significant level, EBIT values are more correlated with SP values than EVA. Then, hypothesis 2 is rejected.

5. Conclusions and Final Remarks Attractiveness

This research determined some of the most important factors affecting on the attractiveness of stock markets. Using these affecting factors, the attractiveness degree of the TSE was evaluated. The results show that, from the view points of the experts and the financial analysts of the TSE, despite of several recent attempts, the TSE is not yet attractive for foreign investors. In order to improve the attractiveness of the TSE, It is recommended to Iranian financial policy makers to implement the following actions:

- improve the efficiency and the quality of the accounting standards,
- improve the accuracy, the precises and the facility of accessing to finacial and non financial information,
- reduce the trading/transaction costs,
- increase the market capitalization,
- increase the TSE liquidity,
- improve the analysts' coverage of the TSE,
- increase the degree of the openness of the TSE,
- remove the transaction barriers,
- reduce the regulatory costs,

- improve the jurisdiction,
- increase the degree of investors protections, and the enforceability of the ontracts,
- decrease the bureaucratic delays and increase the efficiency of the bureaucracy,
- improve the quality of the business laws,
- improve the languages proficiency level of the TSE practitioners,
- improve the degree of automation of trading system,
- increase the integeration of its capital markets .
- apply continious opening rules and procedures,
- improve the leadership role of the TSE at least among the middle east stock markets

CONCLUSIONS AND FINAL REMARKS EVA

Several researches have been implemented to evaluate the ability of EVA in companies performance evaluation and to determine EVA corelation with companies' SP. Some researcher, as Stwart, regards EVA as the most efficient criterion and propose It as one of the the best mesures for companies'performance evaluation. He claimes and empirically confirmes that EVA, as a powerful economic performance measure, outperforms acounting performane measures. On the oher hands, Biddle's empirical research show that although EVA outperforms CFO, but It is dominated by EBIT in terms of their correlations with companies' shares market values. Finally, Biddles concluded that yet some accounting performance measures, as EBIT, do more powerful than EVA.

In our resreach, using the data gathered from the TSE, first we measured the correlations among EVA with SP, EBIT with SP, CFO with SP. The statistical results show EVA performs CFO but is dominated by EBIT. Our research results quitely confirms Biddle's empirical test results. In other words, as Biddle concluded, we believe that yet some accounting performance measures, as EBIT, do more powerful than EVA.

Abstract: Some researchers, as Stewart, believe that the Economic Value Added (EVA) is the best measure for companies' performance evaluation. On the other hands, Biddle' research shows that although EVA may be better than Cash From Operations (CFO), but some accounting performance evaluation mesures- such as Earning Before Interest and Taxes (EBIT)- may outperform EVA in terms of companies' market value (MV). This paper is aimed to provide the results of an empirical study implemented in the Tehran Stock Exchange (TSE). The research detemined and compared the correlation coefficients among Economic Value Added (EVA), Earning Before Interest and Taxes (EBIT), Cach From Operations (CFO), and Shares Market Value (MV) of different companies and industries were randomly selected from the TSE. Using 221 year-company data, the empirical results clearly show that at 95% confidence level (or %5 significant level), although EVA is more correlated to companies'share MV than CFO, but EBIT outperforms EVA. In the other words, the results completely confirm the results of Biddle's research. It means that although EVA is a good economic measurement and performance indicator, but it may be meaningfully outperformed by some prevalent accounting measures as EBIT.

References Attractiveness

Amihud, Y. and H. Mendelson, (1986) "Asset Pricing and the Bid-ask Spread" *Journal of Financial Economics*, Vol. 17, 223-249.

Bancel, F., and U. R. Mittoo, (2001) "European Managerial Perceptions of the Net Benefits of Foreign Stock Listings" *European Financial Management*, Vol. 7 No. 2.

Biddle, G. C., and S. M. Saudagaran, (1989) "The Effects of Financial Disclosure Levels on Firms' Choices among Alternative Foreign Stock Exchange Listings" *Journal of International Financial Management and Accounting*, Vol. 1, 55-87.

Brennan, M. J., and A. Subrahmanyam, (1996) "Market Microstructure and Asset Pricing: On the Compensation for Illiquidity in Stock Returns" *Journal of Financial Economics*, Vol. 41, No. 3, 441-464.

Centra Bank of The Islamic Republic of Iran, (Winter 2002) "*Major Economic Indices*", No. 31,.

Cochrane, J. L., (1994) "Are U.S. Regulatory Requirements for Foreign Firms Appropriate? " *Fordham International Law Journal*, Vol. 17, S58-67.

Comerton Forde C., (1999) "Do Trading Rules on Market Efficiency? A Comparison of Opening Procedures on the Australian and Jakarta Stock Exchanges" *Pacific-Basin Finance Journal*, Vol. 7, 495-521.

Decker, W. F. (1994) "The Attractions of the U.S. Securities Markets to Foreign Issuers and the Alternative Methods of Accessing the U.S. Markets: from the Issuer's Perspective" *Fordham Iinternational Law Journal,* Vol. 17, 10-24.

Farzin, Y. H., (1995) "Foreign Exchange Reform in Iran: Badly Designed, Badly Managed" *World Development*, Vol. 12, No. 6, 987-1001.

Ferris, S.P, T. H. McInish, and R. A. Wood, (1997) "Automated Trade Execution and Trading Activity: The Case of the Vancouver Stock Exchange" *Journal of International Financial Markets*, Institutions and Money, Vol. 7, 61-72.

Harris L. E., (1994) "Minimom Price Variations, Discrete Bid-ask Spreads, and Quotation Sizes" *Review of Financial Studies*, Vol. 7, 149-178.

Huang, R. D., and H. R. Stoll, (1992) "The Design of Trading Systems: Lessons from Abroad" *Financiual Analysts Journal*, Vol. 48, 49-54.

Lau S.T., and T. H. McInish, "Reducing Tick Size on the Stock Exchange of Singapore" *Pacific-Basin Finance Journal* , 3 (1995): 485-496.

Mcinish, T. H., A.Robert and A. Wood. (1992) "An Analysis of Intraday Patterns in Bid/ask Spreads for NYSE Stocks" *Journal of Finance*, Vol. 47, 753-764.

Pagano, M., O. Randl, A. A.Rocll, and J. Zechner, (2001) "What Makes Stock Exchanges Succeed? Evidence from Cross-listing Decisions" *European Economic Review*, Vol. 45, 770-782.

Pagano, M., A.A. Roell, and J. Zechner, (2000) "The Geography of Equity Listing: Why do Companies List Abroad? Working paper no. 28, CSEF. www. Dise. Unisa.it/WP/wp28.

pdf, and Discussion paper No. 2681, CEPR, London. www.Cepr.org/pubs/dps/DP2681.asp.

Parisi, F., L. Nail, and C. Soto, (2002) "Evidence of a Leadership Role in the Chilean Stock Exchanges" *Journal of Multinational Financial Managemen*, Vol. 12, 191-205.

Shastri, K. A., K. Shastri, and K. Sirdom, (1995) "Trading Mechanisms and Return Volatility Unstable: An Empirical Analysis of the Stock Exchange of Thailand" Pacific-Basin Finsnce Journal, Vol. 3, 357-370.

Saudagaran, S. M., and G. C. Biddle, (1992) "Financial Disclosure Levels and Foreign Stock Exchange Listing Decisions" *Journal of International Financial Management and Accounting*, Vol. 4, 106-147.

Schmidt, H., and P. Iversen, (1993) "Automating German Equity Trading: Bid-ask Spreads on Competing Systems" *Journal of Financial Services Research*, Vol. 6, 373-397.

Stoll, Hans R. and Robert E. Whalcy, (1983) "Transactions Costs and the Small Fim Effect", *Journal of Financial Economic,* Vol. 12, .57-79.

Tehran Stock Exchange, , (2001) "*Tehran Stock Exchange Laws, Rules and Regulations*", Second Edition.

Tehran Stock Exchange, (2002) " *Ten Years Performance Report of Tehran Stock Exchange*", First Edition.

REFERENCES EVA
1. Biddle, G. C.; Bowen, R. M. and Wallace, J. S. (1998) "Does EVA Beat Earning" Evidence on Association with Stock Returns and Firm Values", Journal of Accounting and Economics, 24, 301-336.

2. Biddle, G. C.; Bowen, R. M. and Wallace, J. S. (1998) "Evidence on EVA" University of Washington Business School , Seattle.

3. Economic Value Added: Advantage of EVA (Computer Program) Available at: www.SternStewart.com 2004.

4. Fernandez, P. (2001) "EVA, Economic profit and Cash Value Added Do NOT Measure Shareholder Value Creation", IESE Business School.

5. Ghanbari, A. (2000) "Study the Relationship between the TSEs' Companies' EVA and Their Financial Ratios" Master Thesis, The University of Tehran, Tehran, Iran.

6. Izadniya, N. (1998) "Businuss Firms Performance Evaluation using EVA and FCF models and Determining the Gap between Price and Value" PhD Dissertation, Allame Tabatabai University, Tehran, Iran.

7. Kawoosi, Ali (2001) "Comparative Study of the Relationships between Tobin-Q Ratio and EVA with Companies Wealth" Master Thesis, Allame Tabatabai University, Tehran, Iran.

8. Kevin, C. "Valuation Local Authorities" (Computer Program) Available at: www.theauthority.com.
9. Maximizing Shareholder Value, Understanding Economic Value Added (Computer Program) Available at: www.sternstewart.com, 2004.
10. O'Byrne, Stephen (1997): EVA and Shareholder Return, Financial Practice and Education, Volume 7, Number 1, 1997, S. 50-54.
11. "Performance Valuation Measures" (Computer Program) Available at: www.FPM.com
12. Stewart, G. B. (1991) "The Quest for Value: A Guide for Senior Managers" NewYork, Harper Collin Publisher, pp. 179-222.
13. Nazariyeh, Zahra (2003) "Apprasing the Relationships between the TSEs' EVA and their EPS" Master Thesis, Allame Tabatabai University, Tehran, Iran.
14. Rezai, Gholamreza (1999) "Study the Correlation between EVA and ROE for Performance Evaluation of the TSE Motor Vehicles Industry Companies" Master Thesis, Allame Tabatabai University, Tehran, Iran.
15. Uyemura, D. G., C. C. Kantor and J. M. Pettit (1996), "EVA® for Banks: Value Creation, Risk Management, and Profitability Measurement", Journal of Applied Corporate Finance, Vol. 9, No. 2, pp. 94-113.
16. Young, S. D. and O'Byrne, S. F. (2001)"ErA and Value Base Management: A Partical Guide to Implementation" New York, Mc Gram Hill, pp: 206-252.

After defining the major factors affecting the attractiveness of a stock market to foreign investors, now we are ready to answer to the three important investment questions; 1) what domestic investors value? In other words, what factors are attractive to domestic investors when they trade stocks? 2) what are the relative importance of each factor from the stand points of domestic investors? These questions are important because today's, about 41% of the peoples live in advanced economic countries directly invest in companies stocks. Also, direct and indirect investments in stocks consists 20% and 34% of the total investments in the world, respectively. [14] Because of this importance, study the behavior of domestic investors is an important subject in finance.

Several research implemented on investor's behavior. Some researchers investigated the relationships between psychological and personal characteristics of investors and their investment selections. [23, 24, 25, 27] The study of Warnerd show a strong relationship between investors behavior and their investment selection. Although there are not enough researches on the investors behavior theories, but Solomon and Wilcox explains that financial markets provides an important environments for investors behavior studies.[25, 28] The study of Baker and Haslem show investors have different interpretations about three factors of stock returns, future expectations and financial equilibrium. These differences in investors attitudes are related to investors behaviors and their psychological and personal characteristics.[3] Roger believes the critical factor in investment selection process is the quality of company management.[19]

According to the literature, 13 important factors affecting the domestic investors when they trade stocks are as follows:
- Management (the quality of company management performance in the past, the social and public image of company management and/or company managers personality and morality)
- Price trends (increasing trend, decreasing trend, or on trend)
- Dividend ratio (high, avreage or low ratio respect to industry avegare ratio)
- Stock returns (high, avrege or low returns respect to industry avegare return)
- Industry sector and stage (introductory stage with high returns and risk, growth or development stage with high returns but low risk, or maturity stage with low returns and low risk.
- Knowledge base (consumed company products in the past, having information about company products and/or having experiences in company)
- Price to earning ratio (high, average or low Price to earning ratio)
- Price volatility (high, medium or low price volatility)
- Nature of the stock (high current income, high price growth respect to risk)
- Source of recommenda (brokers advises, financial journals, financial magazines or newspapers, informal information about the company and its stocks)
- Principal place of operation (operate in abroad, domestic or both)
- Dividend per share (Paying dividend per share in regular or irregular intervals)

- Capital increasing methods (issuing the rights or providing stocks to public)

3. Field Research Results

In order to answer the question of what foreign investors value, we have implement a filed research. First of all, we reviewed the literature and determined 36 important factors (variables) affecting stock markets attractiveness. Based on the variables, a questionnaire was developed. After pretesting the validity and the reliability of TSE financial experts and analysts. Finally the data was collected and analyzed. The results show that "from the view points of the TSE experts and analysts, the TSE is not yet attractive to foreign investors".[9] On the other hands, in order to answer to question of what factors affecting domestic investors when they trade stocks in the TSE, another questionnaire (in likert scale) was developed. A number of questionnaires were distributed among 95 randomly selected TSE investors. Finally, to determine the relative importance of each factors in the TSE, we calculated the frequency, the priority and the relative importance of each factors from view point of the TSE investors. Table 1 show the frequency, mean value and the rank of each of factors from the stand points of the TSE investors.

Table 1: Frequency, mean value and rank of each important factor

Row	Important Factors In Investors Decisions	Mean Value	Factors Rank of Importance	Frequency of Factors in terms of their Relative Importance				
				No Important 1	Low Important 2	Avrage Important 3	Important 4	Very Important 5
1	Price Volatility	2.937	8	17	21	25	15	17
2	Price Trend(PT)	4.290	1	2	4	14	19	56
3	Earning Per Share (EPS)	3.368	5	10	16	14	39	16
4	Dividend Per Share (DPS)	3.558	4	4	8	37	23	23
5	Price to Earning Ratio (P/E)	3.305	6	15	16	17	19	28
6	Yield	2.968	7	15	18	27	25	10
7	Capital Increasing Methods	2.610	9	21	28	25	9	12
8	Appreciation Capital	4.021	2	20	20	22	25	8
9	Management	2.432	11	28	29	19	7	12
10	Industry Sector	2.8	10	20	20	22	25	8
11	Knowledge Base	2	13	44	25	12	10	4

| 12 | Source of Recommenda | 3.916 | 3 | 4 | 11 | 15 | 24 | 41 |
| 13 | Principal Place of Operation | 2.126 | 12 | 34 | 30 | 20 | 7 | 4 |

Results of the statistical analyzes show the priority of the quantitative financial factors (price volatility, price trends, earning per shares, dividend per share, price to earning ratio, yield, capital increasing methods, and appreciation capital) to nonfinancial qualitative factors (management, industry sector, knowledge base, source of recommenda and principal place of operation).

1. **Conclusions and Final Remarks**

Because of the increasing role of the foreign investments in stock markets, two important questions that FPMs should answer are 1) what makes stock markets more attractive to foreign investors? 2) what factors are important to domestic investors when they trade stocks. This paper attempted to answer these important investment questions.

We determined important market attractiveness factors and developed a questionnaire to appraise the attractiveness of the TSE to foreign investors. Results of the statistical analyzes show that recently implemented actions plans to enhance attractiveness of the TSE to foreign investors are not yet satisfactory. We also determined what are important to domestic investors when they trade stocks, and using a developed questionnaire, calculated the relative importance of each factors from view point of domestic investors. Results of the statistical analyzes imply that although nonfinancial qualitative factors (Management, industry sector, knowledge base, source of recommenda and principal place of operation) are important when to dometic investors when they trade stocks, but the quantitative financial factors (Price volatility, price trends, earning per shares, dividend per share, price to earning ratio, yield, capital increasing methods, and appreciation capital) are meaningfully more important from the stand point of the TSE' investors.

We believe that the results of this research not only improve FPMs out-of-box insights to determine the relative weaknesses of their stock markets, but it also increasere their understandings of their domestic investors priorities, preferences and behaviors when they trade stocks. Since forign and domestic investors preferences and priority structures and the competition situation of the international financial markets may change over the time, It is required to monitor and manage the behavior of both the foreign and dometic investors to increase the stock market attractiveness and efficiency.

Market Efficiency Literature Review EMH

The extent of predicable variation in assets returns, as stated by Gaunt and Gray (2003), is of great interest to academics and practitioners. To what extent can be past history of a common stock's price be used to make meaningful predictions the future price of a stock? Previous researcher such as fama (1965a), D' Ambrosio (1980), Wong and Kwong (1984), Barnes (1986), Ayodegi (1999) and many more has studied extensively the behavior of equity share price. One of the most important hypothesis that lets to study this behavior is The Efficient Market Hypothesis (EMH).

EMH states that at any given time, security prices fully reflect all available information. Fama(1970) defines a stock market as efficient if stock prices fully "reflect" available information. This definition implies that the available information cannot be used to forecast stock prices in a fully efficient market. The more efficient the market, the more random the sequence of price changes generated by such a market and the most efficient market of all is one in which price changes are completely random and unpredictable. (Lo, 2000). Annuar (2002) notes, "In an efficient market, the prices of stock reflect a rational assessment of the underlying value of stocks. On average, you will make money but the money you make is just enough to cover the risk you have assumed". If market is efficient, the new information is reflected quickly into market prices. Formally, efficient markets are those that do not allow consistent abnormal rate of returns. This suggests that in general, majority of investors cannot consistently profit from any delays in price adjustments reflecting new information.

From these notions, three forms of efficient market hypotheses namely the weak form, semi strong form and the strong form has emerges. Each concern with the adjustment of stock prices against one set of relevant information for instance the historical price, publicly available information and so forth. Under the weak form test, the relevant information is the set of historical prices whereas the semi-strong form test, it is the efficient adjustment of stock prices to publicly available information other than historical prices. Lastly, under the strong form test, the consideration is whether some investors have any access to any information relevant to the formation of stock prices.

The stock price behavior of most developed countries such as US and European countries has been known to follow the random process. (Fama, 1965; Theil and Leenders, 1965; Solnik, 1973, Ang and Pohlman, 1978). Comparisons of these studies showed that because of difference in characteristics (such as stringencies of disclosure requirement, control and inside trades, thinness of market etc of the two markets) the deviation from a random walk is more apparent in European stock markets than in the Us. The lesser the degree of regulations, the greater the degree of deviation from a random price behavior. (Ang and Pohlman, 1978)

Uri and Jones (1990) address the EMH in the USA for the period of 1974 to 1988. They found that the markets are indicated to be weak form efficient based on monthly data. Gaunt and Gray (2003) examined the EMH in Australian equities. Dragota and Mitrica (2004) found the evidence of inefficiency in the Romanian capital market.

In Asia, D' Ambrosio (1980), Wong and Kwong (1984), and Lew (1981) have tested the random walk hypotheses in Singaporean, Hong Kong and Malaysian markets. D' Ambrosio found that in Singaporean stock markets some pockets of efficiency exist. Wong and Kwong fails to support his weakly efficient hypotheses in Hong Kong market but opposite to Singaporean and Hong Kong stock market, he found that Malaysian stock market is weakly efficient. Lew found no significant deviation from weak form of EMH in KLSE. Ayodeji (1999) investigated the weak form efficiency of the Nigerian stock market using correlation analysis. The results of his study support the evidence of weak form efficiency in the sense that technical analysis and other security analysis based on historical prices appear to be valueless in Nigeria. Groenewold, Tang and Wu (2003) examined the weak market efficiency in Shanghai and Shenzen stock exchanges for the period 1992-2001. Their study found evidence of departures from weak efficiency in the form of predictability of past returns. Cajueiro and Tabak (2004) tested the EMH for China, Hong Kong and Singapore by means of the long memory dependence approach. They found that Hong Kong is the most efficient market followed by Chinese (type A) shares and Singapore and finally Chinese (type B) shares. They also suggest that liquidity and capital restriction may play a role in explaining results in EMH tests. Gunasekaraga and Power (2001) analyzed the performance of technical trading rules for four emerging countries South Asian capital markets (the Bombay, the Colombo, the Dhaka and the Karachi Stock Exchanges). They found that technical trading rules have predictive ability in these markets. The results suggest that the employment of these techniques generates excess returns to investors in South Asian markets.

The random-walk version of the EMH for Istanbul stock exchange is tested by Buguk and Brorsen (2003). The results parametric test indicate that the composite, industrial and finance index of Istanbul stock exchange are a random walk but a nonparametric test provides evidence against a random walk.

Norli (2004) investigated the randomness of Bursa Malaysia share price movements after the currency turmoil 1997. He looked at the behavior of Malaysian stock after the currency turmoil and the conformity of the Malaysian stock market at that time to the week form of EMH. The results of the study seem to support that the Malaysian market is at least weakly efficient.

References:

Annuar, M.N. 2002. Is the KLSE efficient? Efficient Market Hypothesis Vs Behavioural Finance. Syarahan Inaugural, University Putra Malaysia.

Ang, J.S., and Pohlman, R. A, 1978. A Note on the Price Behavior of Far Eastern Stocks. *Journal of International Business Studies*, 9:103-7.

Ayodeji, R. (1999). Weak Form Efficiency of the Nigerian Stock Market: Further Evidence. African Development Bank, Blackwell Publisher, pp 54-68.

Bachelier, L. 1964. Theory of Speculation. In "The random character of stock market prices, pp 17-78.

Barnes P, 1986. Thin Trading and Stock Market Efficiency: The case of KLSE. *Journal of Business and Accounting*, pp 609-17.

Berkman, Neil. 1978. A primer in the random walks in the stock market. *New England Economic Review*, pp 32-49.

Buguk, C. and Brorsen, B.W. (2003). Testing weak-form market efficiency: Evidence from the Istanbul Stock Exchange. *International Review of Financial Analysis*, pp 579-590.

Cajueiro, D. O and Tabak, B. M. 2004. Evidence of Long Range Dependence in Asian equity Markets: The Role of Liquidity and Market Restrictions. *Physica A* 342 (2004), pp 656-664.

Gaunt, C. and Gray, P. 2003. Short-term Autocorrelation in Australian Equities. *Australian Journal of Management*, Vol 28, No. 1.

D' Ambrosio, C.A. 1980. Random walk and the stock exchange of Singapore. *Financial Review*, 15: 1-12.

Dragota, V. and Mitrica, E. 2004. Emergent Capital Market's Efficiency: The Case of Romania. *European Journal of Operational Research*, 155 (2004), pp 353-360.

Dryden, M. 1969. Share price movements. A Markovian Approach. Journal of Finance, pp 49-61.

Fama, E.F. 1965. The behavior of stock markets prices. *Journal of Business*, pp 34-105.

Fama, E.F. 1970. Efficient capital markets: A review of theory and empirical work. *Journal of Finance*, pp 383-417.

Fama, E.F. 1976. Foundations of Finance, Basic Books New York.

Gibbons, M., and Hess, P.J. 1981. Day of the week effects and asset return: Journal of Business, pp 579-596 in Othman, Y. and Ismail, I. 1993. Understanding the Behavioral Patterns of Stock Prices. Leeds Publication.

Groenewold, N., Tang, S.H.K. and Wu, Y. (2003). The efficiency of the Chinese stock market and the role of the banks. *Journal of Asian Economics*, pp 593-609.

Gunasekaraga, A. and Power, D.M. (2001). The profitability of moving average trading rules in South Asian stock markets. *Emerging Market Review*, pp 17-33.

Hong, H. 1978. The random walk in stock markets: Theory and evidence. Securities Industry Review, pp 25-29 in Othman, Y. and Ismail, I. 1993. Understanding the Behavioral Patterns of Stock Prices. Leeds Publication.

Lew, T.L. 1981. The efficient market hypothesis and weak form test on the KLSE. Unpublished research, University of Shieffield.

Lo, A. W. 2000. Finance: A Selective Survey.

Nagayasu, J. (2003). The efficiency of the Japanese equity market. *International Financial Review*, pp 155- 171.

Officer, R. 1975. Seasonality in the Australian capital markets: market efficiency and empirical issues. Journal of Financial Economics, pp 29-52 in Othman, Y. and Ismail, I. 1993. Understanding the Behavioral Patterns of Stock Prices. Leeds Publication.

Othman, Y. and Ismail, I. 1993. Understanding the Behavioral Patterns of Stock Prices. Leeds Publication.

Roll, R. 1981. A possible explanation of the small firm effect. Journal of Finance, pp 879-888 in Othman, Y. and Ismail, I. 1993. Understanding the Behavioral Patterns of Stock Prices. Leeds Publication.

Sarno, L. and Thornton, D.L. 2003. The Efficient Market Hypothesis and Idenification in Structural VAR s. Working paper 2003-032A, Federal Reserve Bank of St Lousi.

Solnik, B.H. 1973. Note on the validity of the random walk for European stock prices. *Journal of Finance*, pp 1151-9.

Theil, H. and Leenders, C.T. 1965. Tomorrow on the Amsterdam stock exchange. *Journal of Business*, 38:227-84.

Theobald, M. and price, V. 1984. Seasonality and estimation in thin market. *Journal of Finance*, 39: 377-92.

Uri, N.D. and Jones, J.D. (1990*). Economic Modeling*, pp 388-394.

Wong, K.A., and Kwong, K.S. 1984. The behaviour of Hong Kong stock prices, Applied Economics, pp 905-917 in Othman, Y. and Ismail, I. 1993. Understanding the Behavioral Patterns of Stock Prices. Leeds Publication.

Wong, K.A and Tan, J. 1987. An assessment of risk and return in the Singapore stock market. Unpublished paper.

Promoting Organizational Agility: An Applied Framework

AMROLAH AMINI (Ph.D)

Associate Professor, Allameh Tabatabaei University (ATU), Tehran, Iran.

aminij@atu.ac.ir

ALIREZA EMAMI

Master of Science, Tehran University, Tehran, Iran

memami@alumni.ut.ac.ir

MOSTAFA EMAMI*

Master of Science, Michigan Technological University (MTU)

memami@mtu.edu

***Corresponding Address**

Applied Research and Technology Office, Michigan Technological University

1400 Townsend Dr, Houghton, MI 49931

Tel & Fax : +1-(816) 237-0018

E-mail: memami@mtu.edu

Abstract

Purpose: prepare new methodology for agility in which organizations can respond to the business change drivers through new advanced technologies and procedures.

Design/ methodology/ approach: in this paper, we presented first main definitions and concepts of agility. Then, with literature review process on agility's models, main models of agility are determined to the further investigation. Following, some of the critiques on agility are discussed and analyzed and finally, the step-by-step and new methodology is presented as a comprehensive and holistic approach to agility evaluation and enhancement in any organization.

Finding: in this paper, holistic definition of agility, as well as step by-step method for agility evaluation and enhancement are discovered and explained.

Originality/value: because of environmental divers and need for achieving competitive advantage(s) through encountering challenges and opportunities, organizations need to be agile so that they can respond quickly (by attaining new and powerful capabilities) to changes in customers' demands and market conditions.

Implications and further investigation: the proposed conceptual methodology is applicable for any organization but it is based on literature review and therefore, need to be deployed and tested in real life organization in order to gain validity and functionality.

Keywords: change, agility, literature review, approaches, applied framework

1-Introduction

Uncertainty and change in the business environments had been a major topic in management research for a long time. Thompson (1967) stated that one of the most important functions for any organization is to manage uncertainties. Drucker (1968) described the concept of entrepreneurial task as the search for change, response to change, and exploitation of changes as opportunities. In existing era, many factors have pressures on organizations to get adaptability and flexibility about changes that occur in their business environment. As Hayen (1988) has pointed out, there is nothing new about change. However, today's change is taking place at a much faster speed than ever. The first set of conditions or factors that have pressures on today organizations are the series of socio-economic, financial and political changes that occurred in the last quarter of the twentieth century. Further drivers for change are Changes in cost and efficiency; the adoption of agile manufacturing and industries' best practices; a need to manage supply chains more efficiently; a market shift from standardization to differentiated products; de-regulation or new regulatory policies and/or government regulations; changing societal concerns, attitudes and lifestyles; and; changes in the degree of uncertainty. Therefore, to respond effectively to the above drivers, organizations need to be truly agile.

As it can be observed in following literature review, many agility models have been proposed for enhancement of responsiveness and flexibility, but noon of them (except Sharifi and Zhang, 1999) doesn't suggest practical methodology to agility evaluation and enhancement. On the other hand, many authors have proposed different concepts and components for agility and don't agree on its implementation or evaluation process. Meanwhile, their proposed frameworks are mainly based on manufacturing area and don't present holistic and comprehensive approach to agility evaluation and improvement in other organizational context (such as service and public sector organizations). As a new framework, our proposed

This paper is organized as following. At the first, definitions of agility and agile manufacturing are discussed so that the basic concepts and ideas of agility are explored and discussed. At section two, literature review on more cited and relatively practical models and approaches to design, implement and enhance agility's practices is presented. Following, critiques on agility concepts and frameworks are presented and then, we propose a practical methodology for agility implementation, which is based on above models. Finally, some recommendations for agility implementation and enhancement will be presented to the interested managers and practitioners.

2. Literature review
2.1. Definitions and Drivers of agility

At the beginning of the 21st Century, the world faces significant changes in almost all aspects, especially marketing competition, technological innovations and customer demands. Mass markets are continuing to fragment as customers become increasing demanding and their expectations rise. These developments have caused a major revision of business priorities and strategic visions (Sharifi and Zhang, 1999). Organizations have realized that agility is essential for their survival and competitiveness. Available literature on agility, scarce as it may be, has provided many conceptual overviews of its dimensions and has further conceptualized related elements. Also, a preliminary empirical assessment of management attention for agility is available to further indicate the relevance of the general agility concept as recognized by management (Naylor et al., 1999). Obviously, different facets of agility have been emphasized by various authors and this has lead to varied views reflected in the literature. According to Gunasekaran (1999), agility is the ability of surviving and prospering in a competitive environment of continuous and unpredictable change by reacting quickly and effectively to changing markets, driven by customer-defined products and services. Kidd (1994) defined agility as a rapid and proactive adaptation of enterprise elements to unexpected and unpredicted changes. The creators of ''agile manufacturing'' concept at the Iacocca Institute, of Lehigh University (USA) defined it as: A manufacturing system with capabilities (hard and soft technologies, human resources, educated management, information) to meet the rapidly changing needs of the marketplace (speed, flexibility, customers, competitors, suppliers, infrastructure, responsiveness). Main characteristics of agile manufacturing are delivering value to customers, being ready for changes in terms of market and technologies, and Prospering from the turbulent environment emerging (Helo, 2004). Also, Maskell suggests the most important aspects of agile manufacturing as customer prosperity, people and information, cooperation within and between firms, and fitting a company for change (Maskell, 2001). Likewise, Li Jin-Hai and et.al identify critical elements of real agile manufacturing as strategic processing, core competencies, multiple winners, integration, and information technology.

Yusuf et al. (1999) proposed that agility is the successful application of competitive bases such as speed, flexibility, innovation, and quality by the means of the integration of reconfigurable resources and best practices of knowledge-rich environment to provide customer-driven products and services in a fast changing environment. Despite the differences, all definitions of ''agility'' emphasize the speed and flexibility as the primary attributes of an agile organization (Gunasekaran, 1999; Sharifi and Zhang, 1999; Yusuf et al., 1999). An equally important attribute of agility is the effective response to change and uncertainty (Goldman et al., 1995; Kidd, 1994; Sharifi and Zhang, 2001). Some authors (Sharifi and Zhang, 1999) state that responding to change in proper ways and exploiting and taking advantages of changes are the main factors of agility. The next common component of published definitions of agility is a high quality and highly customized products (Gunasekaran, 1999; Kidd, 1994). These definitions should be considered simultaneously in order to gain a better understanding of what constitute agility. In other words, although various definitions of agility are available in literature world, these definitions do not contrast with each other. Sarkis (2001) express that the concept of agility is in the process of being defined by both practitioners and researchers. Even a number of definitions for agility have been posited within the last few years, a common thread focuses on being able to function and compete within a state of dynamic and continuous (in table-1-, some of the best definitions of agility have been presented briefly).we define agility as organizational ability to sense, perceive, analyze and respond to the changes that occur in the turbulent environment based on competency, speed, cost, quality, responsiveness, team building, virtual structure, participation, knowledge and learning and at the same time, exploit from those changes.

Table-1- definitions of agility

Author(s)	Definition
Iacocca institute (1991)	A manufacturing system with extraordinary capabilities (Internal capabilities: hard and soft technologies, human resources, educated management, information) to meet the rapidly changing needs of the marketplace (speed, flexibility, customers, competitors, suppliers, infrastructure, responsiveness).
Sharifi and Zhange (1999, 2000)	Agility is a basic ability for any organization that is sensing, perceiving and anticipating changes in the business environment. Also, Ability to sense, respond to, and exploit anticipated or unexpected changes in the business environment is called agility.

Maskell (2001)	Agility is the ability to thrive and prosper in an environment of constant and unpredictable change.
Vernadat (1999)	Agility can be defined as the ability to closely align organization systems to changing business needs in order to achieve competitive performance.
Helo (2004)	Agility is a capability of responding to change in a dimension beyond flexibility.
Goldman et al. (1995)	Agility, for a company, is to be capable of operating profitably in a competitive environment of continually and unpredictably changing customer opportunities.
Hormozi (2001)	Agile organizations are flexible and quick to respond to fast moving market conditions.
Dove (1996)	Agility is the ability to manage and apply knowledge effectively so that an organization has the potential to thrive in a continuous changing and unpredicted business environment.
Kid (1994)	To operationalise agility, it can be defined as 'the synthesis of a number of enterprises that each have some core skills or competencies which they bring to a joint venturing operation thus enabling the cooperative enterprises to adapt and respond quickly to changing customer requirements.
Naylor and et.al (1995)	Agility means using market knowledge and a virtual corporation to exploit profitable opportunities in a volatile marketplace.
Power and Sohal (2001)	Agility means using market knowledge and a virtual corporation to exploit profitable opportunities in a volatile marketplace
Youssuf et.al (1999)	Agility is the successful exploration of competitive bases (speed, flexibility, innovation, proactivity, quality and productivity) through the integration of reconfigurable resources and best practices in a knowledge rich environment to provide customer driven products and services in a fast changing market environment.
Prince and Kay (2003)	Ability to respond to sudden changes and meet widely varied customer requirements in terms of price, specification, quantity, qualify and delivery is called agility.

Agility as a new paradigm for enhancing competitiveness has been widely researched since its inception in the early 1990s. The concept, in its various forms, is now recognized as a winning strategy for growth if not a basic one for survival in certain business environments. Agility implies not only the ability to respond to unanticipated change (responsibility) but also to act proactively with regard to change. You have frequently heard that if there is one constant thing, it is certainly change. Here, the most important question is what factors or drivers force organizations to get agility? Many researches place primary importance on the external changes. Nagel and Dove (1991) identified some of the key drivers that shape the future competitive environment of the twenty first century as information availability, technology acceleration, globalized market and competition, wage and job skills shifts, resource limitation, and increasing customer expectation. Yusuf, Sarhadi and Gunasekaran (1999) determine drivers of agility as automation and price/cost consideration, widening customer choice and expectation, competing priorities, integration and proactivity, and achieving manufacturing requirements in synergy. Sharifi and Zhang (1999) also classify changes as due to market, competitive, customer requirements, technological, and social factors. Summarizing previous studies, Christopher (2001) identifies the general areas of business environment change as market volatility, intense competition, changes in customer requirements, accelerating technological change, and change in social factors. *In sum, it can be concluded from above that the main drivers of agility are increasingly competition, enhancing customer expectations, technology and innovation acceleration, globalization, social and cultural factors, market variability, information technology, special and loyal human resource scarcity or limitation, and so on (figure-1-)*.

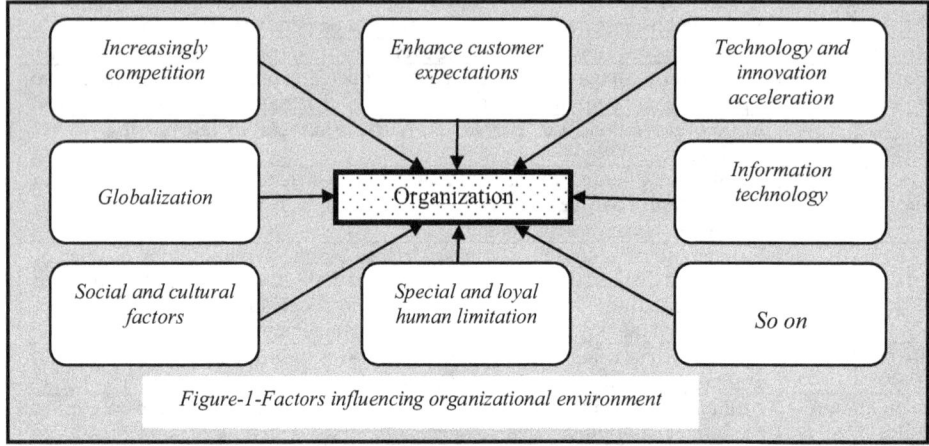

Figure-1-Factors influencing organizational environment

2.2. Agility models and approaches

Agile organization has been advocated as the 21st century's organization paradigm, and is seen as the winning strategy to become national and international leaders in an ever increasing competitive market of fast changing customer requirements (Youssuf et al., 1999). However, the ability to build agile organization and enhance it has not developed as rapidly as anticipated, because the development of technology to manage agile organization is still under way (Sharp et al., 1999). Thus, in embracing agile organization many important questions concerning agility need to be asked, such as what precisely is agility and how can it be measured? How will organizations know when they have it, as there are no simple metrics or indices available? How and to what degree does the organization's attributes affect companies' business performance? How to compare agility with competitiveness? If a company or organization wants to improve agility, how can it identify the principal obstacles to improvement? How to assist in achieving agility effectively? Answers to such questions are critical to the practitioners and to the theory of agile organization design. To assist managers in better achieving an agile organization, there have been numerous studies dedicated to design, implement, and improve the agility of an organization. In this section, we introduce some of the most cited and applied models of organizational agility so that the practical methodology of agility implementation process can be extracted and developed based upon them. It must be taken into account that election of following models is based on their conceptual and operational methodologies as well as their citations in relevant journals and books.

2.2.1. Goldman and et.al approach: researchers believe know Goldman, Nagel and Preiss (1995) as the first ones permeating the agility concept in the business world in order to respond successfully to the turbulent and changing environment. They described agility in the book "agile competitors and virtual organizations" (1995) as dynamic, context-specific, aggressively change-embracing and growth oriented. From this point of view, agility entails a continual readiness to change (sometimes radically) and there is no time when a company has completely fulfilled the goal of being agile. According to above definition, Agility is context-specific in that differences among markets limit the generalizability of detailed rules for becoming agile. Agile firms embrace change as they understand not only their current markets, product lines, competencies and customers, but also understand the potential for future customers and markets and the necessity of changing to meet those opportunities.

They identified four key dimensions of agile organization. The first dimension is enriching the customer. This entails a quick understanding of the unique requirements of each individual customer and rapidly providing it. The second dimension entails co-operation (intra-organizational, interorganizational co-operation such as supplier partnerships and perhaps emerging virtual relationships with competing organizations) in order to enhance competitiveness. The third dimension utilizes new organizational structure(s) to master change and uncertainty through techniques such as concurrent engineering and cross-functional teams. The fourth dimension leverages the impact of people, information and technology and recognizes the importance of employees as a company asset, placing greater emphasis on education, training and empowerment.

Figure-1-four principles of agility (Goldman et.al, 1995)

2.2.2. Ramesh and Devadasan model: Based on twenty agile manufacturing (AM) criteria, Ramesh and Devadasan (2007) concluded that agile manufacturing is function of flexible and lean manufacturing systems. They believe various definitions of agile manufacturing are not contrast with each other. But commonality among most of them is the enunciation that AM is the ability of manufacturing enterprise to quickly respond to the market requirements. Thus, AM calls for radical changes in the system, culture and management styles being currently followed in traditional manufacturing environment. They introduced twenty criteria on agile manufacturing as organizational structure, delegation of authority, manufacturing set ups, status of quality, status of productivity, employee's status, employee participation, nature of management, customer response adoption, product life cycle, product service life, design improvement, production methodology, manufacturing planning, cost management, automation type, information technology, integration, change in business and technical processes, time management, and outsourcing. Then, they designed the procedure to attain and enhance agility in organizations, which some the most important phases of their model are top management support and commitment, organizational structure study, studying the existing practices with reference to twenty agile criteria and estimating the deviations, identifying and implementing vital few activities, expand implementation based on the impact of preliminary efforts, and finally, analysis the result of implementation process.

2.2.3. Meredith and Francis model: Meredith and Francis (2000) have proposed the 16 dimensional reference model for implementing agile manufacturing, including components such as strategy, linkages, people, and processes (figure-2-). This reference model provides a tool with which to audit each company on its degree of agility and provides an integrated definition of the components of agility. The reference model is presented in the shape of a wheel to demonstrate that its components are interdependent. A wheel is weakened if any spoke is absent, broken or fragile. It is the same with agility. That is, if any of the 16 components is under-developed, then the firm's agile capability is weakened. In sum, the purpose of the wheel is to assist managers to audit the agile capability of their firms, identify agility blockages and develop a focused development plan.

The first quadrant focuses on strategic aspects of agility. Four policies/practices are specified: wide-deep scanning, strategic commitment, full deployment and agile scoreboard. The second quadrant focuses on organizational processes that support agility. Four policies/practices are specified: flexible assets and systems, fast new product acquisition, rapid problem-solving and rich information systems. The third quadrant focuses on outside linkages. Four policies/practices are specified: agility benchmarking, deep customer insight, aligned suppliers and performing partnerships. Finally, the fourth quadrant focuses on people and the management of the human resource of the firm.

Four policies/practices are specified: adaptable structure; multi-skilled, flexible people; rapid, able decision-making; and continuous learning (Meredith and Francis, 2000).

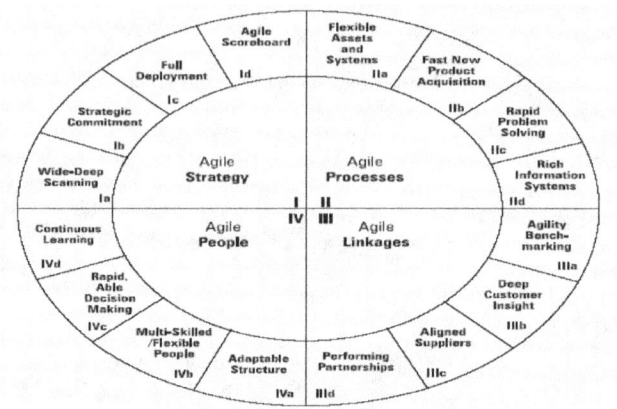

Figure-2- reference model of agility (Meredith and Francis, 2000)

2.2.3. Dove's model: Rick Dove (1994) is one of the first to discuss agility as the capability of a process to respond to the unanticipated change. Dove (1999) prefers to define agility succinctly as the ability to manage and apply knowledge as well as master to change proficiency. Though both knowledge management and change proficiency are still immature practices, he feel a sufficient foundation exists to guide an organizational engineering project to success. Figure-3- represents the key relationships and dynamics his investigations have revealed so far. In this model, infrastructure of agility are System Integrity Management, corporate change agents, Reusable/Reconfigurable/Scalable (RRC) or (CAS) architecture principles, culture, learning science principles, IT, network and repository, KM change agents. As you see in following model, agility has two sides: change proficiency and knowledge management. At the left hand, processes, procedures and people of change proficiency are place on. Ant the right hand, competency and strategy of knowledge management are place in order to acquire, transfer, store and use of knowledge. According to Dove (1999) agility is achieved when change proficiency and knowledge management are balance.

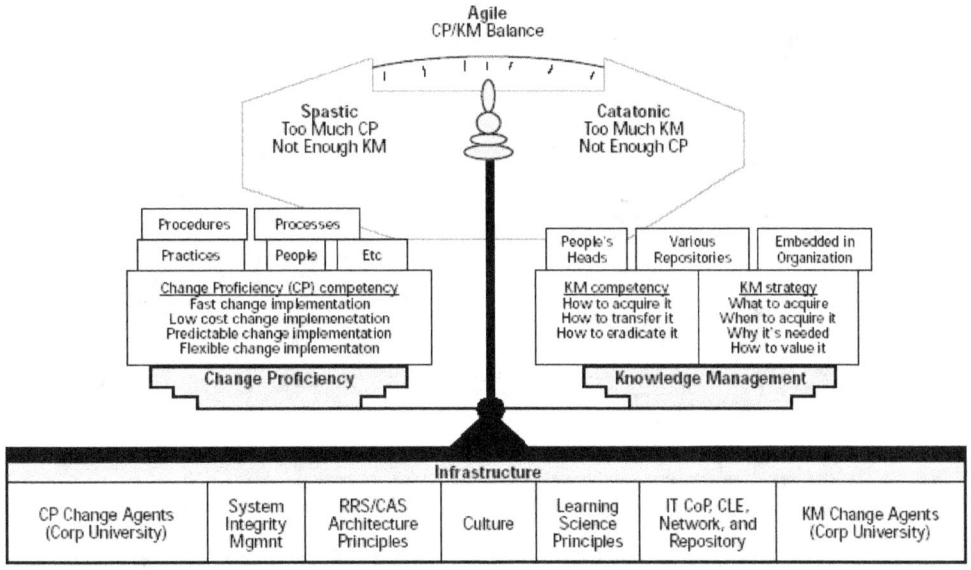

Figure-3- agility: knowledge management and change proficiency (Dove, 1999)

Dove and et.al (1996) define an agile enterprise as one that is broadly change-proficient; i.e., it exhibits competency at causing and dealing with change in the important competitive business practices of its business sector. According to them, there are three key concepts involved in this definition: change proficiency, critical business practices, and competency assessment. Sponsored by the Agility Forum, Rick Dove and et.al (1996) design a reference model structure that effectively captures and displays the essence of enterprise-wide competency at both proactive and reactive change(figure-4-). The reference model spans 24 interrelated critical business practices in 6 categories: strategic planning (3), business case justification (3), organizational relationship management (7), knowledge management (4), innovation management (4), and performance metrics (3)[1]. The seven organizational relationships focus on business units, employees, partners, suppliers, customers, information systems, and production systems. Each of the 24 practices is presented in a 3–5 page structure that provides: a generic definition, the framework and modules of a case-study practice that fits that definition, a set of generic proactive and reactive change issues, case-study responses for each issue, and finally, a change proficiency maturity synopsis that evaluates and displays the competency of the case example using the recently developed Change Proficiency Maturity Model (Dove and et.al, 1996). Figure-4- shows the change proficiency maturity profile for Remmele Engineering Corporation.

---

[1]- The numbers into ( ) represent amount of practices in each category. For example, "strategic planning" category has three practices as Strategic plan vision, Strategic plan dissemination, Strategic plan buy-In.

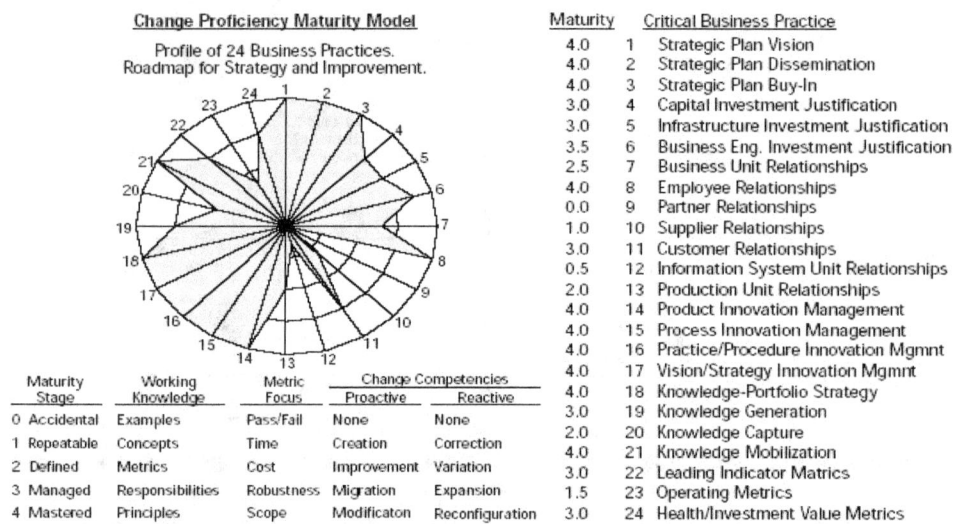

Figure-4 - Change proficiency maturity profile for Remmele Engineering (Dove and et.al, 1996)

A five-stage maturity model framework was recently developed as a tool to assess existing corporate competency at change proficiency, as well as to prioritize and guide an Agility transformation or improvement strategy. The framework is based upon a progression through five stages of working knowledge and strategic focus for practices and procedures, with separate competency tracks for both proactive and reactive proficiencies. The framework is used to build a Change Proficiency Maturity Model for a specific business practice. They focus on change proficiency as a necessary and fundamental enabler for the agile enterprise. They also recognize that an agile enterprise can be as simple as a portfolio management company that constantly reshuffles the in-agile resources it controls, or as complex as a vertically integrated organization concerned about the Agility of each of its operating units, which in turn are concerned about the Agility of each of their key business processes. Complexity aside, all enterprises have frequent occasion to weather change, and each does so with its own degree of proficiency, or lack thereof. Some deal with each event as they come, some learn naturally from each event and get better at the next change, and some recognize competitive value in mastering the process of change.

Dove and et.al (1996) do not gauge a company's progress toward timeless mastery at change proficiency by accumulating points for practices like teaming, mass customization, virtual partnering, integrated product/process development, and other such very important concepts of the day. Instead, we look for more fundamental capabilities that allow a company to adopt and integrate whatever operating concepts are important today as well as those yet undefined that will become important tomorrow. Implementing today's competitive practices says nothing about the ability to implement tomorrow's.

2.2.5. Sharifi and Zhange methodology: In developing a model for achieving agility in manufacturing organizations, Zhang and Sharifi (2000) used three elements. Elements of their model are: (1)Agility drivers which are the changes/pressures from the business environment that necessitate a company to search for new ways of running its business in order to maintain its competitive advantage; (2) agility capabilities which are the essential capabilities that the company needs in order to positively respond to and take advantage of the changes; and (3) agility providers that are the means by which the so-called capabilities such as could be obtained (practices, methods, tools, techniques facilitating a capability for agility). As a result of surveying 1,000 companies, and conducting case studies in 12 of them, they concluded that practices related to people and organization issues were both more effective and important for manufacturers. They also found that the Internet, mass-customization and virtual organizations were only used by a small percentage of respondents, and usually only partially (Power and Sohal, 2001). Figure-5-presents conceptual model of agility implementation from point Sharifi and zhange view.

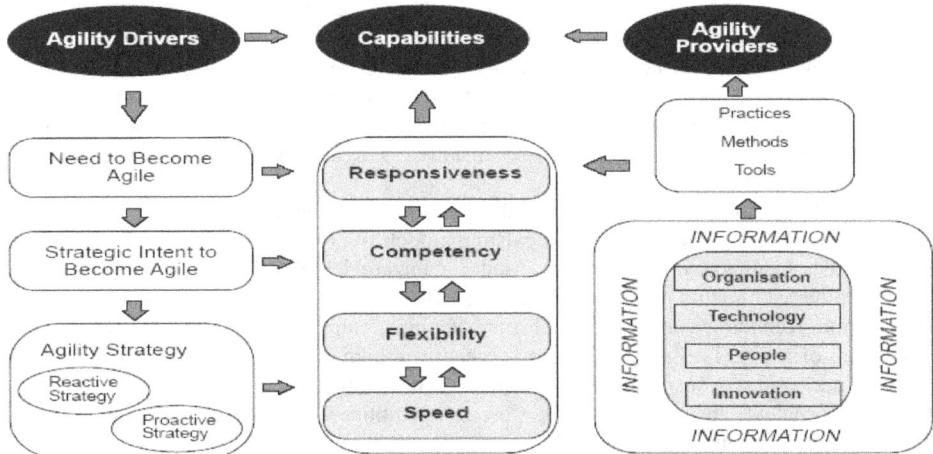

Figure-5-conceptual model of agility implementation (Sharifi and zhange, 2000)

As changes and pressures faced by companies may be different, the degree of agility required by individual companies will be different. This degree is defined as the ``agility need level'', which is a function of various factors such as turbulence of the business environment, the environment that the company competes in, and the characteristics of the company itself. Once the agility need level is determined for a company, the next step is to assess the current agility level of the company, i.e. how agile the company is now. The difference between the level of agility required and that the company already has may then be analyzed to provide a basis for further decision making. The next stage following the analysis of agility needs is to determine the required agility capabilities in order to become agile. This would require the detection, recognition and classification of changes faced by the company, as well as the analysis of the impact individual changes will bring to the company. The agility capabilities required may then be determined from the changes. The final stage in the methodology involves identifying agility providers that could bring about the required capabilities, implementing the identified providers, determining the level of agility achieved (through performance measurement), and formulating corrective measures to further improve the performance. A number of tools are being developed to assist manufacturing enterprises to carry out the above process, which have already been discussed. In sum, Sharifi and Zhange (2001) have proposed a methodology to examine the business environment of the company, determine the level of agility needed by the company, speculate on the strategic alternatives available for the company to pursue, determine the abilities of the company in response to unpredictable changes, determine the capabilities and priorities in implementing the capabilities required by the company to respond to changes (according to the specific circumstances surrounding it), identify the practices that could support the company's approach towards agility.

2.2.6. Youssuf, Sarhadi and Gunasekaran model: According to Youssuf and et.al (1999) agility is the successful exploration of competitive bases (speed, flexibility, innovation, reactivity, quality and profitability) through the integration of reconfigurable resources and best practices in a knowledge-rich environment to provide customer-driven products and services in a fast changing market environment. As we mentioned in definitions of agile manufacturing part, Youssuf and et.al (1999) have identified core concepts of agile manufacturing as core competence management, knowledge structure, virtual organization, and capability for reconfiguration(figure-6-). They propose three parallel steps to base competitive position in order to achieve agility: metrics, agility attributes and pathways or obstacles. Gunasekaran (1999) has proposed a conceptual model for the design of agile manufacturing systems based on the four key dimensions of strategies, technology, people and systems. He notes that most of the literature in this area focuses on strategies or techniques, but there is little or no focus on the integration issues. He also states that there is a lack of empirical studies testing hypotheses based on theory in this area.

Youssuf and et.al (1999) have stated that an agile organization must develop a strategic plan to launch new products in succession. Launching a single product hastily without a follow-up could be counter-productive. According to them, collectively literature reviews provide insights to what constitutes agile practices and attributes of an agile organization. As mentioned above, attributes of agility are integration, competence, team building, technology, quality, change, partnership, market, education and welfare. Competitive bases, the pathways and obstacles to achieving these attributes are important issues for consideration if progress is to be achieved in moving towards agility. Also important is the metrics for the processes that are required for achieving agility.

2.2.7. Youssuf and Crocitto model: Youssuf and Crocitto (2003) have presented a human based model of organizational agility. They decided to expand on existing models of organizational agility by incorporating the role of people, advanced manufacturing technology, and organizational characteristics in organizational success; especially in the delivery of quality products and services. Their model emphasized on elements such as leadership, culture, information technology, organizational memberships, suppliers, customers, and reward system as fundamental aspects of agility. They suggest that above generic or human factors, along with advanced manufacturing and information technologies, can enhance flexibility and responsiveness of company gaining the agile manufacturing in the context. Then, if company reinforces capabilities such as quality, cost and speed, is can achieve agility in the turbulent environment (figure-7-).

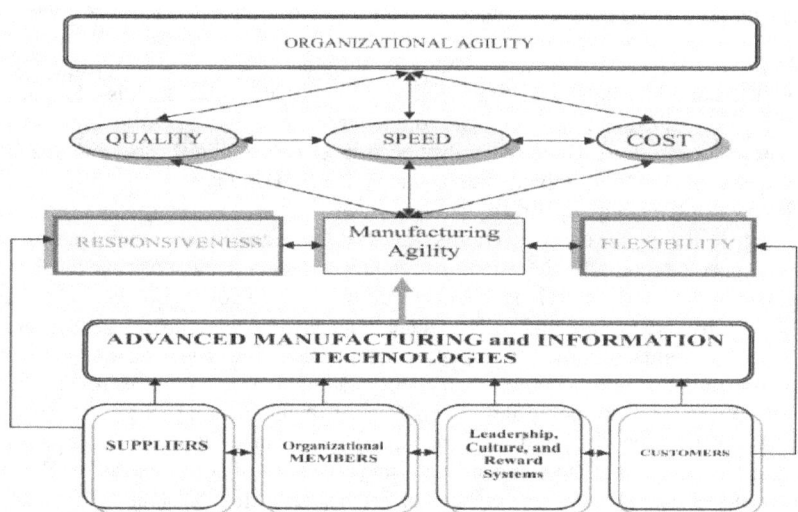

Figure-7-human side of organizational agility (Youssuf and Crocitto, 2003)

2.2.8. Chin-Torng Lin et.al model: According to Torng Lin and et.al (2005) the purpose of agile organization is to enrich/satisfy customers and employees. The main driving force behind agility is change. Even through change is nothing new; today's change is taking place at a much faster speed than ever before. Turbulence and uncertainty in the business environment have become the main causes of failure in the manufacturing industry. The number of changes and their type, specification or characteristic cannot be easily determined and are probably indefinite. So, they have developed a model containing four aspects to be truly agile. The first aspect is that customer requirement, competition criteria, market, technology, and social factors are changing competition in business environments (Agility drivers). In the second aspect, agile organization tries to Enrich and satisfy customers based on elements such as cost, time, function, and robustness. Agility capabilities included in the third aspect are flexibility, quickness, responsiveness, and competency. Finally, to be agile, organizations need to reinforce the agility enablers/pillars such as integration, competence, team building, technology, quality, change, partnership, market, education and welfare by leverage people and information technology (Foundation), master change and uncertainty (Control), and collaborative relationships (Strategy). However, these enablers have been presented earlier by Youssuf and et.al (1999). See figure-8-.

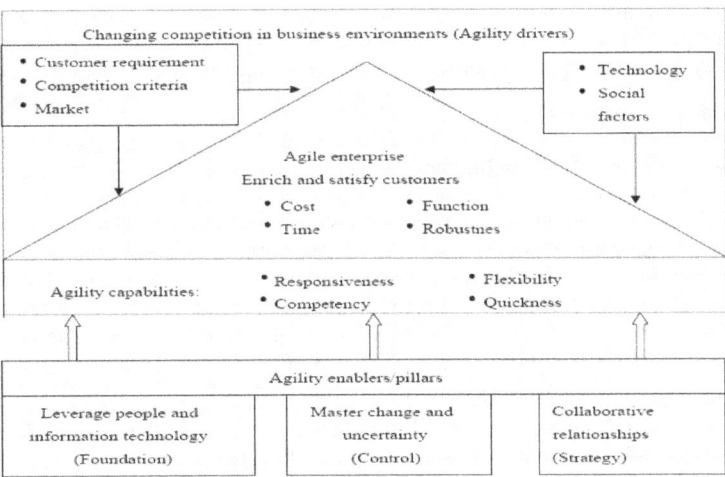

Figure-8- conceptual model of agile enterprise (Torng Lin and et.al (2005)

3. Critiques on agility conceptualizations

Organizations have realized that agility is essential for their survival and competitiveness. As mentioned before, available literature on agility has provided conceptual overviews of dimensions and has further conceptualized related elements. Obviously, different facets of agility have been emphasized by various authors and this has lead to varied views reflected in the literature. Despite the differences, all definitions of agility emphasize the speed and flexibility as the primary attributes of an agile. Thus, There is no commonly accepted definition of agility, and there are a large number of opinions concerning the meaning of this term. The term of agility is used in the research on how organization can cope with unpredicted and dynamically changing environment. An equally important attribute of agility is the effective response to change and uncertainty as Dove (1996) believe that agility is equal to knowledge management and change proficiency. Also, there is large number of publications on agility that are concerned with the specific strategies, techniques, and manufacturing and/or management practices. There is also a vast number and variety of strategies, techniques, and manufacturing and/or management practices described as a part of the agile enterprise. Only a few studies address the conceptualization and development of an integrated view of the agile enterprise concept. Although, some agility frameworks make an attempt to present a more integrated and holistic model, it still presents a view mostly focused on production and the technological aspects of enterprise. Moreover, most agility related publications are focused on the theoretical descriptions of agility and agility frameworks, mainly in manufacturing context. Only few of those metrics and frameworks were investigated in empirical research (Sherehiy and et.al, 2007).

Two main approaches to understanding and defining agility have been distinguished among reviewed literature. The first approach is a very broad and imprecise concept that encompasses all definitions and description of various practices and technologies that have been implemented in industry during last two decades. For example, Yusuf et al. (1999) stated that agility is the synthesized use of the developed and well-know technologies and methods of manufacturing. This view is supported by Goldman et al. (1995), who describes AM as the assimilation of all flexible production technologies, together with experience gained from total quality management (TQM), "JIT" production, and lean production. Thus, according to this approach, agility is mutually compatible with lean manufacturing, CIM, TQM, materials requirement planning II (MRPII), JIT, and employee empowerment. Conversely, Gunasekaran (2002) also noted that AM is not lean, or flexible manufacturing, or CIM. To clarify the differences between the AM and current practices, Sanchez and Nagi (2001) stated that the lean manufacturing is a collection of operational techniques focused on productive use of resources, whereas agility is an overall strategy. Those authors contrast agile and flexible manufacturing in reference to the type of adaptation: flexible manufacturing is reactive adaptation, while agile is proactive. According to Tsourveloudis and Valavanis (2002), the flexibility is a capability of the whole factory to change from one task or production route to another, and agility is a strategic ability of the whole enterprise to adapt to unpredicted and sudden changes in the market.

The second approach to agility is much more narrow and focused. In this approach, the main emphasis is placed on the ability of rapid adaptation; however, it is not simply the speed of response. Agility is a rapid and proactive adaptation of enterprise elements to unexpected and unpredicted changes, and represents a new and radically different manufacturing business model. Enterprise elements are the goals, objectives, technology, and organization. It has been argued that since most of currently applied and well-known practices are not adjusted well to uncertainty and unpredictability of the dynamically changing business environment, those methods cannot be included into the concept of agility.

The development of an agile organization framework presents a serious challenge. First of all, the agility concepts are not yet clearly defined and conceptualized. Although the main and most important attributes of agility have been identified, those attributes are supposed to be applied to such complex structures as an enterprise. It has been proposed in the literature that, in reference to agility, the following components of the enterprise are most important: organization, people, and technology. Each of these elements is multidimensional and complex itself. Thus, numerous agility related concepts, practices and characteristics proposed in the literature can be summarized and classified in two main ways. First, it can be classified into groups according to the adherence or relevance to the main attributes of the agility. In the reviewed literature, a large diversity of agility attributes has been identified. Based on the review, the following main attributes for an agile enterprise can be distinguished: (1) flexibility and adaptability, (2) responsiveness, (3) speed, (4) integration and low complexity, (5) mobilization of core competences, (6) high quality and customized products, and (7) culture of change. It should be noted that among those attributes, the core and global characteristics of agility that can be applied to all aspects of enterprise include flexibility, responsiveness, quickness, culture of change, integration, and low complexity. These core characteristics should be reflected in most important aspects of enterprise: production/service, organization, and workforce. Flexibility is considered as the ability to pursue different business strategies and tactics, to quickly change from one strategy/task/job to another. The strategies should be of course different in some reasonable extent, which will not endanger the integrity and main mission of the enterprise. Responsiveness is an ability to identify changes and opportunities and respond reactively or proactively to them. The term ''culture of change'' is a description of environment supportive of experimentation, learning, and innovation and is focused on the continuous monitoring environment to identify changes. Culture of change is an environment where people on all organizational levels have positive and fearless attitude to changes, different opinions, new ideas, and technology. In order to respond to changes the management and workers at all levels have to continuously scan the business and work environment to identify changes and opportunities related to customers, suppliers, and competitors that may be exploited by the enterprise. The market and business environment have to be monitored in order to determine new technologies, practices and methods of production, management, and organization that can be used by the enterprise to successfully respond and adapt to the changes. The speed is ability to complete requirements of all other agile characteristics in shortest possible time. The ability to learn, carry out tasks and operations and make changes in shortest possible time. The integration and low complexity dimension is defined as close and simple relations between the individual system components, easy and effortless flow of the materials, information and communication between the system components, organizational structures, people, and technology. The described general attributes have to be translated into specific indices for each of the main enterprise structure: organization, workforce, technology, and operations.

The other classification of agile organization concepts and characteristics is based on their adherence to the enterprise structures. The global agility attributes can be established as goals for the high-level management and are applicable to whole enterprise. Starting from these general goals of agility, the more specific sub-goals and the means to achieve them could be derived. The more specific goals and ways to achieve them would depend on the specificity of the each particular enterprise. However, at the highest and global level of the enterprise can be established few domains that should be the main focus for enterprise while trying to achieve agility. These main domains are focus on customer satisfaction; cooperation, learning and knowledge management, and development of culture of change.

4. Organizational agility framework

As you saw in literature review section, Agility as the term is the ability of an organization to respond quickly and successfully to the changes and also exploit them. Hormozi (2001) acknowledges that successful implementation of agile manufacturing requires changes in five areas as government regulations, business cooperation, information technology, reengineering, and employee flexibility. Sharifi and Zhange (2000) state that any organization firstly should identify agility level need it based on agility drivers' identification. To determine the current level of agility the organization has, capabilities of organization to respond the changes occurring in the turbulent environment is assessed and determined what capabilities the organization lack. After determining agility level the organization needs and the level of agility it has, strategic intent to become agile is necessary and then strategy development and formulation is started. By determining current and desired level of agility, as well as strategic planning, the providers help the organization to enhance existing abilities and capabilities are specified and promoted. In this section we are going to develop a practical methodology for agility's practice implementation in any organization. Indeed, as you have seen and recognized in the above materials, researchers suggest three main phases to agility. Those are agility drivers, agility's capabilities, and agility enablers or providers. Researches have introduced many factors about drivers, capabilities, and enablers in the field. Here, we combine those elements to form new and complete model of organizational agility areas. Figure-9-shows this model.

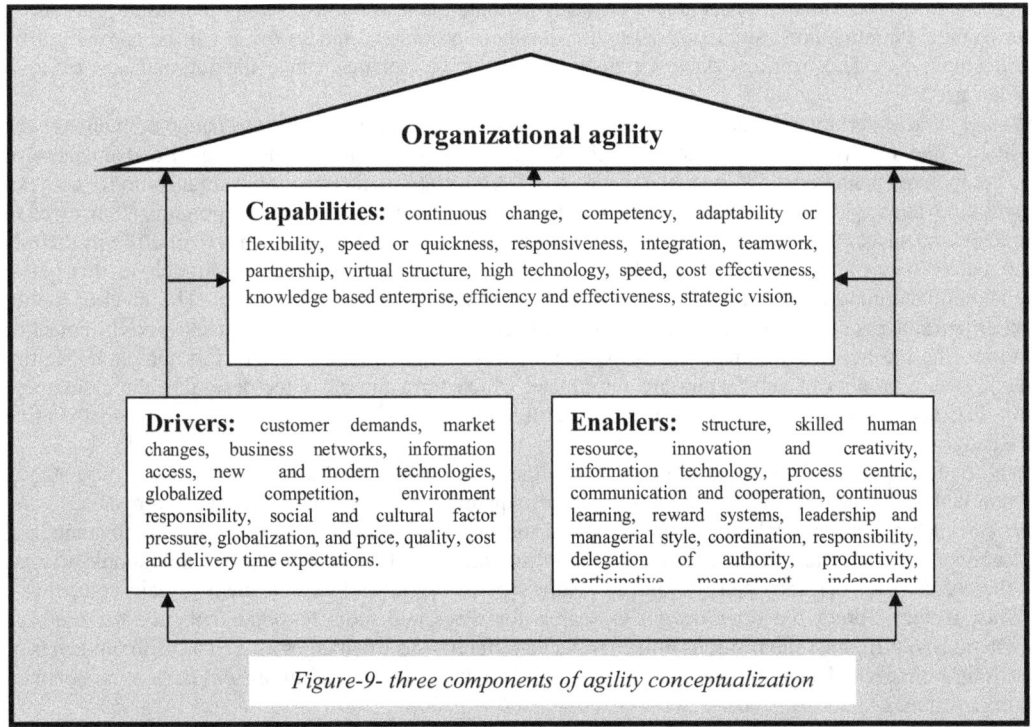

Figure-9- three components of agility conceptualization

As you know, the aim of this paper is to prepare a conceptual model for agility evaluation and enhancement to respond rapidly to the changes in the environment. In other words, we are going to combine previous models and approaches to propose step-by-step methodology upon which organizations can improve their performance based on agility. In literature, previous models and methodologies don't prepare any step by step process for agility implementation (except somehow Sharifi and Zhange (1999) model). Although those models indicate three part of agility as drivers, capabilities, and enablers but don't agree on elements of these basic parts. Furthermore, steps such as strategy formulation, public and special environment consideration, performance measurement process, and developing action plans sometimes aren't clearly identified and stated. As you saw in agility approaches section, authors have stated many different definitions for agility concept and don't have agreement about defining it. We define agility as an organizational ability to respond to the business drivers using enablers in order to gain useful capabilities. In summary, main characteristics of this methodology than previous models are:

This model has step by step and systematic approach and guides organizations to implement easily and successfully.

Internal drivers of change is considered and determined in this model

Many factors, capabilities and providers have been identified in this model

Strategy formulation and action plans are highlighted in order to move away from current state to desired state.

After given period, it is needed to be measured performance (or level of agility that organization has gained) to re-analysis conditions and design improvement initiatives.

Some agility frameworks make an attempt to present a more integrated and holistic model, it still presents a view mostly focused on production and the technological aspects of enterprise, but, this model can be applied to any organization (whether profit, nonprofit, service, public and private).

Figure-10- presents the practical methodology of organizational agility measurement and enhancement. Based on below presented model, any organization needs to analyze the dynamic or static state of organizational environment (as a first stage). Through considering mission and vision statement, goals and objectives, policies and procedures, rules, market change, liquidity flow, strategies, structure, business processes, and so on, it can be carried out by managers and employees. This work is done for determining the factors that cause the internal and external environment is varied.

At second stage, it is important to be determined the drivers that press on organization to change or challenge the organizational life and survive. These are factors such as market environment's changes, level and intensity of competition, competitor characteristics; customer need, social and cultural factors, intra-organizational context, technology and innovation, globalization, environmental responsibility, and so on. Therefore, organizations need to determine quickly and successfully agility's drivers as they face with these factors and survive and life of them is being challenged. Results of this and previous stage can be placed into SWOT analysis model. In this place, organization should determine the level of agility they need to respond change or pressures. The level of agility needed for an organization is considered to be equivalent to the degree of turbulence of the business environment of the organization. The business environment is, as explained before, broken down into factors which are agility drivers, and for each a number of sub-factors are introduced which form the basis for designing the assessment questionnaire. The questions basically address the degree of turbulence of each sub-factor for the organization (Sharifi and Zhange, 2001).

Then, it can be identified and fostered capabilities to readiness for changes and to overcome them (third stage). The most important and comprehensive elements of agile capabilities are flexibility, speed, competency, and responsiveness. Sometimes, agile capabilities were identified such as speed, flexibility, cost, quality, innovation, and proactivity, teamwork, participation, knowledge and skills, virtual structure. In general, organizations should attempt to reinforce these factors so that they can respond to changes or pressures and exploit them to gain competitive advantage. This, in turn, forces the organization to search for ways and tools to obtain/enhance the required capabilities. Obviously, different organizations will experience different sets of changes as well as different levels of pressures resulting from each change. Consequently, different combinations of capabilities will have to be obtained for different organizations.

Fourth stage compromises generic enablers or providers as culture and values, leadership, organizational change, performance measurement, information technology, and customer service. As with capabilities, organization can improve mentioned factors so that their potential to survive and act as a leader in the competitive markets is enhanced. In sum, based on results of third and forth stages, organization can informed with the condition of organization from agility's perspective. In this place, existing level of organizational agility is determined.

With recognizing organization's states, top managers can formulate and develop the best strategies to improving conditions with many development approaches so that the level of organizational agility is enhanced or reinforced. After given period, managers carry out performance evaluation process to determine that the results expected are attained and to determine deviations from objectives and aims. By this, organizations again repeat this cycle (after given or specified period) to find deviations and gaps through environmental and gap analysis so that they respond to changes, uncertainties and turbulences and gain a sustainable competitive advantage.

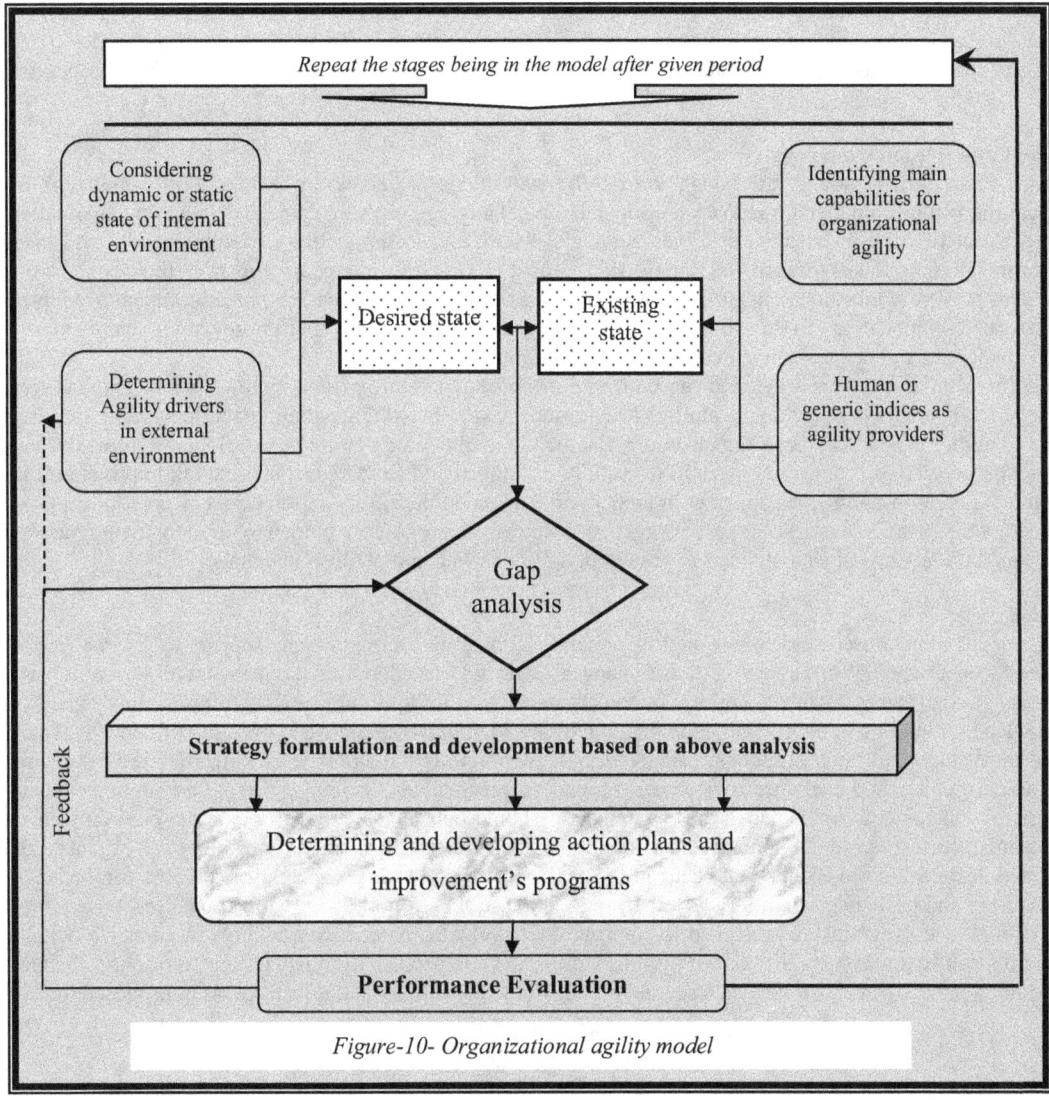

Figure-10- Organizational agility model

By combining the results of previous stages, it can be implemented gap analysis to compare desired state with current state of organization. For improving conditions, many development approaches are designed so that the level of organizational agility is enhanced. After this, managers carry out performance measurement process to determine that the results expected are attained and to determine deviations from objectives and aims. By this, organizations again repeat this cycle (after given or specified period) to find deviations and gaps through environmental and gap analysis so that they respond to changes, uncertainties and turbulences and they can gain a sustainable competitive advantage.

5. Suggestions and Recommendations

Nowadays, many organizations are facing constantly and intensely increasing competition stimulated by technological innovations, changing market environments and changing customer demands. This critical situation has led to a major revision in business priorities, strategic vision, and in the viability of conventional and even relatively contemporary models (Sharifi and Zhang, 1999). In an increasingly competitive market, there is a need to develop and improve organizational flexibility and responsiveness. In the past decade, most companies adopted business process re-engineering (BPR) and total quality management (TQM) and other improvement approaches in response to challenges and demands; however, these were not always successfully.

Although the methodology was developed based on a review of the literature pertaining to the subject, it was seen as necessary to validate its practical applicability. A comprehensive methodological approach to strategy building with regard to agility is needed among organizations and such a methodology could be developed in practice. The methodology proposed in this paper, though still to be fully developed and validated, constitutes an important effort in this regard and helps to bridge the gap between theory and practice in the agility's literature. For practitioners, the proposed methodology provides a basis for assessing their business situations and a guideline for recognizing missing capabilities and building up strategic policies in pursuit of agility as well competitive advantage.

6. Conclusion

Today's organization must operate in a highly dynamic competitive environment subject to internally and externally induced change. While many of these changes could be considered continuous, there are some very disruptive changes that can dramatically impinge on the organization's ability to survive. Therefore, in this paper, we firstly introduced definitions of agility and agile manufacturing to understand the basic meaning of concept. Then, several and most important models and approaches to implement and retain agility in organization are presented. Based on above models and literature review, we propose a practical methodology for agility implement and improvement. As mentioned in this paper, any organization should consider internal and external environment to recognize changers that press on it. So, managers must improve and enhance capabilities and abilities of organization to respond and also exploit the change that occur in the environment. After this, gap analysis process can be act to determine current and best state of agility's level. If there is constrains to improve organizational responsiveness, corrective actions and programs are designed to improve the level of organizational agility. In sum, we believe proposed model can help managers to enhance responsiveness and competency of organizations to respond changes and also exploit them. However, we suggest researchers to examine the validity and effectiveness of proposed model.

References

At. Kearney Institute (2002). How Governments Can Improve Public Sector Performance, LSE public policy Group, London.

Brown, N; Bessant, J (2003).The Manufacturing Strategy-Capabilities Links in Mass Customization and Agile Manufacturing, International Journal of Operations and Production Management, 5(4), p.p 707-730.

Burgess, T (1994).Making the Leap to Agility, International Journal of Operations & Production Management, Vol. 14 No. 11.

Christopher, M; Towill, D (2001).An Integrated Model of the Design of Agile Supply Chains, Journal of Distribution & Logistic Management, V.31, N.4, p.p 235-246.

Crocitto, M; Youssuf, M (2003).Human Side of Organizational Agility, Industrial Management & Data System, 103/6, pp.388-397.

Dove, R ; Hartman, S and Benson, S (1996). An Agile Enterprise Reference Model, US Agility Forum, Bethlehem University.

Dove, R (1999). Knowledge Management, Responsibility, and the Agile Enterprise, Journal of Knowledge Management, 3 (1), pp.18-35.

Drucker, P (1968). Comeback of The Entrepreneur, Management Today, April, pp.23-30.

Hage, J., Aiken, M (1969). Routine technology, social structure and organizational goals. Administrative Science Quarterly, 14, p.p 366–376.

Fliedner, G and Vokurka, R (1997). Agility: Competitive Weapon of The 1990's and Beyond?, Production and Inventory Management Journal, Vol. 38 No. 3, pp. 19-24.

Giachetti, R; Martinez, L; Saenz, O; Chen, C (2003). Analysis of the Structural Measures of Flexibility and Agility Using a Measurement Theoretical Framework, Journal of Production Economics, 86 (1), 47-62.

Goldman, S.L., Nagel, R.N (1993). Management, technology and agility: the emergence of a new era in manufacturing. International Journal of Technology Management, 8 (1/2), 18–38.

Goldman, S; Nagel, R; Preiss, K (1995). Agile Competitors and Virtual Organizations, Kenneth: van No strand Reinhold.

Gunasekaran, A (1999). Agile Manufacturing: A Framework for Research and Development, International Journal of Production Economics, Vol. 62 No. 1-2, pp. 87-105.

Hayen, G (1988). Change, Challenge and Continuity: An Entrepreneurial Vision from an Electronics Multinational, International Journal of Technology Management, Vol. 3 No. 3.

Helo, P (2004). Managing Agility and Productivity in the Electronics Industry, Industrial Management and Data systems, v.104, n.7: 567-577.

Hormozi, A.M (2001). Agile Manufacturing: The Next Logical Step, Benchmarking: an International Journal, 8 (2): 132-143.

Iacocca Institute (1991). 21st Century Manufacturing Enterprise Strategy, V.1, Lehigh University, Bethelham, USA.

Jackson, M; Johansson, C (2003). An Agility Analysis from a Production System Perspective, Journal of Manufacturing Systems, vol.14, No .06: 482-488.

Kid, P.T (1994). A 21st Century Paradigm in Agile Manufacturing: Forging New Frontiers, Addison-Wesley, Wokingham.

Levary, R (1992). Enhancing Competitive Advantage in Fast-Changing Manufacturing Environment, Ind England: 21-8.

Lin, Ching-Torng; Chiu, Hero and Chu, Po-Young (2004). Agility Index in The Supply Chain, International Journal Production Economics, 100(2):1-15.

Lin, Ching-Torng; Chiu, Hero and Chu, Po-Young (2005).Agility Evaluation Using Fuzzy Logic, International Journal of Production Economics, 101(2): pp.1-16.

Maskell, B (2001). The Age of Agile Manufacturing, Supply Chain Management: An International Journal; Vol.6, No 1: 5-11.

Meredith, S; Francis, D (2000). Journey Towards Agility: The Agile Wheel Explored The TQM Magazine, Vol.12, No. 2: 137-143.

Naylor, J.B; Naim, M.M and Berry, D (1999). Leagility: Integrating The Lean and Agile Manufacturing, International Journal of Production Economics, 62(1-2): 107-118.

Nagel, R., Dove, R. (1991), 21st century manufacturing enterprise strategy: an industry led view, Iacocca Institute, Lehigh University, Vol. 1.

Narasimhan, R; Swink, M and Soo Wook Kim (2006). Disentangling Leanness and Agility: An Empirical Investigation, Journal of Operations Management, No. 24(5): 440-457.

Power, D; Sohal, A (2005). Critical Success Factors in Agile Supply Chain Management, International Journal of Physical Distribution & Logistics Management, 31(4): 247-265.

Prince, J; Kay, J (2003). Combining Lean and Agile Characteristics, International Journal of Production Economics, 85(3): 305-318.

Ramesh, g; Devadasan, S (2007). Literature Review on the Agile Manufacturing Criteria, Journal of Manufacturing Technology Management, 18(2): 182-201.

Ren, J., Yusuf, Y.Y., Burns, N.D (2000). A prototype of measurement system for agile enterprise, International Conference on Quality, Reliability and Maintenance, Oxford, UK, pp. 247–252.

Ren, J., Yususf, Y.Y., Burns, N.D (2003). The effect of agile attributes on competitive priorities: a neural network approach. Integrated Manufacturing, 14 (6): 489–497.

Sanchez, L.M., Nagi, R (2001). A review of agile manufacturing systems, International Journal of Production Research, 39 (16): 3561–3600.

Sarkis, J (2001). Benchmarking for Agility, Benchmarking: An International Journal, 8, No. 2: 88-107.

Sharifi, H; Zhang, Z (1999). A Methodology for Achieving Agility in Manufacturing Organizations, International Journal of Production Economics, 20(4): 7-22.

Sharifi, H and Zhang, Z (2000). Agile Manufacturing in Practice: Application of a Methodology, International Journal of Operations & Production Management, 21(5/6): 772-794.

Sharp, J; Irani, Z; Desai, S (1999). Working Towards Agile Manufacturing in The UK Industry, International Journal of Production Economics, 62(5): 155-169.

Sherehiy, B; Karwowski, W and Layer, J (2007). A review of enterprise agility: Concepts, frameworks, and attributes, International Journal of Industrial Ergonomics 37(5): 445–460.

Thompson, J (1967). Organization in Action, McGraw-Hill, New York, NY.

Tsourveloudis, N.C., Valavanis, K.P (2002). On the measurement of enterprise agility. Journal of Intelligent and Robotic Systems, 33 (3): 329–342.

Vernadat, F (1999). Research Agenda for Agile Manufacturing, LGIPM, ENIM/University, International Journal of Agile Management Systems, 1(1): 37-40.

Vokurka, R; Fliedner, G (1998). Journey toward Agility, Industrial Management & Data Systems, 98(4): 165–171.

Youssuf, Y; Sarhadi, M; Gunasekaran, A (1999). Agile Manufacturing: The Drives, Concepts and Attributes; International Journal of Production economics, 62(1-2): 33-43.

Service Quality Measurement: An Empirical Investigation and a Critical Evaluation

AMROLAH AMINI (Ph.D)

Associate Professor, Allameh Tabatabaei University (ATU), Tehran, Iran.

aminij@atu.ac.ir

ALIREZA EMAMI

Master of Science, Tehran University, Tehran, Iran

memami@alumni.ut.ac.ir

MOSTAFA EMAMI*

Master of Science, Michigan Technological University (MTU)

memami@mtu.edu

***Corresponding Address**

Applied Research and Technology Office, Michigan Technological University

1400 Townsend Dr, Houghton, MI 49931

Tel & Fax : +1-(816) 237-0018

E-mail: memami@mtu.edu

Service Quality Measurement: An Empirical Investigation and a Critical Evaluation

ABSTRACT

Service quality has strong effects on customer satisfaction, loyalty, retention, and firms' performance superiority. This paper has two aims. The first is to show the differences between customers and employees' evaluations of service quality by implementing an empirical investigation in one of Iranian leading Banks. The second aim is to criticize the existing service quality measurement models in terms of two important difficulties with these methods 1)Simple Additive Relationships between service quality dimensions and 2)Under Achievement Constraint. This paper suggests General Criterion Methodology as a more effective and interactive methodology in order to remove the weaknesses of the existing measurement.

Key y words:

Bank Service

Service Quality

Customers and Employees' Evaluations

General Criterion Methodology

Critical Evaluation

Effectiveness

1. INTRODUCTION

It is well known that the quality, in service industries, is an important strategic factor that strongly effects on customers' satisfaction, loyalty, retention, and finally on firms' performance superiority. Because of the importance of the quality in service industries, one of the most important questions is that how the quality of services can be measured, *effectively?* This question is important because what we consider as high quality, in reality may not be so high or even may be low (what we get may not be what we see).

Several instruments have been developed to facilitate the quality (as SERVQUAL, INTERSERVQUAL, and SERVPERF) have been widely used in different service industries, but they have also been widely criticized.[23] For instance, the validity and the reliability of the difference between expectations and performance have been questioned. Several authors have also suggested that perception scores alone offer a better indication of service quality.[17,39,49,54] One of the other critiques explained by GroÈnroos is that it is required to takes into account the role of expectations from a dynamic perspective.[24] Also, there are some critiques on the simple additive relationships between service quality dimensions.[17,54] The other critics is their under achievement constraints. Several of these critiques have been explicitly addressed by Zeithaml.[57]

This paper has two aims. The first is to show the differences between customers and employees' evaluations of service quality by implementing an empirical investigation in one of Iranian leading Banks. The second aim is to criticize the existing service quality measurement models in terms of two important difficulties with these methods 1)Simple Additive Relationships between service quality dimensions and 2)Under Achievement Constraint. This paper suggests General Criterion Methodology as a more effective and interactive methodology in order to remove the weaknesses of the existing measurement.

2. THE LITERATURE

Quality, as a key strategic indicator in service industries, strongly effects on customers' satisfaction, loyalty, retention, and firms' performance superiority.[20] In literature, common research objectives for services are

- to identify dissatisfied customers
- to discover customer requirements or expectations
- to monitor and track service performance
- to assess overall company performance compared to competition
- to assess gaps between customer expectations and perceptions
- to gauge effectiveness of changes in service
- to appraise service performance of individuals and teams for rewards
- to determine expectations for a new service
- to monitor changing expectations in an industry
- to forecast customers' future expectations.

Results of several researches clearly confirm that:

- ❖ there is a positive relationship between the quality of services and customer satisfaction,[31,37,51]
- ❖ there is a positive relationship between customer satisfaction and loyalty/retention.[46,47]

[Insert Figure 1 near here]

- ❖ finally, there is a positive relationship between customers' retention and firm performance.

To days, almost all researchers confirm the positive relationship between the service quality and the firms' performance. But two more important questions are

1)what is the nature of the service quality? 2)how the quality of services can be measured, effectively?

What is the quality? Service quality often defined as the comparison of service expectations with actual performance perceptions (GAP analysis). [43] The central idea in GAP models is that service quality is a function of the different scores between expectations and perceptions. In other words, service quality is the customer's judgment of overall excellence of the service provided in relation to the quality that was expected

[Insert Figure 2 near here]

. But what components create customer expectations? Three important components of customer expectations are as follows:

1. *Desired Service Level:* wished-for level of service quality that customer believes can and should be delivered.
2. *Adequate Service Level:* minimum acceptable level of service.
3. *Predicted Service Level:* service level that customer believes firm will actually deliver
4. *Zone of Tolerance:* range within which customers are willing to accept variations in service delivery.

[Insert Figure 3 near here]

How can we measure the quality of services, effectively? On an operational level, research in service quality has been dominated by the SERVQUAL instrument, based on the so-called GAP model.[43] Some researchers have used GAP model to measure internal service quality (INTERSERVQUAL).[21,30,33] As shown in Figure 3, service quality is naturally a multi-dimensional concept.[40,41]

[Insert Figure 4 near here]

Five key dimensions of service quality have been identified as reliability, responsiveness, assurance, empathy and tangibles. Reliability is defined as the ability to deliver the promised service dependably and accurately. Responsiveness is described as the willingness to help customers and provide prompt service. Assurance is the service quality that focuses on the ability to inspire trust and confidence. Empathy is described as the service aspect that stresses the treatment of customers as individuals. Finally, tangibles focus on the elements that represent the service physically.

Assessing service quality is a hot subject for recent researches. [14,42,45,48,50,51] For example; several researches have been implemented on Hotel and Hospital industries. [9,10,32,55] Nitecki assessed the service quality of the university library.[36] Doholbkar et al. and Finn et al. applied SERVQUAL method in retail sector.[15,18,19] There are also a lot of papers on the measurement of the quality of bank services.[1,2,3,4,5,8,12,31,35] We can also find a lot of papers in different countries around the worlds that focused on the important and hot subject of service quality measurement and assessment. [11,27,28,29, 35,53]

Are the existing measurement methods effective? One of the critical questions in service industries is that how the quality of services could be measured, effectively? Although the classical multi-dimensional service quality measurement methods have been widely used in several service industries, but they have also been widely criticized.[13,17,24,39,49,54] Two critical difficulties with all existing quality measurement methods are related to considering simple additive relationships between service dimensions and under achievement constraints. This paper is aimed to relax these weak points by developing GMSQM.

3. RESULTS OF AN EMPIRICAL INVESTIGATION

In 2004, a field research has been implemented to measure bank service quality in one of Iranian leading banks (Bank Refah).[7] The primary objectives of this research were to answer the following research questions:

1. What factors affect on bank service quality?
2. What are the relative importance weights of bank service quality dimensions from stand points of the customers and employees?
3. How about the gaps between customers and employees expectations and bank actual performance?
4. How customers and employees score bank service quality?
5. Statistically, is there a meaningful difference between two sets of the relative importance weights were defined by customers and employees?

First question was answered by literature review. To answer the second and the third questions, an adjusted SERVQUAL questionnaire was designed and distributed among bank customers and employees. (See Appendix 1) The questionnaire was included 8 quality dimensions with 32 quality factors or elements. To answer the fourth question, four classical service quality measurement methods (SERVQUAL, weighted SERVQUAL, SERVPERF and weighted SERVPERF) were applied. Also, in order to determine the relative importance weights for weighted SERVQUAL and weighted SERVPERF models, Shannon Entropy Method was used. Finally, the fifth and the sixth questions were answered by using statistical methods.

[Insert Table 1 near here]

In summary, this research had the following implications:

❖ Both customers and employees have defined different average relative importance weights for all 8 quality dimensions and all 32 service quality factors.

❖ Statistically, there was a meaningful difference between the sets of the average relative importance weights were defined by the customers the employees.

❖ Both customers and employees evaluated bank service quality higher than average.

❖ Customers' average scores were meaningfully higher than that of the employees.

The lessons we learned from this research were:

• Service quality measurement problems are naturally multi-dimension and complex problems. The problem is one of value trade-off that requires the subjective judgment of the DM.

• Mostly, customers' preference structure is different from that of the employees

• Classical service quality measurement methods can not incorporate DM preferences, effectively. They are not interactive.

• Designing a new general approach for service quality measurement is a necessity in order to remove the classical models weak points.

4. GENERALIZED CRITERION METHOD

Service quality measurement problems are naturally complex. Complex problems involve multiple and mostly conflicting objectives or criteria and often no dominant alternative exists that is better than all other alternatives in terms of all objectives. In this case, the problem is one of value trade-off that requires the subjective judgment of the DM. Such problems are complex, because improving achievement with respect to one objective can be accomplished only at the expense of the other.

Service quality is naturally a multi-dimensional concept.[40,41] Five key dimensions of service quality are reliability, responsiveness, assurance, empathy and tangibles. In other words, to solve a service quality measurement problem, we need to render a Multi Attribute Decision Making (MADM) model. In reality, DM should assess each alternatives based on several dimensions or a set of multi-attribute alternatives. Defining a vector A (A1, A2, …., Am) for all possible alternatives each with k relevant attributes or dimensions, DM seeks to identify each alternative's service quality score and rank them from one with the highest score to one with the lowest score.

As mentioned in literature, there are some difficulties with classical service quality measurement methods. Two important critiques are *the simple constant additive relationships between service dimensions*, and the other constraint we named it *under achievement constraint*. Under achievement constraint implies that all existing service quality measurement methods just try to measure the undesirable deviations from the customers' expectations. These methods suppose that a service provider performs equal or lower than customers' expectation (not higher than expectations) in terms of a given quality dimension. In other words, classical GAP models just determine d^-_i in their complex multi-dimensional service quality measurement process. Mathematically, respect to *i*th quality dimension and considering G as an expectation, it is possible for a firm to perform lower P1, as P1, between P1 -G, as G, or even between G-P2.

[Insert Figure 5 near here]

In a real world service quality measurement problem, DM seeks to calculate the value of one of the following four equations for each alternative j:[6]

$$(1)\ Z_j = \sum_{i=1}^{k} \left(W_i^+ d_i^+ + W_i^- d_i^-\right)$$

$$(2)\ Z_j = \sum_{i=1}^{k} P_i \sum_{l=1}^{ni} \left(W_{il}^+ d_i^+ + W_{il}^- d_i^-\right)$$

$$(3)\ Z_j = \sum_{i=1}^{k} P_i \left(d_i^+ + d_i^-\right)$$

$$(4)\ Z_j = \sum_{i=1}^{k} \left(F_i^+ d_i^+ + F_i^- d_i^-\right)$$

Where $f_i(X) - d_i^+ + d_i^- = g_i$
$X \in C_s$

Considering a quality measurement problem with k quality dimensions, where gi denotes target levels or customer expectation for *i*th quality dimension (i:1,2,...,k), let define the following symbols:

W_i^+, W_i^- : nonnegative constants representing the relative weights to be assigned to the respective positive and negative deviational variables

W_{il}^+, W_{il}^- : nonnegative constants representing the relative weights to be assigned to each of the $l = 1, 2, \ldots, ni$ different classes within the ith category to which the value of Pi is assigned.

Pi: priority factor as a ranking symbol that can be interpreted to mean that no substitutions across categories of goals will be permitted and no combination of relative weighting attached to deviational variables can produce a substitution across categories.

d_i^+, d_i^-: positive and negative deviational variables.

$f_i(x)$: actual performance in terms of ith quality attributes.

Accordingly, a lower total undesirable deviation from customers' expectation or a higher total desirable deviation from customers' expectation can be translated as a higher quality. In other words, this approach lets DM to consider performance that is higher expectation in terms of some or all desirable attributes or dimensions.

As mentioned, service quality measurement problems are naturally complex multi-dimensional problems. In these cases, the critical question is that how DM trade-offs different attributes? Determining the trade-off ratios for different attributes is regarded as a difficult step of formulating multidimensional problems. Several methods have been proposed in order to determine the trade-off ratio s and define the proper form of objective function. For example, Charnes and Cooper[16] suggest the interval methodology, Gass [22] proposes the normalized vector method based on the AHP of Saaty, O'Leary[38] proposes the conjoint analysis, Sakawa[44] suggests to utilize the concept of the fuzzy set and membership function, and Takeda and Yu[52] provide a good discussion on the pair wise comparisons. Hannan [25,26] suggests value function method. According to Hannan's suggestion and well known generalized criterion method of Promethee, Martel and Aouni [34] propose an approach that the DM can build his preference functions along with the goals. Also an effective procedure of incorporating the DM's preferences provided by Anvary Rostamy and Tabata.[6]

According to General Criterion Methods (GCM), for each criteria i and for each pair of performance (x,y), a function Pi(x,y) can be defined to measures the intensity of the DM's preference. In other words:

$P_i(x,y) = 0$ for indifference case, $f_i(x) \approx f_i(y)$

$P_i(x,y) \approx 0$ for weak form of preference, $f_i(x) \succ f_i(y)$

$P_i(x,y) \approx 1$ for strong form of preference, $f_i(x) \succ\succ f_i(y)$

$P_i(x,y) = 1$ for absolutely preference case, $f_i(x) \succ\succ\succ f_i(y)$

Defining $d_i = f_i(x) - f_i(y)$ as the difference in performance between the action x,y in relation to criterion i, this performance function can be defined by two criterion or value function noted by $F(d_i^-)$ (a decreasing function for undesirable deviation from target or goal) and $F(d_i^+)$ (an increasing function for desirable deviation from target or goal). According this method, in a service quality measurement problem with k dimensions or quality elements, a DM can define k two-sided attributes with probably different preferences functions.

[Insert Figure 6 near here]

General speaking, a DM can calculate firms' service quality scores and rank them from one with the highest value of Z to the one with the lowest by using the following equation:

$$Z = \sum_{i=1}^{k}\left[w_i F_i d_i^+ + w_i F_i d_i^-\right] \quad \text{where} \quad d_i^+ \times d_i^- = 0 \qquad (2)$$

It is clear that the preference functions may be different for negative and positive deviations from targets or expectations and for the different criteria (different service quality dimensions or elements). The functions may also change with time horizon of decision making. Figure 7 shows some samples.

[Insert Figure 7 near here]

5. CONCLUSIONS AND FINAL REMARKS

Quality is a critical success factor in service industries. To days, it is well known that quality has strong effects on customer satisfaction, loyalty, retention and firms' performance superiority but the question is that how the quality of services can be measured, effectively? To answer the question several methods have been developed in literature. Although these models are widely used in service industries, but they have been also widely criticized. Two important critiques on existing service quality measurement models are the simple additive relationships between service quality dimensions and under achievement constraint. In order to relax these critical weak points and improve the effectiveness of the service quality measurement process, a GMSQM is developed. According to this method, a lower total undesirable deviation from the customer expectations or a higher total desirable deviation from the customer expectations can be translated as a higher quality. This methodology allows DM to define different preference functions for negative and positive deviations from expectations, for the different criteria (different service quality dimensions or elements) and also for different times. The difference between fuzzy method and the proposed GMSQM is respect to the philosophy that underlies the DM's input its power in incorporating DM's preferences in an easier and more effective manner.

REFERENCES

Aldlaigan H, Buttle F. (2002) SYSTRA-S Q: A New Measure of Bank Service Quality, *International Journal of Service Industry Management*, 13(4), pp. 362-381.

Allred. A.T. (2000a) Employee Evaluations of Service Quality at Banks and Credit Unions, *International Journal of Bank Marketing,* 19(4), pp. 179-185.

Allred A.T., Addams H.L. (2000b) Service Quality at Banks and Credit Unions: What do Their Customers Say?, *Managing Service Quality*, 10(1), pp. 52-60.

Allred A.T. (2001) Employee Evaluations of Service Quality at Banks and Credit Unions, *International Journal of Bank Marketing* 2001; 19 (4)/4:179-185.

Angur M.G., Nataraajan R., Jahera J.S. Jr. (1999) Service Quality in the Banking Industry: An Assessment in a Developing Economy, *International Journal o f Bank Marketing*, 17(3), pp.116-23.

Anvary Rostamy A.A., Tabata Y. (1998) Appraising the Effectiveness of GP in Incorporating the Decision Maker (DM)'s Preferences, *Journal of the Operations Research Society of Japan*, 41(2), pp. 279-288.

Anvary Rostamy A.A., Torabi Goudarzi M, Alimohammadlou M. (2005) Comparative Study of Bank Service Quality From View Points of the Customers and Employees, *Journal of Modares Human Science*, Special Issue, 42, pp.53-78 (In Persian)

Avkiran N.K. (1994) Developing an Instrument to Measure Customer Service Quality in Branch Banking, *International Journal of Bank Marketing,* 12(5), pp. 10-18.

Babakus E., Mangold W.G. (1992) Adapting the SERVQUAL Scale to Hospital Services: An Empirical Investigation, *Health Services Research*, 26, pp. 767 -86.

Barsky J.D. (1992) Customer Satisfaction in the Hotel Industry: Meaning and Measurement. *Hospitality Research Journal*, 16(1), pp. 51-73.

Berry L.L., Parasuraman A., Zeithaml V.A. (1994) Improving Service Quality in America: Lessons Learned. Academy o f Management Executive, 8(2), pp. 32-52.

Blanchard F.R., Galloway R.L. (1994) Quality in Retail Banking, *International Journal of Service Industry Management,* 5(4), pp. 5-23.

Boulding W., Kalra A., Staelin R., Zeithaml V.A. (1993) A Dynamic Process Model of Service Quality: from Expectations to Behavioral Intentions, *Journal of Marketing Research*, 30, pp. 7 -27.

Brady M., Cronin J.J., Brand R.R. (2002) Performance-only Measurement of Service Quality: A

Replication and Extension, *Journal or Business Research*, 55, pp. 7-3.

Carman J.M. (1990) Consumer Perceptions of Service Quality: An Assessment of the SERVQUAL Dimensions, *Journal of Retailing*, 66, pp. 33-55.

Charnes A., Cooper W.W. (1977) Goal Programming and Multiple Objective Optimizations, *European Journal of Operational Research*, 1, pp. 39-54.

Cronin J.J., Taylor S. A. (1992) Measuring Service Quality: A Reexamination and Extension, *Journal of Marketing*, 56, pp. 55-68.

Daholbkar P.A, Thorpe D.I., Rentz J.O. (1996) A Measure of Service Quality for Retail Stores: Scale Development and Validation, *Journal of the Academy of Marketing Science*, 24, pp. 3-16.

Finn D.W., Lamb C.W. (1991) An Evaluation of the SERVQUAL Scale in Retail Setting. In Solomon, R. H. (Ed.), *Advances in Consumer Research*, Vol. 18, Association of Consumer Research, Provo, UT,.

Fitzsimmons J.A., Fitzsimmons M.J. (1994) *Service Management for Competitive Advantage*, McGraw-Hill, New York, NY.

Frost F.A., Kumar M. (2000) INTSERVQUAL: An Internal Adaptation of the GAP Model in a Large Service Organization, *Journal of Services Marketing*, 14(5), pp. 358-377.

Gass S.I. (1987) The Setting of Weights in Linear Goal Programming, *Computer and Operations Research*, 14, pp. 227-229.

Gremler D.D., Brown S. W. (1996) Service Loyalty; Its Nature, Importance and Implications. in Edvardsson, B., Brown, S.W., Johnston, R. and Scheuing, E. (Eds), QUIS V: Advancing Service Quality: A Global Perspective, ISQA, New York, NY, pp. 171-81.

GroÈnroos C. (1993) Toward a Third Phase in Service Quality Research: Challenges and Future Directions. in Swartz, T.A., Bowen, D. and Brown, S.W. (Eds), Advances in Services Marketing Management, Vol. 3, pp. 49-64.

Hannan E.L. (1981) Linear Programming with Multiple Fuzzy Goals, *Fuzzy and Systems*, 6, pp. 279-288.

Hannan E.L. (1985) An Assessment of some Critic is m of GP, *Computer and Operations Research*, 12, pp. 525-541.

Hoxley M. (2000) Measuring UK Construction Professional Service Quality:The What, How, When and Who, *International Journal of Quality & Reliability Management*, 17(4/5), pp. 511-526.

Jannadi O.A., Al-saggaf H. (2000) Measurement of Quality in Saudi Arabian Service Industry, *International Journal of Quality & Reliability Management*, 17(9), pp. 949-965.

Kandampully J., Menguc B. (2000) Managerial Practices to Sustain Service Quality: An Empirical Investigation of New Zealand Service Firms, *Marketing Intelligence and Planning*, 18(4), pp..175- 184.

Kang G., James J., Kostas A. (2002) Measurement of Internal Service Quality: Application of the SERVQUAL Battery to Internal Service Quality, *Managing Service Quality*, 12 (5), pp. 278 -291.

Lasser M., Walfried C.M., Winsor R.D. (2000) Service Quality Perspectives and Satisfaction in Private Banking, *International Journal of Bank Marketing*, 18(4), pp.181-199.

Lewis R.C. (1987) The Measurement of Gaps in the Quality of Hotel Services, *International Journal of Hospitality Management,* 6(2), pp. 83-88.

Kang G., James J., Kostas A. (2002) Measurement of Internal Service Quality: Application of the SERVQUAL Battery to Internal Service Quality, *Managing Service Quality,* 12(5), pp. 278-291.

Martel J.A., Aouni B. (1990) Incorporating the Decision Maker's Preferences in the GP Models, *Journal of the Operational Research Society*, 41, pp. 1121-1132.

Newman K., Cowling A. (1996) Service Quality in Retail Banking: The Experience of Two British Clearing Banks, *International Journal of Bank Marketing,* 14(6), pp. 3-11.

Nitecki D.A., Hernon P. (2000) Measuring Service Quality at Yale University's Libraries, *The Journal of Academic Librarianship*, 26(4), pp. 259–273.

Oliver R.L. (1993) A Conceptual Model of Service Quality and Service Satisfaction: Compatible Goals, Different Concepts. In Swartz, T.A., Bowen, D. E. and Brown, S. W. (Eds), Advances in Services Marketing and Management: Research and Practice, Vol. 2, JAI Pres s, Greenwich, CT, pp. 65-85.

O'Leary D.E., O'Laery J.H. (1984) The Use of Conjoint Analysis in the Determination of G P Weights for a Dec is io n Support System. In Dec is io n Making with Multiple Objective. Y. Y. Haimes and V. Chankong Eds . Springer, New York, pp. 287-299.

Orwig R.A., Pearson J., Cochran D. (1997) An Empirical Investigation into the Validity of SERVQUAL in the Public Sector, P AQ ,pp. 54-68.

Parasuraman A., Zeithaml V.A, Berry L.L. (1985) A Conceptual Model of Service Quality and Its Implication for Future Research, *Journal of Marketing*, 49, pp. 41 -50.

Parasuraman A., Zeithaml V.A, Berry L.L. (1988) SERVQUAL: A Multi-item Scale for Measuring Customer Perceptions of Service, *Journal of Retailing*, 64(1), pp.12-40.

Robledo M.A. (2001) Measuring and Managing Service Quality: Integrating Customer Expectations, *Managing Service Quality*, 11(1), pp. 22 -31.

Rosene F. (2003) Complacency and Service Quality: An Overlooked Condition in the GAP Model, *Journal of Retailing and Consumer Services*, 10, pp. 51– 55.

Sakawa M. (1984) Interactive Fuzzy Goal Programming for Multiobjective Nonlinear Programming Problems and Its Application to Water Quality Management, *Control and Cybernetics*, 13, pp. 217-228.

Siu N. Y.M, Cheung J.T. (2001) A Measure of Retail Service Quality, *Marketing Intelligence & Planning*, 19(2), pp. 88-96.

Spreng R. A., Mackoy R.D. (1996) An Empirical Examination of a Model of Perceived Service Quality and Satisfaction, *Journal of Retailing*, 72(2), pp. 201-214.

Stank T.P., Goldsby T.J., Vickery S.K. (1999) Effect of Service Supplier Performance on Satisfaction and Loyalty of Store Managers in the Fast Food Industry, *Journal of Operations Management*, 17, pp.429–447.

Stanley L., Wisner J.D. (2002) The Determinants of Service Quality: Issues for Purchasing, *European Journal of Purchasing and Supply Management*, 8, pp. 97-109.

Strandvik T., Liljander V. A. (1994) Comparison of Episode Performance and Relationship Performance for a Discrete Serv ic e, in Kleinaltenkamp, M. (Ed.), Dienstleistungs Marketing: Konzeptionenund Anwendungen, Gabler Edition Wissenschaft, Berlin.

Sureshchandar G.S., Rajendran G.S., Anantharaman R.N. (2002) Determinants of Customer-perceived Service Quality: A Confirmatory Factor Analysis Approach, *Journal of Services Marketing*, 16(1), pp. 9 -34.

Sureshchandar G.S., Rajendran G.S., Anantharaman R.N. (2002) The Relationship between Service Quality and Customer Satisfaction: A Factor Specific Approach, *Journal of Services Marketing*, 16(4), pp. 363-379.

Takeda E., Yu P.L.(1995) Assessing Priority Weights from Subsets of Pair wise Comparison in Multiple Criteria Optimization Problems, *European Journal of Operational Research*, 86, pp. 122-136.

Teas R. K. (1993b) Consumer Expectations and the Measurement of Perceived Service Quality, *Journal of Professional Services Marketing*, 8(2), pp. 33-54.

Teas R.K. (1993a) Expectations, Performance Evaluation, and Consumers' Perceptions of Quality, *Journal of Marketing*, 57(4), pp.18-34.

Tsang N., Qu H. (2000) Service Quality in China's Hotel Industry: A Perspective from Tourists and Hotel Managers, *International Journal of Contemporary Hospitality Management*, 12(5), pp. 316-326.

Zeithaml V.A., Parasuraman A, Berry L.L. (1990) *Delivering Quality Service: Balancing Customer Perceptions and Expectations*, Free Press, New York, NY.

Zeithaml, V.A., Berry L.L., Parasuraman, A. (1996) The Behavioral Consequences of Service Quality, *Journal of Marketing*, 60, pp. 31-46.

Appendix 1 Bank Service Quality Measurement Questionnaire

Bank Service Quality Factors (1)	Quality Fctors Importance Weights (2) 1 2 3 4 5	Assess Bank Actual Performance 1 2 3 4
Tangibles:		
1. Employees who have a neat, professional appearance	☐ ☐ ☐ ☐ ☐	☐ ☐ ☐ ☐
2. Work environment being comfort and attractive, visually appealing facilities	☐ ☐ ☐ ☐ ☐	☐ ☐ ☐ ☐
3. Visually appealing materials associated with the service	☐ ☐ ☐ ☐ ☐	☐ ☐ ☐ ☐
4. Easily to find a branch, easy to locate and contact	☐ ☐ ☐ ☐ ☐	☐ ☐ ☐ ☐
5. Material being visually appealing	☐ ☐ ☐ ☐ ☐	☐ ☐ ☐ ☐
Reliability		
6. Perform the service right and accurate especially at first time	☐ ☐ ☐ ☐ ☐	☐ ☐ ☐ ☐
7. Providing services at the promised time	☐ ☐ ☐ ☐ ☐	☐ ☐ ☐ ☐
8. Willing to help and correct the mistakes and errors	☐ ☐ ☐ ☐ ☐	☐ ☐ ☐ ☐
9. Dependability and the ability of employees in handling customers' service Problems	☐ ☐ ☐ ☐ ☐	☐ ☐ ☐ ☐
Responsiveness		
10. Being polite and kind especially when employees are very busy	☐ ☐ ☐ ☐ ☐	☐ ☐ ☐ ☐
11. Keeping customers informed about when services will be performed	☐ ☐ ☐ ☐ ☐	☐ ☐ ☐ ☐
12. Willingness to provide advises and suggestions to guide customers	☐ ☐ ☐ ☐ ☐	☐ ☐ ☐ ☐
13. Easy to meet or have a session to bank managers or supervisors	☐ ☐ ☐ ☐ ☐	☐ ☐ ☐ ☐
14. Prompt service to customers, Respond quickly and efficiently	☐ ☐ ☐ ☐ ☐	☐ ☐ ☐ ☐
Confidence or Assurance		
15. Employees who instill confidence in customer, making customer feel safe in their transactions	☐ ☐ ☐ ☐ ☐	☐ ☐ ☐ ☐
16. Employee who have the knowledge to answer clear and understandable	☐ ☐ ☐ ☐ ☐	☐ ☐ ☐ ☐
17. Providing appropriate, accurate, clear communication and informing customers of their accounts changes	☐ ☐ ☐ ☐ ☐	☐ ☐ ☐ ☐
Empathy		
18. Employees devote enough times to their customers	☐ ☐ ☐ ☐ ☐	☐ ☐ ☐ ☐
19. Sincerely concerning about the problems and willing to help customers	☐ ☐ ☐ ☐ ☐	☐ ☐ ☐ ☐
20. Providing services in holidays to remove customers' problems	☐ ☐ ☐ ☐ ☐	☐ ☐ ☐ ☐
21. Giving individual attention to customers and having the customer's best interest in heart	☐ ☐ ☐ ☐ ☐	☐ ☐ ☐ ☐
Process		
22. Using standard processes in providing banking services	☐ ☐ ☐ ☐ ☐	☐ ☐ ☐ ☐
23. Employees who provide the services with an appropriate speed	☐ ☐ ☐ ☐ ☐	☐ ☐ ☐ ☐
24. Modern equipment and having up-to-date equipment	☐ ☐ ☐ ☐ ☐	☐ ☐ ☐ ☐
25. Reasonable waiting time	☐ ☐ ☐ ☐ ☐	☐ ☐ ☐ ☐
26. Enough number of employees to meet the demands	☐ ☐ ☐ ☐ ☐	☐ ☐ ☐ ☐
Responsibility		
27. Being polite and kind and behavior rationally	☐ ☐ ☐ ☐ ☐	☐ ☐ ☐ ☐
28. Appropriate geographical distribution of the branches in different area	☐ ☐ ☐ ☐ ☐	☐ ☐ ☐ ☐
29. Willing to accommodate special request of the special customers,	☐ ☐ ☐ ☐ ☐	☐ ☐ ☐ ☐
Service Organizational Factors		
30. Bank reputation compare to the other banks	☐ ☐ ☐ ☐ ☐	☐ ☐ ☐ ☐
31. The ability to meet customers' different needs and request, service diversification		

32. Balancing branches services to the different requested services

*Numbers 1, 2, 3, 4, 5 in column (2) denote not important, relatively important, average importance, very important and high important, respectively.
*Numbers 1, 2, …,9 in column (1) denote bank actual quietly degree.

Priority Ranks of the Bank Service Quality Factors From View Points of Customers	Priority Ranks of the Bank Service Quality Factors From View Points of Customers	Adjusted Relative Importance weights of the Quality factors (Determined by Customers) W'_{je}	Adjusted Relative Importance weights of the Quality factors (Determined by Customers) W'_{jc}	Relative Importance weights of the Quality factors (Determined by Employees) λ_{je}	Relative Importance weights of the Quality factors (Determined by Employees) λ_{jc}	Relative importance weights of the factors (calculated by Shannon Entropy method using employees' questionaire data) W_{je}	Relative Importance weights of the factors (calculated by Shannon Entropy method using customers questionaire data) W_{jc}	Bank Service Quality Factors
	24							1. Employees who have a neat, professional appearance
26	26	0.03291	0.02964	0.03218	0.03046	0.0143	0.0256	2. Work environment being comfort and attractive, visually appealing facilities
24	31	0.0334	0.03069	0.03242	0.03099	0.0199	0.0251	3. Visually appealing materials associated with the service
29	20	0.03373	0.03201	0.03258	0.03165	0.0488	0.0336	4. Easily to find a branch, easy to locate and contact
28	28	0.03214	0.03184	0.0318	0.03157	0.0184	0.0265	5. Material being visually appealing
25	29	0.03307	0.0335	0.03226	0.03238	0.0162	0.0202	6. Perform the service right and accurate especially at first time
27	25	0.03397	0.03497	0.03269	_0.03309_	0.0126	0.0152	7. Providing services at the promised time
3	3	0.03508	0.03408	_0.03322_	0.03266	0.0141	0.0146	8. Willing to help and correct the mistakes and errors
30	30	0.03288	0.03319	0.03217	0.03223	0.0133	0.0158	9. Dependability and the ability of employees in handling customers' service problems
22	22	0.03423	0.03413	0.03282	0.03268	0.0143	0.021	10. Being polite and kind especially when employees are very busy
_32_	17	0.03132	0.0324	0.03139	0.03185	0.0188	0.0242	11.Keeping customers
31		0.02954	0.03005	0.03049	0.03067	0.0201	0.022	

_32_								informed about when services will be performed
4	18	0.03017	0.0306	0.03081	0.03095	0.0188	0.0182	12. Willingness to provide advises and suggestions to guide customers
10	14	0.03037	0.03163	0.03091	0.03146	0.018	0.0186	13. Easy to meet or have a session to bank managers or supervisors
2	12	0.02979	0.03064	0.03062	0.03097	0.0235	0.0229	14. Prompt service to customers, Respond quickly and efficiently
21	19	0.0349	0.03337	0.03314	0.03232	0.021	0.0183	15. Employees who are confidence and making customer feel safe in their transactions
9	21	0.03477	0.0318	0.03307	0.03155	0.0179	0.0155	16. Employee who have the knowledge to answer clear and understandable
12	10	0.02957	0.03245	0.0305	0.03187	0.0322	0.0192	17. Providing appropriate, accurate, clear communication and informing customers of accounts changes
5	11	0.02751	0.02968	0.02942	0.03048	0.0222	0.0197	18. Employees devote enough times to their customers
23	23	0.02454	0.02771	0.02779	0.02945	0.0237	0.024	19. Sincerely concerning about the problems and willing to help customers
19	16	0.01215	0.02164	_0.01955_	_0.02603_	0.0951	0.0924	20. Providing services in holidays to remove customers' problems
11		0.02286	0.02881	0.02682	0.03003	0.038	0.0491	21. Giving individual attention to customers, and having the customer's best interest in heart

Rank A	Rank B	V1	V2	V3	V4	V5	V6	Item
8	18	0.03	0.03128	0.03072	0.03129	0.0318	0.0331	22. Using standard processes in providing banking services
27	14	0.03243	0.03115	0.03195	0.03123	0.0165	0.0192	23. Employees who provide the services with an appropriate speed
13	*1*	0.03568	0.03337	0.0335	0.03232	0.0795	0.0725	24. Modern equipment and having up-to-date equipment
6	7	0.03328	0.03175	0.03236	0.03153	0.0432	0.0389	25. Reasonable waiting time
9	16	0.03559	0.03311	0.03347	0.03219	0.0688	0.0772	26. Enough number of employees to meet the demands
15	8	0.03519	0.03227	0.03328	0.03178	0.0251	0.04	27. Being polite and kind and behavior rationally
4	17	0.03379	0.02959	0.0326	0.03043	0.0575	0.0467	28. Appropriate geographical distribution of the branches in different area of the city
5	16	0.03117	0.0293	0.03132	0.03028	0.0529	0.0485	29. Willing to accommodate special request of the special customers
7	13	0.03218	0.03103	0.03182	0.03116	0.0309	0.0327	30. The reputation of the bank compare to the other banks
2	15	0.03061	0.03103	0.03104	0.03116	0.0455	0.0259	31. The ability to meet customers different needs and request, service diversification
1	20	0.03114	0.03128	0.0313	0.03129	0.0269	0.0235	32. Balancing branches services to the different requested services

Table 1: Results of Empirical Study in Bank Refax

www.ingramcontent.com/pod-product-compliance
Lightning Source LLC
Chambersburg PA
CBHW080538220526
45466CB00010B/2965